FRIEDRICH RITTELMEYER (1872–1938) was a Lutheran minister and theologian who led the founding of The Christian Community. Rittelmeyer came to prominence as a leading liberal theologian and preacher early in the twentieth century, advocating a socially engaged 'Christianity of deeds' (*Tatchristentum*). During the First World War he became one of the most high-profile clergymen in Germany to oppose the war publicly. From the 1910s his thinking was gradually influenced by the philosopher, spiritual researcher and teacher Rudolf Steiner. In 1922 a group of mainly Lutheran pastors and theology students founded The Christian Community, a Movement for Religious Renewal. Rittelmeyer remained at the helm of the movement until his death.

I0794725

Dutch Delftware tile portraying Christ writing in the ground during the scene with the Woman taken in Adultery (John 8)—(Private collection)

LETTERS ON JOHN'S GOSPEL

Friedrich Rittelmeyer

Translated by Margaret L. Mitchell

Revised and edited by Neil Franklin and Alan Stott

TEMPLE LODGE

Temple Lodge Publishing Ltd.
Hillside House, The Square
Forest Row, RH18 5ES

www.templelodge.com

First published in English with supplementary material by Temple Lodge in 2022

Originally published in German as individual essays, 1930-32. First published as a single volume under the title *Briefe über das Johannes-Evangelium* by Verlag Urachhaus, Stuttgart in 1938

A CIP catalogue record for this book is available from the British Library

ISBN 978 1 912230 96 9

Cover by Morgan Creative
Typeset by Symbiosys Technologies, Visakhapatnam, India
Printed and bound by 4Edge Ltd., Essex

Contents

Editor's Preface

From the Preface to the first edition of these *Letters on John's Gospel*, which appeared in instalments 1930-32, the author wrote:

> These *Letters on John's Gospel* are conceived as a study to extend over several years ... Their aim is to make John's Gospel accessible to people today as their own gospel both as a whole and in the details; to illuminate it with the spiritual knowledge of the age and to make it fruitful for life, not only for meditation but also for practical ordering of destiny.

On his original intentions, Rittelmeyer adds:

> There lies over John's Gospel an indescribable glory of revelation of love. This glory has such purity, delicacy and spiritual power that in it one has the material with which a marvellous new world may be built. Perhaps it is only after much study of John's Gospel that one can receive this *substance of transfiguration* into oneself in such a living manner. With this purpose these studies have been written. Anyone who lives in this realm, in this essence that has come down out of heaven to the Earth, and which is yet the fulfilment of earthly history—lives in Christ [from *Letter* 9].

*

The Gospel according to St John takes a primary position for Friedrich Rittelmeyer (1872-1938). Early in his career as a Lutheran pastor—as noted in his autobiography (1937)—he was drawn to and preached on John's Gospel (*Aus meinem Leben*, Stuttgart 1986, p. 175). He sought as an expositor to plumb its depths to the best of his abilities. In these *Letters* he shares the meditative fruits of many years. With his own suggestions, teachings and insights, Rittelmeyer also introduces those of his revered teacher, the spiritual researcher Rudolf Steiner (1861-1925).

In his day as a Lutheran pastor in the *Johanniskirche*, Würzburg, the *Heilig-Geist Kirche*, Nuremberg and later in the *Neue Kirche*, Berlin, Rittelmeyer was famous for his engaging sermons. A habitual homiletic style may appear discursive, occasionally irksome by some present standards; the author's intentions, however, survive the years. To make the Gospel accessible, Rittelmeyer habitually looks to find examples from experience to illuminate textual details, but also to attempt reaches of the imagination, at times of a surprising boldness. This is perhaps understandable, bearing in mind the difficult times in which he worked, with the urgent need to get beyond the depressing and stifling materialism causing the social problems. However, what the author writes reflecting the times sounds surprisingly relevant to our own day. For Rittelmeyer, dedicated to spiritual renewal, nothing short of recognition aided by deep meditation could supply answers, nourishment and inspiration. And nothing compares with John's Gospel as a source of present help.

Parallel cases in the English-speaking world of some kindred spirits at the beginning of the Michaelic Age (began 1879) might be worth mentioning. In his masterly survey of Anglican theology, A. Michael Ramsey (1904-88) defended Henry Scott Holland's (1847-1918) 'ardent personality, mesmeric preaching, exuberant language, zeal in social reform'. Holland's work on John's Gospel, *The Philosophy of Faith and the Fourth Gospel*, ed. Wilfrid Richmond (London 1920), is still one of the best introductions in the language.

Certainly, on the continent theological researchers of John's Gospel acknowledge the insights first noted by Rittelmeyer in these and other eloquent addresses, initially his colleagues Rudolf Frieling (see 'Sacred Number in John's Gospel', in *Frieling Rarities*, forthcoming) and Rudolf Meyer, later Christoph Rau (whose works on the literary form and rhythms in the gospels is outstanding) and other scholars. This concerns research into the *profound rhythms of the writing*, begun in the present work and emphasized here through the layout. Certainly one of the spiritual joys of exploring John's Gospel—regarded by many as the most important document of humanity—is to find commentators to whom the devotional, meditative, indeed *musical* approach is taken seriously as a means to acquire spiritual *knowledge*. Here Rittelmeyer's homiletic expositions hold their own; the chapters unfold many insights for meditation, culminating in a remarkable and detailed exposition of the Great Intercession, the High-Priestly Prayer. The author, we are often reminded, lived in a 'time of transition'—but then so does every scholar, teacher and creative personality, learning from the past, and reaching into the future. The rhythm of such 'new treasures as well as old' (Matt. 13:52) is what drew Rittelmeyer, the theologians with whom he worked and others who acknowledge his insights.

For a detailed survey of the ultimate sources of revelation of the gospel, Rittelmeyer's colleague, the universal scholar Hermann

Beckh (1875-1937) occupies a class of his own, not least for the questions it opens up with his two-volume work, *Mark's Gospel: The Cosmic Rhythm* and *John's Gospel: The Cosmic Rhythm* (both Temple Lodge 2021). An appreciation of Dr Rittelmeyer in English is given by Adam Bittleston, who, at the Priest Seminary in Stuttgart, studied under both men: 'Friedrich Rittelmeyer as Forerunner of a Christianity of the Future', in *Counselling and Spiritual Development*, Edinburgh, Floris 1988, pp. 252-68 (reprinted from *The Golden Blade* 1988. 131-39). Although most appreciative of Beckh's work—not least concerning a new spiritual knowledge of the stars, now available in English, *The Language of the Stars*, TL 2020—Bittleston unfortunately did not pen an appreciation of Prof. Beckh. The still continuing publishing project, the *Collected Works of Rev. Prof. Hermann Beckh*, may contribute to rectify this situation.

The translation of these *Letters* is a revision of Margaret L. Mitchell (1937), to whom we are also indebted for Rittelmeyer's *Meditation*, one of two works that explores the Johannine 'I-am' sayings that he was the first to expound as an organism of seven. (Another important text on this subject is the posthumously published *Ich Bin*, 1951.) The occasional omissions of the translator here, one of which is serious, have been rectified, mistakes corrected, and the copy-editing first begun by the late Charles Davy (a former editor of the London weekly *The Observer*) and the present writer (my occasional footnotes marked '*Tr. note*'), completed by Neil Franklin with numerous helpful suggestions (as main Editor mostly unmarked, sometimes for clarity marked *Ed.*). For a sake of completion, Rittelmeyer's account of the Prologue of John's Gospel has been freshly translated from *Vom Johanneischen Zeitalter* ('The Johannine Age', Eng. trans. in MS) and his exposition of John 21 are added here as separate items, with other cited articles from the weekly *Das Goetheanum*. Some subtitles and occasional bullet points have been added throughout in an attempt to help the reader. The result is a complete, corrected translation, revised, expanded and edited for the twenty-first century.

For New Testament quotations, the Revised Standard Version is mostly used as the best for the present purpose. Rittelmeyer's own translation contained in the German book, influenced by the time-honoured translation of Luther—which he sometimes calls to task—has been consulted. The English equivalent to Luther, the AV/KJV also based on the Received Text, contains what a modern reader would call 'archaisms'. The RSV, working from a better original Greek text dispenses with 'thou', 'thee' and 'thy' verbal forms, except for the High-Priestly Prayer, the Great Intercession (John 17).

My gratitude, as usual, is due to my wife for checking large passages of the translation and for helping to translate the five additional chapters and articles, and to Neil Franklin for taking time from other projects to add from his knowledge and wisdom in preparing this edition. Needless to say, all surviving blemishes derive from my shortcomings.

Alan Stott, Palm Sunday 2017

Introduction: Friedrich Rittelmeyer and John's Gospel[1]

'Books have their destiny.' This applies in a special sense with a significant book. For the 'destiny' of a book not only consists in how many copies are sold and how it is received by public opinion. To the destiny of a book there belongs above all what souls inwardly experience through it. The existence of such a book is incomplete if one does not take this effect into account.

This can be truly felt with regard to John's Gospel. It meets us as a being explored by many souls. What has been experienced through it during the course of now two millennia cannot be separated from the book itself. Whether we think about it or not, John's Gospel comes to us in the aura of these its destinies. Wherever its text is heard, there in a hidden manner there re-emerges how once out of these words the early Christian community heard the voice of the revered Apostle of Ephesus; how in the Middle Ages for the devout persons in their lonely cells, silently immersed in these words, the miraculous mystic flower bloomed; how for the great idealistic philosophers of past centuries the eternal Logos spoke spiritually awakening words.

To these destinies of John's Gospel the name Friedrich Rittelmeyer also belongs. Certainly, his experience of John in the mature figure of the last two decades would not have been possible without Rudolf Steiner's fundamental new discoveries in the gospel. Yet it can be clearly seen how there always runs a thread of independent work; moreover, in all the abundance of light arising from the new insights, his own voice in no way becomes lost. Through the meeting with the new knowledge Rittelmeyer's own personal experience of John is not 'dissolved' but is 'fulfilled'.

*

In his autobiography, he tells how he received an initial deep impression out of the world of John's Gospel. It was notably a musical experience, for in particular John's Gospel in an exact sense is through and through the 'musical' gospel in which the sound-ether is heard. On the waves of sound a saying from the Farewell Discourses reached the inner world of the then twenty-two-year-old. 'What then sounded like a prophecy: "I will see you again and your hearts will rejoice, and no one will take your joy from you" [John 16:22]—this was fulfilled completely inwardly and completely spiritually ...' writes Rittelmeyer, looking back on this experience (*Aus meinem Leben*, 3rd ed. Stuttgart 1986, p. 126f.). 'As a new higher world slowly opened for me under these first impressions, discovering Christianity, it was the Christ of John's Gospel Who greeted me with the prophecy of a reunion.'

During the time in Würzburg—he preached as deacon 1895 to 1902 at the *Johanniskirche*—he gradually began to 'discover' John's Gospel. 'Now as deacon, John's Gospel repeatedly beckoned as a higher world destined for me, in which, however, I could still not find a full entrance' (ibid., p. 175).

One should not forget the academic, theological background of those years. The 'genuineness' of John's Gospel was cast into doubt. 'I recall I was unaccountably aroused when the genuineness of John's Gospel was doubted ... Such a feeling is indeed often a sign that one feels with the soul something which with the understanding one does not as yet grasp' (ibid., p. 175f.). A gentle feeling for knowledge hindered him from dismissing the objections without more ado and to take on blindly the traditional belief; he possessed in full measure what Nietzsche demanded as intellectual 'honesty'. But in the depths of the soul he nevertheless felt that in the apparently so assured critical judgment there lurked a capital error.

Johannes Müller in his way treated it more lightly. In Heidelberg, challenged once from the critical side concerning John's Gospel, he simply said: 'The gentlemen themselves are not genuine'—otherwise they would actually not doubt the genuineness. Rittelmeyer, proceeding cautiously, consequently arrived later all the more splendidly to a fundamentally based, justifiable knowledge. Yet this is to anticipate. We would rather follow the path that he himself gradually pursued to reach fulfilment.

Rittelmeyer possessed quite a special organ for what is called 'personality'. He was particularly open always to feel the miracle of the individual nature of human beings. With an unusual ability he was able to live into the most varied personalities. An excellent example for this is his involvement with Friedrich Nietzsche, at a time when this name in critical circles was simply felt as a red rag. With delicacy and a clairaudience of soul Rittelmeyer sought to understand this radical opponent of Christianity.

In a devoted manner he occupied himself with Tolstoy and with Buddha. It is worth noting what he says in his lecture '*Religion und*

Persönlichkeit' ['Religion and Personality'] (1913) concerning the nature of personality:

> It is completely individual and unique and nevertheless endlessly rich. It is transparently clear and yet unfathomable. It is securely self-enclosed and yet full of active life ... Behind all this the actual riddle confronts us, the actual miracle, the actual Mystery of the 'I', the wondrous flowering that the universe has brought forth for those who have eyes to see, a flowering that before all other blooms has the advantage that it lives before us a life in spirit and soul. It blooms, yet also shares with all the other blooms the Mystery that from here there proceeds a completely delicate, tender fragrance of soul, indescribably inwardly appealing ...

A person with this open organ for the 'I' could not avoid John's Gospel: he has entirely to pass over the objections of all premature criticism to perceive the special vibration of the unique Individual Whom it proclaims.

All his concern with remarkable personalities was for Rittelmeyer basically but a preparatory exercise, in order finally to be permitted to realize the figure of Jesus of Nazareth. Precisely for his acute sense for the revelation of an 'I', this Figure became ever more unforgettable, ever more full of riddles and full of mystery. What kind of 'I' can so speak and act? What was the special thing about Him? He saw himself, as he later expressed it, as if before a steep, massive mountain wall, where the means of gaining knowledge up to now simply did not progress any further.

By feeling the Mystery of this Personality at work in Jesus as a riddle of knowledge that became increasingly weighty, he had worked to formulate the right questions, in order really to meet as the 'answers' the communications of spiritual science. This took place around his fortieth year. So much indeed depended on the mutual finding of question and answer. A knowledge that is not met as the answer to a burning question, that after the strenuous toil of searching is not met as the word that carries the solution, is not able to touch the soul in its depths—just as a drink means nothing for those who experience no thirst.

The insights now opening up concerning the essence and significance of the 'I' within a living, ordered and structured spirit-world within world-evolution, in organic connection to the new view of the being and significance of the Christ and His deed—the 'I' as the meaning of Earth-evolution, the Christ as the meaning of the 'I'—how that must have been received by a person like Rittelmeyer! Not as a teaching, which one learns as a pupil and repeats like a pupil, but as an insight that was 'meant' for him, for which he paid attention, for the reception of which he had become mature. Now his earlier labours could become truly fruitful.

Thereby the hour had also finally come for John's Gospel. The 'I-AM', that is expressed so grandly out of this gospel, hitherto not realized by theology, or miserably misunderstood, grew increasingly sublimely for him in all its divinity and spirituality, as something 'that also in us as individuals intends to be the seed of light of a new human being'. This 'I-AM breathing in the spirit' was no doubt the central experience of Rittelmeyer with John's Gospel. Rittelmeyer was the first publicly to say that it was differentiated into a septenary of 'I-AM-sayings' (the Bread of Life; the Light of the World; the Door; the Good Shepherd; the Resurrection and the Life; the Way, the Truth and the Life; the True Vine).

Doubts concerning the 'genuineness' were finally resolved; the inadequate materialistic assumptions of a self-styled 'assumption-free' science could be clearly exposed.

Thus the last two decades were for Rittelmeyer a time in which he was allowed to experience a deeply satisfying joy of discovery with John's Gospel, which precisely in its organism, in the composition of its parts right into the finest textual details, opened up ever more clearly to his meditative immersion. He frequently spoke about the joy of such work.[2]

Through the sacramental life of The Christian Community there came a further emphasis. What 'liturgical word' and sacred text are in the sounds of speech and its rhythm, how the 'Word' finds the way to become 'flesh', he was allowed to realize full of vitality in a life with the Act of Consecration.

The literary fruits of this new work on John's Gospel are available in the publications: *Vom johanneischen Zeitalter, Meditation, Briefe über das Johannes-Evangelium, Christus* [and the posthumously published addresses *Ich Bin*], ['The Johannine Age', 'Meditation', 'Letters on John's Gospel', 'Christ' and 'I AM']. But also all the other writings fundamentally contain the Johannine influence. It is not here the place to discuss all this in detail. One may but briefly mention some motifs, which take a place in this life's work, unforgettable impressions that can be retrieved from hearing and reading him.

Let us take a walk through John's Gospel and recall how all this content lived in Friedrich Rittelmeyer, beginning with the Prologue with its symphonic musicality; then the seven signs shining like stained-glass windows in a church, glimmering in a divining, subdued light; the spiritual organism of the seven I-AM sayings; the consecration of the Farewell Discourses; the cathedral-like splendour of the Great Intercession, the High-Priestly Prayer; the sustained mystical ardour of the story of the Passion; the etheric tenderness and awakening power of the Easter-chapters.

We may from now on feel connected with the individual and unique manner—how this is reflected in the spiritually bright, inwardly religiously devoted soul, in Friedrich Rittelmeyer's experience of John's Gospel—and with the destiny of this profound book of humanity.

Rudolf Frieling

The 'I-AM' as the Midpoint of Human History[3]

It was a decisive hour in the history of John's Gospel when Rudolf Steiner pointed out the special emphasis in which the word 'I' appears, for the 'I' spoken in John's Gospel gains recognition as taking the central place in the history of human ego-development. Hitherto, in recent decades amongst theologians, one often met the mood: John's Gospel cannot be genuine, because Jesus speaks so much about himself (which is 'something that is not done'). It did not strike anyone that this objection is suspiciously similar to the objection that the opponents of Christ raised in His time—'You are bearing witness about yourself' (8:14).

One of the most beautiful tasks that Rudolf Steiner gave to those working in spiritual science [anthroposophy] is through the key given by his research to open up the individual shrines of John's Gospel that are still closed. One detail may be related here, others could follow.

One can in a special way call John 8 'the I-AM chapter'. After the narration of the adulteress, in which is revealed the consequential effect on human life lived under the law, the revelatory word is spoken, 'I am the light of the world'. During the course of the following sayings of Christ, three significant words about the 'I-am' follow, in which we can discover the actual interpretation of the preceding word of revelation. These three words carry, as it were, the whole new proclamation of the 'I'. Through the usual translation, 'I am he', these truths are obscured. Whatever Luther might have seen for linguistic reasons in such a translation, it seems that through these words the true meaning of the sentences has been withheld from humanity. We quote these three sentences in the order they appear:

- 'You will die in your sins unless you believe I am' (8:24).
- 'When you have lifted up the Son of man, then you will know that I am he' (8:28).
- 'Truly, truly, I say to you, before Abraham was, I am' (8:58).

Regarding the inner structure of these three sayings, one initially sees that the first saying relates to the present, the second to the future, and the third to the past. And clearly it can be realized that really the highest truths meet us concerning the present, future and past of humanity.

(1) 'You will die in your sins unless you believe in me.' If one wants to reach a true understanding of this saying, one first has to free

oneself of all the false notions of 'belief', and the concepts of belief that have arisen in the history of Christendom. One may recall that the word *πιστεύειν* belongs to the same root as the German word *fest*, 'firm'. It does not concern a 'holding for true', a conviction, but in the sense of John's Gospel with 'grounding oneself'. One could translate: 'If you are not grounded in the "I" which I am, then you will decline in your errors.' It is sufficiently well known that the best Israelites suffered heavily under the 'nature of sin'; they saw their people and themselves entangled in the law. The opinion existed, for example, that were the Sabbath truly held on only one occasion by the whole people, then Messiah *has* to come. What is said here we can express in more detail—there is only one single way humanity can get beyond its doom: it has to be endowed with a new 'I'. Through this alone everything is changed from within. This new 'I' has now come. Christ himself is this new 'I' and can bestow it on every human being. There is only *one* condition for this—that the human being really lays his existence into this new 'I', really grounds himself. If this happens then man is saved; if it does not happen he is doomed to decline. It is the highest insight the human being of those days could gain concerning the present in which he lived. And always, it is the deepest and innermost insight of his existence as long as man lives on the Earth. In this way the light of the world illumines the 'present'.

(2) The second saying speaks of the future: 'When you have lifted up the Son of man, you will know that I am He'—'that I-am', 'the one, who I am', 'the I, which I am', however one could translate it. Christ is immediately confronted by the hate of His opponents which outwardly will destroy Him. But this means, spiritually seen, only that they will 'raise up the Son of man'. From 'belief' the saying, now with full intention, goes over towards 'recognition'. For this recognition—that Christ is the true 'I' of humanity—will in future not only be given to the friends but also to the enemies. How this will happen, the same John to whom we owe the gospel, has placed before humanity with his mighty visionary pictures in the Apocalypse. It is truly *the* knowledge towards which the whole of humanity progresses. Again, one could express it in detail: You believe you destroy the Christ? In reality, for Him you will prepare His throne; He will henceforth live as the true human being over humanity; this will be evermore *realized*; from the friends as well as in a different way from the opponents. It will become ever clearer in the future of humanity that there the true 'I' of humanity has revealed itself. This is the highest knowledge that is given to humanity. Thus 'the light of the world' illumines the *future*.

> (3) The third saying looks back to the past. 'Before Abraham was, I am'. What is expressed here in the context of the Israelite history of religion is valid for all pre-Christian history of religions. For you—thus one could elaborate—Abraham is the celebrated primal beginning of your people, and with it also the essence of your religion. But Abraham would not have been called out had not a greater divine Thought hovered over humanity; behind Abraham stood Another, Who one day should appear and Who led the whole history of the Israelites towards their aim. Abraham, the whole Israelite nation and essence of their religion were all preparation and prophecy for Him. As it is with you, so it is with all the other religions—a greater view about the whole past of humanity has never existed than this: everything is preparation and prophecy towards the divine 'I' that appeared in Christ and which secretly was already guiding all religious history. Whoever realizes this, begins to understand the history of humanity. Thus, 'the light of the world' illuminates the *past*.

In the Churches 'the light of the world' has been edifyingly preached innumerable times. But the interpretation Christ Himself gave in His address that directly follows is not at all noticed. It is indeed not a subjective, ethically edifying address. It is of universal, 'cosmic' greatness. With this example, it may be seen how anthroposophy and the gospel are in harmony, how the truths of anthroposophy are indeed to be found in the gospel, how the gospel is illuminated in its depths through the insights of anthroposophy.

Christianity as a Mystery Religion[4]

In the early religions, great Mysteries concern the snake, or serpent. Today, the staff with its entwining snakes is still known, signifying the god of healing. But this staff [of Hermes, or Mercury] with the snakes is in many ways an ancient sacred symbol. It is hardly possible to review the whole abundance of ideas and feelings that were connected to the snake and which—along with the picture of the dragon—penetrated and governed the whole of China and the Americas. But access to the central essential core can be found by following the story told as a picture in the biblical Book of Numbers 21:5-9.

The Children of Israel, dissatisfied with their leader, are plagued by fiery snakes, or serpents, who bite them. Moses, following the command of Yahweh, fixed a bronze snake on to a pole. Whoever looks up to it is saved. Those who do not look up perish. Whatever might have happened then—and there are several narratives concerning the 'burning snakes' of that geographical area—such a story only becomes fully comprehensible if it is seen as a picture that was to imprint itself into the childlike soul of the Israelites of that time, and should become meaningful for all time. One can no longer speak of an arbitrary recounting of legends when such a story has begun to render its deeper meaning.

The snake is the animal of the earth. It crawls on the earth. It inhabits the earth. It lives with the earth. Snakes with their flickering tongues directly become a picture of human passions rising out of the Earth's being. Also the quiet, deceitful, poisonous being of the snake adds to the picture. People can perish through these earthly creatures. Only one thing can save them. Human beings do not need to deny this earthly creature. But it can give them the upward direction. He has to take the direction upwards *with* the earthly creature and go *beyond* the earthly creature. The human being looking up to it in reverence when it is 'raised', is raised beyond his decline.

If one has not yet learned to allow pictures to speak to oneself as pictures, then these thoughts will be thought an artificial interpretation. With childlike forces of the soul, people at one time looked through such pictures into the governing intentions of prophetic forethought. The upward path of humanity was repeatedly presented to them in impressive, lasting pictures. From this picture from folklore one has access to all pre-Christian 'initiation'. Just this principle, appearing here as a picture before the people, lived as a basic principle in all the early Mysteries. Human passions that bring man destruction are overcome by presenting the earthly creature in the direction upwards. In elevating it beyond the Earth, the earthly creature is beheld in prayer. Rudolf Steiner frequently spoke of the snake as the symbol of ancient initiation. How from this insight the path leads also to the snakes of the staff of Mercury, the ancient serpent of Paradise, as well as the snakes of Laocoön, will not be pursued here. But it should be pointed out how Christ Himself relates His work to ancient initiation.

In John's Gospel Christ speaks several times about His being 'lifted up'. With this the crucifixion is always meant, not, for example, the ascension. This is proved in John 12:33, 'He said this to show by what death He was to die'. The early religions took pains not to vary their verbal expressions in their documents. It is very significant that Christ in John's Gospel speaks of His lifting-up only as of His crucifixion—and of His crucifixion only as of His raising up. This was made easier, since in Aramaic the word for raising up and for crucifixion is the same.[5]

Christ speaks three times about this lifting-up. And in the first saying He links directly to the lifting-up of the serpent.

- 'As Moses lifted up the serpent in the wilderness, so must the Son of man be lifted up, that whoever believes in Him may have eternal life' (John 3:14, 15).
- 'When you have lifted up the Son of man, then you will know that *I am*' (John 8:28).
- 'And I, when I am lifted up from the Earth, will draw all men to myself' (John 12:32).

The lifting-up is shown as having a threefold effect:

- The human being receives 'super-temporal life'.
- He knows the 'I-am'.
- He unites with others to form a human community.

From here we can now look back to early initiation. In these three contexts it stands precisely in contrast to the new work. It isolates individuals, especially people prepared—it was not for 'everyone'. It brought the human being to an exceptional condition of soul in which he lost his 'I'-consciousness and his free 'recognition' born out of the 'I'. And it gave to the human being only a transitional union with the higher world, nothing 'permanent', 'beyond time'.

Already in his first book concerning Christianity, *Christianity as Mystical Fact and the Mysteries of Antiquity* (GA 8. 1902), and then again in many lectures, Rudolf Steiner points to this characterization of initiation and contrasts it to the new union with the divine-spiritual world that is opened up through Christ. In John's Gospel we have presented in these three sentences, point for point, in all clarity—as clear as it can be in a document meant for general reading—the character of Christianity as differing from the earlier path of initiation. The first of these sayings actually expressly links to the essence of the Mysteries and is spoken by an elder, who is probably a representative who proclaims the Mysteries to the folk.

The fulfilling of the Mysteries has arrived. They step into public view for 'everyone'. They take place with full 'I'-consciousness, indeed they first bring the true 'I'. They give the human being permanent union. That is the significance of Christ's work in the innermost story of humanity.

An historical detail, hardly noticed, may be presented here in this context. In the Old Testament the account is found that the Israelites still burnt incense to the bronze serpent in the Temple, until the time of King Hezekiah, who ruled around 700 BCE and was a contemporary of the prophet Isaiah. Only then was the bronze serpent removed from the Temple (2 Kings 18:4)—despite the respected memory of Moses. Whoever can read such reports understands what they actually are intended to say. Right into the time of the rising prophecy the connection still existed to the early Egyptian initiation. It was set up through Moses and was lost at the time of the prophets. The removal of the serpent out of the Temple, however, was the preparation for that which seven centuries later would link to the earlier initiation.

First 'the Son of man' had to come. But then the *human being* stepped into the place of the *Earth*. In this contrast the last word is spoken concerning the difference of the times. A new symbol of initiation appeared before the whole of mankind.

The Nascent World[6]

When Renan's *The Life of Jesus* appeared,[7] a German historical researcher is supposed to have said: 'One single word of John's Gospel throws this whole construction of dust into the dust.' In such a judgment, though it may not see anything in Renan's brilliant mental gifts and the historical importance of his work, something nevertheless rears up of the Teutonic spiritual manner that seems to be fundamentally related to John's Gospel. It is still uttered out of the knowledge that the great spirits of our greatest period were inclined in reverence to John's Gospel. No one would force entrance into the sanctuary of humanity who did not know how to direct a deep force of reverence towards it. Only to these people are the gates opened.

'In the primordial beginning the Word already was' (1:1).[8] If we just want to experience this sentence as it resounded in John's spirit, we would have to write a long history of humanity. There was a time when the word was much more alive, and consequently what was alive was much more 'Word'. Creation still spoke to man; it was not a neutral creation, but mighty living beings around man told him of their existence and activities. This was the world at that time. Slowly the cosmic word became mute. The outer world became ever quieter and lifeless, finally became mute in profound silence. It allowed human beings to speak. The earlier time had already passed when the evangelist began his narration. But its ceasing, still resounding in his soul, allowed in his spirit the deepest music of all existence to be heard through a mighty divining. Like an awakening to Christ of all the ages of the early Mysteries, like a dawning of the archetypal memory of tremendous processes of cosmic creation, is the saying: 'In the primordial beginning the Word already was.'

Our eye is evermore bound by the picture before us, deep in meaning. Here is a disciple of Christ in whom the will becomes alive to write down the story of Christ. With his gaze directed to Christ, he puts his quill to work. He searches for the first word. He finds nothing that seems to him worthy. His spirit circles over the earthly events like an eagle. Finally we see him move his quill. What does he write? 'In the primordial beginning.' This very first phrase of the gospel should already silence the thoughtless talk about the 'simple gospel'. What would John say concerning such talk? He has already answered: you lack reverence for the gospel. The simplest person can find in his own mineshafts and galleries all the gold to make himself rich. But only the gaze of wisdom that has awoken to penetrate the world will worthily realize what has been given to it, that both have been united, the loving-kindness towards the least and the overabundant wisdom for the greatest. Precisely this is the essential nature of this gospel.

It is a festive experience to perceive deeply how in the soul of the evangelist the certainty arises: if I want to write about Christ in adequate dignity, then I have to find the courage to write a new story of creation. Or is it that the evangelist did not know, when he stepped aside and writes, 'In the primordial beginning', he challenges the memory of the sacred book of his compatriots, when, with his first words, he imitates the great Moses [traditional author of Genesis]: 'In the primordial beginning'? He dares to confront the old account of creation with a new account of creation, because he knows that the Holy Spirit has illuminated his vision. He has to dare this because he knows only in this way can he worthily speak about Christ. What challenges to the spirit of humanity sound alone in these words!

People frequently regarded the four evangelists, how each of them presents the entry of Christ into the earthly world. Matthew rests his gaze on the youth in whom all the prophecy of the elders becomes true, is greeted by all the wisdom of the world. Luke remains full of devotion before the heavenly gift in the crib, above which the choirs of angels are heard. Mark looks at the divine Son, Who at the Baptism miraculously descends. But John has the drive to experience the light of Christ as the great 'Let there be light' of the primordial beginning. He has the drive to see the being of Christ ascend out of the archetypal silence of the divine pre-worldly tranquillity. This wrestling for a greatest Christendom of all embracing all the widths of the world, illuminating all the depths of the world, brings us contemporary people so close to this evangelist. This keen courage of spirit has to awaken when Christendom shall become active again if it is at all to survive. Out of the innermost depths of the world, Christ has to meet us, Who wants to lead us into the future.

'In the primordial beginning the Word already was.'

The gaze of the seer goes back into the depths of time, as far as only it can go, resting on a most sublime picture of all, from which it can hardly wrench itself away. He dare not speak of it in an uncouth, wordy manner, but also not in one single, brief sentence. What does he help us to see? The Holy Trinity! The poorness of spirit today may take this for some playful gimmick. It deeply illuminates the religious documents when we realize that here the beholding is at the same time a participation in the Mysteries; here the experience is at the same time a being taken hold of by a higher life.

Thus, through the true clairvoyant deep truths of the world are expressed in all clarity, which his cognitive understanding could not have sufficiently fathomed. It is not a teaching of the Trinity that is proclaimed to us, but for one moment a participation of its life is movingly presented.

- 'In the primordial beginning the Word already was.' Here spirit-vision rests in Being, in ultimate existence, in the Father,
- 'and the Word was with God'. Here the beholding spirit touches as in passing on the relationship, on Love, on the Son,
- 'and the Word was a[9] God'. Here it meets a breath of the Being, of the Spirit, of Holy Spirit.

For one moment a human being breathes with the sacred harmony of the primordial, divine life. For one moment has awoken with the Holy Trinity itself. Thus he was—baptized by Christ Himself in the name of the Father, the Son and the Holy Spirit. Thus at the beginning of his gospel he radiantly places the aim of all Christendom, participation in the life of the Holy Trinity, in a wonderful illuminated vision.

'The same was in the primordial beginning with God' (1:2). The seer is granted another view of the world above. But it is as if its gates are slowly closing. And these gates seem to be nothing else than choirs of angels singing praise, who reverently and piously cover again the uncovered Grail and carry it aloft. The play of world-events begins.

At first a sacred play of the creation of the world. The number two appears, taking the place of the number three, that number which carries the struggle of 'the Yes and the No' in thinking as well as in the will, carrying in itself logic as well as ethics. 'All things were made through him, and without him was not anything made that was made' (1:3). This saying is the opposite of the phrase 'to be with God'; it is immediately divided into an opposite. The division, the archetypal law of world-becoming, begins its activity before us. Softly into the primordial, sacred world falls the first shadow of evil, but in such a way as evil can exist in the world above, as a spiritual possibility of the opposite, as '*Gottes Gegenwurf*—God's counterstroke', as Jakob Boehme expresses it.[10]

The beginning of Wagner's *The Rhinegold*[11] helps us to experience how the primordial world-becoming is grandly set into movement.

Out of the primal musical sound, profoundly at rest, there develops an ever increasing lively and richer play of waves and worlds. The master brings to musical expression a time of revelation, sacred to himself. Particularly in this context the time of revelation in John appears so tremendous. In Wagner it rises from below upwards out of the resting primal tone at rest in the depths and unfolds into the world. In John it sounds from above downwards, out of the divine harmony of heaven which in itself is pure spirit filled with life.

Word—life—light—flesh. In these words the seer of all world-becoming lets the innermost history pass before us. In his lectures on John's Gospel, Rudolf Steiner presents what is revealed here. It is cosmic days that pass before us, the sequence of embodiments of our complete solar system, the cosmic days that in esoteric science of earlier times were called Ancient Saturn, Ancient Sun, Ancient Moon and Earth, the greatest cosmic days that the human being can perceive. It is truly a higher creation story facing the creation story of Moses [in Genesis] that will speak to us. For these cosmic days are mirrored—as all becoming that ever was can be seen today in that which is—in the story of Christ prior to His appearance, which the evangelist wants to tell us. And that he has beheld this story of Christ right into the depths, that behind it the countenance of the greatest cosmic days themselves becomes visible: this is precisely the sign that he did behold the cosmic Mystery itself in the Mystery of Christ. In Christ he discovered all the cosmic richness, proclaiming in Him the richness of all divinity.

- 'I am the life', Christ spoke during His earthly course. He was able to speak in most profound truth because He contained the world, because according to His being He *was* the world that once in distant primordial times gave life to the precursor of man.
- 'I am the light', Christ said. He could so speak in most profound truth because according to His being He was also the world that later, still in our far distant primordial past, was developing towards the light for the precursor of man.

He was light and life in highest splendour, and at the same time in deepest depths. From such deep foundations of life, which at the same time are divine depths of life, the words of Christ were born. When today science wants to explore what life is and what light is, then it approaches the light [as a product] from outside, from below through experiments. But as certainly we learn what is 'man' rather from Goethe than from the *Pithecanthropus erectus*, so certainly the evangelist is right when he says: If you want to know what life is and what light is, then look at the One Who, out of the deepest depths of the world and the highest divine heights, has spoken to you: 'I am the life'; 'I am the light.'

'In him was life, and the life was the light of men. The light shines in the darkness, and the darkness has not overcome it/comprehended it' (1:5). In divine heights there sounds for the first time, darkly and seriously, the Passion motif as if from afar carried by cosmic trombones.

And now there enters into this highly sacred, primordial cosmic song, the head of a human being. Do we not feel how it ennobles man, just to be mentioned in these heights? And is not each word that he speaks as if shone through, as if in this light of the heights the Mystery of man itself wants to be solved? 'There was a man sent from God, whose name was John—the grace of God.'[12] 'He came for testimony, to bear witness to the light' (1:6, 7). Of whom does the evangelist speak? Does he speak of John the Baptist? Does he not tell us in these words what and how he himself would want to be? Does he point to us as in the clear light of the stars what man himself is and what he should be?

Earthly existence had begun with a 'Let there be light'. In the present time a science has appeared, anthroposophy, which unfolds to the human being how light is not only a 'condition of vibrations', of some kind of ether, but is itself of the finest out-streaming nature; how all matter, and in particular the human being himself, has been condensed, darkened out of light. Divine is the teaching that proclaims: O Man, you are born of light. How does man gain that for which this knowledge makes him long? How does he become light again? The light, which he had betrayed, has sought and found him on new paths. He can become a listener of the light, a proclaimer of the light, a witness of the light. And thus he can return into the light. The human being, who is 'transfigured', who is light again, brings creation back with him. The new aim is to become light, the highest aim of the darkened world.

> He was not the light, but came to bear witness to the light. The true light that enlightens every man was coming into the world. He was in the world, and the world was made through him, yet the world knew him not. He came to the individual human being, and the individual human beings did not receive him [1:8-11].[13]

We have descended into human regions. More mighty and penetrating sounds the Passion music. But as in the opening chords of a music drama all the motifs are gathered, which afterwards carry the great event, so here in these opening sounds of the gospel, we too already perceive announcements of other melodies.

- 'But to all who received Him'—Christmas is announced;
- 'He gave full power to become children of God'—Easter hymns enter mightily;
- 'who believed in His revelation'—Pentecost jubilates from afar;
- 'who were born, not of blood nor of the will of man nor of the will of man, but of God'—the melody of a new world is here where there will be no physical nature independent of God, no etheric life independent of God, no astral will independent of God, where there will be roaring ever more mightily that which is heard here for the first time, 'born of God'.

Now everything is prepared, especially with these words 'born of God', that all the music can be gathered and concentrated into the main melody—'and the word became flesh and dwelt among us, full of grace and truth; we have beheld His shining glory, glory as of the only Son from the Father full of the grace of devotion and the power of truth.' If one could but give people an impression how these words live in the Greek, already expressed in their sounds! Although already an ancient language, the Greek of the gospel still appears to us as if we are looking into the eyes of a fresh youth, where in a modern translation, especially after the changes of recent decades, we become much more intellectual; we feel we see the extinguished gaze of an old person. 'We beheld'—*ἐθεασάμεθα*—the word itself is already a gradual opening of the eyes, a pure look of wonder, a slow festive closing of the eyes with a living afterglow. 'And the Word became flesh'—*ὁ λόγος σὰρξ ἐγένετο*. The threefold sound itself forms a threefold strong upbeat; from above a heavy, mighty impact, a rumbling on to ever further spheres. The gospel thus weaves out of the sounds of human language its first earthly garment. The Word out of which everything once originated conjures a new world to rise before us, the world of the fine spirit-figures of the sounds of speech. Those who think about this find the world of the Liturgy, where the Word has become flesh, where all flesh wants to become Word again. To take seriously the Word, the world-creating Word, leads to the Liturgy.

With reverence we listen into the miracles of such a saying of the gospel. It is as if the angels in it 'ascend and descend'. It descends in a sacred rhythm of three:

- 'The Word became flesh
- and dwelt among us
- and we beheld His glory.'

In a sacred rhythm of three it ascends again:

- 'We beheld His glory
- the glory of the only-begotten of the Father
- full of the grace of devotion and the power of truth.'

The angels that descend and ascend sing again the song of Holy Trinity.

- They tell us of *being*—'the Word became flesh';
- they tell us of *love*—'and dwelt among us';
- they tell us of the *essence*—'we beheld His glory'.

And again it echoes back to the Son after resting only for a moment on the word 'glory' in earthly existence—'glory as of the only-begotten of the Father'. And it continues to echo in the primordial existence—'grace of devotion and power of truth'. The song sounds out like the echoing of distant high cosmic vaults. All this is not thought out [as a construct of the evangelist], but experienced out of the innermost truth of participating in the divine, creative life.

In Christ was light and life. Light and life in Christ come now to earthly man in such a transformed and concentrated form, as in his life he can now freshly receive from the Spirit. Out of light has become power of truth. Life appears as grace of devotion. Alone these words 'raying of being filled with grace of devotion and power of truth' are already a baptism.

- In the power of truth, if one deeply experiences it, lives the Spirit.
- In the grace of devotion there shines the Son.
- In the raying of Being lives the Father.

Whoever merges into such words receives a secret baptism.

With all this spirituality one could almost overlook what a firm rock descended into the world of that time as the foundation of a new world. The flesh was despised in the spiritually striving East. It was glorified in the West, where the Earth was acknowledged. Now the East and the West receive in one single sentence their redemption and at the same time their atonement, a new world and at the same time an innermost marriage. That the *Word* became flesh opens up the depths for the West; that the Word became *flesh* opens up reality to the East.

There is no end to what could be said how in this world the Word became flesh, in order that the flesh become Word again.[14] But we continue to follow our Christ-hymn singing into the cosmos.

Again, John the Evangelist mentions John the Baptist. And again it is not the individual John alone. 'John bore witness to him, and cried, "This is He ..."' Thus John the Baptist has remained throughout Church history. Thus he has been seen in uncountable pictures as the man who points towards Christ: This was He! In this picture, he shows the human being himself, who shall become great by serving the One who is greater. 'John bore witness to Him, and cried, "This was He of whom I said, He who comes after me ranks before me, for he was before me"' (1:15). But is it not shamefully little, what the Baptist has to say about Christ?—only for the person for whom the time is so without life, as it is for contemporary people. At that time, in the language of the Mysteries, one beheld in the person's age their spiritual level, the rank of dignity of their being. It is the great 'I-AM' of which the gospel speaks afterwards that the seer experiences here. The evangelist turns his first gaze right through time towards the great 'I-AM'. Is not man forlorn on the Earth because he does not know his origin and his aim? As he strides over the Earth, the Baptist feels as if embedded in a greater 'I-AM'.

And now John the Baptist is joined by another high-ranking figure: Moses. 'The law was given through Moses, grace and truth came through Jesus Christ' (1:17). It is very moving how the evangelist appeals to the greatest figures of the past, in order to make visible to human beings the Greatest of all. It is as if he leads us on to high mountains in order to show the mighty main peak of revelation in His whole exceeding glory. Thus before us he builds up, as it were, the context around Christ—the two mountains Moses and Elijah. Elijah? Indeed, Christ Himself has said (Matt. 11:14; Mk. 9:12; cf. Lk. 1:17), whom we should see in John—Elijah has returned! Moses and Elijah—is it not, as if in the soul of the evangelist, a picture has become alive again, which he had once beheld when he walked with Christ over the Earth—Christ speaking on the Mount of Transfiguration beyond time with Moses and Elijah (Mk. 9:4; Matt. 17:3; Lk. 9:30)? The picture, transformed into history, became active in his spirit when he began to write his gospel. Moses, the law; Elijah, prophecy.

Now is uncovered ever more clearly what we see before us. Pre-Christian humanity had walked on two paths to the Mount of Revelation. They were sent in two directions to seek Christ.

> [1] The Teutons, the Persian and the Greeks were searching in the outer world, in the blowing of the wind, the shining of the light, in the revelation of earthly beauty. The highest they found on the Earth was the human being. But where in the human being is God? Where is the human Son Who is God? The highest thing was hope. Prophecy lived with the Greeks in the statue of Apollo, with the Teutons in the longing of Balder, with the Persians in the proclamation of the appearance of Ahura Mazdao on the Earth.
>
> [2] The southern Semitic peoples searched the inner world, in the Mystery of birth and death, in their destiny, in their consciousness. The highest revealed to them was the divine demand within the human being.

But 'the law' broke down the human being. Only a god can suffice for him. Where is the god who will become man? This is the pertinent question. Thus Moses and Elijah stand before us as the embodiment of all human longing:

- Moses, who on Sinai sought outside for the divine voice (Ex: 3:12), and
- Elijah, perceived the divine Voice within (I Kings 19):

> in the storm like the Teutons,
> in the fire like the Persians,
> in the power of the Earth like the Greeks,
> and who finally perceived it in the soughing, wafting of the Spirit.

They both stand in human history as human longing itself and point towards Christ as the reality. Law became grace; Prophecy became truth. 'Grace and truth' in a radiant glory: this is the fulfilling of all human longing—Christ.

We have beheld sufficiently. The portals of the divine world are slowly closing. And on these closing gates a script, weighty in content, becomes visible. 'No one has ever seen God; the only Son, who is in the bosom of the Father [1:18] has become the Guide in this beholding.' 'Now, earthly man, you know what you have seen—and what you will see in the following narration of the gospel, after the heavenly gates have closed and have released their Messenger on to the Earth.'

> [1] In our translations all the sounds have been extinguished of the Mystery-music of language, in which all this once resounded to man. Who can still sense that the phrase 'primordial beginning' for the Apostle Paul was still the name of an angel?[15] 'Before time began, the Word already was' (1:1). It is as though the first of the high governors of time, which the 'word' summoned in order to breathe world-beginning into him, tells us what he has beheld from his super-earthly mountain of the primordial play of the eternal Holy Trinity. This no longer lives fully alive in our souls. Yet the breath of God still wafts out of the words. What to us today is 'time' and 'beginning'?
>
> [2] A second phrase: 'to these ... he gave power to become children of God' (1:12). 'Power', too, was to Paul the name of an angel (*exousia*). In the language something whispers of a mysterious angelic narration: 'We were once creative powers; in primordial times we had fashioned the human being by divine command. But the work went awry, was spoiled. We stood before it bereft of advice and help. Then, from the heights, sacred power came to us. Then a higher Being began to work in us. Now we are able to complete the earthly task in a divine manner. You human beings will feel our might within yourselves when you become children of God, and within our might His sublime power.' Thus it murmured in the depths of the soul of those who had ears for the Mysteries. What does 'power' mean for us today?
>
> [3] A third phrase. 'From his fullness have we all received, grace upon grace' (1:16). Who senses today that the word 'fullness' [*pleroma*] for centuries was the name for a whole divine heaven, for the sublime choir of creative world-powers? What is 'fullness' for us today? 'When you glimpse Christ', thus the gospel spoke to those who understood more deeply, 'then you behold the living, heavenly gods on the Earth. You are able to enter and leave this heaven of gods, and what you receive is all the splendour of grace. Out of spirit-depths and worlds of spirits there is wafted to human beings a super-earthly music, when you listen to the language of the gospel.'

The words 'light', 'life', too, and that word above them, not mentioned and yet is there as 'splendour of grace' of the 'Word'—'love', for human beings at the time were not spiritually-thin concepts, but they rayed down out of sublime heights.

- There were angelic worlds whose reflection human beings carried in their thinking; in them 'light' was carried.
- There were angelic worlds whose reflection human beings carried in their feelings; in which 'life' flowed.
- There were angelic worlds whose reflection human beings carried in their will; in them 'love' glowed.

And behind these angelic worlds there rayed again the countenance of the Holy Trinity itself:

- 'Light' lived in these highest heights as the Holy Spirit.
- 'Life' streamed from the divine Son.
- 'Love' is the Father.

This threefold, holy and divine, primordial Being shone as reflection from the face of Christ (2 Cor. 4:6). That is His 'radiant splendour of revelation' that we 'behold'. Of this Countenance of Christ the evangelist has, as it were, written the heavenly biography:

- Where the human being carries his thinking, everything is light about him.
- Where in the human being feelings live, everything about him is life.
- Where the human being is will, love glows about him.

Thus he sounds in the flesh as the Word.

When he read the beginning of John's Gospel, it must have felt for the evangelist as though he entered the most holy Mystery-centre, where a highest angel lights one candle after another in him, and each candle is a world. And when in his Mystery-centre through long paths of purification through the realms of 'teaching', 'purification', 'illumination', he rose up to 'communion', then he experienced here that he received all this in fullness through the one Christ.

- What he sought as teaching, came in Christ as divine light.
- What he attempted as purification, he received out of His divine life.
- What he longed for as illumination, that was given him as a gift in Christ through divine love.

As a divine festival of consecration the evangelist experienced Christ Himself. He received in His Mystery-celebration bread and wine and in them the life of the Godhead; he received in Christ grace and truth. Truth is the body of Christ. Grace is the blood of Christ. And both are the splendour of the Father. Communion, the highest Communion, was given to him when he entered the temple of John's Gospel.

John's Gospel, Chapter One
(Revised Standard Version)

In the beginning was the Word, and the Word was with God, and the Word was God. 2 He was in the beginning with God; 3 all things were made through him, and without him was not anything made that was made. 4 In him was life,[a] and the life was the light of men. 5 The light shines in the darkness, and the darkness has not overcome it.

6 There was a man sent from God, whose name was John. 7 He came for testimony, to bear witness to the light, that all might believe through him. 8 He was not the light, but came to bear witness to the light.

9 The true light that enlightens every man was coming into the world. 10 He was in the world, and the world was made through him, yet the world knew him not. 11 He came to his own home, and his own people received him not. 12 But to all who received him, who believed in his name, he gave power to become children of God; 13 who were born, not of blood nor of the will of the flesh nor of the will of man, but of God.

14 And the Word became flesh and dwelt among us, full of grace and truth; we have beheld his glory, glory as of the only Son from the Father. 15 John bore witness to him, and cried, 'This was he of whom I said, "He who comes after me ranks before me, for he was before me."' 16 And from his fullness have we all received, grace upon grace. 17 For the law was given through Moses; grace and truth came through Jesus Christ. 18 No one has ever seen God; the only Son,[b] who is in the bosom of the Father, he has made him known.

The Testimony of John the Baptist

19 And this is the testimony of John, when the Jews sent priests and Levites from Jerusalem to ask him, 'Who are you?' 20 He confessed, he did not deny, but confessed, 'I am not the Christ.' 21 And they asked him, 'What then? Are you Eli'jah?' He said, 'I am not.' 'Are you the prophet?' And he answered, 'No.' 22 They said to him then, 'Who are you? Let us have an answer for those who sent us. What do you say about yourself?' 23 He said, 'I am the voice of one crying in the wilderness, "Make straight the way of the Lord," as the prophet Isaiah said.'

---

[a]John 1:4. Or *was not anything made. That which has been made was life in him.*

[b]John 1:18. Other ancient authorities read *God.*

24 Now they had been sent from the Pharisees. 25 They asked him, 'Then why are you baptizing, if you are neither the Christ, nor Elijah, nor the prophet?' 26 John answered them, 'I baptize with water; but among you stands one whom you do not know, 27 even he who comes after me, the thong of whose sandal I am not worthy to untie.' 28 This took place in Bethany beyond the Jordan, where John was baptizing.

29 The next day he saw Jesus coming toward him, and said, 'Behold, the Lamb of God, who takes away the sin of the world! 30 This is he of whom I said, "After me comes a man who ranks before me, for he was before me." 31 I myself did not know him; but for this I came baptizing with water, that he might be revealed to Israel.' 32 And John bore witness, 'I saw the Spirit descend as a dove from heaven, and it remained on him. 33 I myself did not know him; but he who sent me to baptize with water said to me, "He on whom you see the Spirit descend and remain, this is he who baptizes with the Holy Spirit." 34 And I have seen and have borne witness that this is the Son of God.'

35 The next day again John was standing with two of his disciples; 36 and he looked at Jesus as he walked, and said, 'Behold, the Lamb of God!' 37 The two disciples heard him say this, and they followed Jesus. 38 Jesus turned, and saw them following, and said to them, 'What do you seek?' And they said to him, 'Rabbi' (which means Teacher), 'where are you staying?' 39 He said to them, 'Come and see.' They came and saw where he was staying; and they stayed with him that day, for it was about the tenth hour. 40 One of the two who heard John speak, and followed him, was Andrew, Simon Peter's brother. 41 He first found his brother Simon, and said to him, 'We have found the Messiah' (which means Christ). 42 He brought him to Jesus. Jesus looked at him, and said, 'So you are Simon the son of John? You shall be called Cephas' (which means Peter[c]).

43 The next day Jesus decided to go to Galilee. And he found Philip and said to him, 'Follow me.' 44 Now Philip was from Bethsaida, the city of Andrew and Peter. 45 Philip found Nathanael, and said to him, 'We have found him of whom Moses in the law and also the prophets wrote, Jesus of Nazareth, the son of Joseph.' 46 Nathanael said to him, 'Can anything good come out of Nazareth?' Philip said to him, 'Come and see.' 47 Jesus saw Nathanael coming to him, and said of him, 'Behold, an Israelite indeed, in whom is no guile!' 48 Nathanael said to him, 'How do you know me?' Jesus answered him, 'Before Philip

---

c John 1:42. From the word for *rock* in Aramaic and Greek, respectively.

called you, when you were under the fig tree, I saw you.' 49 Nathanael answered him, 'Rabbi, you are the Son of God! You are the King of Israel!' 50 Jesus answered him, 'Because I said to you, I saw you under the fig tree, do you believe? You shall see greater things than these.' 51 And he said to him, 'Truly, truly, I say to you, you will see heaven opened, and the angels of God ascending and descending upon the Son of man.'

*

LETTERS ON JOHN'S GOSPEL

Letter No. 1

The Mystery of the 'I'[16]

In calling John's Gospel the 'book of the Mystery of the "I", or ego', we are indebted to Rudolf Steiner, and indeed in general for the basic views expressed in these studies. Steiner taught us to feel that the word 'I' when spoken by Christ always receives a special emphasis. It is as if it meant the true 'I', the divine Ego, is speaking. It need not always be so translated, but we ought always to feel this about it.

Here we are reminded that the God Who revealed himself to Moses in the burning bush (Ex. 3) spoke His name thus: 'I am the I am.'[17] This translation of 'Yahveh' is accepted today by historical criticism, which only studies the external documents. The moment in mankind's history when the word 'I' was spoken by God, and moreover, was spoken as God's own name, cannot be overvalued. This would never have been possible in Ancient India, neither in Greece, nor in the Teutonic lands. By this we may be reminded that before Christ the peoples of the civilized world were sent out in two directions upon their search for God. The peoples of the North, whose task was to seek the divine in external revelation, found the highest revelation of the Godhead in light. This was especially true of the Persians, the Greeks, too, and in another way of the Teutonic tribes. The peoples who had to seek more inwardly found the highest revelation of the divine in the 'I'. The Egyptians prepared the way for this. The goddess Isis often revealed herself in the 'I' style to them. But it was the Israelites who experienced this revelation most sublimely and solemnly. These words are prefixed to the law of Israel, 'I am—the Lord your God'.

Monotheism, which is regarded as the great historical achievement of Israel, is very closely connected with this religion of the 'I am'. Different forces and possibilities lie before people according to whether they live chiefly in the free realms of the soul, or of nature. In the realm of the soul, they meet thinking, the feelings and the will; or more particularly, an experience of beauty, intellectual appreciation, feeling for nature, and so on. In the kingdom of nature we find the airy element, water, too, in its various forms, the solid earth, the light. Because people long ago gave themselves up more to the individual details, lost themselves in the details, they were polytheists in religion. In contrast to this, the 'I' arose sovereignly in Israel. No Zeus, no Wotan would have spoken like this, out of pure inwardness. In this way the human being laid hold of himself on the Earth for the first time fully as an individual being, a personality in his own right. It was a marvellous process. To be able to experience God as the 'I', the human being has first to have passed through a certain development towards the 'I', even if unconsciously. This is the case with Moses, who, to begin with, was separated by his destiny from the body of his people. But when a human being in this way becomes capable of hearing the word 'I' as the name of God, then the 'I' as if out of the heights progressively sinks down into his being through the effect made upon him by this divine name.

According to a general law of evolution, if a quality or faculty of soul is to unfold rightly, it has first to emerge to a certain extent in a one-sided way. Consequently, all polytheism was rooted out in Israel. We know from the history of Israel how hard this was, how painfully the people were drawn upward to the heights of that monotheism which spoke of the ego. Israel's prohibition of polytheism might have been expressed in this way: 'The "I" in you, which seeks to evolve, which is the meaning of the Earth's evolving, demands that you should look for once wholly at the One, the Ruler, and not at the individual powers of the soul, and the forces of nature. In this way you will become capable of experiencing God in His highest revelation.'

The same end was served by the way in which the people of Israel were led by destiny to direct their gaze entirely to history. In space, many things can exist side by side. When attention is fixed upon it, time is much more likely to lead one to seek the unity that runs through it. This law was so inexorably strict not only because in the visual and sculptural arts did the ancient gods live, but also because the people of Israel were to be trained to pure inwardness—to conceive of God entirely from within. In what we are saying, we are but developing what Rudolf Steiner was the first to say. The training of the Israelites was a wonderful contrast to the training of the Greek people, who, so to speak, received the commandment, 'Thou *shalt* make pictures and images'. This training of the Greeks, too, prepared the way for Christ. This occurred when, out of an earthly body, the words 'I am' were spoken. And one picture of this union is John's Gospel itself, expressing the divine inwardness—but in the Greek tongue.

In John's Gospel the longings of the northern and the southern peoples are united. 'I am—the light of the world.'

Love is the meaning of the Earth. The incense of love's pure being should rise up from the Earth. But an 'I' must first be there, otherwise love remains only a natural feeling. Love in its highest form, the love of a 'free spirit', taking this word in its best and highest sense, would be wanting. Consequently, people must look up to a God who says 'I'. Consequently, too, all the dangers of egoism, of national egoism and, later, of egoism of the individual person, must be included for better or worse, both then and throughout the evolution of the Israelites in the centuries to come. The central religious saying of Israel has been considered to be, 'Whom have I in heaven but you? And earth has nothing I desire besides you' (Ps. 73:25). This has often been quoted in an appreciative sense, but sometimes the religious egoism expressed in these words has been condemned. In such a saying we can see the greatness, but also the limitations of Israel. It is extraordinarily great not even to ask for heaven when one has the 'Thou' in whom the true 'I' speaks. And yet the limitations of Israel are clear. What is lacking is that for which God asks. He is asking precisely for Heaven and Earth. And in Christ, He has mightily asked for the Earth, simply because He is Love. That was, and still is, His life. This second thing ('Thee', Love) waits, slumbering in the background of such a saying. Initially, the first thing ('I', pure individuality) has to be attained. After Judaism, this second mighty thing appears in Christianity.

We must bear all this in mind if we are to look at the John's Gospel in the right spirit. The 'I' which speaks in it, is the very 'I' which asks for the Earth and for humanity. It has lost all the harshness and exclusiveness of the Old Testament 'I', but the greatness and sublimity are there in all their fullness. Here we can perceive how the Israelite can tragically come to refusing Christ. He does not perceive in Christ the 'I AM', the 'I AM' which spoke to him from Mount Sinai. And yet Christ was the fulfilment of that 'I AM'.

The spiritual investigations of anthroposophy speak of seven Elohim, whose working is the ground of all created existence. The spiritual place of work of these Elohim was the Sun, that is, the spiritual realm whose external expression is the Sun. But one of them, Yahveh, transferred to the Moon, in order to work from there. In a sense, he went there to assume the lordship, and prepare for the work of the others. If one cannot take this statement in any other way, it may be taken in spiritual pictures. Not only in the festivals of the Moon which Israel celebrated, but in the cold, intellectual, hardening element of the religion of Israel, we can see a resemblance to the Moon. And in contra-distinction to this, there is a resemblance to the Sun in the radiance, the mightiness of soul, the self-devotion of the 'I AM', which lived in Christ. The first half of human history serves the purpose of working out the 'I'. The second half serves to fill this 'I' with its content, love. Later, we shall discuss how this is directly expressed in John's Gospel.

We shall begin be making a few preliminary remarks about the more inner world of John's Gospel. We have to start from the fact that the gospel is divided into two parts. The first part ends with Chapter 10. The second part begins with the raising of Lazarus. This second part leads us more deeply into the Mystery of Christ. Steiner shows how this gospel itself points clearly to this division. We read at the end of Chapter 10: 'John did no sign, but everything that John said about this man was true' (10:41). At the end of the second part, we read: 'This is the disciple who is bearing witness to these things, and who has written these things; and we know that his testimony is true' (21:24).

In early sacred writings, such parallel forms always possess significance. Here, they reveal to us the fact that the first half of John's Gospel is close to the tradition of the group of disciples around John the Baptist, but that in the second half we are in immediate contact with the disciple 'whom Jesus loved'. Indeed, he is immediately mentioned, and for the first time, in Chapter 11:3. We might put it like this. The evangelist says in a half-concealed manner corresponding to the language of such documents: What I have previously written can be understood if one has passed through what was revealed in the preaching of John the Baptist, if one has not slept through the historical events connected with the Baptist. But, in order that we may understand what is coming next, Christ must perform a deed upon us such as he did upon Lazarus.

And so, at the end of Chapter 10, before the evangelist goes on to the deeds and events of Golgotha, we expect a kind of summing up of Christ's teaching, and we do find this. Even externally, by all the signs at the evangelist's disposal he points out that we have reached a culmination. 'It was the Feast of the Dedication at Jerusalem' (10:22). As we penetrate into John's Gospel, we find everywhere that the word 'temple' is used in a threefold sense:

- the temple of wood and stone,
- the temple of Christ's body, and
- the temple of the human body in general.

Immediately, at the first mention of the temple in John's Gospel, we are made aware of this ambiguity. 'But he spoke of the temple of his body' (2:21). It would be an entirely false view of the religious writers of past times to think that the evangelist could make such a remark for this occasion alone, without thinking from that time on whether such a variety of meaning might not be present for us. The knowledge of such a fact is valid for one and all.

When it says that 'it was the Feast of Dedication', this means: 'Take notice. Now the temple is really being dedicated. See how Jesus dedicates the temple. Do not think only of the stone temple. Think of the temple of the body. Think of the temple of His body, and think of the temple of your body, and give heed to what happens now.' We do not mean to say, of course, that the evangelist has 'put' this speech of Christ in the temple and that it was not really spoken there. But he would not have thought it worth mentioning if he had merely had to write an historical note, or had wished to create an impression of historical truth. He always sees outward events rich in divine meaning. He tells us that from all sides angels are pointing to what is happening so that human beings may be awake to it.

Rudolf Steiner also said that John's Gospel was really written for the angels.

- Matthews's Gospel was written for the Jews,
- Mark's Gospel for the Romans,
- Luke's Gospel for mankind,
- John's Gospel for the angels.[18]

And so, as no other gospel can, this one can help to make human beings into angels. Angels do not have earthly eyes. They cannot see earthly things in the same way as people can. But they see into people. And their realm begins immediately behind the impressions of the senses. They live, so to speak, on the inner side of the impressions of the senses. So they share in the experiences of the world, but spiritually one stage higher than human beings. If, then, the experiences of the senses are led to the point where they pass into spirit, where they become quite transparent for the spirit, then we go as far as we can to meet the angels. At the frontier between sense-impressions and spiritual impressions we meet the angels. John's Gospel is a continuous meeting of this kind. It describes things in an earthly manner, certainly, but so that the angels, too, can read it. In a certain sense, this is the secret of John's Gospel. Such an indication may say something even to those who do not feel able to speak of angels as realities. They can see in John's Gospel the human being himself 'on the way to the spirit'.

To tell the story as John tells it is only possible after repeated meditation upon the events throughout many years, so that only the spirit of them remains. Everyone who penetrates more deeply sees the meditation of the evangelist, his 'keeping and pondering' of the words (Luke 2:19) as if it were near enough for him to grasp. Thus, conversely, John's Gospel is the real gospel for meditation, and only in meditation can it gradually reveal itself in all its greatness and depth.

Even such a remark as 'it was winter' (John 10:22) is not to be explained as happens today, by saying that it was intended to show why Christ was walking 'in the portico of Solomon' sheltered from the rain and wind, instead of in the open air. This is what the modern journalist thinks, and the modern professor of history, too. For the evangelist quite different facts are important. And if we cannot feel our way into this spirit, we shall not understand at all what he wants to tell us.

'Winter' is also a picture of universal winter. External nature has died. It bears nothing more. It no longer gives any spiritual or religious revelation. The times are passed when human beings received revelations from the divine world with joy, fear and devotion. Even the celebration of the Israelite Feast of the Dedication of the Temple in December, was not only because the temple chanced perhaps to have been finished in winter, the most favourable time for building. It is an historical picture of the new temple which Israel was spiritually building among the nations. It is a picture of Israel's religion amongst all the other religions. They rejected the revelation of nature. They built out of the spirit. The fulfilment came with the dedication of the temple of Christ. When the evangelist looked away from what was happening then at the Feast of Dedication in Jerusalem, out to the cosmic events, he saw universal winter everywhere. This could be shown from the most differing sides; it was true especially of the human body.

And when we read that 'Jesus was walking in the temple, in the portico of Solomon', we have to ask: To what secret does the evangelist indicate? Solomon's portico, on the east side of the temple, was still regarded as the last survival of the earlier temple built by the son of David. The promise which had been given to David rested upon it. Solomon, the son of David, is named here, where the greatest Son of David appears. Of Him Solomon himself was a prophecy, and Solomon had also helped to build His earthly body. Solomon—the Temple—the Feast of Dedication; in the symbolic language which is at the evangelist's disposal, he calls to the world: 'Come ye all hither, ye who have a sense for the divine signs! That for which Solomon fashioned with his body, that for which he built the temple, that of which he himself and his life-work were a living prophecy, now finds its fulfilment in the true Feast of Dedication of the Temple.'

The other circumstances also point very clearly to the meaning of the hour. 'So the Jews gathered round him and said to him, How long will you keep us in suspense? If you are the Christ, tell us plainly' (10:24). We see the whole Jewish people assembled around Christ, as if it were raised for a moment to the heights, lifted about itself. We hear the decisive question coming from its mouth. Now or never, we shall learn in what sense Christ called himself Christ. The gravity of the situation is painted in another picture: 'The Jews took up stones again to stone him' (10:31). As a people they pronounce the final judgment. They will pull down Him who would raise them above themselves, and cause Him to die by stoning and to sink down into the earth, His grave. The living Temple is to be buried under the stones. Their own law, their own religious nature gradually had become petrified. They cannot remain in the heights to which, for a moment, they had been raised. The stones which they bring are really their own selves. It was the hardened nature within them which they piled up there, in an image which is all too expressive. They are revealed. The Temple of stone is defending itself against the Temple of flesh, because it no longer regards itself as temporary and prophetic but has become soulless and hard. In legality, stoning as a capital punishment in Jewish law, meant that the Earth itself destroys those who have committed crimes against it. But here, stoning means that human beings have become stone and do not perceive that the temple of stone has reached its fulfilment in the human temple.

Once again, it is very significant that Christ withdrew from them immediately afterwards, and crossed the Jordan. The 'fulfilment' goes back 'over the river', 'beyond the Jordan' to the place from which it had come. This, too, is a judgment. It is Christ's judgment, as opposed to the Jews' judgment, for one who can read the language of the evangelist. 'I do not deserve to be driven from the Earth by you, but you deserve that I should go away again from the Earth.'

The true 'I'

Within this significant framework we shall now study the words which Christ speaks at this time. There are three sayings in particular in which he tells us in what sense He regards himself as Christ. 'I and the Father are one' (10:30), 'I am the Son of God' (10:36), and 'the Father is in me, and I in him' (10:38).

'I and the Father are one.' From the beginning, Christianity strove to understand the unity of Christ with the Father. But when we study, for example, the Athanasian Creed[19] (which up to now has been regarded as equally valid with the Apostolic and Nicene Creeds) we find:

> The Catholic faith is this: That we worship one God in Trinity, and Trinity in Unity; neither confounding the Persons, nor dividing the Substance. For there is one Person of the Father, another of the Son, and another of the Holy Ghost. But the Godhead of the Father, of the Son, and of the Holy Spirit, is all one, the Glory equal, the Majesty co-eternal.... And in this Trinity none is afore or after other, none is greater, or less than another, but the whole three Persons are co-eternal together, and co-equal, so that in all things, as is aforesaid, the Unity in Trinity, and the Trinity in Unity is to be worshipped. He therefore that will be saved, must thus think of the Trinity.

We see that here the unity is asserted, but not really understood, not experienced in a truly illuminating way. This is connected with the fact, most important to see, that behind this statement there is only logical thought, and nothing more. Logical thought was the achievement of the Greeks, especially of Aristotle. When in his *History of Dogma* [1894-98] Adolf von Harnack shows that ecclesiastical dogma was the offspring of the Greek spirit on the basis of the gospel, he was right. This is a significant truth. Only we must not believe that this dogma was therefore simply a false path and that in its place we have to put a so-called 'simple' gospel. We have to break through into a new spirituality which increases the possibilities of expressing the gospel. We have to understand that the protective mantle of logic, in which the Greek spirit initially enclosed Christian truth, was meant, according to the deep wisdom of the cosmic rulership, to allow Christianity to develop first in people's feelings and will. Here it might express its true nature, and, by the revelation of its nature, might be protected and restrained from spiritually dissipating itself, or changing its spiritual nature. For the essence of Christianity is the principal thing.

We cannot enter into details on all this here. But we can point out that the hour has come when Christianity can be expressed better than through dogma, through a new kind of spirit. What has pointed out the right way to humanity is John's Gospel. It has waited for humanity.

There is a spirituality, which, starting from the words, 'I and the Father are one', seeks to work out from the 'I' the unity in duality. In earlier times, humanity had not yet sufficient power in the ego to do this. Through Christ Himself, the 'I' has first to be strengthened until it is able to walk in such ways. John's Gospel, or rather the disciple of Christ in whom that gospel was born, was the forerunner, who was led so far by Christ as to be able to express these Mysteries in words.

Very much depends on the development at this present time of an insight into the true 'I', that an experience is present among human beings of its secret. When the 'I' has found itself to a certain degree, as it has in our time, then precisely the greatest dangers arrive. One danger, for example, is the feeling of loneliness which drives many people today to suicide. Furthermore, great dangers threaten the 'I' today from outside. Technological processes in industry are beginning to extinguish the human 'I', and to mechanize mankind. Man becomes a part of the machine. And the progress of politics threatens us with collectivization; the individual finds no prospect of asserting himself. He becomes a member of the general human mass.

We are fully conscious that we are fighting an apparently hopeless battle against these baleful forces when, able to do nothing but proclaim a truth—and one that demands much activity from mankind to understand it—we speak here of the Mystery of the 'I' in the name of John's Gospel.

The human 'I'

The 'I' is the real miracle of the Earth. It always sounds from within. No one can apply this word to any other human being. One cannot say 'I' when speaking of another person. The 'I' is the most defined particular fact which could be found. Yet at the same time, it has the most varied forms. It is always only one person who can say of himself 'I' and yet each person who says it is other than the rest. How different are all those people who say 'I'!—the cannibal and the genius, the headstrong child and the old man to whom years have brought ripe wisdom, the Patagonian woman and the Buddha. Out of what heavens and hells 'I' sounds! It differs a thousandfold and is always the same. Man himself has to develop through childhood for years before he can say 'I'. And it is a sovereign moment, even if it is usually unobserved, when a child says 'I'. Then out of his inward self we hear the words spoken, which one can learn from no one else, can imitate from no one else, which one can find only by oneself from the inborn dignity of one's own human nature. People who can say 'I' to themselves, however dull or narrow this saying may be, carry a patent of nobility, which raises them above all surrounding nature.

It is as if the word 'I' is bestowed on human being and all the angels are watching to see in what spirit it is uttered. It sounds forth dully or mightily; it casts down or raises up; it speaks in agony or in rejoicing.

And yet all this is but one side of the truth, and even this side is only hinted at. We find the other side expressed at its greatest in the saying of Master Eckhart: 'No one but the Father alone can speak the little word "I".'[20] To be sure, if we would penetrate this deepest Mystery of the human 'I', then we first have to take several steps.

When we say 'I' in ordinary life—who really speaks? If we closely examine ourselves, in many thousands of cases we shall say, 'But I wasn't there at all! At most, there was something dimly seeking the way to the real "I", a shadowy part of what happened. It was really something else that acted through me—some habit, some accepted opinion, some eternal compulsion, perhaps also some passing impulse that arose out of the dark depths of the body, or a personal wish within the human community, of which I did not realize the nature, or a need whose origin is strange to me. But was it I myself? My "I" was like a feeble flame, moving about among accidental and arbitrary impulses, which springing up within played upon me.'

Everyone, or at least everyone wishing to penetrate the Mystery of the 'I', should make the experiment of asking himself when setting about an action, 'How would my real, true self act?' Better still, immediately after an action, to ask, 'How would my real true self have acted?' For it is easier for a person rightly to gain an insight into what he perceives when he is not immediately obliged or able to carry it out.

If, then, after meeting somebody, we ask, 'How ought I to have behaved towards that person?' If we go more deeply into this question we gradually begin to discover what depths lie below this self. If we do not give up, but go on saying, 'No, that is not yet our true "I", our real self!' —*then at last comes the moment when we become conscious of a deep union with God.* It seems as if divine light breaks into our being. This light breaks in with the pure splendour of the spirit. We begin to see that our 'I' is an organ with which we find the Father—Who is Himself an 'I'. We stumble upon the ultimate Mystery of human becoming. We break into the realm of creation itself. We feel that we can only truly say 'I' when we allow the *Father* in us to say 'I'. 'No one but the Father alone can speak the little word "I".'

God willed that there should be an 'I' upon the Earth. In each of many people there should be an 'I'. And it should stand quite independently before Him. But this independence only comes first so that it may find the very deepest union of all. For there is no deeper union in the world than that a person should be able to say 'I' wholly—and yet the Father is speaking through him. It is of this separation and of this union that Christ speaks when He says, 'I and the Father are one'. This saying takes the 'I' and the Father apart—and unites them again completely. In this separation and union we see into the deepest cosmic Mystery of the human being and of humanity's earthly history. At this point many people will say: 'But it is only said of Christ that "I and the Father are one".'

It is a precisely a decisive moment for us when we perceive that Christ has not come in order to show us something we can never achieve ourselves, but that He has come in order to give us His whole 'I' to be our real self. 'I in *them*.' With this saying, Christ concludes his High-Priestly Prayer, which is the conclusion of His preaching (17:26). Anyone failing to understand this is still taking his Christianity in a pre-Christian sense, for everything emphasizing the distance between God and man, and not equally strongly the union between them, is not yet Christian. Whenever anyone fails to get beyond the opposition of God and man, and takes this 'I and Thou' as real Christianity has not got beyond a pre-Christian position. Those who are acquainted with Christianity and theology know to what extent this is the position today. It is unlike John to say 'I and Thou', but 'Great-"I" and Small-"I"'. The Great-'I' and the Small-'I'—this is the crux of real Christianity, of Christianity in the Johannine spirit.

Christ does not merely win heaven for us, or promise us heaven; He *is* heaven and comes into us as heaven with the 'I' which He gives us. This is heaven's open door.

Master Eckhart was on the track of a very great Mystery. He could not have felt it without Christ. This vision flashed out like lightning within him at a time when the 'I' was generally not yet strong enough for it. Although his mysticism often sinks back into a mood of Neo-Platonism, or of early Indian thought, yet this gleam of the future was there.

If a human being could allow the pure 'I', the deepest, most profound 'I', to speak in himself, then he would be in the Father and the Father in him. Because he cannot do this, Christ enters as 'the light of the world'. In this light the human 'I' is washed clean. Not only does it receive the forgiveness of sins. It bathes in Christ and becomes clean. It kindles its own light at the light of Christ. And so in reliance on Christ, in renewal through Christ, in creation through Christ, although provisionally very sick and feeble, it learns to say, 'My real "I" and the Father are one'. It begins to know a kind of union, a kind of becoming united, such as there is nowhere else in the world. And on *this* path, and never on the path of dogmatic, dialectical definitions, it comes to an inkling of the way Christ and the Father are one.

The German thinker J.G. Fichte [1762-1814] on his abstract path approached these Mysteries. He understood the 'I' as absolute activity, because he sought it in the depths. And he understood the human individuality, when it rightly understands itself, as being filled by the one absolute 'I'. Upon the path of the intellect one cannot proceed further. But John the evangelist went further. Looking at Christ, he no longer speaks in his own person, but takes shelter in the light of this 'I'.

This cannot be expressed more simply than it is in John's Gospel. Every person, at every stage of their development, has something of it. And yet it is the deepest Mystery of humanity. It is characteristic of John's Gospel to bring the ultimate truths so near to us, and to express them so grandly that we become almost afraid. There it stands, perfectly comprehensible in the words used, and yet well concealed, waiting until people are mature enough to understand it.

In the human 'I' the Sun of the Father-God can rise. A person's feeling for their own 'I' can become infinitely sacred the more this dawns on them. God visits us in our 'I'. God has created this organ so that He Himself may speak in it.

And now we have taken our first glimpse at the 'Dedication of the Temple', which took place at that time. The body is the temple of this 'I'. That is its significance. At the moment when an 'I' spoke out of a human body, saying, 'I and the Father are one', *the true 'Dedication of the Temple' took place.* Not only the body was consecrated, but also the Temple which is its prototype.

In order to complete what has already been said, we shall study another passage, at the end of Chapter 12. It is clear that at this point—before passing on to the scene of the Washing of the Feet and beginning the narration of the Passion—the gospel once more makes a tremendous summary. After the chief priests had decided upon Christ's death, the evangelist significantly points to the prophecy of Isaiah, which has been fulfilled in the Israelites (12:37-43).

Immediately after this, the whole of Christ's preaching is summed up in few short sentences (12:44-50). 'Believe in me.' In a mighty gesture, this great passage of Isaiah—by far the largest prophetic passage contained in John's Gospel, and quoted at the turning point of the gospel—is placed between the sayings, 'Believe in the light' and 'Believe in me'. This is the demand with which Christ meets humanity. Believe in the 'I' that stands before you.

The word 'believe' has been spoiled for people today. They connect it to notions of some spiritual compulsion or other. They hold it to denote a lower form of spiritual life compared with knowledge.

All these notions would pass away if they once received into themselves the Johannine way of speaking about faith. In John's Gospel faith is never connected with any particular facts, never with any particular truths but always with Christ Himself. 'Believe in me.' This is repeated time and again in John's Gospel. In accordance with our focus on the 'I', this might also be translated 'Believe in my "I"'. Indeed this one fact out of John's Gospel might be of infinite benefit to people if they would rightly consider it. Believe in Him—that can never be a single article of faith, a mere believing that something is true. It is something quite different. The phrase differs only in that it sometimes says, 'Believe in the light', then again, 'Believe in my name', and again, 'Believe in him that sent me'. In this threefold varying phrase, that which came through Christ is marvellously expressed—a new world of light, a new world of sound and a new world of life. These are the three worlds that are described by anthroposophical spiritual science from the human side as the worlds [of higher cognition], of Imagination, Inspiration and Intuition. We shall meet them more often in the gospel.

It may now become clear to us that to believe and to know may sound together with quite another accord in John's Gospel, compared to that which they have in today's apprehension. The Johannine way is indicated especially in the passage (17:8): 'They know in truth that I came from Thee; and they have believed that Thou didst sent me.' It is a real knowing that takes place, but one by the help of higher forces. One can perceive by the ordinary powers of the intellect that the Christ taught rather differently from the Buddha—but not that Christ came from God. Here one has to enter an element of truth that is accessible to the spirit, though not to the [reflecting] intellect.

When Goethe stood before the Classical pictures and statues of Italy, he put his impressions into words: 'Here is necessity! Here is God!'[21]

A similar impression is made by Christ, when He sends His light into man's soul: 'Here is Truth! Here is God!' Even if a background in theory of knowledge is not drawn on, one nevertheless appreciates that one is moving in a kingdom of truth. In this spirit, the quoted passage in the gospel means: They have perceived in truth that I came from you. This kingdom of truth does not need to be justified before the other truths that people perceive. On the contrary, that which otherwise appears true is only a shadow compared with the light of truth which is in this kingdom. In this kingdom one knows with the 'I' and not with the intellect.

The human 'I' can realize those of other human beings. Had we not ourselves an 'I' we could not know those of others. We are more able to realize those of others since our own 'I' is rich in possibilities. People with a pure nature who find no conscious approach to many existing sins will find it extraordinarily difficult to realize an 'I' that lives in base selfishness. They will always say, inwardly if not outwardly, 'How is such a thing possible!' They will always be inclined to believe people are better than they are. Conversely, a person inclining to common selfishness will be quite unable to grasp a higher 'I' that finds its real homeland in goodness. They will be invariably mistrustful and suspicious. This is only an example of how an 'I' can be an organ of knowledge to perceive the 'I' of others. And so the human 'I', which is of divine origin, is well able to realize an 'I' that has proceeded from God. That is the most sacred act of perception that exists. It must not be thought that we are here entering upon uncertain ground. One can *know*. When we see Christ, how He loves, how He gave Himself in radiant purity, how of Himself He wishes nothing, but lives in the divine Will, then we can *realize* that 'this is from God!'

People can *know* the truth that Christ came forth from God. But—and here is a fine distinction—that God sent Him to us we can only *believe*. The first thing is a *fact*, the second a *deed*. And this deed can only be answered by another deed. I can experience that a messenger has set out to bring me a message. Still, I can close the door on him. The fine, quite personal act that I receive him is something different. This I can do only if I trust in the one who sent him and open my door to him and his message. If the message is to concern *me*, then I have to assent to it. The Johannine relationship between knowledge and faith becomes apparent to anyone who ponders this difference. These persons see that an act of knowing precedes faith. They notice what is really required of us. Certainly, faith is frequently spoken about in such a wide sense that the act of recognition is included. But the real act of faith is this opening of oneself upon which a connecting and uniting follows.

'Believe in me.' Pictures can best say what that means. Let us place before our souls a landscape. Think of the early morning when we wake. Then let us remember Christ. And the Sun arises radiant in our inward landscape. When in an earthly landscape the Sun rises, then everything begins to shine, it cannot do otherwise. Not only in the sea does the Sun mirror itself, but everything that lives endeavours to let the Sun shine back from it again; as well as it can, tree, field and stone. They compete with one another, striving which can do its best. And none is jealous of the other. Some things cannot mirror the Sun, cannot yet mirror it, but they can grow bright. And everything does grow bright. That which happens in nature of its own accord ought to happen freely and consciously in the inward landscape. Our whole world is turned to Christ, growing bright and radiant as much as it can. And this is simply faith. *It is a great and joyful affirmation, a saying 'Yes' with our whole being.* And as such an assent we are to think of faith, and then the word 'faith' will become quite newly dear to our soul.

One can ever repeat this 'yes' during the course of the day, can allow this Sun in the heavens to shine through the clouds into the soul. 'I am come as light into the world, that whoever believes in me may not remain in darkness' (12:46). How relieved one can feel, because *this and nothing else* is faith in a Johannine sense.

So it must come about that the Sun stands still and remains shining in the heavens. Then we have the 'light of life'. As long as this is not yet, we have to allow this Sun freely to shine through our repeated 'Yes!' But we say 'Yes' to the Sun as the sea, in which it is reflected, as the eye in which it shines, as the soul which is transformed into its light. And thus we continue to repeat afresh the act of faith.

We are invited to use this simile when we consider words like these (12:36), 'While you have the light, believe in the light, that you may become sons of light'. The Sons of Light, that is the secret Order of Christ.

Directly after this saying, we read, 'When Jesus had said this, he departed and hid himself from them'. This, too, is said with the greatest significance. The external fact which impressed itself upon the evangelist—that Jesus hid Himself after these words—is to him an eloquent picture of what happened spiritually at that time. And so, full of significance, he continues:

> Even after Jesus had done all these miraculous signs in their presence, they still would not believe in him. This was to fulfil the word of Isaiah the prophet:
>
> > Lord, who has believed our message
> > and to whom has the arm of the Lord been revealed?

Afterwards this summing up the whole of Christ's teaching comes again (12:44-50). Let us take as a completion the saying (16:7-9), the Holy Spirit, 'the Counsellor' will 'convince the world of sin and of righteousness and judgment ... because men do not believe in me'—and we have penetrated to the weightiest point in the whole of John's Gospel. That is *the* sin, that someone should not believe in the 'I' that is there in Christ. In earlier times it may have been sin to break this or that commandment, but in reality that was sin because out of this commandment an 'I' spoke, which was perhaps not yet understood, but which was trying to raise men to Itself. With the coming of Christ, all other sins lost their significance and the real sin is seen—as resistance to the divine 'I' which is in Christ. That is the greatest deepening which the experience of sin can attain. The experience of sin is immediately connected—not with particular commandments that can be transgressed but with the deepest sense of life of the new man. 'What does not proceed from faith is sin', says Paul (Rom. 14:23). In the sense of John's Gospel, that which does not happen out of union with this divine 'I' in Christ is all sin, however righteous and good it may appear.

It can be the most liberating feeling a person can entertain and that which lays on them the greatest responsibility. The obverse side also has to be deeply and vividly felt—all that does not proceed out of the light-'I' of Christ is simply dark and soiled. The more people really feel that they make themselves unworthy by everything that is not born out of the light-'I' of Christ, *the more they are Christian in the sense of John's Gospel.*

Those of us of The Christian Community are often accused of not knowing what 'sin' is. That is one of the superficialities that is opposed to that which is new. People feel pious because they know better what sin is. In reality one ought to learn out of John's Gospel the ultimate force of the feeling of sin, of which Christianity has until now known scarcely anything. 'If you do not believe I am the one I claim to be, you will indeed die in your sins' (8:24).

This is Christ's tremendous demand of people: Believe in Me! Not in the sense of any arbitrary trust, but in the sense, Believe that in Me the true 'I' has appeared, for Whom you have all waited, in Whom you can all find your own 'I', in Whom is fulfilled the meaning of humanity in Earth's history.

It is not without reason that these decisive words of proclamation stand just after the raising of Lazarus. We have brought them into connection with an awakening. It is *the* awakening, the resurrection! We can perform the act of the awakening of Lazarus in ourselves at every moment, if we say 'Yes' to the light of Christ, say 'Yes' with our whole being.

Letter No. 2

The Mystery of the 'I' (2)

Three times in human history has 'unity' been mightily proclaimed:

(1) In early India it was endeavoured to lead people to a feeling of the unity of all creation. That was a very strong religious experience, full of exaltation and blessedness. We can still feel something of it today. It lies, as it were, beneath the threshold of our consciousness. But it is more important to feel that this experience belongs to the past, and that everywhere when it is proclaimed—which happens more often than is realized, in religion, art and philosophy—it is a return to the past. In the early days of the monism of science, this feeling of all-inclusive unity was proclaimed, often with enchanting poetic power, for example, by the late Julius Hart,[22] whose inner relationship to India is obvious.

(2) A second time unity was proclaimed with a historic grandeur was through Israel. Yahveh alone is God, and there is no God beside Him.[23] All other gods were seem to be but sound and smoke when Yahveh appeared in His splendour. If one is to tread with the nations along the road leading upwards to the highest one feels the very different grandeur and severity of this belief in unity. By this proclamation, human beings felt called to that which is highest and hardest. It filled souls with sublime enthusiasm right into the greatest period of Arabism, and is still heard in the philosophies of Semitic thinkers, down to Spinoza and Cohen,[24] in the feeling of superiority which the Islamic doctors have over Christianity, and in the scientific monism which is the mood of the science of our time, in whose foundation the Arabs have played such a decisive role. Here also one must perceive the paths which lead from the past to the future. Even in Protestant theology of today, the first as well as the second of these experiences of unity may be clearly realized.

(3) For the third time unity was proclaimed with ultimate greatness in John's Gospel. In the Great Intercession, the High-Priestly Prayer (John 17) the proclamation of unity is transcendent in its majesty. 'That they may be one as we are one' (17:11). 'That they all of them may be one, Father, just as you are in me and I am in you' (17:21 also vv. 22 & 23). Since then, this prayer for divine unity has risen like a song above all strife and divisions in the world. People who have received this music into themselves bear the song of the Earth's perfecting. These words of Christ's prayer hover over the Earth like consecrating melodies. It is as if

> a Temple built up of singing harmonies were above and around us. Out of this, the ultimate will of Christ, all who have received it draw their highest power to work for mankind—the true fire of divine love.

Considering this unity in its threefold form, one is presented with a historical picture of those aspects of the human soul which are expressed by anthroposophical spiritual science in the three words: sentient soul; intellectual, or mind-soul; and spiritual soul, or consciousness-soul. It does not matter that the times given by anthroposophy, as the classical ages that developed these different members of the soul, do not correspond exactly with the ages into which we have glanced here. The Indian's experience of unity lives in the feelings and consequently it is felt instinctively by the people of our age, to whom it came in an altered form, as not quite suited for the present time. It lived originally in the breathing, which then was revealed as bearer of the feelings. The breathing which is in man—*atman*—and the sacred smoke that rises from the sacrifice—*brahman*—were felt to be a unified divinity revealed in a twofold manner, outwardly and inwardly.

In Judaism, unity was experienced quite differently. Here the element of intellectual knowledge appeared more clearly. The other gods are nought. The intellect realizes, separates and distinguishes. On the other hand, in the Indian world the unity existing among the various gods had been felt and people had been led into a worldwide tolerance. That the understanding separates people, but feeling unites them is known to all orators who wish to move the masses. But besides the element of the understanding, there is an unmistakable element of *Gemut*, of mind and soul, in Israel. In the Psalms, 'Whom have I in heaven but you? And earth has nothing I desire besides you' (Ps. 73:25). In the period of the mind-soul which, according to anthroposophical division of time is developed during the fourth post-Atlantean culture from the eighth century BCE, Judaism found its complete self-expression, whereas the Indian culture being that of the feelings had already reached great heights long before.

It is again very different when we reach John's Gospel. That which must be attained here can only be won upon the path that leads through the 'I'. 'I' in Christ, Christ in the Father; the Father in Christ, Christ in the 'I', all one in Christ, all one in the Father, the Father in all—that is the sublime path to human perfection, as shown us by John's Gospel. Only in free-will, in our awakened consciousness can a person find these heights. It is clearly an ultimate matter that is revealed to us here. We see 'the human being' standing in the glowing light of this highest revelation.

Such sayings as 'all one in me', are usually experienced much too logically and mathematically by us in our refined intellectuality. It is in this way that we come to the experience of John's Gospel. By a roundabout way, through a picture we may perhaps come to an open door which leads into this temple. Volkmann-Leander[25] in his *Träumerein an französischen Kaminen* ['Dreams by a French Hearth'] tells his children that once, at the beginning of the history of mankind, a great sheet of music was torn to pieces in heaven. The single notes fall to earth. And every man found one note. Since then, everyone sings his own note, and they often sound together very discordantly. But at the end of the world, so the poet says, the sheet of music will be put together again in heaven. Then everyone will sing his note at the right place. And then, all at once, one will see that it was the greatest symphony imaginable.

This picture leads us to yet another perception. When the Indian sought and felt unity, it was the unity *before* the world—in all directions. The Indian denies that which is individual, particular, and many-sided. He goes backwards. So, too, this is still evident, even in Neo-Platonism and in the mysticism of Master Eckhart, where the wave of Indian experience breaks, transformed again, into the Occident. The Israelite seeks a quite different unity. He seeks unity *above* the world. And for that reason too his life was conflict. First there was an inner conflict of the soul and in the people against the many gods. Later, in Arabism, it was also already known that this unity above the world is not the ultimate unity, but is only the preparation for a unity which will come one day, will reveal itself one day. And so Judaism shows itself again to be the religion of preparation, the religion of promise. That which is to come is the unity *in* the world, in which the whole of this world's history is to end. Through the whole world, which has now reached its goal, its completion, its consecration, this unity echoes once more: but now it is not unity *before* all plurality, nor is it unity *against* all plurality, but unity *in* all plurality. We see before us the work of Christ in the spirit of John's Gospel, when we perceive that He is the only one who can bring this unity, and that this unity in the highest thing that He has brought.

One cannot and dare not wish to reach this unity too soon. That leads to catastrophe. Much misery caused by personal peculiarities and self-will must be overcome over a very long time. But His true disciples can draw the power of consecration onwards from the invisible temple, which, since Christ, stands above mankind. One note from this resounding temple, and we know once more that this *is* the truth, this *is* the goal, this *is* the divine thought for the world!

Now it is essential that one should see especially the love proclaimed in John's Gospel in the light of this unity. This love is not merely a feeling; it is a breaking through into a higher sphere. It is not simply a single helpful act, but it is the goal of the world. It is not a sentimental 'blessedness', but an awakening in Christ to a higher all-embracing 'I', and a fight for the new Earth, carried on by virtue of this new awakening. This is already contained in the saying, 'Thou shalt love thy neighbour as thyself'. But one is taking John's Gospel into a sphere which is much too human, if one does not carry this love within oneself as a flame out of this invisible temple. Love, as meant by John's Gospel, is the burning wish to fulfil upon Earth the commission given by Christ in His High-Priestly Prayer; to bring this wish into every single act by the power of the spirit, of the Holy Spirit, and by the illumination that comes from the Light of the World Himself, and so to make this love a cosmic battle—*the* cosmic battle. Fire ought actually to fall from heaven to Earth, but not in the way the sons of Zebedee wished—'Lord, do you want us to bid fire come down from heaven and consume them?' (Luke 9:54). 'I am come to cast fire on the earth: and what will I if it be already kindled?' It is characteristic of John's Gospel that fire is never mentioned, but always light. Even where the baptism of Christ is spoken of, in contradistinction to the baptism of John (1:33), it does not say as in Matt. 3:11 and in Luke 3:16, that Christ will baptize with the Holy Spirit and with fire, but only with the Holy Spirit. Even small details show that whereas the three other gospels are meant to be received by the soul, John's Gospel has to be received by the spirit. In John's Gospel, love is a love that not only feels itself marvellously touched by Christ's being, but also joins itself to the light of Christ's purpose for the world, and allows this light to kindle warmth in the soul.

In His prayer of farewell Christ gives us the sublime eternal example for all human love, 'the love wherewith Thou (the Father) hast loved me'. This is the origin of all love. By looking to this eternal love which is the great fact upon which the world is based, love is unfolded in a person's heart. 'That the love wherewith Thou hast loved me may be in them, and I in them!' (17:26). It is one of the chief glories of John's Gospel that here, by the parallelism of the phrases, we have the equation: 'The love wherewith Thou hast loved me', and 'I'. The 'I' of

Christ is filled with the love wherewith it is loved by the Father. It is one with that. It is itself this love. Here we see into the final Mystery of the 'I'. The love of the Father at the beginning of the world's evolving would have no object, if it were not directed to an 'I'. Consequently, out of this love comes an 'I' that can be loved. For 'He speaks and it is done'. The divine will is distinguished from the human will because it does not consist of wishes and impulses that are everywhere limited, but it creates what it wishes.

Nietzsche touched in a distorted way upon this divine will, when in his last period he wished that his own will might become the truth of the century. He expresses his sorrow in *Thus Spoke Zarathustra.* As to the future, he still hopes that, after 'God is dead', according to his meaning, he can cause the future to come forth out of the will. But there is the past. It stands 'eternally still'. And with regard to this, Nietzsche says, 'That it cannot will the past to come back is the loneliest tribulation of the will'.[26] It is necessary to see the divine in such distortions, for such a way of thinking will help to heal Nietzsche's world.

Unity with the Father

> (1) To such heights we may be led by the second saying we quoted from John 10. 'The Father in me and I in him' (10:38). This saying is emphasized by its position at the end of the first part of John's Gospel, which is also the end of Christ's public activity. And its meaning is brought out in a twofold way. It is introduced by the phrase, 'That you may know and believe' (10:38). And immediately afterwards the sentence follows, 'Therefore they sought again to take him: but he escaped out of their hand' (10:39). In place of the inward force they ought to have used for perception, they bring only the external force of reaction. But in this way they cannot reach Him. They only cause Him to disappear from their sight.

In this saying, the Dedication of the Temple, which was then taking place, stands before us again. The Temple ought to be a house of God. 'He shall build a house for my name' (2 Sam. 7:13). But it points to the other house that must be built later. Yes, the Temple helps by its services to build its other house. This house is eternally the human body—inwardly the human 'I'. The place where the Father can dwell is His house. When it could be said with truth, 'The Father in me, and I in the Father', then this house stood before us, and the Father had found His true house on Earth. *The Dedication of the Temple!* And through Christ's saying, uttered at that time, the consecration of the Temple takes place again in everyone who, deeply divining and perceiving, participates in this consecration.

> (2) We find this saying, 'I in the Father and the Father in me' for the second time in the Farewell Discourses in 14:10 and 11. The first time it was spoken with respect to the Israelite world, this second time it has to do with the Greek world. Through Philip, who himself bears a Greek name, the Greeks had come to Christ wishing to see him (12:21). And Philip himself entreats Christ, as if in the name of the Greek world, 'Lord, show us the Father and we shall be satisfied' (14:8). The historical greatness of the Greeks lay in their being able to pray through the eyes. In gazing at the statues of the gods, in viewing the artistic works of the temples, their worship became active. And so it is not without meaning that Christ now points away from sight to faith, and says twice with emphasis, 'Do you not believe that I am in the Father and the Father in me?' (14:10) and, immediately afterwards, 'Believe me that I am in the Father and the Father in me' (14:11). The Greeks have to learn that inward seeing, which is faith. This is the continuance of their history through Christ. This faith then leads to full knowledge, and it is there already in embryo, 'At that day ye shall know that I am in my Father, and ye in me, and I in you' (14:10).

And it is not insignificant that when spoken to the Israelites the words run thus, 'The Father in me, and I in the Father', but when spoken to the Greeks, the order of the words is different: 'I in the Father, and the Father in me.' The Jews believed in the Father, but they had to learn to seek Him in Christ. The Greeks looked at man, but they had to learn to see in him the Father. It awakens in us increasing reverence for the gospel when we see what a revelation it is even in the order of its words.

> (3) This saying appears a third time, in the High-Priestly Prayer, the Great Intercession. 'That they all may be one; as thou, Father, art in me, and I in you' (17:21). Here, one might say, it is spoken for all people, not only for Jews and Greeks, and above all people, in the form of an address to the Father, in a solemn confirmation, far above mankind. And the saying, 'I and the Father are one' re-appears in a changed, heightened form as a prayer uttered before the divine countenance, 'That they may be one, even as we are one' (17:22). Through their return into a higher sphere, these words of revelation have a sacred seal impressed upon them. This is a special characteristic of the Farewell Discourses, and of the Great Intercession in particular, with which we shall yet become more closely acquainted.

Is it mere chance, that this saying of which we are speaking appears exactly three times in the gospel, or that on the second occasion it is repeated three times (14:10, 11 and 20)? Is it pure chance that in the first saying (10:38) the Father stands first, in the second the Son, and in the third (17:21, 22) the Holy Spirit appears, 'That they all may be one'? Or that the last form which appears in the second occurrence of the words already prepares for the third occurrence, and takes it into itself? 'I in my Father, and you in me, and I in you' (14:20)? None of us would dare to assert that this was all consciously present to the evangelist.[27] But such writings are written out of higher harmonies than are contained in the chain of logical thinking. When one repeatedly meets such rhythms, one hears them singing, as it were. One sees angelic choirs hovering above the gospel, and catches in the gospel the echoes of their song. Without this view of the invisible worlds lying behind John's Gospel, one could never receive that gospel rightly.

But when we look into the history of Earth, we should like to bring out two of the many points of view from which this saying can be studied. Ever again we come up against the historical fact that the peoples of the civilized world of that age before Christ were directed in two different directions. The Northern peoples—Persians, Greeks and Teutons—sought the divine more outwardly, in the revelations of nature, whereas the Southern peoples—Indians, Egyptians, Israelites—sought it more inwardly, in the revelations of human destiny and of the human being as such. One need not take this distinction too rigidly. For example, in the cult of Dionysus, as distinct from the cult of Apollo, the Greeks also had a more inward way. Again, besides the way of Atman, the Indians also had a more outward way in their worship of Brahman. But on the whole this distinction is obvious and is very significant.

The highest to which the peoples and religions of the North could have attained would have been that they could have experienced they were in the midst of the divine Father. When the vision reaches through the whole of nature, the whole created world, then the person who is awakened looks into the face of the great, divine Father. They did not yet come so far. The fulfilment of their seeking and longing came in Christ's saying, 'I and the Father'. And in all their searching, the Southern peoples could have found nothing higher than the revelation that the inmost essence in man, the 'I', is capable of, and destined to bear within itself, the fullness of the divine. It is in its nature a reflection of the highest Godhead, and it ought fully and consciously to become so. The fulfilment of their search is in Christ's saying, 'I in the Father, and the Father in me'. Here the peoples are united. The Temple in which they can worship together stands shining before them. This Temple is a living Person—the example for all living people.

Another consideration can help us to see the cosmic greatness of this saying. We think of our time and of the great contrast between the men of the East and those of the West. In the West people have discovered the 'I', but it has become an earthly ego. It is increasingly losing its connection with the higher world. The redemption of the West depends on the 'I' finding itself *in the Father*. If, in the West, the 'I' can be brought into the divine revelation of the Father, then it will be saved. In the East men have retained their ancient spirituality, even if they are now in the process of losing it. But they experience it in a devotion to truths and facts, and thereby they lose the free, awakened 'I'. They are overwhelmed or consumed by the divine nature, as it was revealed to people ages ago. Today other times have come. It is the Father *in the 'I'*, which the East has to experience. It must find its way through to its own free 'I', and yet must not lose the divine essence.

It is a sublime marriage of West and East which may be read in this saying. For really this saying flows together into one in the central saying of all, 'I and the Father are one'; in this sentence we have the highest humanity. Looking into this saying we see the light of the human ideal.

In wishing to meditate upon this saying, we immediately meet a difficulty. This is of a purely external, more a mathematical, logical kind. Conceiving, perhaps unconsciously, the 'I in the Father' as a point within a circle, one cannot imagine how the converse can be true, 'the Father in me'. But this may lead on to a living perception. Think of the air; I can be in the air and at the same time the air is in me. If I imagine myself as a beam of light the I can be in the light and the light is in me. If we want to understand John's Gospel, we have to be accustomed to such a higher way of thinking, and not the lower, abstract, external kind. In its every expression, the thinking of John's Gospel is not the lower, but the higher way of thinking. For meditating on such a saying the simile of the light is very valuable—not the point in the circle, but the ray in the light. We shall experience for ourselves how this picture can work in us.

And now we come to the highest which this saying can accomplish in us. If we place ourselves completely into the divine forces of the Father we are formed anew, created anew by them. We receive a new body, and if we allow the divine Father to govern in us, a new blood streams into this new body. It is not far-fetched, but a sober, real experience is expressed by claiming such a saying is a real Lord's Supper. Only out of such a body as was that of Christ can it be said, 'I in the Father'. That is the background of this Supper. But again, when the 'I' in the Father is spoken with all possible strength and devotion, a new body comes into being. And so only when, in Christ, the purest blood flowed, could He truly say, 'the Father in me'. But again, if with all our strength and reverence we say, 'the Father in me', our blood becomes new. In a living way we feel this new blood flowing in our body like a delicate spiritual striving that is unexpected and quickening.[28]

The greatest Christian truths live very close together. The Lord's Supper, and Christ's word of revelation sound in each other. They are one and the same.

We follow this saying still further in John's Gospel, to see how it lives in Christ's words and deeds.

In reality, these two are not separated in Christ as they are in ourselves. And this, too, is a fact of great significance. Let us study John 14:10: 'The words that I say to you I do not speak on my own authority, but the Father who dwells in me does his works.' This saying is preceded directly by the repetition of the words, 'I in the Father, and the Father in me', and so bears witness to the close inner connection. Deep insight comes when one follows the inner way taken by Christ's soul in such a saying. In the second sentence one might expect to read: The Father, who in me dwells—speaks through me. Yet it does not say this, but: 'The Father who lives in me—does His works.' Such sayings, which in their inner nature are certainly genuine, allow us to see deeply into Christ's inner life. He feels His speaking as a deed, as a creating. He cannot remain at the word 'speak'. That would in no way correctly express the truth. But again, He does not speak of His own creating, but out of the deepest possible feeling for the truth, He continues unexpectedly: '*My Father* does His works.' That He uses here the word 'His' works is something like a prayer. It is a looking beyond to the Father's work, which is done through Himself alone. One may here think of the Act of Consecration of Man, how the blessing of Christ 'streams living through the word'. And one can also think of the saying of the other, the Synoptic Gospels, 'He speaks as one that has authority'. Of this saying from the other gospels that speak of the *external* impression made by Christ upon people, John's Gospel is in a sense the *inner* acknowledgement, out of Christ's life. It is in this way that the first three, the Synoptic Gospels, and the Fourth Gospel frequently complete each other.

In such a contemplation a far, high ideal of human speaking rises up before us. In man's word God continues His creation. Speech is given to us in order that we may grow into fellowship with the creative work of the God of the world. Speech is the tool with which we create. It is not given to man in order that he may 'conceal his thoughts'—people are of necessity driven to do that when they remain isolated, individual selves opposed to the world—but speech is given in order that man may learn to do God's works. We cannot yet do many works. But what we can do is already great and godlike. The *old* world came forth out of the cosmic word (John 1:2); the *new* world ought to come out of the human word which is purified and made alive through Christ. An actual picture of this whole process is given in the prayer before the reading of the gospel in the Act of Consecration of Man. In it the word is first purified. Then it is made alive. It wills to sound as a living thing upon the lips of those who proclaim it, and to pass as such from them to those who should receive it. But then the blessing, the creative blessing of Christ, streams through the living word. The union of life between Christ and man is established. *Consequently, in every celebration of the Act of Consecration of Man we are trained to share in God's work of creation.*

Concerning all this we shall have much to say when we come to speak of 'the word' in John's Gospel. Here we must speak of how in this way also we are trained in Christ's speaking. When in the Ordination of Priests, the prayer in made that those who are becoming priests may live in the speaking of Christ—which is a working and a bearing of the divine creating—we are looking up to the same heights in this prayer. 'I in the Father'—that is the simplest and the final classical expression of such a life.

But the converse is also true, that Christ not only calls His speaking a working, but on the other hand calls His working a speaking. Here again, we confine ourselves initially to a single passage (5:36), 'But the testimony which I have is greater than that of John; for the works which the Father has granted me to accomplish, these very works which I am doing, bear witness of me that the Father has sent me'. Consequently, the deeds of Christ are majestic words spoken by the highest God Himself. As such they must be received. And, looking at John's Gospel, we may certainly say, these deeds are not only a repetition ever again of the one general proclamation that 'this is He Whom I have sent', but they are, even in the smallest details, a speaking, a revelation. Even in the smallest details they bear living witness to the '*I*', to the true 'I' which is there in Christ, and through Christ should come to human beings. To this we are directed by the mighty saying immediately preceding the above passage, but which has been barely noticed, 'For the Father loves the Son, and shows Him all that He Himself is doing; and greater works than these will He show him, that you may marvel' (5:20). We shall look very closely at this when we come to consider the individual acts of Christ. 'The Father in me'—we see this before us now in all its living power.

In this we again find a high and far ideal for all human actions. They ought always to speak. They ought to bear within them a living language. They ought actually to be eloquent deeds. If they cannot speak through the '*what*', through that which they say—and here a person often comes face to face with an overwhelming tragedy, through their relations with other persons—yet they can often speak through the '*how*', through the way in which they are done. The most frightful thing that can happen to a person is that he with his higher 'I' is completely thrust out of his own acts and that through him other powers should act, unacknowledged by him and from which he cannot escape. People today are standing in the midst of this death of the higher 'I'. They can often assert their real nature *only* through what they say *outside* their profession. And even this is often made impossible for them because their business often takes away their strength for anything else. The great upheavals of the present time may be regarded as the despairing struggles of men to be their real selves, to achieve their real actions out of their own 'I', which ought to be the bearer of the higher 'I'. But the people thus fighting the cosmic battle against the oppression of their 'I' by a technological age have frequently lost themselves to a false higher 'I', to a mass-ego, inhabited by a machine-soul.

What can the people of John's Gospel do against this? Many an individual may perhaps be able to do more than they think. But *everyone* can help to create in the world *the true human being* who speaks through deeds. Seeing such people, who are still able by their destiny to speak in some way through deeds, increasing numbers of individuals must come to realize that a person's deeds are meant to be the means whereby he speaks. Or, much rather, they will see that the God of the world speaks and is revealed through the deeds of human beings, as once He spoke through 'the Word', creating the world, expressing and revealing Himself in a world that is moving onwards.

It is a small thing, yet we are laying the foundations of a new humanity, when we repeatedly enter in meditation into this world of Christ's speaking and acting. When Christ speaks, the 'I in the Father' speaks. When Christ acts, then the Father works in the 'I'. One sees how lost and spoiled human nature is, when one sees how far both speech and action have degenerated from this, their divine glory. How festive it must have felt when the word was used in the clear consciousness that the Father of the world was then acting through the word, was continuing His work of creation in it. And people must feel the same dignity, when they accomplish their deeds in such a way that somehow they allow God to speak, and allow the hidden divine world to be revealed. Words may thus acquire an essential strength, and deeds a living spirituality. Many people, at least on Sunday if there is no opportunity during the week, could recall to themselves Christ's speaking and creating, and so unite themselves with Christ. They would then experience in a life-giving sense how word and deed actually put on their Sunday best, proclaiming and bringing about a new Sunday.

Does not our age, which makes void the word and deprives the deed of its spirituality, require such a proclamation? Where Christ's word is, however shadowy it may be, there is Christ Himself. Where Christ's work proclaims Him, even if only in a faint echo, Christ Himself is there. Such a revelation of Christ is more powerful and convincing, conquering more widely, than any description given by man of what occurred on Golgotha. It is not the dead but the living Christ Who passes through the world in such a proclamation. Such a proclamation both bears witness and creates. To enter often, if only on Sundays, into this twofold truth of the creative word and the speaking word, one would soon experience how greatly life gains in weight and value.

In yet another aspect we find the word and work of Christ placed significantly side by side. We return to the saying, 'Truly, truly, I say to you, the Son can do nothing of his own accord, but only what he sees the Father doing; for whatever he does, that the Son does likewise. For the Father loves the Son, and shows him all that he himself is doing; and greater works than these will he show him, that you may marvel' (5:19). Taken seriously, these words lead to an *inner vision* of Christ. Seldom has Christ allowed such a glimpse of His hidden life. What is meant by the words, 'the Father shows him all that he himself is doing'? Into what inner experience of Christ do such words permit us to look? What has taken place to give to Christ the possibility of saying, 'greater works than these will the Father show him'? Here we can look as through a tiny crack into a great, rich house. But a ray of light comes to us out of this house, giving us a glimpse of heaven, 'that you may marvel', and man stands upright, worshipping and marvelling.

We will look at this saying in connection with another:

> 'Truly, truly, I say to you, he who believes in me will also do the works that I do; and greater works that these will he do, because I go to the Father. Whatever you ask in my name, I will do it, that the Father may be glorified in the Son; if you ask anything in my name, I will do it' [14: 12-14].

Here it is indicated that out of the heavenly world Christ will perform through the disciples the greater works as was promised to Him that He should do. This promise and the future of humanity that lies locked up within this we carry with us in our hearts, under a divine seal. We do not forget it; we think of it and await it. Yet this waiting, like all Christian waiting, is active and preparatory. In this connection the most important thing is to learn to see as Christ saw—to see the works of the Father. Is it too much to say that *all* our seeing should gradually become a seeing of the Father's works; that this is the consummation of all seeing; that such a seeing can be developed ever more highly, becoming ever more a seeing of the Father's works? If we were to go through the world as through a work of the Father, in which He shows us all that He does; and were so to move ourselves as to look into the works of the Father and also 'do likewise', then our 'doing God's will' would no longer be only capricious. It would be a copying and a sharing of the works of the Father. We would be walking in the way of Christ, and be His disciples in truth.

Besides learning of Christ's seeing, we learn something about His hearing (8:20). 'I speak to the world those things which I have heard of him'. And similarly, in the Farewell Discourses, it is said of the Holy Spirit (16:13), 'For He shall not speak of Himself, but whatsoever He shall hear, that shall He speak'. There are many similar passages that speak of Christ's hearing. We are to think of Him as constantly inwardly listening to the words of the Father. His *action* flows out of inward *looking* at the *work* of the Father. His *speaking* flows out of an inward *listening* to the *word* of the Father. In meditation we must ever more seek to unlock the inner greatness of the life that is here revealed to us.

Sometimes we find the reverse. Christ says (8:38), 'I *speak* that which I have seen with my Father'. And again, of doing, he says (5:30), 'I can of mine own self *do* nothing: as I *do*, I judge'. But that is not an arbitrary reversal. It reveals to us that we are here in the region in which the human senses came into existence, in which they are still one, as it were, in which hearing and seeing are combined in a deeper unity.

We can also learn from the evangelist John much about this spiritual seeing and hearing hinted at here. In a striking way we see man on his way to Christ. We find new examples of the spiritual way in which John sees all that is external. Thus he sees everywhere in Christ's acts, the 'signs', which tell of higher things. Just as Christ looked at the works of the Father, so does the disciple look at the works of Christ. And finally he 'beholds' in Christ Himself, 'glory, full of grace and truth' (1:14). John's Gospel itself is *a training in seeing Christ*. In it this higher 'I', which sees the works of God, is in process of evolving. But in the same way we perceive in John *the higher hearing*. He penetrates even into the higher hearing. He hears Christ Himself as the 'Word'. Consequently, he also preserves the word of Christ more truly than any other disciple—in the Farewell Discourses, in the High-Priestly Prayer. He hears the deepest revelation of the 'I AM' in the word, whose witness he was (21:24), as John the Baptist was a witness to it (1:7).

Finally, another saying bears witness that we are here in the realm of the higher senses (4:34), 'My food—the nourishment of the "I"—is to do the will of him that sent me, and to finish his work'. Add to this that at the beginning of the Passion the picture is taken from the same sphere. 'The cup which my Father has given me, shall I not drink it?' (18:11). That the will of God should be felt as so tangible and real that it is actually food and drink, and is not merely compared to it—that is the spirituality and greatness to which we aim to rise. *The will of God* is really *the bread of life* for the higher 'I', and is also *the cup which refreshes it*. That is a real communion. We may think ourselves happy when an idea of how one can eat and drink the will of God enters into our life. This indeed agrees with the saying of another gospel, 'Man shall not live by bread alone, but by every word that proceeds out of the mouth of God' (Matt. 4:4).

We are looking into the evolution of the higher 'I', or higher Self, that will learn to feed and live in a higher world, if it first learns from the words of Christ how to hear, and from the deeds of Christ how to see.

Letter No. 3

Son of God and Son of Man (1)

We shall have still much to say about the Mystery of the 'I'. Let us now seek to approach it by considering the third saying, at the end of John 10, the conclusion of Christ's public ministry—and try to become clear about the phrase 'Son of God'.

When the phrase 'Son of God' gradually dawns upon us in its Johannine sense, the way in which that phrase sounds in people's ears today seems to us to be deeply tragic. It is as if an adverse power had dimmed and stained what was to have become for human beings their highest glory and joy. This already began in the first Christian Councils. The phrase 'Son of God' fell prey to the earthly intellect. People disputed bitterly the question whether the Son was of the same substance as, or of similar substance to, the Father; how human beings are related to the divine being; how the Holy Spirit is co-ordinated with the two other 'Persons of the Trinity', and all questions connected therewith. Today one can only say that thereby the power of light is taken from the Word, and it has become at best an impenetrable miracle that must perforce be believed.

So things have remained for many centuries. When one looked up to Christ, the tangible life not only of His human nature but also His divine nature was lost, and one prayed to a rigid dogma. Naturally this did not prevent people from understanding, in this way, the nature of the divine within the earthly world as an extraordinary historical fact, and in absolute concentration upon the Person of Jesus Christ, experiencing it as the event which surpassed all understanding. But in connection with this the phrase 'Son of God' became ever more obscure, rigid and dead, until at last it would no longer fit into their world at all. Today the phrase is lost, unless 'in stubbornness of faith',[29] one sets a biblical phrase against the whole world.

John's Gospel can again come to the rescue. At the end (20:31) we read: 'These things are written that you might believe that Jesus is the Christ, the Son of God; and that believing you might have life through his name.' Consequently, the title, Son of God, is the key that re-opens to us the Gates of Paradise—'life'.

This note sounds throughout the whole of John's Gospel. We recall the passage in the Great Intercession in which Christ sums up His whole work when He says, 'This is life eternal, that they may know you, the only true God, and Jesus Christ whom you have sent' (17:3). In the knowledge of Jesus Christ as Son of God, all the springs of the super-earthly life welled up for the person of those early ages. Have we lost this for ever? Can it be regained from John's Gospel?

We seek a point of departure in the first person to confess the Son of God, made by one of the newly won disciples—Nathanael. From what occurred (1:46-52) we need only pick out this one point, that he felt in his deepest being that he was known by Christ. The way in which his human striving and longing was illumined by a higher light was decisive for him. This took place in the spiritual forms of the world of that day. In our own language one might say: Into his best endeavour a light suddenly fell from above. Brightly shining, He stood there, perceived not in any single characteristic, but in the humanity that was striving within him. This was Nathaniel's experience of the Son of God. 'Rabbi, you are the Son of God; you are the King of Israel.' Thus, alone is the experience of the 'Son of God' both real and great.

But observe how Christ replies to him. He in no way refuses the new name which sounds here for the first time from the mouth of a disciple, and thereby He accepts it. Eastern people generally have a special sense for such indirect speech and action. Christ shows no surprise. He expresses His joy in a gentle and generous way. From the phrase 'Son of God' He leads on to the phrase 'Son of man'.

> 'Because I said to you I saw you under the fig tree, do you believe? You shall see greater things than these.' And he said unto him, 'Verily, verily I say unto you, hereafter you shall see heaven open, and the angels of God ascending and descending upon the Son of man' [1:50-51].

This is the first word of revelation that we hear from the mouth of Christ Himself. Knowing the ways of early authors, and especially those of John the evangelist, we have every reason to expect here most significant disclosures affecting the whole gospel.

First of all, it is significant of John's Gospel that with great awareness it is sparing in its use of the phrase 'Son of God', upon which nevertheless everything depends. With the exception of a single passage, which we shall come to study (10:36), Christ never expressly calls Himself 'Son of God'. He always calls Himself 'the Son'. In a living sense one feels one's way into the fact that this, although the same, is yet something different. The whole feeling of such a saying is quite different from what it would have been had He always called Himself—one might say with dogmatic emphasis—the Son of God. We shall certainly find it hard to feel completely how such a saying sounded at that time. In it there is neither the judicial, legal sense such as appeared in it in the Roman world, nor the physiological, natural sense such as lay nearer in the Greek world with its children of the gods, nor such as continued in dogma and is felt still more strongly in our age of the theories of heredity. But in the saying was something spiritual, like an image or reflection. In earlier times, when the 'I' was not so developed individually, sons were externally more like their father. They were the younger image, full of life. In the background there is the thought of plenary power. When we feel that the Son is the youthful, living image of the Father, endowed with his plenary power, then we come nearest to the feeling of that earlier age. 'The Son.'

John's Gospel must be studied in all its delicate nuances. We may observe how the phrase 'Son of God'—besides the word 'Son', which occurs much more frequently—is also heard sometimes from the mouth of Christ. But it occurs in a certain remoteness from His Person. 'Truly, truly, I tell you, the hour is coming, and now is, when the dead will hear the voice of the Son of God, and those who hear will live' (5:25). Is it an accident that the voice of Him Who appears to men to be especially 'the Son', or the 'Son of man', is realized by the dead to be the 'voice of the Son of God'? In the kingdoms of the dead one hears much more thoroughly. One perceives more truly what is there. And so it is natural that in this passage, as in the story of Nathanael, Christ leads again from the Son of God to the Son of man, when He comes to speak of the living. 'For the Father has life in himself, and has given authority to execute judgment because he is the Son of man' (5:26-27).

It cannot be without purpose that in this passage Christ teaches us to look at, to understand, the Son of God in connection with the Son of man. And so we have first to study the phrase 'Son of man' more closely.

Son of Man

The phrase 'Son of man' cannot have any arbitrary meaning that we may be pleased to attribute to it as we should like it to have. It is an ancient word, used in the Mysteries, and it means something quite definite. The passages in John's Gospel are everywhere meant for ears trained in the Mysteries, who listen, possessing a background of exoteric or esoteric prophecy. In the last few decades, Protestant theology has had much to say about the phrase, Son of man. Special attention has been given to the passage in Daniel (7:13) concerning the coming kingdom, which was seen in a vision of a figure 'like a son of man'. In the apocryphal writings of the Old Testament, the Book of Enoch and 2 Esdras, the Son of man is described as living in heaven long before the world was. He appears, pure and elect, and he is called the Anointed One. He reveals all wisdom. Judgment is given to Him and rulership over all the world. From this it seems very remarkable that with its own methods of research anthroposophical spiritual science comes today to this result, that the boy Jesus, who became the bearer of Christ, had never before been incarnated, but, as it were, had been reserved in the spiritual worlds so that he might enter the world unstained by sinful evolution.[30] Words like those of John 17:24, 'that they also, whom Thou hast given me, may be with me where I am, to behold my glory which Thou hast given me in Thy love for me before the foundation of the world', gain in emphasis from such perceptions, and show clearly how Christ speaks of fulfilment.

We may also recall the vision in 2 Esdras 13. Out of the sea there comes in a storm a man flying upon the clouds of heaven, accompanied by a host of angels. At sight of Him the cosmos trembles. Before His voice the world melts. An innumerable army fights against Him. But with the stream of fire which proceeds from His mouth He destroys His enemies and assembles around Him an army of peace. To a materialistic understanding, such pictures are quite incomprehensible, confused and irreligious. In reality the sea is a picture of the etheric world. Storm and clouds are well-known symbols of that which occurs in the higher worlds. The fire of His mouth, the might of His voice are the true weapons of Him who is the cosmic Word. Also the depths becoming alive and what has hardened becoming soft again, are clearly expressed in the pictures of earthquake and melting. The struggle is not to be understood as taking place in the outer world. It is a mighty world-encompassing occurrence. And so it may remain undecided whether such visions were not soon misunderstood in a materialistic manner. They may even has been misunderstood by those who first saw them. Nevertheless, it may be possible today to fathom their true spiritual meaning.

Today, theology warns us against reading into the expression 'Son of man' the meaning 'ideal man' as we for instance understand it. But this is to take too short a view. The human being reserved in heaven—in this form the ideal man was imagined at that time. When we speak of the ideal man we fill the human image with our highest thoughts and feelings. Moreover, we know of no land as the unreal kingdom of the ideal out of which he could descend—the people of that time meant the same thing, only in a more concrete and real form, when they said that a man is reserved in heaven until his hour has come.

Again, it is a very great and true thought when the Book of Daniel speaks of the kingdom of the beasts that precede the ultimate surrendering of lordship to the Son of man. In the earlier kingdoms of the world there still remained some unfathomed soul-qualities that human beings brought with them out of the past, still linking man and beast. The kingdoms of the world *today* are still on the level of the beast. This can be perceived right into the details with the help of the Book of Daniel. With Christ 'the human being' came into the world. The true human kingdom begins.

Against such a background we would now study the words that Christ Himself speaks in John's Gospel concerning the Son of man. We look into a kingdom transfigured with spiritual clarity.

We see a certain affinity to the old ideas in the first of Christ's sayings, in His teaching concerning the Son of man (according to 1:51). 'No one has ascended into heaven but He Who descended from heaven, the Son of man Who is in heaven' (3:13). This saying concerning the ascending and descending of the Son of man reminds us of that first saying concerning the angels who ascend and descend upon the Son of man. That which is told of the angels is an image of that which is true of the Son of man Himself. As long as He walks upon the Earth, the angels perform above Him that which writ large is *the course of His own life*. This picture of the Mysteries of John's Gospel speaks to us much more deeply than we usually realize. We understand John's Gospel aright when we read above in its first half (John 1-10) the words, 'I came from the Father', and above in the second half (John 11-21), 'I go to the Father'. Both sayings are intermingled. Moreover, in the first half there are several sayings, such as: 'Where I am, you cannot come' (7:34). But the main emphasis lies upon the announcement, 'The Father has sent me to you'. On the other hand, in the second half the mood is not missing that the Father has sent Him. But much stronger there emerges, 'I go to the Father'.

The everyday human being exists between the portals of birth and death. When one day birth and everything connected to it is perfectly illumined so that it is a pure and true confession when someone, looking at their origins, says, 'I come from the Father', and when one day death and everything that it brings is completely irradiated so that someone, looking into their future, sees behind everything only this one thing, 'I go to the Father', then they have indeed become a *human being*. One has truly to drink deeply the sublimity and dignity of this humanity; only then does one see how the human being appears 'reserved in heaven', what picture of the human being lives in the divine thoughts.

We are entirely justified by the spirit of John's Gospel when we say all this not only of Christ, but of the human being himself, before whose eyes we place man's glory, to be obtained through Christ. 'Born of God'—that is the nature of the new humanity that is here created. Already in 1:12 we read:

> But to all who received him, who believed in his name, he gave power to become children of God; who were born, not of blood nor of the will of the flesh not of the will of man, but of God.

Then, those who are 'born of God' are spoken of especially in John 3. This is the '*coming from the Father*'. And towards the end we read again, and applied to human beings, the other sound of '*going to the Father*'. 'I go to prepare a place for you ... that where I am you may be also' (14:2, 3). Again, quite strongly and sounding out above all else in the Great Intercession, 'Father, I will that they also, whom Thou hast given me, may be with me where I am, to behold my glory ...' (17:24).

Birth and death are transformed. They are not only understood differently, they are created anew for the person who is with Christ.

The picture is completed only when, behind the saying 'I come from the Father', we see the divine Father, and behind the saying, 'I go to the Father', we see the Holy Spirit, Whom Christ will send from the Father. This is the living, historical Holy Trinity. This John's Gospel reveals to us, and not any dogmatic systematization. We look up to this picture. Here is the whole history of the world, which is really divided into the time of the Father, of the Son, and of the Spirit. Rather than to seek in an old-fashioned way in John's Gospel for 'proof texts' of the Trinity, one could enter oneself into the living Trinity which, as a plenitude of all Mysteries, is spread above us in John's Gospel like a divine altar picture above the horizon of the world's history.

With regard to the phrase 'Son of man', Rudolf Steiner has said decisively that in early times, 'son' by no means meant simply physical posterity. 'The Son of man' is much rather that which man should one day become, according to the divine will.[31] Up to the time in which Jesus, who was to be the bearer of Christ, was far ahead of his time—human beings were to develop in their own being so that they might receive the divine content into this vessel. *The Son of man grows towards the Son of God.*

In anthroposophical spiritual perception this is stated more exactly. The 'consciousness-soul' [alternative term 'spiritual soul', for in it the spiritual light of self-knowledge is first kindled] is to be developed, in which the 'I' forms the central point. At the time of Golgotha this had been attained only by a few. Most people were still in the stage of development of the 'intellectual soul', or 'mind-soul' [*Gemütseele*]. When the consciousness-soul has been developed with the 'I', it receives from above the higher divine content which is destined for the human being—the Spirit-Self, Life-Spirit and Spirit-Man. This is the content of the 'Son of God'. The 'I' opens like a cup that receives its contents, like a blossom that is filled with the Sun. This is the divine plan for human beings.

With this idea as a background one understands many things in John's Gospel much better. Let us recall the scene with Nathanael, and we have in Christ's words (2:31), 'Truly, truly, I say to you, you will see heaven opened, and the angels of God ascending and descending upon the Son of man', the most living picture of this truth that is before us. Christ leads Nathanael from the details to the thing itself. He shows him in Himself the *fulfilment* of that which Nathanael himself had sought under the fig-tree. He leads him from an abstract, dogmatic conception of the Son of God, which he may have still entertained, even when he stood before the fulfilment of prophecy, to the living reality. These are depths in the narrative that gradually open to us.

If we now link together the early ideas of the Son of man found in the books of the Israelites, the following ideas result:

(1) the Son of man is reserved in heaven, and is revealed from there;
(2) He is destined to hold judgment upon the Earth;
(3) He enters the kingdom of the world;
(4) He reveals all heavenly wisdom.

In the light of these pre-Christian ideas we can study the *twelve passages*[32] in which John's Gospel speaks of the Son of man, and we shall everywhere perceive how the graphic imaginations of the apocalyptic pictures are now fulfilled in the light of the clear spirit.

The passages concerning the Son of man

> [1] The first passage relates: the Son of man is not a product of evolution from below. He is a gift from heaven. He is in heaven. From heaven he descended (5:13). We shall express this in a way which is more approachable by people today by saying, man is not a being out of which one may make whatever one likes, as Nietzsche surmised, but man is *found* when one takes the trouble to discover the divine thoughts concerning man, and to think them with God. Man indeed lives upon the Earth, and finds himself upon the Earth, but yet he feels that he does not ultimately belong to the Earth, in so far as it is a being that passes away. He surmises that he must indeed mature upon the Earth, but only with the purpose of entering a higher world. If this is not realized, then he will never find 'the human being'.

Christ came in order that human beings will reveal what they should become. At the very end of His life Christ says several times with special emphasis that this work is now finished. The first time He says it significantly when the Greeks sought Him, whose whole search was to find the human being (12:23), 'The hour is come for the Son of man to be glorified'. The hour of the fulfilment of all Greek longing has come. From this point of view, we have also to consider the fact that Pilate in the decisive hour speaks the words of fulfilment, 'Behold the human being'. In him there speaks the Graeco-Roman civilization whose task it was to bring man entirely down to the earthly plane.

Another time Christ speaks of the finishing of this work at the beginning of the Farewell Discourses (13:31), 'When he had gone out,'—it is significant that Judas, the betrayer, had, so to speak, also passed out of the picture of man—'Jesus said, Now is the Son of man revealed, and in him God is revealed. If God be revealed in him God shall also reveal him in himself, and shall straightway reveal him'. In this passage and in that which follows, one sees quite clearly *how the consciousness of Christ moves, as it were, ever around the point in which the Son of man and the Son of God meet*. Thus, we read in the first sentence of the Great Intercession, of the High-Priestly Prayer: 'Father, the hour has come, let the Son be revealed that the Son may reveal Thee, since Thou hast given Him power over all flesh, to give eternal life to all whom Thou has given Him' (17:1, 2). That which apocalyptic vision had seen, has been fulfilled. The Son of man is revealed from heaven. But in order to perceive the fulfilment other eyes are required than are required to perceive the prophecy. Spiritual eyes are required, such as can only be formed in nearness to Christ. The evangelist John has become able to see with those spiritual eyes.

It is significant that the last question that the Jews, in a last reminder of receptivity, put to Christ was, 'Who is this Son of Man?' (12:34). If they should find the answer to this question they would come out of their Judaism. Then they would find the true fulfilment of Judaism. Then they would also be united with the Greeks, who had just been addressed, in the true Son of man who bears the Son of God. *The Greeks had to find the Son of God Who fulfils the Son of man. The Jews had to find the Son of man who brings the Son of God.* World history in the very greatest form is expressed in these words.

But for the questioning Jews, Christ has no other answer than, 'While you have the light, believe in the light, that you may become sons of light' (12:36). Here the only possible answer is clearly given. There is no other proof of the truth but the 'evidence' that one should come to 'see'. But only the light can bring one to see. So, in the highest region of all, Goethe's saying remains true, 'The eye is formed in the light for the light'.[33] And we, too, when we seek the human being, must let our eyes be formed for this by the light itself.

> [2] It is in a great inward explanation of His attitude to those concepts then governing the world that we see Christ, when we look at the second group of thoughts—those concerning the Last Judgement. For the people of that time, life was scarcely bearable unless they had before their eyes the thoughts of a Last Judgement. When a single governor for his own benefit in two years could so plunder a whole land that it was left in miserable poverty; when innocent men were destroyed in vast numbers by cruel tortures; when the court of the prince was a place of festivity for all wickedness and no mouth on earth said anything against it, no hand from heaven was raised to oppose it—all this was indeed the daily experience at that time of the pious in a bitterness that we can hardly imagine—then the tormented sense of justice cried out, Is there none who care for human rights? Amongst the Jews in particular all longing for vengeance turned to the hope of a coming judgment. By their sensitive feeling for the Earth and life, by their strong feeling for the 'I', by their trained sense of justice and by their strict logic they were made especially receptive of the ideas of the Last Judgement. And the consciousness of their election, amid their daily humiliations—had the same effect. When the Messiah appeared—so all their expectations of Him led them to expect—He would restore order, would hurl back the enemies of God, and justice would reign once more.

It was a long way from such hopes to the fulfilment revealed to us in John's Gospel. But we have no ground for assuming that the evangelist attributed all these sayings about judgment to Christ only after the Last Judgement had not arrived in the form in which it was expected. It would have been more likely that the evangelist, had he wanted to put a different construction upon Christ's words, would have pointed out that particular judgment—the most terrible in all history—which was carried out before the eyes of all, upon the Jewish people who had rejected their king. One is not to assume that John's Gospel must have been written much later because no recollection on the judgment upon Israel is reflected in it. This terrible judgment did not lie so far back that no impression of it would remain. On the other hand, it is very possible that the words of Christ about the *inner* judgment were not at that time understood by most of the disciples, because their thoughts were governed by totally different ideas.

Everything becomes clear when we rightly understand the saying, 'For as the Father has life in Himself, so he has granted the Son also to have life in Himself, and has given Him authority to execute judgment, because he is Son of man' (5:26, 27).

The saying, 'The history of the world is the world's judgment'[34] is superficial when placed beside the words, 'The Son of man is the world's judgment'. Before Him everything must stand. If a person finds he can say 'Yes' to Him, if he realizes in Him the divine thought of man, then he has found the meaning of the Earth, then he joins the side of those in whom the goal of the Earth can be attained. If he cannot find this 'Yes', then he can no longer be taken into consideration for the meaning of the Earth, or the divine aim for it. This is so, so long as he does not find this 'Yes', and it is so for the real goal of the Earth—the making real of love in freedom. We do not need to add that this 'Yes' can be entirely an inner one. It can even be quite unconscious, and can be given in complete opposition to the Churches.

This is expressed in the gospel in the following words, 'He who believes in Him is not condemned; he who does not believe is condemned already, because he has not believed in the name of the only Son of God' (3:18, cf. 9:39; 16:8 and 11).

In John's Gospel, John the Baptist, the great announcer of the coming judgment by the Messiah, clearly agrees with this idea of judgment, 'He who believes in the Son has eternal life; he who does not obey the Son shall not see life, but the wrath of God rests upon him' (3:36).

We have still to pay special attention to some words—'has given him authority to execute judgment'. If we stumble over this word 'authority' (or 'plenary power') we have to remember that in the New Testament it is also the name of specific angels. The *Exusiai*, the spirits of plenary power, are called in the more recent esotericism the 'Spirits of Form', corresponding to the Elohim who accomplished the work of creation in the name of God Most High.

From this comes the idea that this world-judgment now being accomplished in the Son, is really the further progress of the creation of the world. The judges of Israel—we shall come to speak of this again—were even called expressly 'Elohim' in the Old Testament.[35] Authority for the decisive world-judgment is given by the appearance of the Son of man. But 'the Father judges no one, but has committed all judgment to the Son' (5:22). For *only by someone who is a true human being* can this deed be accomplished.

Therein lies an answer to the thousand questions that might have been put by the people of that age who were hungering for righteousness. The *Father*-powers, the primal forces of life, fail no one, neither the pious man nor the man who is corrupt; they are not judges. But the decision lies with the *Son*.

Like a mighty symbol of this, we have the story of the man who was born blind, which as we shall see, is in many respects the story of man himself. 'Do you believe in the Son of man?' Christ asks him. 'And who is he, sir, that I might believe in him?' 'You have seen him, and it is he who speaks to you' (9:35-37).

Anyone who hears of Christ—always assuming that the voice of Christ Himself penetrates through that which they have heard about Christ—receives into themselves their own judge. For they receive into themselves their true 'I'. They receive for ever the judge of the world, and ever after carry Him with them throughout life. This is true not only when one has really heard the word of Christ, but also when one has only heard the sayings of Christ. 'He who rejects me and does not receive my sayings has a judge; the word that I have spoken will be his judge on the last day' (12:48). Just as surely as after death, when we awake in the land of truth we shall clearly see that we have our cosmic judge arising out of *our own soul*. And ever increasingly clearly this will be revealed as the *real* Last Judgement. This we can already know. A deep awe before the cosmic judge, whom they hear in their own chest, lays hold of the people who have once fully perceived this. This cosmic Word, the Logos, has already entered into them, and within them has set up His seat of judgment.

But Christ guards Himself with all emphasis against appearing before people only in this role. It must have been one of the chief struggles of His life to draw His hearers away from the external and all-too-human idea of a cosmic judge. John's Gospel is authentic just because it decries this spiritual conflict. If anyone holds that such sayings are unhistorical and subsequently invented must acknowledge one of two propositions. Either Jesus did not hold Himself to be the Messiah, so that He had not to occupy Himself with thoughts of the world-judgment. Or, that He held Himself to be a prophet sent by God, Who only *after* His death was clothed with the Messiah's dignity, and that for this reason He let the old, false ideas of the world-judgment remain as they were—a contradiction of the character of His whole gospel. In the Synoptic Gospels the pure grandeur of the new proclamation of world-judgment has not yet come out fully. What is so mightily convincing in John's Gospel is that Christ, the Saviour, refuses to stand before mankind in the cloak of an executioner; that He says indeed with strong emphasis, that in Him is the world-judgment, but that He places the judge—the Logos—in every person's own chest. You, you alone, can be your own cosmic judge; and you have already pronounced this cosmic judgment in all stillness. Everything further will be only the working out of that which has passed over to your soul, if you do not confess the Son of man, the divine thought of the human being. The expectation of judgment is fulfilled by the Messiah. But the commission of Christ is and remains in all purity, to bring life and salvation (3:17-21).

This does not prevent the external judgment from taking effect. At least this is expressly said of those who are in their graves (5:28f.). But in so far as judgment takes place, Christ says of Himself that He does not judge according to the Ten Commandments; He is silent until He hears the infallible voice of His Father speaking within Him (5:30). The 'life' that He bears within Himself is the one great question that He puts to people, and to which they must find the answer within themselves.

We are placing all these things in detail before ourselves here because we hope thereby to give an answer to the thousand questions—How ought I to live amongst my fellow human beings? Must I not openly say when I think anything is unjust? When may I keep silent? When must I speak? How can I carry on the struggle between good and evil in a really Christian way?

> [3] Let us now study the third hope, that is, that the *kingdom* shall be given to the Son of man. A 'lifting up' above all peoples shall be accomplished. Christ takes this up. In His first conversation with a spiritual leader of His people, He already speaks of it (3:14), and again in His last word to the people (12:32f.). And between these, He speaks of it in His decisive conversation with His opponents (8:29). Consequently, we have again the same saying three times and in three important passages.

- In the first conversation He talks of the deep necessity that exists for His lifting up,
- in the second that it will lead to a decisive perception of the 'I AM',
- in the third that it will lead to the foundation of the true kingdom.
- 'And I, when I am lifted up from the Earth, will draw all people to myself' (12:32).

It is remarkable that these three sayings, without any forcing of their meaning, again reveal in succession the aspect of the Father, of the Son and of the Spirit.

- In the first, Moses is named, and attention is drawn to deep cosmic laws. The lifting up appears as an act of the Father.
- In the second, it is in the Jews who appear as the actors. 'When you have lifted up the Son of man, then you shall know that I AM' (8:28).
- In the third, through the prefixed words 'And I', Christ Himself appears as the real actor, but the congregation whom He will gather together is taken into consideration—consequently, He acts through the Holy Spirit.

Is it by chance that everywhere, where this lifting up is mentioned, it is always the Son of man who is named, and never the Son of God, or simply the Son? Only an inattentive study can pass over such definite expression. That by this lifting up it is not the lifting up to heaven, but the cross itself that is meant, is proved by 12:33, 'This He said, signifying what death He should die'. It is the *only* form in which Christ, in John's Gospel, announces His death. And clearly it has been laid upon the evangelist to point to it, since he has done so equally definitely from the very beginning. In the very first conversation with a leader of his people, Nicodemus, Christ speaks of this death (3:14). And consequently it is so that Christ in John's Gospel *has spoken of His cross only from the point of view of the 'lifting up'—and of this 'lifting' only in reference to the cross.*

The serpent, or snake

To understand this, we must follow up the hint which Christ Himself gives us in the gospel, 'And as Moses lifted up the serpent in the wilderness, so must the Son of man be lifted up' (3:14). What did this lifting up of the serpent mean? One will certainly not understand such stories aright holding only to the words of the external history (Num. 21:8). The very fact that the serpent was given to the god of healing as his symbol in many religions of that age and of that sphere of culture, and that the staff with the snake, the caduceus of Mercury, was a sacred symbol must attract our attention.

What did the ancients think about snakes? How do they come to regard them as symbols of wisdom, since they are certainly stupid?

The snake is the animal of the Earth. Upon the Earth it creeps. Out of the Earth it comes. With the Earth it comes into being. If we take them as symbols of the earthly being, the snakes, with their flickering tongues appear as the picture of the human passions that arise out of man's earthly being. Moreover, that which is dangerous in earthly existence heightened still more by the silent, apparently spiteful being of the snake was imaged in them. What could be done against this? One could not repudiate earthly existence. But one had to give it an upward direction. Yes, more, one had *with* the earthly being, to lift oneself *above* the Earth itself. Then something victorious might come out of this earthly being. There was a twofold earthly being—one which gave itself over to the Earth, and one which drew its forces indeed from the Earth but with them ruled the Earth from above.

If we look with such thoughts in our mind at the ancient biblical story of Moses, it becomes for us a deeply significant picture of the world. Whatever may have taken place then outwardly was not the most important thing. Everything may have happened just as it is described in the Book of Numbers. But the children of Israel to whom this was told still divined that they could look through it with their feelings into a higher event. Moses sees the Children of Israel threatened by fiery snakes that arise from the Earth. And he takes the snake and lifts it up above the Earth. By this it loses its dangerous power, and all who see it lifted up are guarded against it. Let us regard the whole story as but a permanent picture that was received deeply into the childlike forces of a nation's being.

Much is connected with this spiritual background. The snake in Paradise will also be seen in this light. Consequently, the snake was also regarded as the symbol of early initiation. This is reflected in Matt. 3:7, where Christ calls the scribes not 'generation of vipers', but, according to Rudolf Steiner's explanation, 'those that are born of the snake'.[36] In this way, it becomes more comprehensible that down to the time of King Hezekiah (who ruled around the year 700 BCE, i.e. more than 500 years after Moses), the Children of Israel, in spite of Moses, burnt incense to the [bronze] snake. (This snake was broken to pieces by Hezekiah; 2 Kings 18:4.) Considering the absolute authority Moses had with the Jews such a deed is incomprehensible, unless one sees what lies in the historic background. Under Hezekiah the prophetic line conquered. The prophets strove to break the connection with the early initiation, which still reverenced Moses and practised what he taught. The lifting of the snake was a preparation for what we now learn in John 3:14.

Naturally, with this one could discover yet more deep connections. For example, today people can still feel their spinal cord as a kind of snake, passing from an early, not yet fully awakened, consciousness of the 'I'—a consciousness more strongly connected to the system of nerves and the senses—to a new, more awakened and more spiritual consciousness of the 'I'. One then carries the snake with its flickering tongue within, but it now is erect, and is to be conquered by the higher 'I'. One experiences within all that we have been discussing. This may initially suffice to hint at the deeper understanding of Christ's words.

A new cosmic, universal symbol is set up. A new highway is opened. It is not the snake, the unconscious earthly creature leading back into the past, which pictures that to which we are now to aspire—but the Son of man. Thereby the human being becomes really human. Previously, he entrusted himself in initiation to a cosmic force that he had not understood. Now, we are told of the Son of man 'that whosoever believes in Him should not perish, but have eternal life' (3:16). The centre of gravity is now placed within man himself. Without putting too fine a point on it, one might say in our language—in his own 'I'-consciousness.

After all this, one has still the impression that humanity has not yet really laid hold of the healing image that has been set up over it, however much has been said, written or invented about the cross. One must really understand it in the sense of a lifting up, of an elevation to sovereign rank—as Pilate himself wrote above the cross, 'Jesus of Nazareth, King of the Jews'.

John's Gospel, rightly comprehended, contains three mighty paradoxes.

- From Him Who was *destroyed* there proceeds *life,* the true and lasting life. This we are told by the first passage that speaks of the lifting up of the Son of man (3:14).
- From Him who was denied and condemned as one who had no right to exist, the *light* of the 'I AM' is spread abroad. 'When you have lifted up the Son of man, you shall know that I AM' (8:28).
- And He who was *cast out* and deserted by all, will draw all people to Himself and will found the kingdom of *love.* 'And I, if I be lifted up from the earth, will draw all men unto me' (12:32).

This is the real kingdom which the Son of man sets up. In the three sayings that are uttered concerning this kingdom one can easily find the three fundamental words of John's Gospel—Life, Light and Love. In these last three sayings we can also clearly hear the contrast to the early initiation.

As Christ indeed knows that many people will steadfastly refuse Him, this has only a full meaning if it is said to be spoken of 'people in general'. It is not only individuals, as in the early Mysteries, but all people who now have access to Him. We are now led to the question: Are the two other sayings also in contrast to the early Mysteries? In the early Mysteries people lost their 'I'-consciousness when they looked up to the higher world, as we can observe today in mediums. The new Mysteries lead directly to the clear vision of the 'I AM' (8:28). The early Mysteries could give a man at his initiation only a passing taste of the divine world. After that he had to be awakened again out of his temple-sleep if he were not to be destroyed by it. In the new Mysteries people bear eternity within themselves. They possess it, and possess it for ever. And so these three sayings speaking of the lifting up of the Son of man, are at the same time *a sublime doctrine of the Mysteries;*

- *not for individuals, but for everyone;*
- *not in unconsciousness, but in the 'I' that perceives clearly;*
- *not for an hour, but as a permanent possession.*

The deep organic unity of John's Gospel becomes again clear in such a context.

But we will not overlook the fact that here a real Kingdom is founded. The 'Son of man' is 'lifted up', but He is lifted up on the cross, on the cross of the world. In mighty divine paradoxes He bestows Life, Light and Love, He brings salvation into the world of death, darkness and hate. In the same way the true human being in ourselves is also found as we pass out of this world, but return into it again with a higher world within us. Ascending and descending—the great picture of the Mystery of the human being.

> [4] We have still to study the last saying concerning the Son of man. People of that time felt it as a 'hard saying' (6:51-63), 'Truly, truly, I say to you, unless you eat the flesh of the Son of man and drink His blood, you have no life in you; he who eats my flesh and drinks my blood has eternal life, and I will raise him up at the last day. For my flesh is food indeed, and my blood is drink indeed. He who eats my flesh and drinks my blood abides in me, and I in him' (6:53-56).

Such words can only be understood out of a new fulfilment. That the crude material flesh cannot be meant, appears naturally from the fact that such an external eating would have never taken place. Nothing else can possibly be meant but the bodily nature, which is wholly real but spiritual. 'It is the spirit that gives life, the flesh is of no avail; the words that I have spoken to you are spirit and life' (6:63). Why then the crude word 'flesh'? The evangelist never uses the word 'body', but always the word 'flesh'—'the word, flesh it became' [in the order of the Greek]—probably not only because he wished to point to the most concrete reality, but above all because he wished to say that this Body has been taken out of the current of sinful heredity. The point is that it is not the body as it can be in heaven, but the sinful body as it has become on Earth, which Christ takes over, purifies, irradiates and bestows upon us anew.

But what is especially important is that here we have to do with an actual eating and drinking of Christ, and in such a way that through this the actual body and blood of Christ are received. Not only His teaching, but Himself; and again Himself not as a super-earthly being, but Himself as a fully human 'I' in body and blood. This is a part of the 'Mystery of the "I"'. *For the 'I' lives in the blood, and expresses itself in the body.* The earthly self-consciousness of the human 'I' today is bound up with the body and lives in the blood. That which people find so hard to grasp today is simply that there is a body of Christ, that there is actually such today, which is wholly body and yet wholly spiritual. And that there is a blood of Christ, attainable by man, which is blood and yet is invisible. Here the men of the present age lack the experience possessed more or less clearly by people of past ages.

But those who have been touched in a living way by this actual fact, know that in the body and blood of Christ they have access to all the secrets of heaven—but in such a way as *human beings*, sons of man [sons of Adam], need them. And so also the last prophecy of apocalyptic writers is fulfilled, that the Son of man reveals all wisdom. But again it is fulfilled in quite a different way from that in which they themselves represent the fulfilment, that is, in a Mystery of devotion to Christ's whole nature—a Mystery quite unattainable by thought.

The true human being is neither attained by thought, nor by battle, but He is eaten and drunk. This is the ultimate fulfilment of all sacrificial meals. John's Gospel, the 'spiritual gospel',[37] is spiritual, not in the sense that it simply thinks away from that which is earthly—what is coarsely earthly—and places it into the spirit. For the evangelist this is *the real background of the Lord's Supper*, as indeed in this sixth chapter the word 'eucharist', thanksgiving, is used more than once with emphasis (6:11 and 23). And it is of supreme importance for the revival of the Lord's Supper that this connection between Christ and the eating of body and blood should be perceived ever more clearly.

The evangelist remarks, 'This He said in the synagogue, as He taught at Capernaum' (6:59). Where people look from the Jewish to the heathen world, Christ proclaims this truth. And we may again recall that in body and blood the two most inwardly important peoples of that age of the world are united. The Greeks, the people of the body, the Jews, the people of the blood. It was really a communion when the Greeks received into themselves an ideally formed image of a god through sight. Their soul-nature imitated what they saw and was inwardly formed in accordance with it. And it was a communion when the Jews recalling the blood of Abraham flowing in their veins, brought to this blood the feeling of most inner responsibility. To feel in reality the nobility of the blood, and in this the sacred gift of obligation, creates an actual union with the Godhead.

But now, in the Son of man there came the fulfilment of all communion, which was prepared from both here and there. Later we shall speak of the whole construction of John 6, which is especially important. Here in conclusion, let us look one again at the *human ideal of the Son of man*, in connection with the four apocalyptic expectations, from the point of view of the present day.

- The Son of man is not a human thought but a divine gift. Heaven itself is seen in Him. *This is His legitimation.*

- He brings to humanity a mighty decision, *the* decision. One cannot, just as one pleases, be enthusiastic or unenthusiastic about Him, but according to the attitude one takes up towards Him, one reveals whether or not one has grasped the divine goal for humanity. *This is His battle and His victory.*
- He is no external ruler, but an inner king, Who seeks His elevation on the cross. *This is His Kingdom.*
- He brings no wisdom fetched from without, but He bestows Himself in body and blood, only upon those who receive Him directly and not by mediation. *This is His reigning.*

This is the new Kingdom in which the Son of man rules, of which Daniel caught a faint gleam. This is also the Kingdom in which we ourselves find all the hope of true humanity becoming real. Behold the Man!

Letter No. 4

Son of Man and Son of God (2)

The more deeply we enter into the phrase 'Son of God' in John's Gospel the sadder we feel, because humanity has lost this saying with all its glorious powers of light that might irradiate the word 'human being'. In the sense of John's Gospel, the phrase Son of God is simply the entrance into Paradise regained. This is shown in the last sentence [of Chapter 20], 'These [signs] are written that you may believe that Jesus is the Christ, the Son of God, and that believing you may have life in his name' (20:31). With the word 'life', the evangelist always points to Paradise with its Tree of Life. And as to what is meant by 'believing in His Name', we can best represent that to ourselves in the following way. We hear the phrase Son of God used in relation to Christ. Then a whole world is opened before us, a whole heaven, and our inmost being says 'Yes' to this heaven and enters into its shining glory.

If mankind would win back this phrase, 'Son of God', it must first get beyond the false distinction between 'Son of God' and 'child of God', which has crept into Christianity and established itself there. The phrase 'Son of God' has become fixed in dogmatic rigidity, and is used of Christ alone. The phrase 'child of God' was indeed used by the [early] Christians, but has become childish and sentimental in its meaning. To show how false this is, let us hear but one sentence from John's Gospel (1:12-13). 'But to all who received Him, who believe in His name, He gave power to become children of God; who were born, not of blood nor of the will of the flesh nor of the will of man, but of God.' This phrase 'born of God' can help us to get away from the petty human meaning that the phrase 'child of God' has gradually acquired. The very sound of this phrase 'born of God' is like the chiming of a bell. And this is not the only time in John's Gospel where the phrase 'born of God' is applied to Christians and not only to Christ. To the ruler of His people who came to Him by night, Christ says, 'Truly, truly, I say to you, unless one is from above he cannot see the kingdom of God' (3:3). The Luther, AV, RSV, NEB and NIV texts here contain 'born again' or 'anew', instead of 'from above' [as in v. 7], but this translation takes from the saying its strongest content. For at the only place in John's Gospel where Christ applies the title 'Son of God' to Himself, He does not separate Himself from other men, but connects what He says with a passage in the Old Testament in which it is said of the Judges of Israel, 'You are gods' (Ps. 82:6), and from it He proves that He is not guilty of blasphemy when He calls Himself 'Son of God' (10:34).

The phrase 'child of God' has lost its greatness, and the phrase 'Son of God' its living nearness, because these two phrases have been torn asunder. It is true that one can speak of the sons and daughters of God collectively only by using the phrase 'children of God'. But it would otherwise be quite in accordance with the sense of John's Gospel to say, 'The Son of God came that we might become sons of God'. And if anyone should say that by so doing we overlook the great difference existing between Christ and us, then we could only reply that, on the contrary, we acquire in this way a deep reverence for Christ, a living perception of His uniqueness, and of the distance between us and Him. He *was* the Son of God, that we might *become* sons and daughters of God. 'He gave us power to become sons of God, born of God.'

In our age in which man is much more apt to feel his connection with the beasts, and his descent from the beasts, it is of supreme importance that he should be reminded that John's Gospel proclaims that man may become born of God.

This is the main thing to be seen, but the other side of the picture shows the extraordinary delicacy with which John's Gospel speaks of the Son of God. Only through his dogmatic prepossessions could anyone ever have the impression that John's Gospel always speaks of the Son of God in dogmatic sublimity and aloofness, and so is strange to us. Only in one single passage, as noted above, does Christ Himself expressly speak of Himself as 'Son of God', and then only in the form of a question. Elsewhere He speaks of Himself only as the 'Son'. Only when we begin to feel why He says 'the Son' and not the 'Son of God' do we begin to live in the gentle world of John's Gospel, which is the reflection of Christ's own inner life. The few other passages besides 10:36 in which Christ speaks of the Son of God use the word in a delicately objective sense, which removes it a certain way from the Person of Christ Himself.

- 'God loved the world that he gave his only[-begotten] Son' (3:16). And immediately afterwards, 'He who does not believe is condemned already, because he has not believed in the name of the only Son of God' (3:18).
- The second passage is, 'Truly, truly, I say to you, the hour is coming, and now is, when the dead will hear the voice of the Son of God, and those who hear will live' (5:25).

- The third passage is 11:4, 'This illness is not unto death; it is for the revelation of God, so that the Son of God may be revealed thereby'.

If we could penetrate into the more intimate world of John's Gospel, we must study those passages—and let them work upon us—in which Christ, as it were, looks objectively at the Son of God, Who is yet within Himself. Here there lies quite a different feeling of self from one which personally brings some kind of demand into the world. In Him lives an 'I' which, so to speak, with His own self-sacrifice meets a mighty divine necessity. Humanity has not perceived how truly the Son of God has lived within this and yet it might have learned this from John's Gospel.

Further evidence of the delicacy with which John's Gospel speaks of the Son of God is the way in which Christ does not refuse Nathanael's confession of the Son of God, and thereby indirectly accepts it, but yet leads him away from 'Son of God' to the phrase 'Son of man', the name by which He names Himself. If one begins by thinking of the whole style of John's Gospel, and then thinks of the blunt and harsh way in which a confession of the Son of God is often extracted from people, one then sees how much Christians have still to learn from Christ Himself. But one sees, too, that when such a phrase is used with delicacy, it is really living. Only when it is not living, or only lives as a pale shadow, can a harsh and coarse use be made of it.

Another example of delicacy in the use of this phrase is the way in which, with clearly perceptible awe, the evangelist approaches it in the Prologue. First, he speaks of 'the only begotten' (AV/KJV 1:14) then of 'the only begotten Son' (1:18), and not until after that of 'the Son of God' (1:34). The three passages are:

- 'we beheld his glory, the glory as of the only begotten of the Father, full of grace and truth' (1:14);
- 'No one has ever seen God; the only begotten Son, Who is in the bosom of the Father, He has made Him known' (1:18).

It then continues to the first complete and solemn confession the evangelist makes through the mouth of John the Baptist:

- 'I myself did not know Him; but He who sent me to baptize with water said unto me, He on whom you see the Spirit descend and remain, this is He who baptizes with the Holy Spirit. And I have seen that this is the Son of God' (1:33f.).

The word 'only-begotten' (AV/KJV) is one of those words of which we need to gain a clear understanding. It is also a word from the early religious language, the speech of the Mysteries, and it may not be interpreted in any manner we please, but the particular significance it always had at that time is to be perceived. Here again, in his spiritual research Rudolf Steiner has given an indication that may be tested by John's Gospel. He says that the word 'only-begotten' (*monogenes*) does not mean that Christ is to be regarded as the 'only' son, who is born of God, nor that there is none other beside him. At that time people distinguished between the people who derived all their importance from what they were because of their relation to God, and those who were regarded more in their human relationships. The latter would have been called '*duogenes*', born of two, because their origin from father and mother was taken into consideration. But the others were 'born of one'. In these early times it was regarded not only as irrational, but as sacrilegious to take the external circumstances of such people—that which they had in common with all people—into special consideration, and so to investigate the circle in which they lived. Such biographies as are written today, in which all kinds of human, and all-too-human details are dug up, would then have been impossible. In respect of these men what mattered was how they showed by their lives that they came from God.

It may be that academic theology experiences difficulties with such explanations, because it can find no external proofs of them. But, for example, the saying (1:13) quoted before would be an exact definition of such *Eingeborene*, those who are 'born of one—only-begotten', 'who were born, not of blood nor of the will of the flesh nor of the will of man, but of God'. And this is said, not of Christ alone, but of all the sons of God. And in the same way, the whole of John's Gospel is one single proof that all Christ says does come immediately from above. We recall the sayings of Christ Himself concerning His speaking and actions (quoted in *Letter* 2). Of the expression 'Son of man', there is an example in the prophet Ezekiel, showing that this title was by no means applied exclusively to Christ. No fewer than 40 times Ezekiel is addressed as 'Son of man'. That is no mere phrase that might be applied to any human being. At the moment when he experienced the vision, he was really lifted up above ordinary humanity; he had actually attained to some part of that which a person should become. It is also known that the phrase 'Son of man' ceased to be used in the synagogues after the Christians claimed it for Christ.

All these titles—'only begotten', 'Son of man', 'Son of God'—were later taken away entirely from their earlier contexts and transferred to Christ alone. Thus they acquired a stronger, but narrower meaning. The other sons of God were lost when the one Son of God was found. But because of this, Christ became a dogma to humanity. The names given to Him had lost their nearness to the Earth and their living meaning. We need not fear that we will lose sight of Christ's uniqueness when we give back to these names their early meaning. On the contrary, it is just when we look impartially and honestly at all the 'sons of God' of that time and of the recent, that we acquire a lively sense that Christ is *the* Son of God. And John's Gospel calls Him this quite clearly, although it still allows the early usage to show through its words. He is *the* Son of God, Who revealed what it is to be a son of God, through Whom it becomes possible to become a son of God.

Just as in the Introduction, in what is called the Prologue, we meet with three confessions that are consummated in the Baptist's words of witness, so in the main part of the gospel we find three confessions made by disciples. They are the confession of Nathanael (1:50), the confession of Martha (11:27) and the confession of Thomas (20:28). In the confession of Peter (6:69), which is usually regarded as a culmination point, the AV/KJV reads, 'And we believe and are sure that Thou are that Christ, the Son of the living God'. But the earliest texts that are accessible have neither 'Christ' nor 'Son of God' here, but read '... and have come to know that you are the Holy One of God' (RSV).[38] The meaning is not different; and in any case this is an important turning point. But we have to leave it out of consideration for the time being.

The three confessions of the disciples are found at the most important stages in Christ's life:

- The first, Nathanael's confession comes immediately after the appearance of Christ;
- the second, that of Martha, at the raising of Lazarus, and
- the third, that of Thomas, at the resurrection of Christ Himself.

Looking at the inward progress one feels:

- in Nathanael the [Jewish] folk-soul of the people confessed Christ;
- in Martha, the soul of humanity, and
- in Thomas, the universal soul, as it were, confessed Him.

We shall have to go into this in detail. These three confessions lie between the confession of John the Baptist at the beginning, and the confession of John the Evangelist at the end of the gospel, that Christ is the Son of God.

Nathanael

The story of Nathanael (1:45-51) with its position in the gospel points back in a special way to the confession of the Baptist. And in this first chapter, we feel how first the soul of prophecy, in John the Baptist, and then the soul of the living people, in Nathanael, confess Christ. Before we are told how 'the Jews' fail to find their way to Christ, we are informed that 'the Israelite' confesses Christ. 'Rabbi, you are the Son of God! You are the King of Israel!' (1:49).

How did Nathanael arrive at this confession? Like a great lesson, whose echoes reach our own time, are the words Christ spoke of him, 'Behold, an Israelite indeed, in whom is no guile!' (1:47). For all time the two characteristics are laid down, which are a precondition for someone standing out in the face of his/her circumstances to find Christ. First, s/he must have 'no guile'. The pure impression which Christ makes in the light of truth would shine into people's souls if there were not so much falsehood in them. People are deceived, and do not realize all the forms of self-interest that thrust themselves forward, making it impossible for them to allow the simple truth to act upon them. This is true, to a much higher degree than people are aware even with regard to ordinary truths, but most especially with regard to Him Who is *the* truth. If we wish to find Christ, the Son of God, we have first to resolve to follow resolutely what we feel to be true, even for example, against all the 'theories of knowledge' which we have built up for ourselves. It is not that we must 'make believe' that something is true when we wish to make this confession, it is rather as if until then we had actually interposed something between ourselves and the Sun, and the Sun could not consequently be reflected in our eyes.

But in addition to honesty, which must be deep and all-inclusive, there must be something else present—the will to be a warrior of God; to enter combat and toil for that which is highest. We must not wait for grace to reach our souls somehow, some day; but we have to fight for the truth. A mild and passive preaching of the all-sufficiency of grace is in fact one of the greatest hindrances that lie upon the way to God. This is especially true at the present time. No one need be surprised at not reaching ultimate and assured conviction, without the attempt to find it through real struggle and effort. In the way customary in early biblical and other texts, the evangelist places, Christ Himself places before humanity the two things necessary to real discipleship: honesty and resolve, both in a higher sense than that in which they are practised in ordinary life.

We shall see this warrior-hood still more clearly before us if we see behind our story the courses of the proceedings that took place in the Mysteries. Rudolf Steiner has brought this to our notice in connection with this story. Today many people doubt whether amongst the Israelites there existed what we increasingly see amongst the other nations—esoteric doctrine and esoteric schooling. Naturally, our present task cannot be to go into the details of this question. But we are of the opinion that such accounts as are found, for example, at the beginning of the Kabbala, have to be received as far more genuine than they are considered to be today. There it is related that after the destruction of the Temple, Rabbi Simon [Simeon bar Yochai] broke out into heartrending lamentations that there was now no place where esoteric knowledge could be preserved in the right way. If we turn to our story, the word 'fig-tree' may attract our attention, when we recall that in the East the fig-tree was a kind of symbol for 'initiation', for the way to a deeper knowledge of the divine world. Buddha, too, found enlightenment 'under the fig-tree'. In India this suggested to the Indians the fig-tree whose boughs grow down into the Earth and there strike new roots. This is a fine picture of 'being born again from above'.

What is the usual explanation of this saying about the fig-tree? It is said, when historical value is generally ascribed to the story that Christ, perhaps glimpsing Nathanael praying under his own fig-tree, realized in the spirit that he was praying about the coming of the Messiah. Or it is said that in a kind of spiritual vision Christ became aware of Nathanael's prayer, whose fulfilment He was to be. Even if this was the only meaning, yet it would be remarkable that it is a fig-tree that is mentioned—a tree connected to initiation. But that Christ should see such a thing would not have seemed so wonderful to the people of that time. They often had such experiences. And it would not have explained how it immediately led to the recognition of Christ as the Son of God. The story has quite a different aspect if Christ is saying to Nathanael that He realizes him to be a man who in his earlier life was 'under the fig-tree'—was a pupil who was being prepared for initiation. In an age when the strictest silence concerning all the processes of the Mysteries was a stern duty, it was possible to speak of such a thing only in a language comprehensible to the initiates alone. The word 'fig-tree' was such a word. At the moment when the word was spoken, Nathanael knew that his inmost striving was realized and understood. His whole past life was clearly perceived by this Master.

Even the heads of the schools of initiation at that time were no longer able in this way to see into a person.

Everything that has a connection with the Mysteries will only be approached if the technical expressions are investigated, which here and there, half concealing and half revealing, rise to the surface in the reports. The Freemasons today realize each other by a special kind of handshake, which is a last remnant of the customs of a bygone age. It is told of the Rosicrucians that down to the eighteenth century they were accustomed to go on Easter Sunday morning at sunrise through the eastern gate of the town in which they lived. If they saw another man going in the same way through the eastern gate, they had a special greeting, to which a special answer has to be given. Thus they recognized one another. Thinking of these things, we become very doubtful whether we may take this word 'fig-tree' in a trivial sense.

There is a second thing to be noticed. 'Behold an Israelite indeed'—this fits into another connection. We know that in the Mysteries of Asia Minor, the initiate of the fifth grade was called by the name of his people, a Persian, an Egyptian, an Israelite.[39] There was a hidden justification for this. For the divine in them had grown until it governed within them to such a degree that it could be realized as taking the form in which it existed in the nation, the form of the national god. They had got beyond what is narrow and personal, and had become the representatives of the Godhead in their own people. It is known that in Egypt the initiates were simply called Osiris. In this respect, the three final stages of initiation are interesting—Persian, Sun-hero, Father. The man who had reached the fifth stage was united to that which is divine in this Earth, as it is revealed to his nation. He who had reached the sixth stage was united to that which is divine in the whole world of our whole planetary world; he lives, so to speak, with the Sun. But the man who had reached the seventh and last stage was united to the highest divinity in the whole universe, the Father. It was in this way that a man ascended in earlier times. And a last, faint remnant of this lives on among us today, when a monk is called 'Father'.

We are not necessarily making Christ either a pupil or Master of the Mysteries when we seek to understand the story of Nathanael by such considerations. It must have seemed to Nathanael as if he were entering a light that was wholly pure, in which he was wholly revealed. His deepest seeking and longing were perceived; but his real nature—the true state of the evolution of his personality—was also revealed.

He saw not only single details, but he saw: Here I stand before One Who is as the light of the truth itself. The sunlight falls into me from above, and here I stand. What I have attained and what I have not yet attained is fully known. My whole human nature is permeated by the light. Only if the depths of Nathanael's being were stirred in this way, could we explain the overwhelming impression that made him confess, 'Master, you are the Son of God! You are the King of Israel!' (1: 49).

This, we may observe, really means, 'You are the King of the warriors of God'. Christ had said, 'You are in truth a warrior of God.' In the Arabian world it was this warrior-hood that gave Israel its name, which had by now ceased to be spiritual, and become earthly in its meaning. And the warrior of God himself answers Christ: You are the King of this order of warriors for God. If Israel were what its name affirms—thus John says, thus says Christ—then it would have realized Christ. And the story at the end is a terrible contrast, when the leaders of the people call out, 'We have no king but Caesar!' (19:15), and the representative of the Roman power writes above the cross: Jesus of Nazareth, the King of the Jews. One must not fail to observe those powerful dramatic gestures that are in John's Gospel.

In John the Baptist there speaks the spirit of prophecy, and he speaks of that for which all prophecy had yearned, of the Holy Spirit which descended upon Christ from above and made Him known as the One Who is come from God. In Nathanael spoke the spirit of the Mysteries, and he tells how in this Holy Spirit that which is lower is illuminated, namely man himself. Thus the sacred folk-spirit of Israel speaks in a twofold way. He confesses Christ, the Son of God, before the struggle with 'the Jews' begins upon the earthly stage.

Attempting to adapt this story for our own time, we discover that here is actually described a way to Christ that is available for all time, the way of knowledge, or perception. One can know things in the external world in such a way that the knower stands before the thing known and fulfils towards it the act of knowledge, or perception. The more deeply one penetrates into that which lies within, the more does knowing become a becoming known. I can really know a person in his deeper nature only when, at the same time, I see myself from his point of view, and thus acquire a new knowledge of myself by knowing him. Of God there is no knowledge in the external sense, as science 'knows', but knowing Him grows to be a becoming known oneself.

We must now seek in different ways to make this clear. Rudolf Steiner relates that when we meditate strongly and ever more strongly upon a truth, we finally experience that we seem no longer to think the thought, but the thought thinks us. The thought, or rather the truth, acquires a completely objective character. But then the person is not far from experiencing that this truth is really something objective, not in the sense that is over above the Earth as a truth, but in the sense that it is supported by knowledge. One comes to experience that higher beings think in us. And this is the only way, Rudolf Steiner reports, by which one can come to a sure conviction that higher beings exist. They are there objectively, the upholders of the spiritual world that appear in ourselves in ordinary life as thought.

The Medieval mystics meant something similar by their saying, 'The eye with which I behold God, is the eye with which God beholds me'.[40] It is the feeling: Here I step into the light of truth, but this truth is not only a light that shines upon me, but also an 'I' that looks on me; in it I am revealed, with my deepest longing and striving, and also in my condition at the moment in which I am defective. One cannot come into the sphere of Christ without seeing oneself standing in the purest light. This I am; that I ought to be. In this 'I ought to be', lies the confession of the Son of God; but it is not a dogmatic confession, in any abstract sense. It is an actual discovery. One sees before one the true life, the true person, the true definition of being. If people came in this way to the confession of the Son of God, their confession would be something quite free, personal and living. It would be as if they stood under the dome of a vast cathedral, but this cathedral is a human being, only He is a man born of God, a Son of God. Here I am known, here I am understood, here I am filled—so one might express these feelings—but I am not only known as a single individual; I am known as a human being, as a son of man who is illuminated by the Son of God. In saying this, we draw quite close to the experience of Nathanael.

It will have been noticed that we are now near to those words in the Bible that again touch upon this experience.

- 'For now we see in a mirror dimly, but then I shall understand fully, even as I have been fully understood' (I Cor. 13:12).
- 'As the Father knows me and I know the Father' (John 10:15).
- 'You did not chose me, but I chose you' (15:16).

We experience the same fact in a picture when Mary at the grave of Christ realizes Christ because He names her by her name (20:16).[41]

It would be a great thing for humanity if it was seen that there is, and can be, no other way to a knowledge of Christ as the Son of God. This way is made hard only because we know of knowledge in general, only in the form of external investigation, or of logical proof. By this way we can never come to a knowledge of Christ, for He is neither an object of the sensory world, nor a truth of mathematics and logic. Should we perceive Him in this way, we would not realize *Him* as Son of man and Son of God. The way is made hard also because the phrase Son of God has been so overlaid with history and dogma that we must win it back with all its living forces of light. For this reason, one is inclined to seek for some other phrase than 'born of God'. I myself have for a long time found help in a saying which I had formed, basing it on the theologian [Alois] Biedermann: 'The Man in whom God found His human reality and man his divine truth.' The only kind of evidence that can be expected from the fact that Christ is the One Who is born of God is that through Him the Son of God from above calls to the lost son of God in us. The prophecy that we bear within us, deep in our souls, is fulfilled. We see our true being shining out in Him. In a very deep sense, He calls to us by name—by our human name, and by the name of our 'I'. Our real nature is illuminated in Him. Our 'I', which has never until now felt itself wholly filled, is understood and at the same time, kept safe in the clear light of truth, under the eye of a higher 'I'. Perhaps it is the divine will that one should only be able to speak brokenly of such experiences. Each must attain to them by themselves. But one cannot lay hold of God without being laid hold of by Him. One cannot know Him without feeling that one is known by Him. One cannot choose Him without being chosen by Him. And Christ is the light through which God shines into our lives.

Martha

Martha and Mary appear in Luke's Gospel as two sides not only of the soul of woman, but of the human soul generally. They are completely personal, but also representative figures. At the grave of Lazarus they are like the sorrow (Mary) and the doubt (Martha) that are always present when people stand by an open grave. One can see deep wisdom in the way Christ combats doubt by the word (11:21-27) and sorrow by the deed (11:32-34). But the word which Christ opposes to doubt is not discussion but proclamation, 'He will rise again!' 'I am the resurrection and the life!' Martha's vision cannot follow Christ on His inward way. But her whole faith in Christ breaks out, 'Yes, Lord, I believe that you are the Christ, the Son of God, He who is coming into the world' (11:27). This is a beautiful confirmation of what we said in the first *Letter* about faith—that it is an inner saying 'Yes' to Christ, not with hand and tongue, but with the whole being. In the Greek text the word 'I' is even stressed, as when in everyday life we say, 'I, personally'. That which is translated, 'I believe' is in the Greek text 'I have believed' [*ἐγὼ πεπίστευκα*], and in Greek the perfect tense is often used as a kind of strengthening of the statement, and not as a simple past, but as if to say, 'I am determined to believe', or 'I firmly believe'. And in the whole sequence of words and thought: 'Yes, Lord, I...' we see the whole process of belief as clearly as possible.

Martha's confession comes at the highest point of Christ's activities on Earth. Following the whole course of the narration with inner attention, we receive the impression that Christ wishes to lead her at this hour to a confession. And the question arises, does Christ require the confession made by a human soul in order to do His deed for Lazarus? Does He require to find the strength for His final earthly miracle in the echo from a human soul? Was it necessary, or at least good, that at this moment an earthly being gave its support to the deed that lay before Him? Did this cause the deed to be done not above the Earth, but upon it, or did the deed thus become more intimate? Was this confession granted to Christ at this hour as a kind of human assistance, just as at the marriage at Cana in Galilee, the mother of Jesus was present inwardly when the miracle was performed? We are only asking. But when we recall how when the act of awakening the initiate in the Mysteries was performed, the head priest had to be supported by a circle of assistants, we have the right to ask such questions.

In his confession Nathanael spoke of the 'King of Israel'; here it is a question of the *world* which was expecting the Son of God. So the confession rises to a higher level, just as now a higher level of revelation is reached. And consequently we may say that here it is no longer the folk-soul that is speaking; it is the human soul that confesses its redeemer. We see it, as it were, living before us in Martha, who cannot yet fully understand the sublime words of Christ, but hears Him and opens herself to Him, meeting Him with a whole-hearted 'Yes', in which we hear the whole Earth speaking. It is not only Israel and its King, but the whole Earth and its Redeemer that now stand face to face. The confession reaches cosmic greatness.

Nathanael's confession is a model for all time of the way in which the human spirit finds its way to Christ. Martha's confession shows us another way. It leads the human soul to Christ. The soul also has eyes and ears, just as do the spirit and body. We can sit facing another person and as soul meets soul we can know that we should not be alone with this person in a dark wood. And with another, we may be sure that we could go with him through the loneliest desert. Deceptions often occur when one trusts another in this way, because out of unknown regions of one's soul something enters into one's feelings and falsifies them. The eyes of the soul have been opened, and they have known where they can safely trust. There are deeper convictions than those springing from sensory impressions, or from the conclusions of the intellect, and sometimes the soul also knows when to trust, that it is safe to trust.

If people should wish in this age to take this way to Christ, the great men of history may pass before them—Buddha, Plato, Goethe, Jesus Christ. A self-questioning can take place: Whom would you trust most; to whom would you prefer to trust yourself? Whose work is most important for humanity and ought to 'come into the world'? It can then happen that a great trust in Jesus Christ stirs in their soul, so that they feel, 'That is what matters!' Moreover, they feel, 'Only for the sake of Christ, is life, the Earth, even man himself, of value to me. And if Christ were not there I would not know why I should be alive.' This is what the Buddha felt when, looking at the whole world, he saw what it really was and uttered his great 'No!' No, it is not in this world that a man can feel he is in his right place. And if there were only this world, then the only solution for an awakened human being would be to go out of this world. That was humanity's phrase for the Earth before Christ. And Buddha was really the most awakened of all people. To pass through this feeling of the Buddha and come to the feeling of the Christ, to come to say a joyous 'Yes' to the world for Christ's sake, is one way to confess the Son of God; Christ is then really the 'only begotten Son of God, who is to come into the world'.

Martha puts aside the spiritual question. To Christ's question, 'Do you believe this?' she has no direct answer. But out of her soul's need and doubt, she finds the great 'Yes' to Christ, although she does not grasp it all metaphysically. Her 'Yes' does not come out of the sphere of synodical discussions, but out of the bitter needs of life, and is half a guess, but wholly a deeply understanding and arresting act.

It is good repeatedly to put to oneself the question: For what are you living? What makes life worthwhile for you? What is it that entices you to stake your whole life upon it? In this way we can experience how the 'eternal Yea' of which Carlyle spoke [in *Sartor Resartus*], arises in one's own soul. The world lacks that which Christ has willed for it, and consequently that which He willed must come into the world! One may find that only through Christ can one learn to say 'Yes!' to man, to the Earth, to the world. Christ Himself is the great Yea. And in the Bible He is called by something like that name, 'the Amen' (Rev. 3:14, cf. 22:20).

Thomas

Quite different, still more inclusive and greater is the third confession—the confession of Thomas (20:28). Here we meet doubt again, but in a male form more of doubt of spirit than doubt of soul. And it is a gift of God that he, too, is among the disciples.

The legend relates that Thomas later became the Apostle of India. And it is noteworthy that the few traits of his character the gospel does give us, show him to be related in spirit to India. When Christ sets out to go to Judaea in order to raise Lazarus, Thomas says, 'Let us also go, that we may die with him' (11:16). This already brings him close to the Indians, who saw death everywhere and knew only how to die. Thomas appears again, when Christ bids farewell to His disciples at the Last Supper. 'Lord, we do not know where you are going; how can we know the way?' (14:5). This may remind us how in India, for thousands of years, men sought for the 'Path'. This asking for the 'Path', for the way back to the lost world of God, was more usual in India than anywhere else in the world. 'Then the venerable Ananda went out from his home into homelessness, to seek the path of release.' Passages like that are found countless times in Indian texts. And in what seems a great saying spoken to India, a saying that the Indian 'mission' could have lit up beforehand is Christ's answer—'I am the way'. Buddha said, I teach you the path. Christ says, I am the way. Again, after the events of Golgotha, we find that Thomas is the disciple who walks alone. Like an injured wild animal, he withdraws into solitude. This also was the Indian way, to isolate oneself and seek one's solitary path alone. And then, when he wants to 'see' and makes everything depend on seeing, this also is characteristically Indian. It was in India that a man gave up everything in order to see, and in seeing to become one with the divine world. That is why Christ's manner of leading this disciple beyond seeing is significant.

The wish of Thomas's soul sounds in the Greek text more penetrating and intense than we know from the usual translations. 'Unless I see in his hands the print of the nails, and place my finger in the mark of the nails, and place my hand in his side, I will not believe' (20:5).

Yet we would not think of Thomas simply as being an intellectual or a spiritual man. There are people who require the spiritual atmosphere to be quite clear before they will exert their will. Think of Nietzsche's saying, which should never be forgotten, 'If men are to believe, they must believe quite differently, and thus the everyday Christian becomes a miserable figure'.[42] Do you hear what underlies such a saying? A man like Nietzsche knows that his world would crash about him if he were to speak this 'Yes', which is faith. He knows that it would bring with it a radical reversal of his whole life—something which would be completely different from the lame 'conversion' that he had otherwise seen. And he could not reach this 'Yes', could not yet reach it. He could come to it only with most extreme caution, for this decision is final, and its consequence cannot be foreseen. For *this* reason many people remain far from Christianity. And one may be certain that one's 'No' is no final word, just as Nietzsche clearly betrayed in the notes and memoranda of his last days of illness, that he had not yet found his final word about the Crucified One.

And the Buddha, too, although his spirit was clear and penetrating, was greater still as a man of will. His significance for India and for humanity does not consist only in the knowledge that he gained. Others have gained knowledge richer than this. His knowledge is the preparation for a deed. And the Western person can scarcely imagine how mighty was the power of will the Buddha needed in order to overcome all the inclinations in his soul.

When we see Thomas at the end of the story casting himself down before Christ with the words, 'My Lord and my God' (20:28), we would also believe that this man had only been waiting for the moment when his soul could give itself entirely, when it could become wholly one with its new divine content.

But when Christ revealed Himself, it may not have been Thomas's external conviction which threw him down so much as the inward impression of Christ's overwhelming goodness, which came to meet him there—'My Lord and *my God!*' Just as Goethe in Italy, looking at the Italian works of art, called out, 'Here is necessity! Here is God!'—so Thomas felt, not from the external but from the internal impression, 'Here is God!'

We must not, however, overlook the fact that Christ really appeared to him in bodily form—in bodily and yet not physical [material] form.

Today, thanks to the spiritual aid given to us in anthroposophy, we are able to understand that there is a body that is not visible and yet is really and entirely bodily in its nature. And there is also a seeing that is not of the bodily eye, and yet is really seeing. We can fully understand the appearance of Christ to Thomas, exactly as it is described to us, and can know, and not merely subscribe to another man's opinion, that such a thing was possible and may become possible again.

But when Christ himself leads Thomas away from the seeing that He makes possible for him, to a higher seeing, as one can surely say, it is indeed a seeing in the sense for which Thomas longed but was not the decisive thing for Thomas himself. The 'my'—of 'my Lord and my God'—is evidence enough. One might say that Thomas is the redeemed Indian. When the Indian meets overpowering love, then and only then is he released from his 'No'. This for him is the sunrise over the Earth. Buddha had a vision of the coming of this sunrise when, in his famous song of love, he says:

> All the means by which religious merit can be obtained in this life, O monks, did not amount in value to a sixteenth part of the value of love, which is the redemption of the heart. Love, the redemption of the heart, takes all these means into itself and glows and shines out with radiance [Itivuttaka 27].

But this saying of Buddha's was only a promise, not yet a fulfilment. Buddha showed his friendly kindness to all beings, but not yet flaming, redeeming, transforming love. This love met Thomas at that hour, and he greeted it in the way that man had long greeted the Sun—My Lord and my God! One might, in the spirit of John's Gospel, express this saying in the strengthened form: Lord of the 'I', and God of the 'I'!

This confession putting 'God' as a name for Christ, only appears here; it forms the summit of John's Gospel. And yet again, this confession is the answer to a saying placed at the very beginning of the Prologue—'And the word was a God'. This correspondence in the wording should be noticed. With this, Thomas's confession reaches beyond what is merely human. Here, if anywhere, we have a confession made by the world-soul, as Nathanael's confession was made out of the folk-soul, and Martha's out of the soul of humanity. Out of all the widths and depths of the universe this cry comes. It sounds in the kingdoms above the Earth, like an angelic song of praise. It is the answer to Christ's resurrection, as Martha's confession was the answer to the raising of Lazarus and Nathanael's to the appearance of the Christ. He who was the greatest doubter finds words for the greatest of confessions.

This story of Thomas may lead us by a third way to Christ. Nathanael shows us the way of knowledge, Martha the way of the feelings. Thomas shows us the way of the will. He finds his 'Lord', Who becomes his 'God'. Man's will may seek for a content that fills it completely. Like [St] Christopher, he may be in search of the strongest lord, in order to serve him. If love meets him, then, he may feel, here is a real aim for this Earth—an aim that is greater and more all-embracing than any other. To enter combat for love means to enter combat for the highest of all kingdoms. The meaning of earthly history, the goal of Earth's struggle can be none other than the revelation, the unfolding of love, the perfection of love upon the Earth. On the way which leads through the Lord Whom I seek, I come to know the God Who reveals Himself to me. The person who knows that Christ has brought love to the Earth, and that love alone gives an aim to the Earth and its history, the person who stands for this with his own life and with his whole 'I', in doing so, confesses the One Who was born of God, and this is a confession made by the will. The will becomes an organ of perception. It tells that person that for which he was created, for which he has been waiting, and by which he must be perfected. And he then brings his homage to Him Who now is enthroned in the human will.

Looking over the whole course of such a gospel, one sees what sublime harmonies it contains. We have not the slightest intention of asserting that all we have said must have been present in the evangelist's consciousness. It follows, rather, from the inner rhythm of the gospel itself. The 'composition' of such a gospel, full of wisdom as it is, is an image of cosmic harmonies that can today perhaps for the first time, fully enter into human consciousness. But they permit us to listen to a cosmic music, by which we are led more deeply into the primal nature of the divinity than mere words can take us.

The three confessions we are studying also correspond to the Johannine trinity of light, life and love. This too can be shown without artifice.

- In the story of Nathanael it is a question of seeing. A *light* falls from above into the image of Nathanael, and illuminates him, so that he stands before Christ in a clear light.
- In the story of Martha, Christ Himself spoke of resurrection and *life*. Only trust in Christ makes our life worth living.
- But in the story of Thomas, in the repeated 'my', there is the connection with *love*. The will of man receives its content, indeed, it receives

its greatness, warmth and power only through the love that lives in it. And if this is love of Love, then the will has reached its greatest heights. What we have now seen before us is the eternal way of the Son of God, the way to the conviction that Christ is the Son of God and the way of a person's evolution into a Son of God.

Christ's own witness

In conclusion, we turn to a passage in which Christ Himself, speaking to all the people, bears witness expressly to Himself as the Son of God. In the Synoptic Gospels it is the witness to Himself that He gave before the Sanhedrin that brought about His death. In John's Gospel there is placed beside this the confession that Christ made in the presence of the people, and that also brought about the decision. For from that time forth open activity was no longer possible for Christ, and it comes to an end, until we find an echo of it only in John 12.

Looking more closely at Christ's words (10:34-36), 'Is it not written in your law, "I said, you are gods"? If he called them gods to whom the word of God came (and scripture cannot be broken), do you say of him whom the Father consecrated and sent into the world, "You are blaspheming", because I said, "I am the Son of God"?' (in the Greek, 'Son of God am I.').

To many things in this passage but little attention has been paid, and chiefly to its inward delicacy and restraint. This decisive confession of Christ is not put in the form of a challenging statement, but in the form of a question. Neither does He say, 'I am the Son of God', but 'the Son of God am I'. Elsewhere He speaks always in the 'I am' style: 'I am the light', 'I am the bread.' Here He puts the phrase 'Son of God' first. Let us recall what was said at the beginning of this *Letter* about the awe with which He approached this phrase, and how He, as it were, wrapped Himself and his 'I' in it. If one can feel why Christ does not say here, as He said in his other words of revelation, 'I am ...', but 'the Son of God am I', one may find one's way into deep intimacy with Christ's life of feeling. The overwhelming force of the phrase, Son of God, overshadows the human 'I'. We come into a world where even that 'I' that was most full of the divine shrank back from its own content. And it is also evidence of this human delicacy of His when, immediately after this confession, He adds these words:

> If I am not doing the works of my Father, then do not believe me; but if I do them, even though you do not believe me, believe the works, that

> you may know and understand that the Father is in me and I am in the Father [10:37-8].

He shows them the possibility of proof, but the way in which He points to the witness of His own life is so humble and yet so sure that by such a revelation one cannot fail to realize the truth of Christ's inner life. Then Christ withdraws Himself once more into His own life's holy of holies. 'The Father in me, and I in the Father.' As long as we are unable to penetrate into the fathomless human delicacies and divine revelations of John's Gospel, as long as they are expounded so externally, as is usual today, so long will we gain no idea of this great human book.

Connected with what we have said is the fact that, in making this confession, Christ pointed to the only passage in the Old Testament where human beings are definitely called gods (Ps. 82:6). Of course, there are other passages where the judges of Israel are addressed as gods, for example, Ex. 21:6 and 22:8, 9, 28. Here in his Bible Luther has been unable to avoid translating the word 'Elohim' in the plural 'gods', which he elsewhere translates in the singular, making the plural seem to be only the expression of majesty—as a monarch says of him/herself 'we'. Here we cannot say otherwise than here an older and freer use of the word Elohim appears in the Old Testament. The judges were called 'gods' in Israel, because they were considered to bear within themselves the word of God and 'to know what is good and what is evil' (Gen. 2:9, 17); for to have the knowledge of good and evil is said in the story of creation 'to be like God' (Gen. 3:5). Possibly in Christ's time such passages were not willingly discussed, for this seems to be the most enlightening explanation why Christ, as if in warning, here adds the words, 'and the scriptures cannot be broken', why at this very place He applies the Pharisees' most important precept to themselves—that not one word of the Old Testament may be taken away. Here we find ancient opinions, which were once full of living meaning, entering into the Old Testament with their meaning not yet hardened. The man whom the divine word overshadows, by that divine word itself, is raised above himself and made equal to God.

We are consequently confronted by the fact, which we should often keep in mind, that Christ has picked out the place in the Old Testament where men are most incontestably said to be gods. For in other passages, we may assert, the 'God' Who stands behind the judges is meant. And we have before us this other fact that Christ did not place Himself as Son of God in opposition to men, as an isolated miracle or a fixed dogma, but pointed to the inner connection with that which is said of other men. Until now, these facts have not been taken seriously enough. It is still true that Christ is *the* Son of God, even if He Himself does not use in this place the definite article 'the'—for the same reason, His modest reticence. For if those to whom the Word of God came are called 'gods', why should not He, Who was Himself the Word of God, be called the Son of God? This is in accordance with the deepest meaning of John's Gospel itself. And if the judges, having the knowledge of good and evil, are called 'gods', why should not He in Whom came judgment itself, in Whom the true decision between good and evil came among men, be called the Son of God? This, too, is entirely in the sense of John's Gospel.

We are still true to the inner spirit of this passage when we now ask whether we are not here shown the true way by which we may become born of God. And we are given three hints.

> [1] If the word of God comes to us, too, if we let the word of God dwell in us, if we let the word of God not only shine within us, but create in us, then we are on the way to become sons of God. We need scarcely point out that this thought accords with all that Christ has said, especially in His parting words to the disciples (for example, 14:23 and many other passages). To bring back the word of God in us, to its original force, so that it may again become creative—that is the way by which we may become gods. From this point of view, we may estimate anew the deep significance of strong meditation!
>
> [2] The second indication Christ gives us is His pointing out that the Father has sanctified him. This is one of the sayings in which Christ points back to His pre-earthly existence. Buddha has on occasion pointed back to his earlier incarnations. 'Then the sublime one recalled one life, then two lives, then a hundred lives ...' [as in the *Lalitavistara*]. Christ gently points back in this saying to His existence with the Father. But 'sanctification' does not simply mean to make wholly moral, as we are inclined to understand the word, but also 'to give oneself entirely to God'. It has a wider meaning that includes the moral meaning. It is something like the meaning of our word 'consecration'. Christ is He Whom the Father has consecrated—if we rightly understand this last word. And it is in this sense that the saying is for us the way to being born of God. The more we inwardly sacrifice ourselves to God, give ourselves to Him wholly, to be entirely His own, the more (to use a saying of Master Eckhart) we make ourselves into places where God can dwell and work, and do not wish to be anything of ourselves—the further we are on the way to being a son

of God. It is the way of sacrifice that is shown us. From here we may look back again to Peter's confession (6:69), 'And we believe and are sure, that you are the Holy One of God'. And we may here allow to echo with this the words of the High-Priestly Prayer: 'Sanctify them through Thy truth; Thy word is truth. For their sakes I sanctify myself, that they too may be sanctified through the truth' (17:17 & 19). And also 15:3, 'Now you are clean through the word that I have spoken to you'.

[3] The third way of becoming a son of God is to feel increasingly that one knows one has been sent by God into this world, and increasingly to take this attitude to life. This also is emphasized by Christ as the basic fact of this life, not in order to shut Himself off from other men, but in order to reveal to men the true life of which they too may partake. Even if Christ was sent, as of course He was sent in a higher sense, as it will be with us, then we can indeed, for example every morning upon waking up, accustom ourselves to feel sent down, as it were, from the divine world to the Earth. Thus we may connect with that which is above, gradually freeing ourselves from the feeling that we have ascended from below, so common in this age with its favourite theory of the ascent of man. To feel we are ambassadors on Earth from the divine world, to be its representative—that is the feeling in which we find our real human worth. Thus we grow into being truly born of God.

Looking back on these three indications that Christ gave, as if by the way, we may say again:

- there is a way for the spirit—the saying that is alive and at work in us;
- a way for the feelings—to give oneself inwardly to God and to sanctify oneself;
- a way for the will—to feel one is sent to the Earth,

that Christ Himself shows us, so that we may again become—let it simply be said—that which was once said of human beings, and that there should again be made out of human beings through Christ: gods. We do not really need to add that this is an immensely long and difficult path.

Christ has uttered the exceptional confession—such a confession has in truth hitherto never been spoken before humanity. Now it seems as if the whole of John's Gospel enters a state of breathless expectation. Christ Himself is waiting for that which the Father will say in answer to His confession. Now it is the Father's turn to speak.

Then Christ receives a simple message. 'He whom you love is sick.' And in this apparently unimportant announcement Christ perceives the approach of the Father. 'This sickness is not unto death; it is for the glory of God, so that the Son of God may be glorified by means of it' (11:4). Again, He speaks of the Son of God in this objective manner. And how He goes to meet the deed of the Father. It is the divine answer to His words of confession. 'Father, I thank Thee that Thou hast heard me' (11:41). This public answer is the end of Christ's public activity. One has to study the raising of Lazarus—which we shall have to study again in other contexts—for once from this viewpoint alone: the Father has been challenged by the confession of Christ. Christ is now waiting for Him. And the Father does not let Himself be waited for; He now speaks His word, the great and final word of confirmation. He grants to the Son to give life out of death, as He Himself is the life.

Christ makes His confession; the Father makes His confession. It is now the turn of the nation. And it, too, speaks: 'We have a law, and by that law he ought to die, because he has made himself the Son of God' (19:7). The great dramatic force underlying this trinity of confessions has to be taken deeply into our souls.

- Christ confesses that He is the Son of God.
- The Father reveals Christ to be the Son of God.
- The people reject Him, as Son of God.

World-history now passes from the Jews to the Romans. Trembling seizes the Roman's heart when he hears the phrase Son of God. But this weakness is combined with hatred, and the judgment is pronounced. But, as the first sign that the Romans are now taking over Christianity from the Jews, Pilate writes above the cross: Jesus of Nazareth, the King of the Jews.

Letter No. 5

Son of God and Son of Man (3)

How may the ancient names 'Son of God' and 'Son of man' come to life within us again? We should not let ourselves be led astray by the fact that the name 'Son of God' is monopolized by dogmatics and the name 'Son of man' by history. Today people think of and treat 'Son of man' only as an outworn name for a Messiah, with no longer any meaning for us; and they make 'Son of God' a frigid title of honour that comes into our own experience as a 'confession of faith', not as a living example. But the truth is that in the interchange of Son of God and Son of man, as we see it in the gospel, there lies the secret of humanity and of human history. Just as the consciousness of Christ, as it is shown in John's Gospel, always circles around the point where Son of God and Son of man meet, *so in our meditation, we ought to seek this sacred centre point and experience in this the Mystery of God's thought of man*. That in this we are conscious of our distance from God and of our own defilement is self-evident, if we are living in the light of truth.

How has man been thought of by the divine order? Out of the welter of fluctuating emotions called up by the outer world, by his own body, and by his spiritual impressions, the human being through the course of history has gradually surrounded himself with a perpetual durable scaffolding of custom and experience. Little by little this layer of experience and custom crystallized more plainly round an 'I' that appears to be the bearer of this perpetual, complex life-Mystery. This 'I' is prepared from the very beginning through the individual body man possesses—the body which separates one from everybody else. This 'I' increasingly tends to dominate. The real person lives in his 'I' and out of his 'I' he freely handles his customs and experiences. In his own unique self, which penetrates all he says, does and thinks, lies man's dignity and greatness.

In anthroposophical spiritual science, this period of time during which the unsteady emotions still dominate is called the age of the 'sentient soul'. The time in which lasting customs appear is the age of the rational, or 'mind-soul'. All the religious laws and ordinances of past ages went to form this intellectual, or mind-soul. Then follows the age of the 'consciousness-soul', or 'spiritual soul', when man feels he is within his own 'I', seeking to make his own free decisions independently of external ties. We are living today in this age of the consciousness-soul. Human beings wish to understand and freely assent to laws and ordinances when they are necessary.

The human 'I' has sovereign qualities, but it is also a question. It is unique and lonely. What will be its content? It is free. But the question of freedom is less 'free from what?', more 'free for what?' This is consequently the great question: what will be the destiny in human history of the divine thought—the human being?

For this reason the central point of human history has been reached when an 'I' has come so far that from its own centre it penetrates the entire person. At this point it yearns to discover what its content can be. It 'cries aloud in the desert'. Then the Son of God comes to unite Himself with the Son of man, to bring him to fulfilment. One could graphically present the process like this:

Heaven
Son of God
I
Son of man
Earth

The Son of God is one born from above, Who wills to enter as a new man into mankind.

It can perhaps be doubted whether all this is really contained in the biblical words. But one cannot be in doubt when one has once understood that this is the divine idea for man. The Son of man is evolved from below until his 'I' is complete within him. The Son of God, Whose will is to fulfil this 'I', descends upon it from above.

What we here describe is also the process which was carried out at the baptism of Jesus in the River Jordan. The description Rudolf Steiner gave of Jesus making his way to John describes this event from within.[43] Jesus had gathered up his whole soul into one single all-pervading will towards devotion to God. Like a mighty sacrifice this 'I' rose up to God. Then the Son of God descended and henceforth filled all that remained of the man Jesus.

What happened then is the prototype of all 'being made man'. Only, it happened at that time in a classically consummate way, so that the super-earthly Christ-'I' really came upon the Earth in all His greatness and purity. We are still very far from possessing an 'I' that we could wholly offer up. We offer always single feelings and fractions of our will. Our 'I' does not penetrate our entire human self in the way that the 'I' of Jesus had to do when he willed to sacrifice it wholly at his baptism. But even if we had such an 'I', yet our task is different. Since Christ did come at that time in the whole fullness of the Godhead, out of this fullness He can bestow upon every human 'I' that is presented to Him, its own individual ray. He can illumine and perfect it in its own individual 'glory'. Thus every person becomes wholly *him- or herself,* as when they lived a divine thought in the divine light at the beginning, and yet *all are one* in Christ. This goal, however, to be a Son of man in whom the Son of God lives, is the goal of every person. The more a person develops an 'I' that embraces the total human being as an integrated personality, the more it is possible to allow oneself to be wholly 'born of God' in this 'I', to allow oneself to be filled entirely with divine life. That is why we said that the 'I' is the real organ for Christ.

The purpose of the first half of human history is that the Son of man should be born. And the purpose of the second half of human history is that the Son of God should learn to live in him. We can see that we can best understand the biblical passages concerning the Son of man and the Son of God when we approach them with these thoughts, that we have to express in our spiritual language. For example, the repetition of the saying that the Son of man must be lifted up—referring to the death on the cross—expresses the life-necessity of the Son of man being sacrificed in order that the Son of God, He Who is 'lifted up', may become a reality.

Moreover, every true prayer circles round this Mystery, that the Son of man in us unites with the Son of God. And the purest prayer is often the outcome of our praying out of the word Son of man, or man. For we must learn to use the word I in its true nature. The precious stone does not shine yet pure and clear in the light of the Sun; it has still many stains and scratches upon it. And consequently the seasonal prayer for Trinity of the Act of Consecration of Man seeks to lead us in the pure 'consciousness of our humanity' to feel the divine Father; then out of this divine Father to feel the 'divine Son'—which is also a uniting of Son of man and Son of God.

It is in accordance with the nature of John's Gospel, this gift of God, that we should find so much in it concerning the life of the Son of God in the Son of man. In the 'High-Priestly Prayer, the Great Intercession' (John 17) especially, we are allowed to see into the holy of holies in Christ's soul. If we think that this precious treasure is intended just for our instruction, or that it 'repeats itself', we do not understand it at all. To understand such a prayer we have to realize that the intercourse of spirits in a higher world cannot be the same as it is in the earthly world. Here we speak words to one another. Our whole nature may be expressed in these words, but it may also be concealed by them, wholly or in part. This is possible because we are embodied spirits, and our body shuts us in and also shuts us off from one another. Where there are no bodies, intercourse can only exist in an outstreaming from one to the other—which is more real than any words can be. Such, after death, will be our intercourse with those others who have died, and this makes possible a much more intimate connection than we have upon the Earth. But our earthly duty is to make our speaking with words as radiant as we can.

When we have once made this clear to ourselves, the High-Priestly Prayer appears very differently to us. Here we become witnesses of the way in which Christ lives with the Father in the purest light. In here we see a grandeur in the presence of God so free and so loving as to be quite indescribable. We cannot be thankful enough that we are permitted to experience this. Sentence after sentence is the answer to a question, coming to Christ from the Father. The very first phrase—'the hour has come'—tells the receptive student that Christ is actually standing before His Father. For the Father is above all time; the Son lives in time. And when the Son, living in time, looks up to the Father Who is above all time, the first feeling He has is that of the difference between time and eternity. And the second is that He seeks the point where He, living in time, can feel He is united to the Father Who lives above time. And this can be, when He is there where the divine will itself has placed Him, at the place where the divine will itself is passing through time. To speak very humanly, at the moment when Christ looks up to His Father, He asks Himself if He is fulfilling the command of the hour. If the hour is marked not by an earthly but by a heavenly chime, then the Son is united to the Father. Everywhere when the 'hour' is spoken of, we are witnessing a sacred pilgrimage through time. And so all through this prayer, Christ spreads out His life before the all-penetrating eye of His Father, and answers for it. The emanation of the Father's being is always followed by the emanation of the Son's being. And we are permitted to be witnesses of this. In the first half of the prayer, it is more the outstreaming of the Father's being to the Son. In the second half it is more that the petitions coming out of the Father's being are streaming back again to Him.

We shall often have to think of this High-Priestly Prayer. But we have first to find in the preceding passage of John's Gospel the places that give us a glimpse of the intercourse of the Father with the Son. From time to time John's Gospel allows us to look as if through a delicate veil into the highest of all things that ever happened upon the Earth. Behind the outer things a radiant world of light appears very clear and very near to us. And then our inmost life feeds upon this ray of light falling upon our soul.

We have often the impression that Christ is standing at the boundary of the sensory world. That which comes to Him from without needs gently to touch His spirit—and divine truths come to light. His inner part is filled with divine revelation, and this breaks forth when the world of the senses brushes even lightly against it. One might recall to mind the Indian Vedic saying, 'Through everything I ascend into thee' [cf. the prayer addressed to Rohita], or the Zarathustra saying of Nietzsche,[44] 'On every allegory you ride here to every truth'. Only, it is the comparison of these two sayings that makes so much clearer the uniqueness of what we see in John's Gospel.

Let us consider an especially characteristic incident: Christ is waiting for His disciples by Jacob's Well (4:1-42). A Samaritan woman comes to draw water. Christ does not avoid entering into conversation with her; neither does He shun making a request, nor expressing quite simply His bodily necessity, His thirst, 'Give me to drink!' What now comes forth from the woman's soul reveals what is within it. She feels the power she has at this moment over another, since she has the bucket in her hand and can draw water; and she makes use of this power. The national quarrel between the Samaritans and the Jews comes to the surface. 'Ah!' she says, 'I am good enough now, but at other times ...?' Her soul rejoices if only for a moment in the petty opportunity for a petty revenge, which the national enemy seems to put into her hand. How revealing is the way in which Christ answers! 'If you knew the gift of God, and who it is that is saying to you, "Give me a drink," you would have asked Him, and He would have given you living water' (4:10). The divine gift by which He is filled—which He Himself is—is so strong in Him that simply the remark of the woman, 'you ... ask me', causes the reality of the inner situation as against the unreality of the outer situation to shine out immediately. He is now in His inner kingdom, and during the whole course of the following conversation He never again speaks of His thirst. It is not by accident that, in the ensuing conversation with His disciples, He says, 'My food is to do the will of him who sent me, and to accomplish his work' (4:34). In the talk with the Samaritan we are spectators of this process.

Nothing in Christ's answer to the woman is a reaction to that which is happening in her soul. One might here again think of a saying of Nietzsche—for how often did Nietzsche touch upon deeply Christian truths? 'Rather remain a debtor than pay with a coin that does not bear one's own impress. Such is our sovereign will!'[45] In this saying we clearly see a vein of right human and earthly feeling. But Christ here and everywhere pays with a coin which bears His own most pure image. By no word of His does He take any part in the state of soul of this woman who is seeking a quarrel. He sees only *her* need there behind her words. And this is a need of mercy. He sees her inner emptiness that He can fill. And He tells her this in a way that cannot make her feel disparaged but translates His gift into a language that is current with her—'living water'. This puzzling saying about water that lives brings out her questioning and longings, without which Christ can give her nothing. And so we can look into the living interplay of outward event and inner being, and also into the reciprocal activity of Christ's inner will and human possibilities. Out of one single saying in a conversation of this kind much can be learnt for our daily conversation—and also much for the right fulfilment of Christ's mission among human beings.

A similar experience is to be had twice more in this chapter, as if the evangelist had meant to describe fully the nature of Christ's spirit once and for all. 'Meanwhile the disciples besought him, saying, "Rabbi, eat" (4:32). But he said to them, "I have food to eat of which you do not know". "My work is to do the will of him who sent me, and to accomplish his work".' (4:33f.) We see how the request that He should eat does not remind Him of earthly things, or make him aware that He is hungry, but recalls to Him an invisible process whose significance so far outweighs that of the earthly process that the latter falls into the background. Eating and drinking become here the outer pictures for a supersensory process. And it is important that starting from these experiences we do not mean simply the single story, but the inner facts of which it speaks—we should look at the Lord's Supper, which Christ gave to His disciples at the end of His life to be their way of worshipping God. And out of these very details which are here given us, we cannot think of the inward processes in Christ in a way that is also sufficiently living and tangible. When Christ saw before Him a divine will which He had to accomplish, at that moment not only were bodily needs forgotten, but out of this will itself delicate life-forces flowed in, which also sustained His bodily nature. So a higher process of nourishment entered into the earthly process. Here again it is only anthroposophical perceptions that can help us to understand. And it seems to us that in this case it is not only the etheric life-forces of the cosmos that are the vehicles of this nourishment, but still higher forces coming out of the astral world that are pure forces of the spirit.

Thus this passage is closely connected with the words of Christ in the next chapter but one of John's Gospel (6:49-51): 'I am the bread of life. Your fathers ate bread in the wilderness, and they died. This is the bread which comes down from heaven, that a man may eat of it and not die.' The manna, which in its derivation points to the spirit—*mens, manas*—is in the Bible the picture of a food which will be sent down from above. And here not only in Christ's words, but in the events around Him that we are privileged to see—how He bears Himself in relation to the woman, how He bears Himself towards His disciples—this is quite clearly proclaimed. We are looking into processes that would evoke our reverence—processes that in the midst of earthly history speak of the far future. A time will come when earthly food will be replaced by the divine will (4:34) and earthly drink by eternal life (4:14). We do not mean to imply that Christ was already able in the earthly body He shared with the people of that time, to live alone by this divine food and drink. He bowed to earthly necessity down to His latest hour (19:28). But even before the Resurrection we see in Him an earthly body on the way towards this future. And we ourselves, too, with our earthly bodies are upon the way to this future every time we share in the Lord's Supper. Indeed, a person may try fully to feel the eating and drinking of the Supper, even in his/her bodily nature. This may be done in all modesty, without seeking to anticipate anything that does not yet belong today. A very lively foretaste of the 'power of this food' may be experienced. What is earthy in it—the bread and wine—is like a kindly bridge reaching into the land of the future, as an earthly link and a release for that which is no longer earthly. In the Lord's Supper we are very close to the life of Christ. Just as Christ could not entirely free Himself from earthly processes, *we* can also not be entirely excluded from the heavenly processes. In this sense, too, the Lord's Supper is a most intimate uniting of ourselves to the life of Christ, not only to His life in heaven now, but also to the life He then lived on Earth. We can well imagine that out of such considerations and experiences the Lord's Supper may appear to many in an entirely new light.

But in this way the Supper becomes a symbol pointing beyond itself to a future that is, of course, still far off, when fulfilled. It *is* fulfilled—fulfilled in the highest sense—when man's bread of life has become the divine will, and his drink eternal life. The divine nature ought to enter into us in such a living manner that we do not always need to rest and recover from it as we so often do now; but that, great and awful as it is, it becomes food and drink for us. This is what we ought to experience, not only in meditation, but in the deed.

By these two examples, we see how we may experience sometimes in meditation that a being filled with the divine fullness of life was so immediately present in Christ that only a slight impulse was required to make it overflow. Outward things did not draw Him away from the divine so that the divine withdrew from Him. Rather were outer things the cause of revelation, and thus themselves became revelation. And thus they were brought back again into the divine—were redeemed.

Here the difference from the Indian saying, 'Through everything I ascend into thee', is obvious, as well as Nietzsche's saying, 'On every allegory you ride here to every truth'. In India it is always the Universal-One (*All-Eine*) in the *feelings*. In Christ it is the living fullness, in *clearness of spirit*. In Nietzsche the capricious human will is not yet overcome.

Christ radiates the pure revelation of the divine will. One might sooner think of the other saying of Nietzsche, of the wish of Zarathustra[46] 'to stand over each and every thing as its own Heaven'. Only, even in this high saying one can see a falling short of that divine spirit which brings its own heaven in everything, and yet causes the heaven that it reveals to be always the same.

Christ's last saying concerning His food helps us see very beautifully into His soul. He had spoken of finishing the divine work. But this was no dark, abstract saying perhaps sustained by inner enthusiasm in the soul. How living it was, the following words (4:35-38) show:

> Do you not say, 'There are yet four months, then comes the harvest'? I tell you, lift up your eyes, and see how the fields are already white for harvest. He who reaps receives wages, and gathers fruit for eternal life, so that sower and reaper may rejoice together. For here the saying holds true, 'One sows and another reaps'. I sent you to reap that for which you did not labour; others have laboured, and you have entered into their labour.

Christ's eyes may have been resting at that moment upon the fields that stretch far across the country from Jacob's Well by the city. But the outer appearance of the fields is not in accord with the feeling in His soul. The outer picture becomes again the impulse to inner sight. And again we may share tangibly and yet intimately in their experience.

It has been said that Christ rejoiced deeply over what He experienced in this meeting with the Samaritan woman. We may take a further view of this experience. In her, too, we find a misunderstanding preventing her from getting away from the external events. We shall later consider the details of this, but at this very moment she is running to the city to tell what she has experienced. In the next hour the people will come out of the city to seek Jesus. And yet, this coming out is only a picture of a much greater and wider truth. The harvest of the world is beginning. All that went before was seedtime. If, for example, the woman at the well and the people to whom she is hastening have formerly known anything about a Messiah who was to come, that was but a seed sown within them. When the woman looked up to the Temple, which lay there on the mountain and was a prototype for praying 'in spirit and in truth', and when she thus gave Christ an opportunity to utter this saying, that again was a seed that had been sown in her by the religious work of earlier generations. Christ looks back with thankfulness at all this toilsome work of preparation that has had to be done. And again it is so distinctive of Him, that He cannot have this retrospective look without also seeing His predecessors as living men who have a right to see the blessing that has come upon their work and to rejoice in it. He has them with Him at this moment. When eternal life is reaped, then they will receive the inner reward of their labour.

Christ feels at this moment that He is the turning point of the world's history, that He is the beginning of the harvest of human beings. But how characteristic it is of the spirit of His love, that He must have with Him those who have gone before Him, and those who are now working with Him. He feels no lonely greatness, no isolated uniqueness. Perhaps He has been listening to the talk of the disciples, as they spoke together about the harvest that would come in four months. Now He adds His own words. So He speaks to them in their own language. No other word; no word more. A man can but show no greater task in the world than that shown here to the disciples. And at the same time one cannot give Him more help towards modesty. Joy over the greatness of the task, insight into what is necessary for such a task, thankfulness to those who have gone before, and modesty in respect of what they have themselves done—that is the spiritual attitude that Christ expects of the disciples.

But over all this lies the light of pure joy, which one ought to drink into one's soul like the sunshine on a spring day. The shadows of Golgotha have not yet begun to fall. Cosmic day shines in the soul of Christ, filling it with its glory, radiating joy and power into the hearts of His fellow workers.

It seems to me that in such a passage we look more deeply into the way in which parables are born in Christ's soul. John's Gospel, indeed, gives us few parables in the style of the other evangelists. But at this and at other places it helps us see how parables sprang up in Christ's mind. The parables of the sower, of the seed, and of harvest are all connected with an experience of which we here receive a kind of reflection. Outer things approach an exceedingly rich inner life and out of this inner life the corresponding truths flash forth. And the most pure inner greatness of Christ's soul flows in a striking way into these parables. One ought always to turn one's gaze again towards this pure greatness when the truths contained in the parables have been grasped. Christ's walk through the outer world is for Him the gentle impulse which the divine world within Him awaits in order that it may be revealed. If here, so to speak, we have the process before us, then in the other three gospels we have before us in rich measure the results of this walk through the world. John's Gospel completes the other gospels also in this respect, that it preserves the innermost intention of the parables in which Christ expresses Himself. In the book *Meditation*, I have described how the 'I' of Christ is illuminated within by the experiences of the world—light, bread, the shepherd's life, vine-growing—how His own 'I' is thus led to an earthly consciousness and all the world's depths, and His 'I', too, are made to shine forth. It is the greatest good fortune for us that we are permitted to share in this experience. And the comparative simplicity of the world of that time made it possible for great and enduring pictures to be set before us—pictures that shine into the deepest relationships of human existence, and illumine the greatest possible widths and depths of the earthly world.

We shall now study one more of the many sayings that help us see into Christ's relationship to His Father.

> For this reason the Father loves me, because I lay down my life, that I may take it again. No one takes it from me, but I lay it down of my own accord. I have power to take it again; this charge I have received from my Father [John 10:17f.].

Such a saying lets us see into that which is most inward, lying beneath the death on the cross, and the Resurrection. For 'charge' is not to be thought of as given during this life, but before this life! 'No one *has taken* it from me.'

One day the greatness of human life will consist in this, that people will come to the Earth with a duty laid upon them. They will feel that their angel has whispered to them at birth something they are to accomplish on the Earth. They will experience an unrest that they cannot explain otherwise than that they have not yet found the thing they were to find. And when they find their life's work a feeling of deep joy will come over them. What we have just said about the angel who prophesies something to us at birth takes us, according to anthroposophy, into times lying still further back—into the time before birth. The more awake people become to the deep things of the spirit the more they will be convinced that their life's work points them back to a pre-natal life. And this knowledge stands here with great clearness before us in Christ.

The passage under consideration is not the only one in John's Gospel that speaks of these facts. But what on the one hand is a duty laid upon us, on the other hand is a power lent to us. The word 'power' recalls the 'powers', the Spirits of Power, called 'Elohim' in the Old Testament. These are those Spirits who carry out the creation in the name of God Most High. In the deepest sense of John's Gospel, we may say, it is the continuing and completing of the work of creation that the human 'I', with whose evolving the divine cosmic powers were concerned, should freely offer its life at the height of humanity's evolution, and as freely take it again. So the nature of the 'I' is revealed in its depths, as it ought to be. And its true life is accomplished. One must think of this saying as if inscribed above the cross: 'No one has taken my life from me, I myself give it away'—then the sovereign nature of such a saying becomes manifest. In giving away, and taking up again, the true life of the 'I' consists. In everyday life, too, in every conversation, the 'I' gives itself as it listens, and lets the other 'I' speak, and recollects itself within as it replies to the other. In every professional practice, every accomplishment of a deed, the 'I' sees itself against an object, its duty, for example, and it devotes itself to that object, showing itself in it. Then is exercised the 'power' to 'take itself up again', enriched by its relationship with the object. Every time we read anything the same mysterious process goes on. We lose ourselves in it and then take ourselves back again. If all the processes of life were worthily performed, then people would come from every one of their deeds greater and richer than they were before. They would really find that the more they have died into the act, the more their coming from the act becomes a resurrection. What Christ says here is the innermost impulse of His life; it is also the miracle of the life of every 'I', whenever people are really living out of their 'I'.

The most commonplace, everyday fact, however, is closely united with the very highest. 'For this reason the Father loves me, because I lay down my life.' What is translated, 'This charge I received from my Father', could also be translated, 'This my father said in me'. It is the innermost conversation of the Father with the Son that we hear in such words. It is the conversation that endures. It is the Father's revelation of Himself in the Son.

When a man loves, he always in truth loves himself. This is not meant trivially, but in the highest sense. A man likes to call his beloved 'his real [or better] self'. Only, because of the tragedy of his nature, a man sees at first his 'real self' outside himself, because he has lost it. And he frequently sees it falsely—distorted and falsified—when, for example, he loves riches, or power. But it is the characteristic of love that in it love of another and love of self here coincide. In the highest and purest sense one sees this in the love of the Father to the Son. The Father loves His own Image. So He loves the Son and at the same time loves His own divine nature. For as the Son gives Himself, so has the Father given, and so He still gives Himself.[47] For this reason He thereby speaks of it in the Son. So in this passage we look into Christ's nature, into the Mystery of the 'I', into the transfiguration of everyday life and into the nature of the Father; into the historical life task of Christ and into the most fundamental underlying reality of the world, into the love of the Father to the Son, and of the Son to the Father. This is a picture of what the world itself ought to become, that is, a divine Son who rays the Father's glory back to the Father. It is the most underlying reality that can become the soul of every act that anyone performs. 'That the love with which Thou hast loved me may be in them, and I—the true "I"—in them.' This is the birth of the 'Son of God' in the 'Son of man'.

Letter No. 6

The Book of Joy

Four Johannine words

The great and solemn words in John's Gospel are: *Word, Life, Light* and *Love*. We meet them in the first sentences. The word 'love', of course, is hidden at first in the sentence, 'And the word became flesh ... glory, full of grace and truth'. The four words are interwoven, one with another, in a multitude of ways. We have already pointed out that the words, taken in the order, word, light, life, love, correspond to the content of the four parts of the Act of Consecration of Man.

- In its opening prayer a whole history of the *word* upon the Earth passes before us;
- in the Offertory we hear repeatedly the word *light*;
- in the Transubstantiation bread and wine are awakened to *life*;
- there is Communion, union, when the fulfilment of the *love* that is between Christ and His own is accomplished.

It has to be expressly said that, for example, the order of the last two words, life and love, can also justifiably be reversed. Then the Transubstantiation would be the great act of love, and the Communion the awakening to true life. On might reflect how often this word 'life' is spoken in the fourth part of the Act of Consecration of Man, and how often the word 'love' is repeated in the third part. There is no need for confusion by such possibilities of interchange. The chief thing remains untouched by them. In this case, we have these possibilities, because a much closer connection exists between the feelings and the will than between thinking and the feelings, or thinking and the will. Love can be studied from the side of the feelings, and can also be studied from the side of the will. Life, too, can be viewed from both these sides.

The human being studied in the light of these words should show *light* in his thinking, *life* in his feelings, and *love* in his will. The more this is so, the more he himself becomes *word*. He then rightly expresses the word 'human being', not only with his mouth, but with his whole nature. The human being becomes a divine word. And the Word became flesh, so that flesh, the human being, might become word.[48] This is consecration to manhood—the Act of Consecration of Man. One can offer the threefold life of the human being in thinking, the feelings and the will, to the divine world to be consecrated in the Act of Consecration of Man. This is also a baptism. Light is the Holy Spirit, love is the Son, life is the Father. 'For as the Father has life in himself, so he has granted the Son also to have life in himself' (5:26). 'That the love with which Thou hast loved me may be in them, and I in them' (17:26). We are now looking into the deepest ground for the possibility of this interchange. It is the *love* of the Father to the Son, and of the Son to the Father, by which the process of *life* passes back and forth between them. 'All mine are thine, and thine are mine' (17:10).

... also in cultural development

Let us now point out another living order of these words. It is known that in anthroposophical spiritual science four cultural periods are distinguished: the early Indian period, the Persian, the Chaldean-Egyptian, and the Greco-Roman. To the question whether these periods may be connected with the four Johannine words, then clearly the Persian is the religion of light. The Persians looked up to the holy light and became warriors of light in the war against darkness. Clearly, too, we can see the relation of the Greek world to love. This is connected with the Greek way of going right down to the Earth. And thus Eros, the god of love, was worshipped, and the greatest artistic work of Greece, Plato's *Symposium* ('The Banquet'), is a glorification of love.

Only a little less obvious is the relationship of the Egyptian world to life. In that world, people struggled with the question of death. Even the mummies represent a struggle of life with death. And now, for India, there still remains 'word'. Indeed, this is the one of the four words that comes nearest to Indian culture. There, people do not ask for 'life', but seek rather to release themselves from the eternal process of life and death. They speak, instead, of light, too, but not in the sublime manner of the Persians. Of love they knew, but only in the form of mild benevolence to all creatures. But they sought the word, the mantric word, as a way to the divine. And they spoke of the primordial word *va*, out of which everything has come. The priest at the altar spoke the sacred word, and those who meditated lived in the breathing, the creative spirit of the word.

And thus, for the four cultures, we would have the following order: word, light, life and love. It is the same order as we meet in the Act of Consecration of Man. In the age in which people were seeking for love, the great act of love, Christ's deed on Golgotha, took place. The descent of the word as described in the first verses of John's Gospel has consequently the image of the descent of the four cultures into the earthly world—except that here life and light exchange places—and yet they do not change places, for in the Persian period people saw in light, the true divine life, and in looking up to life after death people in Egypt received the true light for earthly existence. Such crossings over prevent us from falling into a system that does violence to real life.

For the present we shall go particularly into one word in John's Gospel, less noticed but yet one that leads well into the centre—the word 'joy'. Here again a saying in Nietzsche comes to mind: 'Ever since there have been human beings, they have enjoyed themselves too little: that alone, my brothers, is our original sin!'[49] In such a saying lies the deep consciousness that man is born for joy, that joy exists for his soul as the Sun for the flowers, and that the soul on Earth is continually withering away, because it has not enough joy. All human longing for joy is expressed in such a saying. And the connection with original sin is also expressed. But people can't escape original sin by suddenly beginning to be joyful. For it is just through sin that man fell from the joy that was intended for him. The Bible calls it Paradise. Sin does not consist of joylessness, but joylessness comes from sin. Consequently, Christ, Who came from the worlds of Paradise, clearly always thought that human beings were in need of joy, that joy must be brought to them.

Fullness of joy

We should look at the principal passage, 'And now I am coming to thee; and these things I speak in the world, that they may have my joy fulfilled in themselves' (17:13).

Let us bring fully into our consciousness the moment when these words were spoken. Christ, Who is standing now before His disciples, will be betrayed by one of them—and He knows it (13:18). He will be denied by the chief of His disciples, and He knows it (13:38). He will be deserted by all His 'faithful followers', and He knows it (16:38). He is going to the most terrible death. He is leaving behind upon the Earth nothing but a troop of frightened disciples whom He must leave among the hate and persecution of men (17:14, 15). *And He speaks now of fullness of joy! He radiates fullness of joy!* The whole High-Priestly Prayer is a super-earthly radiance of joy. 'These things I speak in the world, that they may have my joy fulfilled in themselves.' Yes, the whole of John's Gospel, which here reaches its highest point, is a radiance of joy, far above earthly joy.

One would think that henceforth no one in the world would ever say again, 'In my destiny there is no joy at all'.

The flower of life has thus been planted in the darkest spot of Earth and everyone who seeks for joy may pluck that flower at this place. It is just for dark times like those in which we are living, that such a study as we are now undertaking may become of the greatest value for our whole future life; for it lifts us out of the present into the kingdom of joy, from which we can receive true strength for this present time.

Three times does Christ speak of fullness of joy in His Farewell Discourses. Besides 17:3 there is also 15:11, 'These things I have spoken to you, that your joy may be full'. One could also translate it, instead of 'my joy', 'the joy that I AM'. And then 16:24, 'Ask, and you will receive, that your joy may be full'—with the fullness of God. We see how important for Christ the filling of mankind with joy really was. The Farewell Discourses are meant to be an initiation into joy. It is consequently like an answer when we read, 'Then were the disciples glad when they saw the Lord' (20:20).

But now we have to look carefully to see upon what the joy of Christ rests, which, as He expressly says, He wishes in His last hour to leave behind upon the Earth. We discover this when we listen to the last words that Christ spoke to His disciples, 'I made known to them Thy Name, and I will make it know, that the love with which Thou hast loved me may be in them, and I in them' (17:26). This saying is the highest peak of the High-Priestly Prayer. If one should ask, what is this name of God which Christ has make known? One must not think of a name in our sense of the word. But if a word should be mentioned, a name, which one ought most certainly allow to shine in one's soul, it would be no other than the name 'Father'. In the name 'Father', when it sounds forth rightly, complete joy is shining.

According to John's Gospel, consequently, Christ lets a ray shine out of the highest relationship that exists between Father and Son. This is the ray of joy that He leaves behind upon the Earth into which He enters. The duality between Father and Son is the prototype of all love. Only we must take this seriously. Christ wills, as His words say, that we should feel something of this love, that we should partake of it, should live in it. *Through Him, for so He wills, we ought to feel this love; this ought to remain within us, shining in our souls*. It seems to me that until now, no one has taken these clear words of Christ as seriously as they are meant to be taken. It is not only that God loves us, which is the ground of our joy, but that the Father loves the Son, and that we may 'see His glory'—this is the radiance that we ought to carry with us in our souls.

If we should wish to place before us a picture, which, of course, brings the truth to us only from another viewpoint, let us assume that the Sun is alone in space, and no other heavenly body is present. Then the Sun itself would not shine. It would not see itself. It would not be conscious of itself. Nor would it have anything upon which it could radiate the fullness of its life and love. Only the planets are certainly much poorer creations of the Sun than the Son is in relation to the Father. But let us imagine that in the place of one of the planets there is a great mirror reflecting back to the Sun the Sun's own life and light. And let us imagine, too, that this mirror is not made of glass, but is like the Sun in form: furthermore, that this mirror-world receives into itself all the life of the Sun and recreates it. That would be a picture resembling what takes place between the Father and the Son. 'The Father loves the Son and shows Him all things that He Himself does' (5:20).

If this is brought to consciousness, that truly the light itself would not shine, could not be revealed as light, if there were no object upon which it could shine, one has the closest picture for the God hidden in Himself at the beginning, and for the living fact of love. Here we approach the thoughts which Rudolf Steiner often expressed. In other contexts, he pointed out that when one stands with one's back to the light, looking out into space, so to speak, with the light itself, one can see nothing, because the light only becomes luminous against the objects upon which it falls.[50] This physical fact also points to very profound Mysteries. And, indeed, in the picture of the Sun and the mirror, we may call to mind that Steiner used a like simile for the relation of God the Father to the world in his lecture on the Lord's Prayer.[51]

We can scarcely come much nearer than this to the original Mystery of the world. This picture, too, is only a hint, which must be followed out in one's own mind, as the glance follows the hand pointing out a star in the sky. Then the eye can leave behind the world in which the hand has to remain.

Often in our lives, our human joy felt in its highest moments seems to point to another joy that we do not yet possess. But here, in the gospel, the primal joy is clearly shown us, than which none is greater. The more there is of the love of the Father to the Son, in our single human joys the more does God see Himself in the act we perform, as the light sees itself in the mirror, and consequently loves the Son in us. And so much the more are we then in the kingdom of true joy.

This may seem initially incomprehensible—but we shall understand it better as we give heed to what Christ says concerning the mysterious divine interweaving between Him and His Father. 'The Father loves me because I do all things that he commands me' (cf. 15:10, 10:17f.); 'All that the Father has is mine' (16:15). This saying is strengthened by a phrase in the High-Priestly Prayer, 'All mine are thine, and thine are mine, and I am glorified in them' (17:10). Such words of fellowship express the great joy of Christ over His unity with the Father, in such a way that one can learn from them all one's life long, and can rejoice in them. In such passages, the curtain is withdrawn, as it were for a moment, from before the holy of holies. Here we are experiencing spiritually that which the people of past millennia experienced when they were permitted to look into the inmost part of the Temple. It was not expressed in words of rejoicing. But *joy itself speaks*. And it speaks so gently and with such grandeur that in one single sentence cosmic symphonies slumber, for which we have yet to develop an ear to hear them. It might also be said, 'Here speaks Christ's cosmic voice'. It speaks softly, and yet it penetrates through the world. The person who hears it knows what joy is. But since joy, real joy, is not merely a feeling that makes us happy, but is a source of life and power, we have a right, we have every reason, to listen ever again to this joy and to bathe in it as in the river of Paradise. What are all the joys we know on Earth compared with such a saying—when one dares to take it seriously—that one of us, a human being, can speak to the greatest being of all, saying, 'All mine are thine, and thine are mine'. The love of the Father to the Son, and of the Son to the Father, is here revealed as perfect community.

Here we break off to point out this joy in another place in the gospel. When we read the High-Priestly Prayer, we feel that Christ is standing here upon the threshold between two worlds. He says expressly that He has already crossed this threshold. 'And now I am no more in the world, but they are in the world, and I am coming to thee' (17:11). This saying follows immediately after the other saying concerning thine and mine. Now it is a part of the glory of this High-Priestly Prayer that in it we see Christ passing back and forth between the two worlds. Sometimes it seems as if out of the higher world He were being called, 'Come hither!' And He hears the call. And He answers, 'Yes, I come!' But then He looks back at His disciples again, and seeing them He blesses them, sealing them once more with a word of help. To see how Christ's glance is turned now upon the glory into which He is going, and now upon the disciples whom He is leaving behind—to watch this is to look as deeply into the divine being as is possible for us.

If one would experience this ever again, one has to accustom one's ear to the heavenly music that sounds in the background, as He repeatedly says, in answer to the call that He alone hears, 'I come to thee' (17:11 & 13). Or one has to see how His eye rests upon the glory which He had with His Father—full of joy, yet with no shadow of a feeling of selfishness; full of sureness, yet with a soul that moves towards His disciples (17:5 & 24). Or we have to listen to the primal tones from the life of the divine love, with which the prayer ends, 'Thou in me, and I in Thee' (17:21, 23 & 26). If we can feel even remotely what is in a spirit that can so speak, then we know what joy is.

But we have to return to Earth and out of what we have just been looking at, seek to understand better Christ's life upon the Earth.

It might be said: In Christ there passes over this Earth the Human Being who was illuminated by the Father's hidden sources of light.

> Jesus cried out and said, 'He who believes in me, believes not in me, but in him who sent me. And he who sees me sees him who sent me. I have come as light into the world, that whoever believes in me may not remain in darkness' [12:44-46].

> 'Have I been with you so long, and yet you do not know me, Phillip? He who has seen me has seen the Father; how can you say, "Show us the Father"?' [14:9].

From these heights, let us look down on our life. If we succeed in any small deed in making the Father shine forth, then, at that moment, the Father is loving the Son. Every such deed is in a certain sense itself such a Son whom the Father loves, because He is reflected in it. The divine life shines forth out of its hidden depths, and perceives itself in this deed. When, for example, anyone does a kind deed to a child, out of real love, it is then as if in such a deed the world became for a moment perfect. When someone speaks a word in full, deep honesty, then a light breaks forth out of higher worlds, illuminating that hour.

Many Christians today seek to rejoice only in the essential experience of grace, and by doing so to feel their own unworthiness as a background. It is certainly always true in our lives that a person would never be worthy by himself alone, and that Christ had to come, that everything is pure, undeserved grace. But besides the grace that saves, there is a new life, into which grace will transplant us and which is itself pure grace. No honest person will ever even think that we can reach any sort of perfection upon the Earth. If only *that* has real value which is like Christ, it is *always* little enough. But we are speaking here of that wherein likeness to Christ consists, so that we may learn to see it, and may be able to give it more place in our lives.

From such thoughts, we now look to single sayings, such as:

> 'Are we not right in saying that you are a Samaritan and have a demon?' Jesus answered, 'I have not a demon; but I honour my Father, and you dishonour me. Yet I do not seek my own glory; there is One who seeks it and he will be the judge' [8:49f.].

In the light thrown by such words, the word 'glory' becomes new to us.

Let us try the following meditation: Let us imagine that we carry in our human nature the 'I' like a radiant star in the middle of our forehead. But this light of this star is like a flame that has been kindled out of cosmic spaces and is fed evermore by the glory of this highest and most all-embracing Godhead. So one has a kind of picture of how the 'I' lives in Christ. This 'I' shines forth in Him, as at His baptism the words were heard, 'You are my well-beloved Son, upon whom rests the light of my revelation' (cf. Mark 1:11; Matt. 3:17). In this 'I' He had joy. In this 'I', we also can feel it meditatively.

Christ needed no joy that came from outside. None could give Him anything higher than He already had at every moment, when He was fully conscious of Himself. Nor could He look for joy in the form of any glory that could be bestowed upon Him from without. He bore the deep, eternal source of all joy within Himself.

The Father was 'glorified' in Him; that is to say, Christ went through the world in such a way that all the radiance of the divine world rested upon Him, and was revealed in Him. This was [Gk.] *doxa* (glory). But in the radiance that rested upon Him, He saw the love of the Father for Him, for the Father saw Himself in Him and gave Him Himself!

Here again we return to the fact that in John's Gospel the Mystery of the 'I' is proclaimed. What can be the highest joy in the 'I'? That it is a ray coming from God. That is the most comprehensive joy. For it embraces the very deepest nature of this 'I'. That is the most enduring joy. For it fills every moment during which this 'I' lives. It is the highest joy. For it bears within itself the highest God and His love.

This joy is more than what one commonly sees in Christianity. It does not consist only in God's announcing to us His love, in spite of our sins, as a grace given to us in Christ's death and Resurrection.

It consists in this, that the 'I' walks through the world in the glory of light and the warmth of love, as *the* earthly revelation of God Himself.

Moreover, when Christ thinks of the world after death it is this joy that stands before His spirit, 'And now, Father, glorify Thou me in Thy own presence with the glory which I had with Thee before the world was made' (17:5). With translations using the ancient words such as 'glorify' we must always feel that every vestige of personal glorification has been removed from them. We are speaking here of the hidden glory of God coming to be revealed, of the coming of the primal, invisible light to radiance, as we have described it above in a picture. When the Israelites spoke of the Shekinah,[52] they might have imagined that somewhere there is a radiance of glory that people may one day come to see. The Greek word *doxa,* is the translation of Shekhinah, but it is also the translation of all that is external into what is inner, of all that is spatial into that which is personal, of all that is temporal into that which is eternal, and of all prophecy into fulfilment.

Consequently, Christ had nothing higher to promise to His disciples, or to wish for the future after death than that which is found in John 17:24, 'Father, I desire that they also, whom Thou hast given me, may be with me where I am ... in Thy love for me before the foundation of the world'.

What we are saying here sounds cold and dark compared with how the reality can be in the soul. One might confuse it with some oppressing edification that stirs the soul in passing, but is not really taken in earnest. Nothing has spoiled Christianity more than the way in which the highest truths pass so slickly across people's lips, only stirring the soul a little, as if the divine revelation were meant only to let people entertain a few pleasant feelings soon forgotten as they return to everyday life. It cannot be said clearly enough that what all this means and what we are talking about will only be understood when one takes courage and has the patience to assimilate these truths as real truths, as personal facts. One is to *go into Paradise* by the way Christ shows—by the way which *is* Christ. Then, whatever 'heaven' may bring, however spiritually richer and clearer the world into which we enter may become, it is Christ Who has brought the inmost ray from the Sun down from heaven to Earth. He is here. He shines in John's Gospel waiting for people to kindle from Him the light of their lives. In other words, there is in all heaven no higher joy than that which is spoken here—joy over the love of the Father to the Son. It is of this joy that Christ says,

'The glory which Thou hast given me I have given to them, that they may be one even as We are one' (17:22). Here it is clearly said that this glory is upon the Earth today, and all the heavenly future can only bring greater clarity, power and security to this glory.

Thus one might also call John's Gospel the Book of the Mysteries of Joy. It begins, indeed, with the beginning of Christ's ministry at a wedding. And joy is always born for us in looking towards Christ. John's Gospel, moreover, ends the public ministry of John the Baptist in such a way that the earnest, threatening man is transfigured into joy.

> You yourselves bear me witness, that I said, I am not the Christ, but I have been sent before him. He who has the bride is the bridegroom; the friend of the bridegroom, who stands and hears him, rejoices greatly at the bridegroom's voice; therefore this joy of mine is now full. He must increase, but I must decrease [3:28-30].

Into this radiance of joy John disappears. Only twice more is witness given of him, as he himself had previously borne witness (5:33-36; 10:40f.). With these retrospective glances at John the Baptist, first by Christ and then by the Evangelist, the account given of John is finished, with sovereign gratitude. Let us mention only the last words with which John, at the joyful place already mentioned, takes leave of the reader (3:35f.):

> The Father loves the Son, and has given all things into his hand. He who believes in the Son has eternal life; he who does not obey the Son shall not see life, but the wrath of God rests upon him.

It has been felt as a stumbling block that in John's Gospel the Baptist, too, the preacher to the people, the strong speaker in pictures, should pass over into the language of the Evangelist. He speaks here, not of the 'kingdom of heaven', but of 'life'. So much the finer does it seem here that still, in the last words of the Baptism, the thunders of judgment should roll from afar once more over the world. He was the man who had to emphasize the obverse side of the gospel. When such earnest men rejoice at one time with their whole soul, it is a very special occurrence. It is in this light that we have to see the radiance of joy into which John passes away.

The second personality who comes to rejoice is Abraham (8:52-59). It is remarkable that this passage has not attracted more attention. 'Your Father Abraham rejoiced that he was to see my day; he saw it and was glad.'

How are we to understand such a saying? From the Old Testament we learn only that Abraham rejoiced over the promise of a son (Gen. 17:17). Of course, one may assume that the promise of a son took place in such significant circumstances that he saw in them more than the prophecy of an heir. But does this explain our passage? What does the sentence mean—'He saw it and was glad'? Unless one is willing to overlook such a sentence, one cannot but assume that the Evangelist is speaking of a spiritual meeting between Christ and Abraham. It may have taken place in a vision during Christ's life on Earth, or before Christ came to the Earth. Rudolf Steiner reports that people with a special task to perform upon the Earth, before their birth spiritually converse with those whose work they have to carry further. Since Christ does not speak of the present 'he sees it and rejoices', but of the past, we may be permitted to think of such spiritual experiences. As in the story of the transfiguration, Christ speaks with Moses and Elijah, so, before His birth, He may have spiritually passed by Abraham and received from Abraham's shining appearance the confirmation of the fact that Abraham's joy also rested upon His work. If anyone holds such an experience to be impossible, let him see how he can explain this passage in another way. The whole certainty of fulfilment that underlay the whole of Christ's work will also have been strengthened by such tangible experiences. But for us it is especially important here that Abraham's joy rested upon his *seeing* Christ. He saw it, 'my day'—the day in which I am—the day in which the Sun of the 'I AM' arose—'and was glad'.

John, the prophet, rejoices and with him all prophecy rejoices. Abraham, the great patriarch, rejoices and with him the folk-spirit. Moreover, it is said of men that they rejoice; it is said of the disciples, of the new congregation (20:20), 'Then the disciples were glad when they saw the Lord'. John's Gospel is economical with great words, as all men are who have had great experiences. In all the stories of the Risen Lord we find the word 'glad' used at this place alone. And yet people who are deeply receptive find that the radiance of joy lies over all these narrations, like the light of spring lying over a world to come. To bathe in the light of this world of sunshine is really to experience what joy means. 'Eternal joy shall be upon their heads.' It may have been a special gift of God that the narrator was young when he took part in them. These recollections shine with the magic light of youth into his old age,[53] and thus awaken a breath of eternal youth. They do not speak of rejoicings, of jubilation, of shouting for joy. But all that, as it were, lies behind the pictures passing before us. Yet it is not present as a loud outburst, but as a quiet self-restraint that fears to disturb the angelic songs of joy. We know that we are listening to the blessedness of a world that is still hidden when we have once acquired a sense for the joyful music of these last revelations in John's Gospel. The content of this joy is also clearly named. 'Then were the disciples glad when they saw the Lord.' To *see* Christ is the content of pure joy.

And, finally, Christ Himself says the same:

> When a woman is in travail she has sorrow, because her hour has come; but when she is delivered of the child, she no longer remembers the anguish, for joy that a human being is born into the world. So you have sorrow now, but I will see you again and your hearts will rejoice, and no one will take your joy from you. In that day you will ask me no questions. Truly, truly, I say to you, if you ask anything of the Father, he will give it to you in my name. Hitherto you have asked nothing in my name; ask, and you will receive, that your joy may be full [16:21-24].

In these solemn and glad words, too, all the joy of the disciples is contained in their *seeing* of Him. Just so long as we do not ourselves bear within us the 'I' of glory—which is all joy because it shines in the light of love—so long does our joy depend on our *seeing* this 'I' of Christ. And this same *possessing* is but another manner of *seeing*.

But here this seeing of Christ is illuminated in two ways. With what wonderful purity a mother's love is here described. 'A human being is born into the world.' Not a child, not my child, but a human being [Gk. *anthropos*]. The child is to be regarded here simply as a human being. And the joy that one has been permitted to bring a human being to birth, should be greater than the joy that one has received a son or daughter. Even in such a picture humanity is restored to purity, is redeemed. The mighty wonder that suddenly a new human being is there, that s/he is beginning her/his earthly course, the marvelling over the Mystery of human existence and of human development, and the joy at being so ennobled as to be allowed to share in the making of a human being, would far outweigh all personal considerations if people realized what really happens at a birth. But does one not experience the same joy upon a higher level upon discovering Christ; when one *sees* Him? *The* human being is born into the world. We share in the joy of the divine thought of creation when we see its fulfilment in Christ. This is *joy* itself. For it is the joy of the Father in the Son.

In the same way it is a seeing of Christ, only now quite spiritually, when one receives in His name the fulfilment of a request. In His name—one hears in the fulfilment the voice of the bridegroom, as John the Baptist heard it. He is there. And we experience Him, in His intercourse with the disciples, when we receive gifts through Him. That is the way to walk with Him—to ask and to receive. But the joy does not depend upon the fulfilment of any single wish, but on our experiencing in this way *His* existence.

To sum up: true joy is lacking in people. Christ came to bring joy to men. The love wherewith the Father loves Him is for Christ the highest joy in heaven and upon the Earth. It lives in His 'I'. He wills that people should share in this joy. In John's Gospel the rays from this joy shine forth for us. This revealing of the Father is the transfiguration of the Father through the Son. Consequently, for us, all true joy consists in our perceiving the transfigured Son of man. Thereby true joy enters into our hearts.

Letter No. 7

'I am the Light of the World'

When the evangelist John considered how he could place the fact of Christ before mankind, when, as it were, he was seeking for a historical setting for the picture he carried in his soul, then the creation of the world came into his mind, and he began his gospel with the following sentences:

> In the beginning was the Word,
> and the Word was with God,
> and the Word was a[54] God.
> He was in the beginning with God;
> all things were made through him,
> and without him was not anything made that was made.
> In him was life,
> and the life was the light of men.
> The light shines in the darkness,
> and the darkness has not overcome it [1:1-5].

When wishing to speak these words, one feels one must draw a deeper breath. In order that they may live rightly in us and be rightly repeated by us, they demand a greatness of soul that is beyond us. To allow these words to echo within us means to bathe our souls in the solemn Song of Creation. We listen to these words with all their depths of meaning and we seem to see the faces of angels looking out from them and to hear angelic voices speaking in them. Humanity has still much to learn before a human spirit can cause these words to break forth into music, or human souls are able to receive them into themselves. Just as if a spring of water flowed before our house, and we did not always hear it consciously although it accompanies our daily work with its music, so we receive into our being the song of the eternal source of all being when we repeatedly allow these words to come to life in us in meditation.

There is something of an exalted spiritual inducement when we compare this story of the creation as it is told by John, with Moses's story of creation (Genesis 1). We then see a path before us, trod for centuries by humanity, from an inspired pictorial vision to a conception of reality that has come from pure thought. John also takes an essential step beyond Moses—into God. For Moses did not dare to say anything about what was in God before the world came into existence. John lifts the innermost curtain. 'In the beginning was the Word, and the Word was with God, and the Word was a God.' He lets us behold the sacred movement of the Holy Trinity within itself. We once pointed out—in the monograph *Das johanneische Zeitalter*[55] ['The Johannine Age']—the way in which the Trinity here is revealed, not as a doctrine but as a Being breathing life.

- The first sentence, 'In the beginning was the Word', allows us to look into the world of *being*, of the Father.
- The second sentence, 'And the Word was with God'—into the world of *love*, of the Son.
- The third sentence, 'And the Word was a God'—into the world of *realizing*, of the Spirit. Not that the evangelist need have been conscious of this. But the fact that he wrote these words prove in itself that he began his gospel in a region where he lived in the rhythm of the world's ultimate Mysteries, and felt the ultimate facts of the world move and express themselves within him.

That John was able to take this step beyond Moses, he owes, as he himself confesses in his gospel, to his Master, Christ. 'Father, I desire that they also, whom Thou hast given me, may be with me where I am, to behold my glory which Thou hast given me in Thy love for me before the foundation of the world' (17:24). In John, this last promise of Christ has begun to be fulfilled. He perceives a glimmering of the glory which Christ possessed in the love of God before the wheel of the creation of the world was first set in motion.

'God said, Let there be light!' What is said here returns again in John's Gospel. But it extended into a long story: God, Word, Life Light.

- Out of *God*, the Word proceeds—'God said!'
- Out of the Word comes life: 'God said, *Let there be!*'
- Out of life proceeds light: 'God said, Let there be *light!*'

When we see here how the same primordial events are told here in a twofold way, we can penetrate more deeply into the way in which the Bible speaks of these ultimate Mysteries, in the first case pictorially and in a way that appeals to the people, in the second to the human understanding.

But from this first passage, where it speaks of the light, we can already clearly see how very differently the people of that time must have experienced the light. 'In him was life and the life was the light of men.' How far can life be light? We think we understand the words of such a sentence, but thereby we deceive ourselves. We do not understand their meaning. And when such words have been known to us as texts from the Bible, from our youth onwards, then we have no longer any idea how far we have inwardly departed from the Bible, even when we 'understand' its words. How far life can be light, we must learn anew. And here also lies the real key to understand the saying, 'I am the light of the world'. But let us not imagine that we can lay hold of this key without further thought.

The saying about the Light of the World (8:12) is usually considered too much by itself. But we must also perceive how the motif of light runs through the whole of John's Gospel. It is then well worth carefully observing how this motif of light evolves, unwinding and unfolding itself. Directly after the saying concerning the Light of the World, there follows the healing of the Man Born Blind (Chapter 9), described in exact detail and emphasized by being placed immediately before the raising of Lazarus. Indeed, it is even connected with the miracle of Lazarus by Christ's words (11:9 & 10): 'If any one walks in the day, he does not stumble, because he sees the light of this world. But if any one walks in the night, he stumbles, because the light is not in him.' Here is another example of how easily a person of that time could pass over from the external light which the eyes behold, to the inner light, which shines within. These words pass quite directly from the external light of day to the inner light of God, in whose shining a person walks.

And in order to emphasize once more the significance of this proclamation of the light, the whole of Christ's quite open preaching ends with these words concerning light: 'Walk while you have the light, lest the darkness overtake you; he who walks in the darkness does not know where he goes. Walk while you have the light, believe in the light, that you may become sons of light' (12:35f.). Between these two significant sayings stands the powerful reference to the prophet Isaiah (Ch. 6) who saw the glory of God, but the eyes of the men were blinded.

At the beginning, at the highest point and at the end of John's Gospel, stands the proclamation of the light.

People today as a rule do not yet have the faintest conception of how literally all these sayings about the light are to be taken. We of the present age might perhaps find a point of departure towards understanding this in a saying taken from Goethe's *Faust*, Part 2, V. 5, 'Midnight' (tr. van der Smissen):

> *Faust (now blind):*
> The night comes on with deeper penetration,
> Yet in my soul there shines a radiant light.

In a genial cosmic conception Goethe has spoken here of earthly human destiny. The outer light of the eye, noble as it is and wonderful the world that it shows us, is increasingly losing its significance as future millennia approach. An inner light is arising within people. This inner light, seeking to be born in the human being, will show a new world shining out from within. Human beings themselves will become miniature Suns, directing the light of their spirit upon everything they wish to behold. The Sun-worship and veneration of the god of light of bygone ages could pass away. Their day is past. But we live in an age of transition. Where Christ is, there is the new sunrise. He is truly a new 'Let there be light!'—as majestically great as the ancient process of creation. Thus He wishes to be experienced. This is the message of John's Gospel. That Christ is the light means neither 'enlightenment', nor any merely abstract truth; it actually means the dawn of a new world. When one puts this into words, it remains obscure, naturally, for anyone who has not already experienced at least a glimmering of this dawning glory of creation.

For this reason Christ ever repeats, 'Believe in the light'. The ancient process of creation was accomplished without the cooperation of any human being; this new process of creation calls human beings to be co-workers, to be co-creators, thereby raising them to the highest rank of nobility. By our wills, by our 'Yes', we invite ourselves to the first ray of the Sun of this new creation, and, as it were, give it our life as material by which it can shine. If we sometimes suddenly speak the word 'Christ', inwardly in our meditation, and come so far as to surmise that this is seeking to be a sunrise in the inner heaven of our souls, then we are on the way by which John's Gospel is seeking to lead us. Much depends on whether we can come so far as to bear within us the miracle of this sunrise as our own experience.

John 8 helps us to do so. For this chapter on the light is also the chapter of the 'I'. Is it by chance that here the 'I AM' appears so expressively, three times?

- '... you will die in your sins unless you believe that I am he' (8:24). This is the way it is usually translated, but the Greek has only 'I am'.

- 'When you have lifted up the Son of man, then you will know that I am' (8:28).
- 'Truly, truly, I say to you, before Abraham was, I am' (8:58).

To anyone who knows little about John's Gospel, it may perhaps seem rather odd when we say that these sayings together form an organism. Here is no intention of the author and scarcely a full awareness, but an inward configuration of the truth, placed before us here on the Earth out of the realm of Inspiration.[56]

> [1] The first of these three sayings speaks of the present time, the second of the future, the third of the past. The human being, humanity, will perish in a state of sin[57] unless it receives into itself a new 'I', by the devotion of faith. That is the position at the present time. This demand, upon which hangs the destiny of mankind, hits the mark now as it did then. This is no piece of sermonizing, among other such pieces; it is a decisive illumination of human history. Next after this saying concerning the present, comes that other saying concerning the future. Here again, we have the absolutely decisive perception that has to be acquired in the future, that the Son of man is now there, enthroned above the Earth, and that in Him the new 'I' of the coming humanity is waiting for us. Ever and again what we first received by the heart's power of faith will become 'realization'. But next, the past is also illuminated for us by this light. It becomes ever clearer that behind all the religions that have ever existed the 'I am' appears, revealing itself as the secret of the development of everything that has ever been. We look into the present: 'I am.' We look into the future: 'I am.' We look into the past: 'I am.' The great sermon of the 'I am', embracing the entire history of the world, is contained in this, the 'chapter of light' in John's Gospel. One can never finish learning from the sermon of these three sentences alone. They illuminate the whole of human history. We are once again in the Mystery of the 'I am'.

Once again we have to ask: Is it chance that now in John 9 we hear of the only person besides Christ to speak in John's Gospel the words 'I am'—and that this person is the man born blind but is now healed? The context is too full of meaning for us to be able to take this 'I am he', spoken by the man who was born blind, in any trivial sense. We see again a remarkable connection in John's Gospel. Twice men appear who say, 'I am not' —at the beginning of the gospel John the Baptist says 'I am not' in an important passage (1:21); and

> [2] at the end of the gospel, Peter, standing by the coal fire, says, 'I am not' (18:17 & 25). We see the man who has not yet the new 'I', John, and

> the man who has no longer the new 'I', Peter. Shall we allow ourselves to be persuaded that these pictures have no meaning? Except in Christ there is no true 'I'. But even within the kingdom of Christ one can lose it again. Out of the depths of inspiration, of which the author need not necessarily have been conscious,[58] the truth of the 'I' is here proclaimed, in the midst of history.
>
> [3] And between these two men there now stands the third, a nameless one, an insignificant person who has only one advantage, that Christ has given him the light. And he can, he may say, 'I am'.

At the beginning of the story of salvation God says, 'I am'. Now man is saying it! The healing of this blind man is also introduced by Christ saying: 'As long as I am in the world, I am the light of the world' (9:5). And it is ended with these words, 'For judgment I came into this world, that those who do not see may see, and that those who see may become blind' (9:39). Those with eyes to see, let them see!

If we study these contexts, they are really pictures that are transparent for immeasurably important things lying behind them. We are not denying the immediate meaning of the words of these stories. But we refuse to be hampered by, or confined to, the literal meaning. Taken together, they again contain in a trinity a very great sermon of world-history. The highest to which man can come before Christ and out of Christ, both then and today, is the knowledge that *he is not*, that he lacks the true 'I'. When this is realized, he is knocking at the door of Christ's world. And the worst that can come to the man who is inside Christ's kingdom, is that by lacking the courage of his faith he should renounce the true 'I'. This is true for all people and all ages of the world. But with absolute purity, out of the modest quietness of the nameless one, there arises the confession, 'I am'. It arises in him to whom Christ has given the light of the world.

It is precisely this connection between the new light and the 'I' that people of the present day need. To see into the 'I' of Christ means to see the Sun of a new world. It is, certainly, quite different from our Sun, for it is a spirit-Sun. Before it, though, the outer Sun becomes a mere picture, a prophecy.

There are two ways of entering the new kingdom of the Sun.

- One is learning to experience the outer light ever more spiritually, until, so to speak, it disappears into Christ's being.

- The other is to experience Christ in a way that becomes more living and more filled with light, until He really shines as a light of our life, as *the* light of our day.

In the book *Meditation*,[59] we have described the first way in detail. The best guide on this way are Christ's seven deeds of light in John's Gospel. What He did historically the Sun does naturally. To feel its purity and purifying power, not only on the body but in the soul, leads us on the way to Christ. This can be pursued into measureless depths. And it is a near way to Christ. And so is the experience of its power to heal, the experience of its power to feed us inwardly, its mighty power of satisfaction, its power of illuminating us spiritually, its power of transforming, and its power to awaken us. Seriously to pursue such ways actually leads to experience the Sun as if it were the earthly countenance of Christ. The word 'countenance' is not, of course, used here in the sense of portrait-painting. Today by means of a prism one separates the physical sunlight into its various colours; similarly there is a separation of the revelation of light into its different ways of working by meditation, which here, as often, is comparable to a prism. Goethe still had a much more living, more spiritual way of regarding the world of the senses when he spoke of the 'deeds and sufferings of the light'.[60] We can study these deeds and sufferings of the light directly in ourselves when we enter into the kingdom of light in the way described above.

Here is also a possibility of attaining a deeper understanding of John's words about the creation, if we go, as it were, backwards the way creation took forwards. We seek the LIFE in the LIGHT, the WORD in the life, and in the word, GOD. The simplest ray of sunlight falling into our room can help us to do this. One can accustom oneself to experience as an echo the ancient word of creation, 'Let there be light!' If one always greets the Sun's ray consciously, in such a spirit that one seeks to feel with reverence the growing light in one's soul, then a religious element gradually enters into our whole relationship to light, raising our life into quite another sphere and form of worship. To approach closer to Christianity in all its fullness, we have to receive into ourselves all the greatness and reverence brought to the Sun in the early Persian religion of light. The cosmic feeling of Zarathustra livingly preserved within us remains as an inkling, a prophecy of the fact of Christ. And every ray of sunshine calls us to these altars. Quite inwardly, yet with equal greatness, the feeling is born in us that the priest of the Sun had when he saw the Sun break forth from behind the mountains: 'Let there be light!'

Three ways lead today into the kingdom of reverence:

- the starry heavens,
- the sunrise,
- the ray of sunlight.

Unfortunately, the dwellers in great towns experience the sunrise but seldom, as an exception. Thus they lose a very strong fundamental experience, meant to awaken in humanity all religious feelings. An idea of the true experiencing of the Sun is found among the Moravians at Herrnhut, when on Easter morning, rising while it is still dark, after climbing the Hutberg, up there upon the heights, they regard the Sun, as it rises in might above the mountains through the door of their graveyard, upon which are inscribed these words: 'Christ is risen from the dead', and on the inside, 'And has become the first fruits of them that sleep'. Someone who once has really devoutly felt the impression made by the rising Sun can never again in his life become entirely irreligious. Standing on a mountain and flooded with light, penetrated by light, feeling the irresistible blessing of the power of light upon the Earth and upon oneself, one is near to the original Mystery of the Godhead, as if the Father were showing the Son what He does. The soul begins to live in a feeling for the whole world, which is far above the purely personal sphere, and by which a person feels he is ennobled, as by the trust reposed in Him by the Father, Who is showing Him His work. The soul feeling its way from this promise into fulfilment through Christ finds itself directly within the true significance of Christ's saying about the Light of the World. A greater and broader Christianity begins to dawn within it. Infinitely great receptivity for divine holiness can be acquired from the light.

The Stars

The starry heavens cannot be entirely taken away from people today, unless they themselves are willing to lose it. It surrounds us with a greatness that awakens awe. If with this greatness one experiences restraint, and a waiting in readiness, one is living once more right in the heart of God. It is all there for us, but it all conceals unfathomable Mysteries. It is all resting quietly; it does not thrust itself upon us. Surrendering oneself to this impression, it is as if one felt the nearness of the breath of God. So near, and yet so great! Today an age begins for humanity in which the starry heavens begin to speak. That it has spoken and still does speak to astronomers of its dizzy greatness is only a beginning. It starts to reveal anew its innermost Mysteries and creative power. And one can clearly see a Christianity drawing near that lives amid starry worlds, and weaves the web of everyday life out of the divine forces of the stars.

Such a Christianity will certainly have to develop powers of reverence to which the proud man of today is little accustomed. It would have 'the stars in his hand' (Rev. 1:16) and would work with their powers. Do people believe that such a Christianity is no longer Christianity? Then unworthy and petty thought is given to Christ. When John the Evangelist speaks of 'His fullness', that word 'fullness' at that time did not have the *emptiness* it has today. Concerning what was understood of the *pleroma* in the speech of the Mysteries, we have a last, distorted reflection in Gnosis. The living riches of the divine world was meant, not, however, a richness of colour and form, but a tremendous fullness of life, proceeding from the divine Father and mirrored in inconceivable richness of being. All this fullness, this *pleroma*, came to us in Christ. And when we divine something of this *pleroma*, we are looking into Christ, as it were, from the other side.

It is only when we know Christ to be over us in such a way that we see in Him the revelation in human form of all the starry worlds so that John's saying about 'receiving of His fullness' is fulfilled that gives us 'grace for grace' (John 1:16). Grace as meant in John's Gospel is a much greater and above all a much richer world than was known in the age of Protestantism. The Sun and the stars belong together; together they show us two sides of Christ's divine nature.

- In the Sun we see the power of light concentrated, and turning towards the Earth in blessing.
- In the stars we see the fullness spread abroad—in our language 'star' and 'strew' are connected in their derivation—we see the rich divine background of being, out of which, as it were, the Sun has been sent forth and to which it seeks to fetch us back, waiting to bless us.

Sunlight

Also every ray of sunlight visiting our room can become for us a key to this kingdom of light. We ought not to allow this esteemed guest to enter our house and leave it again unrealized; even when we are at work, our soul can often walk with it upon its spiritual way. Every ray of sunlight can become for us personally like a divine act, and also an unfathomable revelation, through which we feel with increasing astonishment the wonder of the light, and the wonder of the eye. In his well-known cycle of lectures given in Helsingfors [Helsinki],[61] the content of which is a rare spiritual feast, Rudolf Steiner shows how, for example, one can allow oneself to be swung up through the blue of heaven into the spiritual world. One lets the blue work strongly and deeply upon oneself. Then one may eliminate from this experience all that is sensory, viz. the impression of colour, and look only at the spiritual impression that has entered into one's soul along with the colour. This is a suggestion pointing to many similar ways. One can also rise into the spirit through the ray of sunshine. One can investigate from the outer impression its deeper spiritual background, and afterwards give heed to this background alone. In the ray of light, one can look away together from the *light*, and listen only to the *life* which lives and moves in it. This is really looking with human eyes not at colour and form, but through them both at the soul living in them. In many poems in world literature, we find an expression of how people have divined the life of the gods in the movements of light. Certainly they did so ever more out of depths that grew darker. To engage in the spirit with the ray of sunlight already means having a share in the divine life.

But it is equally valid not only to find the way from the light to the life, but also from the life to the *word*. For this, it is valid not only to pay attention to the eye, but also to listen to the voice. One can then feel that for God, human speech would be an inadequate instrument, and that He speaks in rays of light. *The* word, the mighty word, resounding throughout the ages, with its inconceivably rich content can be experienced in the light, of which the Sun is only one bearer. One hears the Father speaking—in the Son. The nature and life of the Father are hidden from us in immeasurable depths. But in the light, He proclaims Himself to us. In the light, He tells us of Himself. He tells us not only what He wishes of us, but also what He is. Thus we come from the Light to the Life, from the Life to the Word, from the Word to God. We look at His countenance, then we penetrate through the eye into the soul, and through the voice into the human spirit. In the end we hardly notice the eye and voice, but we find the human 'I' revealing itself directly to us. Indeed, in the eye itself, even in this alone, we can retrace our way. For the 'I' does not only live, it speaks, and does not only speak, but reveals. We see that all around us there is much at hand to help lead us back into the divine world.

All that has been said here is only *one* way to the saying, 'I am the Light of the World!' But we are compelled to seek this way when we wish to show a contemporary person an initial way of approach to Christ's temple of light. For it is necessary first to climb the height to reach this temple, lying high above the present way of thinking. For us, such a free, decided practice of meditating on the ray of sunlight may take the place of what was experienced in the ancient Mysteries, which involved being shut up in a dark space and then suddenly everything became radiantly bright around one. Then, because the mind came back to itself more quickly than the eye, for a short moment people came very close to the Mystery of the light. Today, the simplest attic may become such a sacred place of the Mysteries.

'I—am—the—Light—of the World!' (again spoken three times in a similar fashion, 8:12, 9:5, 12:46). When people have once gained such a saying in meditation, it will seem to them as if this sentence itself lived in them, like a temple of light into which they could enter at all times. They will go from one word in it to the next, seeing in it a new 'I', a new 'being', a new 'light', a new 'world'. They will discover with astonishment what one single saying of John can be for them. The comparison with an earthly temple will indeed fail. But, if we go in reverse direction through this saying, then we mount upwards, and at the same time build a new temple over the whole world. We see before us, first 'the world' as it is and think that it is destined to be temple of Christ. Then we fill this temple with a new 'light'. Then through this light we hear the sound, the music of a new 'being', of an 'am' of light. And lastly, through this sound we get an idea of the divine nature, of the sacred 'I'. Rudolf Steiner often spoke of the three kingdoms above man, which man has lost and which Christ has regained for him:

- the kingdom of etheric light;
- the kingdom of etheric sound, and
- the kingdom of etheric life.

These words are not to be conceived according to the soulless laws of natural chemistry, but rather of the three kingdoms as 'kingdoms of heaven', peopled by living beings. Then such a saying as this, about the light of the world, is a living witness to this truth—and at the same time a practicable way into these worlds.

In natural science today the light is, so to speak, laid upon the dissecting table and cut into pieces. Its vibrations and its waves are investigated. But through this anatomy of light one learns just as little about the real life of light as one learns of man's true nature through the anatomy of his body. The laws of the corpse are not the laws of life. To find them we have to pursue other paths.

In attempting to follow the individual sayings Christ has spoken about 'life in the light', we now find that we rediscover the same on a higher level in Christ's kingdom of light. We find again the three gifts that the natural light bestows upon human beings: *seeing*, *walking*, and *becoming*.

Seeing

Light makes it possible for human beings to *see*. When one sees into the Mysteries of the gospel, one often receives the impression that Christ felt people were living in deep darkness. In John's Gospel we hear the words, 'walk in darkness', walking 'in the day', and 'in the night'. What do human beings know today about their origin? What do we know about our purpose? What do we know, in the present time, about right walking? We need only let the saying about the light of the world be of use to us, and then we will find all the illumination we need. In the word 'I' we look back towards our beginning, to our Mystery in God. In the word 'world' we look towards our destiny, towards the purpose of the Earth, which John the seer describes in the words, 'And the city had no need of the Sun, neither of the Moon, to shine upon it; for the glory of God is its light, and its lamp is the Lamb' (Rev. 21:23). And from the word 'am' if we understand it in the sense of Christ, in the sense of self-sacrificing love, we can draw true life at every moment. It is only necessary that we should really 'believe' in the light. This believing is a new form of seeing; it is a spiritual seeing, which inwardly and actively always says 'Yes' to this new light. For 'to believe' in the biblical sense, is not only a sentimental feeling, which remains dully confined within itself, as people sometimes think. It is rather the 'Yes' said with all the force of our heart to a new world; and it lives continually in the spiritual conception of Christ if it is to be honest and full of life and power. With this 'Yes', we are taking a share in the new creation itself.

We can actually practise this new 'seeing' by studying a person, or his/her position in life, and then allow the light of Christ to rise up in our souls and fall upon that which we behold. By such practice one can most easily become citizens of the new kingdom of light that will come one day in place of the present earthly kingdom of the Sun. 'The Light of Life!' The light of Christ seems then so definite and so compact, one would almost like to say—as something so clear and distinct in its nature that we can well understand how it can become ever more a new 'daylight' to us. To learn to see in the light of Christ is one of our most real life-tasks.

Walking

But then, as a second and higher life-task, comes the 'walking in the light'. Here much depends upon our having the experience: there is a sphere of light in which one can live, but then many things become impossible for us, which otherwise might happen, but that which happens in this sphere of light is all good. It is as if some things could not breathe in this sphere of light. Only out of such experiences do we understand completely what is written in 3:19-21:

> This is the verdict: Light has come into the world, but people loved darkness instead of light because their deeds were evil. Everyone who does evil hates the light, and will not come into the light for fear that their deeds will be exposed. But whoever lives by the truth comes into the light, so that it may be seen plainly that what they have done has been done in the sight of God.

An instinctive dislike of the sphere of light is in all those who will not let go of evil. But only those who dare to live in this sphere of light find their real way. All this we have also to represent to ourselves in a more real and living way than as it sounds to those who hear the words from outside. The outside daylight shines upon the good and upon the evil. The new, inner light is of quite a different kind. It is granted only to that which is of like nature to itself, and which is related to itself in its being. In all other cases, it grows dark at once. 'To walk as in the day', will become a quite tangible, real experience. Do not think here of any moral knowledge or enlightened thinking. It is actually a secret world of light in which a person goes their way. What is called 'enlightenment' in the usual sense, is something quite dark and abstract when compared with it, a pocket-lamp against the daylight. I have experienced this sphere of light most strongly in Rudolf Steiner. When, for example, one spoke with him about sexual questions, one received the impression that he had within him a crystal to guard that might be tarnished by every breath. So carefully and purely did he guard the inner light of his spirit.

Becoming

But, besides seeing and going, there is a third thing, *becoming*. We grow and develop in the light. If light were taken altogether away from us, we should die. Inner light, which is not only a mystical stillness, as it is among the Quakers, but the Sun of a new day demanding more of us. 'While you have the light, believe in the light, that you may become sons of light' (12:36). And even of John the Baptist, concerning whom it is said at the beginning, 'He was not that light, but was sent to bear witness to that light' (1:8), Christ later says, 'He was a burning and shining lamp' (5:35). But much as Christ praised the Baptist, He asks for more from His disciples. Children of light—there are people who are felt to be related in their inmost nature to light. To become light is today scarcely a goal after which people strive. And yet there may be people who seek to gather more light into themselves day by day. Those who are born of light in whom the light of Christ shines brightly. Those who fight for the light, in whom the struggle against cosmic darkness continues, those who conquer by the light, whose natures have force to affright evil, to stir it up and yet to beat it down—those people are a form of future Christianity; they are a part of future Christianity. A deep love of the light would change itself so much in an inward direction, would change *us* in such a way that we should become soldiers in that army. This is what one might call the way of consecration by the light; it is the simplest and the deepest—to learn to see, to learn to walk, and to learn to become.

And it is not only the Evangelist John who speaks of this. The Apostle Paul also speaks of 'the inheritance of the saints in light' (Col. 1:12). The Apostle James also speaks of the 'Father of lights, with whom there is no variation or shadow due to change' (Jam. 1:17). Above all, however, we find in the Letters of John himself how the seed of light has sprung up sown by the preaching of Christ Himself. 'The darkness is passing away, and the true light is already shining' (I John 2:8). This is the clear confirmation of what was said above. 'This then is the message we have heard from him and proclaim to you, that God is light and in him is no darkness at all' (I John 1:5). 'If we walk in the light, we have fellowship with one another, and the blood of Jesus his Son cleanses us from all sin' (I John 1:7). All these words are still like a strange language to mankind. To a people of light they will one day become the best-known sounds of home.

To end this study, I may perhaps be allowed a personal recollection. As I was working at it, a recollection arose out of the darkness of the past. Thirty-five years ago, as a young deacon of twenty-three in Würzburg, I had to preach my first sermon for Pentecost on the passage of the gospel appointed of old for the second day of Pentecost (John 3: 16-21). After the fashion of that time I formulated a well-constructed discourse; 'Christianity as a new creation' was the subject. And it was regarded in three successive groupings: 'God said, let there be light!', 'God divided the light from the darkness' and 'God called the light day'. Over this sermon and over many similar sermons on John's Gospel, I felt that I had broken into a new world. But there was no one there who received it, or who reacted to it. So, as one had to preach for people as they were, other means had to be sought. And yet today I could not express better the preaching of light that John's Gospel contains.

God said …

It is as a new 'Let there be light!', as a new creative word, spoken by God, that Christ desires to be experienced. And so one comes near to the greatness lying in the fact of Christ. We are face to face with a spiritual Sun, seeking not only to lighten our day, but actually to cause a new world to proceed out of it. The 'light from heaven' that shone around Paul (Acts 9:2) shows us the same reality. It was a wonderful hour in the history of humanity when from Christ's mouth the word broke forth, 'I am the Light of the World!' That was the climax of all the past religions of light—and at the same time it did away with them. In meditation one can even seek to experience these thoughts of Christ—right into their details—as a sunrise. And the more one does so, the nearer one will come to this pregnant saying of the First Letter of John, 'The true light is already shining' (I John 2:8). This first light-event would also correspond to the first proclamation of the light in John's Gospel, in the first chapter, culminating in the words, 'The true light that enlightens every man was coming into the world' (1:9). This first light-event would also bring about within us consecration into light—*seeing*.

God divided …

But in John's Gospel the second aspect of light is also sublimely brought out. 'God separated the light from the darkness.' The power of judgment strides through the whole gospel according to John. In the first chapter this motif of judgment, or verdict, is already intertwined with the music of the spheres. The verdict seems to approach people in a threefold repetition:

- 'The darkness comprehended it not/ has not overcome it' (1:5).
- 'The world knew him not' (1:10).
- 'His own people [the *'ich-Menschen'*, the 'I'-people, as Steiner translated it[62]] received him not' (1:11).

In the living river of the history of Christ, this motif of judgment repeatedly sounds in the warning, 'This is the verdict, that the light has come into the world, and people loved darkness rather than light, because their deeds were evil' (3:19). And at the close, it rolls with full weight, like thunder over the Earth, 'For judgment I came into this world, that those who do not see may see, and that those who see may become blind' (9: 39). Amid lightning and thunder—whilst he lets the 'light' shine forth once more, and the thunder of judgment speaks, Christ withdraws Himself from His ministry among the people (12:35 & 36; 12:44-50). This second proclamation of light in John's Gospel corresponds to the second act of creation, and also calls us to the second act of consecration to light—*walking*.

God called …

'God called the light Day.' 'The true light is already shining.' Ever again we find 'the day' mentioned (9:4, 11:9, 10). Into this 'day' the man who was born blind enters when he says 'I am' (9:9). Then this 'day' shines over the Farewell Discourses. Then there is the new name. Christ no longer calls Himself the Light of the World, but He says, 'Now is the Son of man glorified, and in him God is glorified' (13:31). Christ says this, and immediately beforehand stand these words as Judas goes out: 'it was night.' Just as the outer Sun lives above us, and at the same time seeks to live in us, whenever, as an example for our eyes, it finds a possibility of being mirrored, so Christ is present henceforth in a twofold way. He lives in His Spirit, the 'Spirit of Truth'. This again is announced three times (14:17, 15:26, 16:13)—just as Christ opposes the Roman world as the King of Truth (17:22-24). There He accomplished that which the outer Sun could only make defective attempts to accomplish—to change us into Himself, to make us 'children of the light'. This is the great 'day', the third stage of the consecration into light, the 'new creation'.

Following these thoughts inwardly, we are on the way to unfold our souls to the greatness of the event of Christ. In the old creation, light was *the great likeness of God*. Hence came the great religions of the light. Quite truly and actually, Christ is *the Sun of a new creation, which is already among us*.

Letter No. 8

'I am the Life'

The Teutonic spirit is deeply connected to John's Gospel. It would be a delightful occupation to trace the shining of John's Gospel in the spirit of great Teutonic personalities. One would find that John's Gospel hovers over them like a premonition, like a prophecy.

The saying of *Luther* [1483-1546], that John's Gospel is 'the one delicate gospel, the chief of gospels',[63] is well known. Yet in Luther's Bible [1545] we repeatedly meet passages that clearly show us that Luther has not been able to let the shining depths of John's Gospel appear in his words. An example I have often quoted is Christ's saying (8:31), which Luther translates: *So ihr bleiben werdet an meiner Rede.* ['If you continue in what I say.']—which, however, truly says, 'If you dwell in my word—in the word of life, the word which I am'. How differently does this latter translation speak in comparison with Luther's duller translation that conceals the real meaning! However great one realizes Luther's translation to be, yet, if one wishes to prepare the way of a new translation of the Bible, one has to speak openly about it.

In the age of the classical German writers, John's Gospel can often be felt as shining through in the background. In an article,[64] we wrote how *Goethe* [1749-1832] in his *Faust* points to John's Gospel. One admires Goethe's genial spiritual instinct, searching, as it were, on its very threshold, pointing to it as a closed book, a book waiting for the hour which has not yet come.

And what did *Herder* [1744-1803] wish to say when he caused to be written on his tombstone the words 'Light, Love, Life'? Was it not as the request with which he knocked at the gates of a higher world in which he expected to find revelation and fulfilment? Herder was the greatest spirit that Protestant theology has given to the world. What he has handed down is deeply significant.

And last of this group, let us name *Fichte* [1762-1814] who in *The Way Towards the Blessed Life, or, The Doctrine of Religion*, dedicated one chapter especially to John's Gospel. In these lectures almost nothing is quoted except John's Gospel. Standing before this gospel, Fichte's proud spirit appears as before an acknowledged genius for the purpose of justifying himself. When one considers all this then one can well say that the Teutonic mind and spirit feels it has a mission to John's Gospel, and John's Gospel has a mission to it. This feeling is expressed at the zenith of its spiritual history, but at the same time it is felt that the historical hour has not yet come.

We would add that this historical hour did come when a Teutonic spirit, *Rudolf Steiner* [1861-1925], placed afresh the 'I am' of John's Gospel as a light upon the altar of a new Christianity. Moreover, it was just for this 'I am' that the Teutonic spirit was especially prepared. It was prepared religiously when it said, in Luther, 'Here I stand, I can do no other'. It was prepared poetically when, in Goethe, it transformed all literature into a great 'confession', into the self-confession of the 'I'. It was prepared philosophically when, in Fichte, it realized the 'I' to be the divine key to the cosmos.

We could say much of the way in which, in Rudolf Steiner, the Teutonic spirit entered into John's Gospel as into its own world. But really these *Letters* are everywhere a living witness, for they follow Steiner's lead in this.

To the question which of the three words 'Light', 'Life' or 'Love' speaks most closely to the Teutonic mind, then, perhaps contrary to our expectation, history answers us with the word 'Life'. In Goethe's cosmically great poem of confession, in *Faust*,[65] the Teutonic spirit seeks for *life*.

> When to the moment I were to say:
> 'Linger awhile, thou art so fair!'
> Bind me in fetters fast that day;
> Then, e'en perdition I will dare!

It is life that Faust seeks, first in earthly pleasures, then in activity that brings blessing.

Turning from Goethe to Fichte, of all the most representative thinkers of the Teutonic genius, we find two poems of his that have been preserved. Twice his thinking mind, clear as light, raised itself into that sphere in which enthusiasm can be expressed only in the words of a poet. Both poems speak of 'life'.[66] [A translation reads:]

> That which to mine eye the power did give
> That all misshapenness should from it run,
> And nights therefore should turn to joyful Sun,
> Disorder change to order, corruption turn to life,
>
> What through the web of time and space doth drive,
> Safe leads me to eternal springs, whence flow
> Beauty and truth and goodness, and anon
> Extinguishes all that for which I strive,

Is this: since I looked deeply in Urania's eye,
Which is itself clear, blue and still, and pure
A flame of light, in which myself I see.

Since then, in deepest depths in me this eye
Rests, and within my being doth endure the one eternal,
Live while I live, and sees whate'er I see.

*

Nought is than God, and God is naught but life,
Thou knowest, and with thee I do agree:
Yet how could knowledge overcome to be
If it were not the knowledge of God's life!

How gladly would I dedicate myself thereto, but alone,
Where shall I find it? When somehow it flows
Into knowledge, it changes then by radiant light
Mingled therewith, surrounded by its mantle.

Clearly this mantle is before thee rising,
It is thine 'I': let the mortal perish
And only God live henceforth in thy striving.

If thou canst see what doth surround this striving,
The mantle will reveal itself as covering only
And lo! unveiled before thee is God's life!

In this poem we cannot fail to realize the thinker. We may possibly feel the thought as halting and stiff. But one thing is clear—it was 'life' that brought to him the fulfilment of all his struggles.

This longing for life breaks out again in a unique manner in *Nietzsche* [1844-1900]. This is the more significant because Nietzsche had rejected Schopenhauer's [1788-1860] 'will to life' as the meaning of all that takes place in the world. 'Ah, and then you opened your eye again, O beloved Life! And into the unfathomable I seemed to be sinking again.' 'Into your eye I looked of late, O Life: gold I saw in your night-eye glinting.' 'Was *that* life? Well then! One more time!'[67] When we look at what we have already discussed, we cannot understand this longing of Nietzsche for life simply in connection with his personality and his destiny. An impulse that lives deep in the Teutonic spirit here pushes its way into the cold age of intellectualism—in which indeed the Teutonic spirit also had its special task—and prophesies the future.

We would perhaps have wished that the Teutonic spirit had rather chosen the word 'light', or the word 'love'. But we remember how these words are divided among the periods of the world's history (see *Letter 6*). The Persian Age was the age of serving the light. The Greeks sought for the secret of Eros, of love—yet this is a threefold flame upon a single altar, an image of the Trinity itself. This may remain in our minds when we distribute the three words among humanity today, in the Centre, the West and the East. It is light—new spiritual light—which the West needs if it is not to sink down into materialism. It is love that the East is seeking, even if upon ways that are too external in the Communism of today. It is life that the Central European strives after, for primary reasons, for example, when it speaks today of the life of the people as a whole that overflows its boundaries. And yet it may be said that the East will only find love when, in a way of which it does not dream, the *light* of the spirit shines upon it fresh. And the *light* in the West will first illuminate and bring to its true fulfilment many of the instinctive strivings of the people of the West, after openness to the world, and universal fellowship have come—that is, after *love*. The centre unites. For light seeks to exist as life and to work itself out in love.

Before we now turn to the word *life* as it lives in John's Gospel, we will once more glance at the present age. It is directly characterized by its great longing for life, without having the smallest knowledge of what life is. We need only recall to mind in what sense the word 'life' is used, for example, in such a saying as 'live and let live'. The consequence of this seeking for life of a degraded type, is on the one side a deep fear of death that is found in the souls of almost all the people of the present day, and which frequently breaks out unexpectedly in the moment of danger. Whilst Goethe still knew—as is proved by the saying from *Faust* quoted above—that even *one* moment that has been really lived makes it easy to say farewell to life, people yet reveal their lack of true life by their attitude towards death.

On the other side, and closely connected with the above, is the general striving to prolong life by all kinds of rejuvenating means, also of very degrading nature. If then the profound consciousness supervenes, that this is not real life after all, then suicide assumes threatening proportions.

Today, science is being led gradually ever nearer to the question of life. This is already sown by such words as 'vitamin' and 'neu-vitalism' (*vita* means 'life'); moreover, by all words compounded with *bios*, the Greek work for life. But when one begins to examine life, it is believed that one has to turn to its very simplest forms. Just as it is stupid to study the people of Tierra del Fuego, wanting to find out what it means to be a human being, and as one learns much more about mankind if one looks at the highest human beings—so in relation to 'life', the way of John's Gospel is the very reverse of the modern way of investigating life.

'Life' in the gospel

And now we are standing before the central word spoken about life in John's Gospel—'I am the life!'

Has anyone ever yet marvelled enough at the magnitude of this saying? That a being walked the Earth and said, 'All life upon Earth—and above the Earth—is really seeking Me, in order to find in Me its fulfilment!' Again, 'Look at my "I", feel my "I" in its true being, and you will experience what life is in reality!' Not only, 'I know life', 'I preach life', 'I have life', but 'I *am* life!' Only in so far as you can enter into my 'I', and live in it, will you know about life! All else is only apparent life, or at best, a longing!

In any passage of John's Gospel has Christ spoken of what life really consists? He has done so during the Farewell Discourses in the High-Priestly Prayer. 'This is eternal life, that they know Thee the only true God and Jesus Christ whom Thou hast sent' (17:3). Of course, totally different experiences are to be connected with the word 'know'; a totally different knowledge has to be possessed from that of this age of abstract intellectualism. Let us imagine that a person who comes into a strange land recognizes among the people waiting there upon the quay—his mother; or that a man who feels alone in the world perceives among the guests in a great hall the figure of the woman who has always appeared in his dreams as the one who is his own; or that man who, lost in a primeval forest sees a house before him, realizing it as the picture of the new home he is seeking, and the voice that calls to him as the voice of his father who went there before him—and perhaps through such experiences of perception the contemporary person can begin to guess the meaning of the work 'know' as it is used in John's Gospel.

When we really 'know' God, not only in our thinking brain, not only dully in our feelings, but as the all-prevailing reality shining into and penetrating all things, then a living ray always passes through us, and with it the life of heaven comes to us. It is for *such* a 'knowledge', or 'recognition', of God we ought to strive, even when we only look at a tree in blossom, or an apple. And also for *such* a 'knowledge', or 'recognition', of Christ we ought to strive, that we may be permeated by His life and unite ourselves with it. No other knowledge is any knowledge, as understood by John's Gospel.

But not only 'knowledge', but also 'life' receives a new character through this saying of Christ. We do not bear life in ourselves. We have it constantly bestowed upon us. Out of our contemplation of the Father-God, out of our contemplation of Christ, it constantly breaks forth upon us in all its fullness. What springs up within us when we *behold* Christ in a living way, and through Him the Father-God—that is the beginning of life. And the beginning already bears within itself all its fullness. Once Fichte said that from the moment when the consciousness of God dawned upon him, he never again lost that consciousness. What Christ expresses here in the word 'know' is much more than the consciousness of God in this sense. But when we think of people who feel God to be constantly present within them—such people have awakened to true life. Like a confirmation of this saying of Christ from out of a quite different life, is the well-known saying of Goethe, 'To realize God, wherever and however He reveals Himself that alone is blessedness upon the Earth'.[68] The concord of these two entirely different sayings is deeply moving!

The historical greatness of this saying of Christ can also be shown by looking at an ancient legend. This legend tells that after Adam and Eve have been driven out of Paradise, Seth, the third, last-born son of our first parents, was allowed to return again to look for a brief moment through the open gates of Paradise. There he saw that the tops of the two trees, the Tree of Knowledge and the Tree of Life, had grown into one another. This comforting vision is like a prophecy hovering over the human race. When knowledge and life become one, then the hour of return has come. We now hear with quite different ears Christ's saying, 'This is *life* eternal, that they may *know* thee'. Paradise has come back again. Seth's dream has been fulfilled. The tops of the two trees have grown into one another. Our task is but to seek *the* knowledge in which dwells life, and to seek *the* life that comes from knowledge that realizes God and Christ. Here the Johannine age is waiting for our age that thirsts for knowledge. Every moment when the thought flashes through us, 'There is God!', is a breath from heaven.

Today much is talked about 'knowing life'. The Bible never speaks of 'life' in that way. Even when John's Gospel speaks of the outer life lying between birth and death, the word 'life'—and this is very significant—is used only in the sense of 'leaving one's life', or of 'giving one's life'. Can one not also learn to 'know life' in a sense which can look John's Gospel in the face? Every outer object and every inner experience is an opportunity to study life in this way. When the soul seeks ever for the eye, the voice, the heart of the Father as it has learned to know them through Christ, then it begins to guess how rich 'life' really is. Such an influx of life seeking to take place will often awaken in us the feeling that it is greater than we can bear. Let us then, in meditation, open our soul so wide that the life of a tree in blossom, or of a child, or of a star-filled heaven can enter fully into us. We shall then be working upon ourselves in the higher sense, that we may really become places of life, temples of God.

Besides the saying, 'I am the life', Christ has left us the other saying, 'Because I live, you will live also' (14:19), or, as it is also translated, 'You ought to live also'. From this saying we may guess that Christ did not then find that people on Earth were at all 'living'. We have, indeed, other indications of this. For example, 'Leave the dead to bury their own dead' (Matt. 8:22) but go thou and preach the Kingdom of God—a saying that breaks forth with such power from Christ's soul when the young man tells Him of his father's death, a saying that can be very valuable to us because it makes clear the immediate reaction of Christ's soul to other human souls. This saying shows how Christ felt the ordinary human life to be a living death. For Him, people 'walked in darkness', and they 'lived' for Him 'in death'. When our eyes become sharp to see this dead life and this living in death, then Christ comes nearer to us. Otherwise He would not have said, 'You *ought* to live also'. So, they are not yet living—not even the disciples! But Christ feels that He Himself is 'living'. He bears the fullness of life within Himself at every moment. Only by fixing one's thoughts upon this does one understand something of what death must have meant for Him. This life of the highest fullness, at its highest point of earthly life, this went into death. 'No man taketh my life from me, I lay it down.' But in this life also lives the certainty of a power that lies above death. 'I have power to lay down my life and I have power to take it again' (10:18).

A sure way to draw nearer to the Mystery of life is to live over again as far as possible the two passages in the gospel where the words 'I am the life' break forth from Christ.

'I am the resurrection and the life'

This happened for the first time in full clarity at the grave of Lazarus (11:21-26):

> Martha said to Jesus, 'Lord, if you had been here, my brother would not have died. And even now I know that whatever you ask from God, God will give you.' Jesus said to her, 'Your brother will rise again.' Martha said to him, 'I know that he will rise again in the resurrection at the last day.' Jesus said to her, 'I am the resurrection and the life; he who believes in me, though he die, yet shall he live, and whoever lives and believes in me shall never die. Do you believe this?'

Here we are permitted to experience the way in which Christ's soul stands facing a soul of His time. It is the belief in resurrection that the Pharisees held that meets Him in Martha. It was a passionate, glowing faith—all the dead, if they have served their God faithfully, will be called out of their graves, will become alive again as they were once, as soon as the hour of the Last Judgement and of fulfilment has come. Fiery and strong as this faith was, a totally different reality is felt by Christ to be within Himself. The resurrection is *in* Him!

How cold and clumsy are the outer facts for which people waited, when compared with this inner reality! And how mightily must Christ have felt His inner reality to be when He could thus place it facing the mighty facts of the end of history, towards which people were looking. How did it feel, this 'I am'? Let us enter in spirit into any grave, or any graveyard and ask ourselves: How would it feel within ourselves if we felt, *I AM* the resurrection! Such an attempt is good, if, encountering such a saying, we wish to feel not only a doctrine, but a living fact. For Christ is not preaching an intellectual doctrine, nor is He expressing a hope, but facing death—and even facing the doctrine of the vanquishing of death, taught by the Pharisees—He is placing a new world, His world, Himself! This is what we can find in the gospels—that all preaching, and all revelation breaks forth from Christ out of the new reality which was Himself. The questions which were brought to Him were largely the same as those we meet. The situations in life into which He was led are little different from the everyday experiences we also meet. But in His way of meeting them and in the answers He gives, the gospel itself is before us.

Even today there remains in Christianity much of the Jewish belief about resurrection. In the funeral sermons of many Christian pastors we find, not Christ's saying 'I am the resurrection', but Martha's 'My brother will rise again'. Wherever a far future is spoken of with hope, instead of the near reality being felt and proclaimed, we have Judaism and not yet Christianity, even when this hope is expressed in Christian words, and based upon the resurrection of Christ. Christ *is* the resurrection. And whoever is in Him, 'is passed over from death into life' (5:24). Here people have still much to attain, and they can attain it only by beginning to live in Christ Himself.

In the first half of this saying of Christ, 'I am the resurrection and the life', an answer can be found to the Jewish belief in a resurrection; in the second half a reply can be found to the other great conception of the life after death, to the Greek idea of the life beyond. In the Greek world, too, a further life was assumed. But at first they looked only for a thin shadowy life with those who had descended into Hades. In Plato we meet the sublime Greek hope of 'immortality'. But the word itself characterises the hope. We find the negative in it, 'immortality', or more exactly 'deathlessness' [*athanasia*]. One may consider the saying 'I am the life' as turned away from the Greek world. Do not merely hope—whether in the philosophic or in the popular sense—to live on after death, but look at *the* life itself, standing before you. Life consists not in a shadowy condition of soul, but in an 'I am'. It does not stand before you as a hope for the future, but as a present reality. It is a rich content that is given you in this 'I' itself, and not a continuation of existence pale as thought. In Christianity today, this kind of idea of what lies beyond death is still present. The Jewish form is found more within the simple 'orthodox' Christian believers, the Greek form more among 'educated' Christians. Christ comes to meet both with this saying at the grave of Lazarus. It is the task of a new Christianity to assert its rights, its very existence in the world for this saying of Christ. This does not only demand a 'faith', but such a life of Christ in ourselves, that in us, too, He has spoken, and still speaks, saying, 'I am the resurrection and the life'; and that through us He can then speak to others, not in words, but in our life. This is said calmly, but it demands a great work in us, all our lives. Christ wills to speak *in* us, one 'I am' after the other. This is the true 'consecration of the "I"'.

We may strengthen in a twofold way our impression of this first saying of Christ concerning 'life'. Among the people of the previous centuries who heard most clearly the trumpet call of the resurrection message was the poet Klopstock.[69] We know that by a mysterious prompting of providence, Klopstock's poem 'Der Messias' produced an effect on the youthful Goethe. This comes out in the Easter scene forming the beginning of *Faust*, but it seems like a respectful leave-taking of Christianity. In what way the hopes of resurrection were present in Klopstock, the verse of his 'Song of Resurrection'[70] best shows:

> Soon I am to rise again,
> Behold, the Lord of Harvest goes,
> Intent His sheaves to gather in.
> He gathers us, those who have died,
> Hallelujah!

[In the original German] these lines bear a remarkable solemnity, as if Klopstock had once been a priest of some solemn Mystery. The lines proceed as in a solemn march, accompanied by the sound of temple trumpets. But when we look through the form of the content of the lines, we find a last noble transfiguration of the Jewish hopes of resurrection. This is no longer anything hasty or impassioned in them. But in calm certainty and cosmic greatness, we may see Christ shining through them. But this is not yet fully Christian. Christianity comes fully when 'the true light shines'. In Klopstock's hymn we find the twilight of morning, when the approaching light is announced by majestic music, as it is in Goethe's *Faust*, but we do not yet find the risen Sun. To feel this difference means to be looking towards the Christianity that is to come.

We can again strengthen within us our experiences of these sayings about the Resurrection, by placing beside them the words of John's Gospel in which Christ speaks of the risen *being* of the disciples.

- One of these saying has already been quoted, 'Truly, truly, I say to you, he who hears my word and believes him who sent me, has eternal life; he does not come into judgment, but has passed from death to life' (5:24). We must look closely at this 'has passed'. Does it not remind us of Christ's words about death, 'I go to the Father'? Such a passing, free, voluntary and calm, can already take place during life, and repeatedly takes place. He who bethinks himself of this has found a 'way' to the resurrection.
- The other saying is found in 8:51, 'Truly, truly, I say to you, if anyone keeps my word, he will never see death'. He will, indeed, pass through death, but in spite of that he will not 'see' it. How different is this seeing of John's Gospel compared to our seeing! And is it not remarkable that here again, in three sayings of Christ we have a way of initiation, similar to that which we discovered in the words concerning light? 'Walking', 'seeing'—and the saying concerning resurrection that Christ spoke at the grave of Lazarus, 'I am', adds the 'becoming'. A new *seeing*, a new *walking*, a new *becoming* are also parts of the victory of life.

'I am the way, the truth and the life'

Now we turn to the other passage in which Christ says emphatically 'I am the life'. To know great people more deeply and to look into their souls is possible by taking notice of special moments when their whole being appears to us, so to speak, in response to some outer stimulus. Such opportunities are to be found repeatedly in the Farewell Discourses. For example, in 14:5-6:

> Thomas says to him, 'Lord, we do not know where you are going; how can we know the way?' Jesus says to him, 'I am the way, and the truth, and the life; no one comes to the Father, but by me'.

Here again a truly external way of thinking of the life yonder was presented to Christ. And we are permitted to hear His elemental reaction to it. The first saying at the grave of Lazarus was a false *temporal* idea of the life yonder—he will sometime arise in a far future—and now, in Thomas's question, a false *spatial* idea of it, as if some change of place in a corporeal sense is connected with death. We do not yet clearly realize how strongly our spatial ideas still prevail today in our thoughts of the life beyond. And so we deprive ourselves of the true experience of the life beyond, and also give a certain ground for many of the objections that are brought against Christianity.

In this second saying about life Christ breaks through *space*, just as in the first He had broken through *time*. When we see this, we are witnessing a divine drama. Not a 'then' but a 'now', not a 'there' but a 'here', but both in Christ, the 'I am', and through Him in us, too. That is the true Christian idea of the 'life beyond', or better, the Christian idea of true life. Unsurpassable in its greatness and simplicity: '*The way—I myself am the way. There is no other.*' Buddha had said, 'I teach you the path'. Christ says, 'I am the Way'. Just to see His 'I am' as a way for us, too, is the great gain that we can receive from this saying. Moreover, this way leads into the lost Paradise. There we see the two Trees of Paradise: 'and the Truth'—the Tree of Knowledge—'and the Life'—the Tree of Life. Paradise has opened and has come down to us, otherwise we would never have found its gates again.

It is never possible to sink oneself enough in meditating such a saying, trying, as it were, to feel step by step how it arose in the mind of Christ. One truly retraces the way with Him into Paradise by endeavouring to feel again why, at this moment, He was obliged to say 'I am the way', why He had to add, 'and the truth' and not stopping there, had to say in addition 'and the life'. The 'I' of Christ expands for us to the whole Paradise, in which we may walk and eat of the trees, as the first human beings did. For us His words are those Trees.

In our seeking for life, it is important to notice that this saying does not simply announce to us that 'Christ is like life', but is meant to lead us by a way, a path. Christ's first saying about life was more a progress in what is subjective, 'I am the resurrection and the life'. This second saying is more a progress in what is objective, 'the way, the truth and the life'. To put it as simply as possible, we may say, 'Go the way that is called Christ, and you come to perceive the ultimate truth of the world, and out of it you will gain life'. Is this not again a path of initiation, walking, seeing, becoming?

Here, too, we can make this experience still stronger and more evident by placing beside it a saying of our own time. We spoke above of Klopstock; now let us recall Schleiermacher (1768-1834) [often called 'the father of liberal liberal theology']. His well-known *Monologen* (1865, 2016) end with these sentences:

> To the consciousness of inner freedom and its action correspond eternal youth and joy. These have I grasped, and I shall never let them go. And consequently I see with a smile that the light of the eyes grows dim and white hairs grow amid the fair curls. Nothing that can happen to oppress my heart, the pulse of inner life remains fresh until death.

In Klopstock we saw a last and noblest transfiguration of the Jewish idea of the resurrection, here the hymn of Schleiermacher breathes rather the spirit of the Greek, but of the Greek spirit in the 'spiritualization' which is a flight, which makes a man talk of 'immortality at every moment'. In Klopstock, as we now see, we find the danger of Ahriman, here the luciferic danger.[71] How much more full of matter and valuable does Christ's saying sound, which now we see in all its greatness. 'I am the way and the truth and the life.' It leads us to the heights of the Holy Trinity. Christ, the way, teaches us the truth that rests in the Father, and He helps us to live the life that the Holy Spirit is seeking to live in us.

Here, too, we meet another saying in John's Gospel, by which Christ clearly shows us from a surprising direction the way we have to go. 'Truly, truly, I say to you, unless you eat the flesh of the Son of man and drink his blood, you have no life in you; he who eats my flesh and drinks my blood has eternal life, and I will raise him up at the last day' (6:53, 54). In this strong and living sense, Christ is the way, so that no one shall attain to life unless s/he receives into her/himself Christ's flesh and blood. Here is the way Christ shows us to life. Not only to perceive a truth, or cultivate a feeling, but in full reality to receive Christ into our own flesh and blood. 'This is a hard saying; who can listen to it?' people said, and they are still saying it. In truth here is the secret of life, the way of redemption. And consequently it is important to take this central saying into ourselves in all its contexts.

Christ had fed the Five Thousand. To the astonished people who gather round Him, Christ says, 'Truly, truly, I say to you, you seek me, not because you saw signs, but because you ate your fill of the loaves'. They were hoping, consequently, that He would give them a time of carefree life, when one did not need to toil for bread. And so Christ immediately continues, 'Do not labour for the food which perishes, but for the food which endures to eternal life, which the Son of man will give to you' (6:26, 27). They do not understand, but ask further:

> 'What must we do, to be doing the works of God?' Jesus answered them, 'This is the work of God, that you believe in him whom he has sent.' So they said to him, 'Then what sign do you do, that we may see, and believe you? What work do you perform?' [6:28, 29].

Then they themselves recall the sign by which Moses revealed himself—the manna in the wilderness. And Christ answers, 'the bread of God is that which comes down from heaven, and gives life to the world'. And so we come to the saying: 'I am the bread of life' (35).

These passages are quoted at length, because it is important fully to understand how Christ here proposes only a new form of work to those who expect to have no work in the 'Kingdom of Heaven', and how Christ Himself described faith in Himself as an inner work, in which man works together with God, and how here too we are not far from the ways of an inner way of meditation, with all the force of our will. And just as it is our 'work' to make faith in Christ govern our lives, so Christ points out as His 'work' the giving of Himself to the world. It is His continuous activity, His work, in the midst of which we stand, to give Himself to humanity—to the world—to eat, as bread gives itself to people to eat.

Many signs point to the fact that today the hour has come when people have to be told in a new way that Christ is willing to be there for people to eat, and how this eating can take place. It is a pity that the word 'enjoy' has such an egoistical flavour. In seeking for experiences by which contemporary people can begin to understand what we mean here, the first picture that arises is the way in which a mother enjoys her child. She can look for hours at her baby in the cradle, rejoicing in the infant and all the details of the small human being. And as she turns away to her other activities, she feels as if she had drunk deep draughts of youth—as if she herself had become a child again in all the beauty of childhood. She sees this glory reflected upon all her surroundings. It is well that people may still experience these things, at least experiences that may be the highest we have, and that may lead to higher experiences in real life. 'Truly, I say to you, whoever does not receive the kingdom of God like a child shall not enter it' (Mark 10:15, cf. Matt. 18:3).

Another first step towards that to which Christ seeks to lead us is the enjoyment of spring. When people walk in a garden full of blossoms, opening their heart to it so that its glory may enter into them, and yet feel that they cannot become open enough or pure enough to bring this glory into existence in their soul; when they feel that they must drink in the spring as a draught of Paradise, and can no longer be mean or self-seeking, then they may reflect that Christ Himself was felt by the first Christians to be 'a new creation'. Or, to take yet another example, when an individual stands under the stars, endeavouring to make his soul a pure mirror for this world of revelation, so that there is nothing in him but the greatness, purity and sublime fullness of peace coming from that which is seeking to shine into him, he may then think of the saying of the Evangelist John, 'we beheld his glory, ... full of grace and truth' (1:14).

Ought one not, indeed, to seek from the best earthly experiences a way of access to such a saying of Christ, as that in which He spoke of the true bread that gives 'life' to the world? Before we know as much (or even more) of the 'enjoyment' of Christ, as we do know in these joys, Christ cannot be to us what He fain would be.

Christ once carried this saying concerning 'eating' significantly further when He told His disciples about Himself. 'My food'—the food that nourishes my 'I'—'is to do the will of Him that sent me, and to finish His work' (4:34). In seeking to imagine what forces of inner feeding proceed from a work concerning which we feel that 'this is a work of God', then we shall know what the 'feeding of the "I"' is, and what sublime manner of nourishment has been appointed for human beings in the future. These are the actual ways of 'life' that Christ has shown us.

With the same clarity Christ also speaks of drinking. We already met (*Letter* 5) the saying, 'Whoever drinks the water I shall give him will never thirst, but the water that I shall give him will be in him a spring of water welling up to everlasting life' (4:14). Everywhere in John's Gospel there are indications of a future life which humanity has not yet reached, has not yet grasped. We have to seek to experience how all our deeply concealed thirst for life ceases when we draw near to Christ; we then notice for the first time what unslaked thirst has always been ours, but how this water now wells up and remains within us. We have ourselves become an oasis in the desert of humanity, and possess our own well-spring. From us, too, people can drink. In the East this picture could be understood better than we can. We are entirely unable to represent all this tangibly enough to ourselves. To drink from water that carries life, is in fact life. After all, the whole sensory world is only there to teach this. As we gradually learn to perceive a shining light within ourselves, so it is with a living water. As our everyday light seems to us dark compared with the new light, so does our daily water seem dead compared with living water.

Here again Christ carries this saying concerning water still further, and affords us a glimpse of His own life. He has shown us unheard of heights. 'He that believes in me, as the scripture has said, "Out of his heart shall flow streams of living water"' (7:38). In that passage in the Old Testament to which these words probably refer, the subject is the future Temple out of which rivers flow that enter into the Eastern and Western sea (Zech. 14:8). Here again we have a prophecy of a temple that is fulfilled in the human body—the new temple. Where has such a promise of Christ been fulfilled in more than a rudimentary conjecture? That this—during the hour in which it was spoken—was fulfilled in Christ Himself, we immediately receive a testimony, in the gentle yet significant manner in which such testimonies are given in the Bible. The officers who were sent to arrest Christ heard His words and reported to those who had sent them, 'No man ever spoke like this man' (7:46). The Greek text says more emphatically, 'as this man speaks *the human being'* [*houtos lalei ho anthropos*]. One can hear in this a gentle indication of the fulfilment of all that is human. And the saying that precedes this immediately proves that Christ, in speaking of the overflowing water of life, is also speaking of Himself: 'If any man thirst, let him come to me and drink' (7:37).With deep astonishment we stand before this testimony of Christ to Himself. Was it *thus* that He felt Himself—as if overflowing streams of life proceeded continually not only from His soul but also from His body? Who can have the faintest idea of what this may mean? And it is promised to *us*. How sublime is the life that has been appointed to people upon the Earth, when they really give themselves to Christ! The Rivers of Paradise are here again, as were previously the Trees of Paradise. Of them both, the last vision of John the seer, speaks expressly (Rev. 22:1ff.).

It is in the glory of such a future for the world that we have to discover afresh the Holy Supper. It is the central sanctuary of Christendom. In it Christ comes as near to us, as near to the Earth, as is possible. The Earth and Christ are enclosed together in it. And consequently it can be regarded as the prayer of the whole of humanity when in John's Gospel two requests are made to Jesus, 'Lord, give us this bread always' (6:34), and 'Sir, give me this water' (4:15). These prayers are different from the request, 'Stay with me!' And the fulfilment of these prayers of humanity, made so urgently to Christ, is the Holy Supper. This very Mystery of life is contained in the saying, 'As the living Father sent me, and I live because of the Father, so he that eats me will live because of me' (6:57).

It is no longer possible to bind people by law to an outer form of divine worship, however much of power it may contain. But one has to preach to them that an eating and drinking of Christ exists in the deep holiness and supersensory nature of meditation. Indeed, all true turning to Christ, also in prayer, must become a Lord's Supper, and it will become so when it is real, even if we are not always conscious of this. But even because one realizes this the liturgy of the Lord's Supper will become free and great. It brings to human beings that which cannot be surpassed, even in the deepest union with Christ in prayer. It is offered to us in a celebration that, as it were, expresses the highest Mysteries of life in earthly reality, and thus consecrates this earthly reality by the revealed secret of the ultimate truths of life. Just as one can feel in a traditional church building the existence of the holiest approaching one from all sides, so humanity ought to feel the existence of the Lord's Supper in their midst to be the holiest of all things. 'Unless you eat the flesh of the Son of man and drink his blood, you have no life in you' (6:53). A new Christianity will be built up around this holy of holies—Christ in body and blood. It also becomes apparent that Christ in immediate connection with these words can also say, 'It is the spirit that gives life, the flesh is of no avail; the words that I have spoken to you are spirit and life' (6:63). A body which is spirit, a spirit which becomes body—it is this that we have to lay hold with both mind and hand. And in the same sense, a life which is blood, a blood which is life. Here we are standing in the Temple of true 'life'.

People's feeling about life are quite extraordinarily varied. If we could be in another's skin for only five minutes, we should learn more wisdom than many books could teach us. When sitting listening to lectures by Rudolf Steiner, I have frequently been conscious that here was a human being who experienced the spirit much more strongly and much more vividly than I myself. The spirit was at work in him, at every moment modelling even his body. How much spirit and life can find room in a human body! A quite different feeling of life flows in a much higher potency in the lives of higher spirits than it does in human beings. And we can sometimes surmise, at least in a dreamlike manner, that it is possible to lead such a bright, living, free and spiritually strong existence that beside it we human beings seem to be living in unspeakable earthly dullness, weariness, darkness and impurity. Christ is the way to the life that lies above us. And for our age, it is Christ especially as He speaks in John's Gospel. We have actually to pursue the radiance of His life and strive to catch it in our life. For this radiance of life—as we have seen in many examples—is to be found in all its fullness in John's Gospel.

People today are constantly discovering new 'death-rays'. They are looking with horror into a future in which those death-rays may be brought into man's power, to be used with deadly results. Consequently, now is the time in which we have to tell people of these life-rays that raise us to heights from which we shall 'no longer see death'. Upon this level, death is nothing but 'a means in the hand of nature, by which we may have as much life as possible'. It is only the revealer of life, the strengthener of life. The very first gift to humanity—'life', one has to wrestle hardest to obtain upon its very highest level—'life'. Between the 'life' that we have received and the 'life' that we ought to receive, the 'life', our life that we now lead—or do not really lead—sways to and fro like a pendulum. If only conscience were awakened in us so that we should not allow to perish those little bits of higher life that shine in us here and there; if we did not constantly destroy the embryo life within us, then we should gradually mount to ever higher stages.

Before its Epilogue, John's Gospel closes (20:31) with the words that in believing on Christ we 'may have life in his name'. When Christ's name really sounds in us, then salvation, life, also streams in us. And faith, in the Johannine sense, is just such a touching of Christ as sets up an enduring connection with His life. Christ's own public ministry, before His Passion commenced, also ends, not only with the preaching about the light, but at the very last, with the preaching of life: 'And I know that his commandment is eternal life' (12:50). The end of Christ's preaching, as well as the end of the gospel itself, says to us: Through all the sayings, through all the deeds, you ought to seek *the life* which Christ brought—which Christ was. So the divine Father, the Father of the worlds, willed when He sent Christ to you.

Letter No. 9

'I am Love'

In meditating upon the three words, 'Light, love, life', as they chime together, one's meditation can be very powerful and effective by dwelling upon Matthias Grünewald's well-known picture of the Resurrection. As in the picture of Christ in the Brera, Milan, that [in reproductions] hangs over many of the altars in chapels of The Christian Community, three circles of colour can be most clearly distinguished around the head of the Risen One. The innermost circle is a shining yellow-gold: *Light*. The next circle is a clear pure red: *Love*. The outermost circle is a light, light-filled green, that passes over into dark blue: *Life*. Recalling that in these three circles of colour the worlds of the Father, of the Son and of the Spirit are also speaking to us:

- in the innermost circle of light yellow, the world of the Spirit;
- in the red, the world of the Son, and
- in the green-blue, the world of the life of the Father

then this picture may also be regarded as a noble representation of *one who has been baptized*. Ever more probable becomes the thought that here an artist with the second sight of feeling may have found *the real 'aura' of Christ*. And this is all the more probable, since, according to spiritual-scientific perception:

- thinking—spiritual activity—is most closely connected with the human body,
- the feelings more loosely connected with the human body, and
- the will is still more free.

In meditating the three words 'light, love, life' in colours, then it might well happen that in our own 'aura' these colours would be purified and strengthened, and our aura—does anyone doubt that we also bear an aura?—would become more like the aura of Christ, if our own nature, of which the aura is only an expression, was also corresponding to this and if it was consequently perceptible to people gifted with clairvoyance, then it would be seen that Christians have been baptized in the full inner sense. Such a meditation would not only make the three words more living and powerful, but conversely, too, would make the natural world appear more spiritual in its wealth of colours. Only the outer colour of the aura upon the picture in our imagination has to pass over more into violet than it does in Grünewald's painting, as is indeed so in the altar-picture in the Brera, and then the whole scale of the rainbow colours, which is the ideal picture of our world of colours, would be gathered up into our souls in such a picture. It would be difficult to find a meditation that would convey to us the nature of Christ in such a comprehensive, natural-spiritual manner as such a meditation, which we must now hold within us, shining and living, yet not rigid or clumsy.

It should not be a stumbling-block that in this image of colours the word appears in a different order to that of our study. This was mentioned above. 'Life' just consists in 'love', and 'love' leads people to 'life', consequently one can use *differing* methods of study. The progress of John's Gospel itself leads to the choice of order: 'light, life, love'. It may actually be said that John's Gospel comes down to Earth by the road love—life—light, and then ascends to heaven by the reverse, light—life—love. The initial sentences of John's Gospel point to the life of eternal love, 'and the Word was with God'. Then love enters upon its world course—'in him was life, and the life was the light of men'. Then in the appearances after the Resurrection the way returns in the opposite direction.

- The first appearance at the grave and in the garden results in Mary being called by name; she is given a message announcing—Light!
- In the second appearance another tone is heard: joy, peace—Life!
- In the third appearance the gospel sounds forth in the question, 'Do you love me?'—Love! 'Like heavenly power ascending and descending ...' [1:51].

But, aside from the beginning and ending, looking at the central part of John's Gospel, we find:

- the healing of the man born blind is bound up with the word 'light'; the opposite is that of darkness and light, followed by
- the raising of Lazarus—death and life, the prelude to
- the beginning of the days of the Passion with the story of the Washing of the Feet—hatred and love.

The history of love is the real history of humanity. In the way by which a people, or an age, conceives of 'love' its deepest nature is expressed. The same is true of the individual person. If we see *what* love is in him, and in what *way* it lives in him, then we will have realized him. Self-love is also a real form of love, and indeed often not only concerning one's *own* 'self'.

From the power of physical attraction that comes from the difference between man and woman there runs a straight road to the highest heights of love, a straight road from which indeed many byways lead. And a force is also there driving one forward along this road. That force is the dissatisfaction coming with every other love, with the exception of divine love. This dissatisfaction arises partly out of the earthly circumstances, such as death and the threat of death that does not permit a lasting 'happiness', but for the most part it arises out of every imperfect form of life itself. It is an all-embracing human perception lying in Faust's words concerning desire that finds no rest in its satisfaction. Nietzsche, as so often in a distorted context, expresses a golden secret—'[Y]our finest love is only a rapturous allegory and painful heat'.[72] If people would only pay close heed to what love itself tells them about love, they would be led in their little lives along the whole human road of love, until they reach John's Gospel.

The book of the history of love in humanity has not yet been written. Books have been written only about the 'Eros' of different peoples, and even they know nothing of what Plato taught concerning love in his *Symposium*. In this master-work the human genius of Plato speaks in the Greek manner of a road for humanity to divine love. Could someone from pre-Christian times ever have a clearer pre-vision of John's Gospel, and yet at the same time make more clear that John's Gospel is not to be reached without Christ?

What Plato attempted to do then in pre-Christian times, could, after its fulfilment, happen again today in much broader proportions and clearer thinking. For great talks of the nations and ages about love could be written down and at the end of them all the evangelist of Christ would take up his parable. As his congregation he would have all of humanity, who would belong to what he has to say.

To see how what the people loved is fulfilled in Christ in the 'grace upon grace' (1:16) that is within Him, would be one of the greatest hours of consecration that a human being could experience. Of this we can only hint.

India

What did the Indians love? They loved the spirit. They loved the spirit so much that all earthly things for them were only a banishment from it. This deep love of human beings for the spirit, as it was lived in India, was of great nobility. But this love of the spirit ended in Indian history—as one can say from one point of view—with Buddha in complete collapse. Pointing to the world, human beings said: All this I am *not*. To all this I must say 'No', if I want to be a human being. I have to say 'No', even to the spiritual content of the world. But as to *what* the content, the *positive* content, of a human being ought to be, 'concerning this the Exalted One revealed nothing'. Now, one has to be able to experience completely with Buddha the majestic helplessness of this 'No', if one is to realize Buddha as humanity's greatest teacher before Christ, as the radically powerful negation of a world without Christ, as the all-judging 'No' that calls for the 'Yes'. If John the Baptist was 'the voice of one crying in the wilderness', then the Buddha is the voice of one crying amid negation. In the former it is more the need of the soul that is crying, in the latter it is the need of the world. Those who understand this reach the certainty that the Buddha will become the great friend of the Christ—not the Buddha as he walked the Earth and, as all great men, was held fast by his own mission, but the Buddha as he advances in higher worlds. The Indian love of the spirit, which cannot be found upon Earth, found its fulfilment when Christ spoke these words, 'I will *send* you the Spirit of Truth'. The Indian age of the world is waiting for a new age in which people will live wholly in the spirit, in which they will seek and acknowledge the spirit just as heroically as the Indians do, but in which they will bring back to the Earth the *Holy* Spirit, which they have found in the Kingdom of Christ. The longing for the spirit led them away from the Earth; the fulfilment of the spirit makes them strong enough to return to the Earth—in order to transfigure the Earth itself into spirit.

Persia

A new light falls upon the course of the world's history, which we have learned from Rudolf Steiner, in the succession of civilizations, as we pass from early India to early Persia. Here, too, is love of the spirit, but this spirit is *present* in the world of the senses as the glory of the light. To look up to the light means to see the World-spirit that has called human beings to a victorious battle against darkness. Here we meet a quite different kind of heroism from that of the Indian world. And a quite different love. Earthly love too was thereby ennobled by the Persians. The Indians, in striving after the spirit practised renunciation, whereas the early Persians, so far as we can still perceive them in the distant historical past, regarded married life as a field that has to be kept clean in order that children of the light might come to the Earth. Looking out from this kingdom to John's Gospel, we find the Persian worshippers of light are called in when, as we have seen, in John's Gospel the consecration in light of the sons of light is described with such high spirituality. 'Believe in the light'—all your powers of love lie in this belief.

Chaldea-Egypt

How was love expressed in Ancient Chaldea, in the third period of the world's civilizations? Here and in Egypt people sought in initiation a life that is above death. People already felt that they had entered more into themselves. Even the degenerate cults of love in the temples of Babylon are a cry for life. Human beings, having learned to feel more within themselves, would fain pass beyond themselves. This is to speak in general terms in order to characterize the whole situation. The striving is now away from the Sun of the early Persians to the stars. The search was for a wisdom ruling space and enduring beyond time. If we could gather around John's Gospel those who had high aspirations among the early Egyptians and Chaldeans, then the words, 'I am the resurrection and the life', would have more appeal to the Egyptians; the other words, 'I am the way and the truth and the life', would speak more to the Chaldeans.

In early China, moreover, this saying appears almost verbally, when Lao-Tze describes his doctrine as 'The way to the true life' [TAO-te]. In early Egypt, however, death has already come more threateningly near than in early China. And in early Chaldea life was already striving with greater longing away from the Earth than for the quiet wise man in the Far East. But in John's Gospel, 'the way to the true life' is shown in such a way that death is not ignored, but overcome, and life lays hold of people, not in a higher mysticism, but in a new creation.

Here we are speaking of the highest love of these peoples. A band of most noble spirits goes before on the way to true love. Other people follow at a considerable distance, or settle down in the valleys and on the lower slopes.

We are confined to but a few hints for further enquiry. Free explorations in the garden of history would yield many spiritual joys. One penetrates deeply into the nature of a people when seeking its 'love'. This characterizes a people more truly and worthily than any limiting description. What, for example, was the love of the Chinese? Are we in error when we say: they wished for order and harmony? They sought for a reflection of the order of heaven; they wished to have it on Earth, both outwardly and inwardly. Their way would lead straight into Christ's saying, 'Peace I leave with you; my peace I give to you; not as the world gives do I give to you' (14:27). Here heaven is streaming down to Earth, and making it in its own image. And morality is redeemed from its subjection to rational law and is born anew from within—from harmony with the will in heaven.

What is the love of the original Americans, as we see it, though in decadence, in the Mexican cult? Magical force. This is expressed even in the American of today, and connected with the peculiar nature of the ground and its subterranean forces. The redemption and transfiguration of this frame of mind would come also from a saying of Christ. 'He who believes in me will do the works that I do; and greater works than these will he do, because I go to the Father' (14:12).

What is the love of the true Germanic people? Much is alive in the world of the mind. But nowhere does the soul speak to us more arrestingly than in their Balder-longings.[73] Their union with nature asks for a new spring, for a new glory of light for a new creation. Consequently, the German people are especially open to the landscape of spring, and to the stories of the Resurrection. There one sees the new world and therein people, freedom, and leadership are at one, rising up to complete humanity.

In a great spirit, John's Gospel must be presented to the world by world history, by the whole of humanity, as *the* fulfilment. Then in it can be perceived how all capacity for love that is possessed by the human race reaches its consecration. This would be the consecrated study of history. We might point to the chapter, 'Promise', in *The Holy Year*,[74] which sketches how among the peoples some centuries before Christ, the idea of love in its highest sense awoke. It was unable, however, to live in this form; it was a last prophetic call for Christ. Another essay, 'Jüngerweihe',[75] on John 21, may be recalled where the progress of the Greek world towards Christ is sketched in connection with the Greek words *eran*, *philein*, and *agapan*.

When we turn from this background to the proclamation of Christ itself, we do not find in the whole of John's Gospel the saying forming the title of this *Letter*, 'I am love'. However, this is very characteristic of the whole gospel. It is a part of the true revelation of love that Christ did not say these words but acted them. In other respects, too, we find in the gospel that Christ is reserved in the use of the *word* 'love'. This reserve is in marked opposition to the misuse, and too frequent use, of the word in later times in Christian groups. The word 'grace', or 'mercy', is never found in the mouth of Christ in any of the four gospels, except in the parable telling of the publican's prayer, 'God, be merciful to me' (Luke 18:13), where also the words 'God have mercy upon me' do not appear in the Greek text. John the Evangelist uses this word only twice, with special force, when he speaks at the beginning (1:16) of 'receiving of His fullness, grace upon grace'. Christ Himself avoids speaking of love, whether in a parable such as that of the Good Samaritan, or in a deed such as the Washing of the Feet.[76]

Nevertheless, there lies over John's Gospel an indescribable glory of revelation of love. This glory has such purity, delicacy and spiritual power that in this one has the material with which a marvellous new world may be built. Perhaps it is only after much study of John's Gospel that one can receive this substance of transfiguration into oneself in such a living manner. With this purpose these studies have been written. Anyone who lives in this realm, in this Being that has come down out of heaven to the Earth, and which is surely the fulfilment of earthly history, that which the whole universe awaited—lives in Christ.

Yet we do find again what we have also experienced in the other words, 'light' and 'life', namely that in a sacred triad love appears at the beginning, at the end, and at the highest point of the gospel. 'The only Son, who is in the bosom of the Father, he has made him known' (1:18). Let us look from this saying across to the last saying of the High-Priestly Prayer:

> Father, I desire that they also, whom Thou hast given me, may be with me where I am, to behold my glory which Thou hast given me in Thy love for me before the foundation of the world ... that the love with which Thou hast loved me may be in them, and I in them [17:24-26].

Here all human speaking ceases. The human heart can only stand before this in deep, joyful reverence. That which Christ experienced in the heart of the Father, the Ground of the World, was brought by Him to the Earth, and therein *we* shall find heaven. Let us be fully aware—it is not only the grace which Thou givest them, not only the love wherewith Thou lovest *them*, but 'the love with which Thou hast loved *me*'! This leads us far beyond all proclamation of grace by Protestantism, and yet it includes it. We are to live in the current of life that flows back and forth between the Father and the Son. No human being can receive this fully into himself. If we only *think* of it, and even *surmise* it out of our consciousness today, we shall be consecrated as nothing else can consecrate us. This is your sublime Kingdom, O man!

A third saying comes at the end of the gospel, to be united to these two, 'Do you love me? ... Follow me' (21:15, 16, 17, 19). The love to Christ that is in our hearts is that part of the divine love between Father and Son that He can leave to us upon the Earth, and it carries us further. In the spirit we see, by the side of this closing of John's Gospel, the closing of Goethe's *Faust*: 'The Eternal Feminine draws us upwards and on'; cosmic depths are opened before us.

A new, greater view of John's Gospel is acquired by seeking out the greatest events in Old Testament history—the greatest events of religious history in general—and one perceives how clearly in John's Gospel three new events are placed facing the three events. We refer to:

- the creation of the world,
- the building of the Temple and
- the giving of the Torah, the law.

These three events, we know, govern the Old Testament. Yet in them the whole of religion in general is embodied. The creation, which also includes the whole of mythology, in the past took the place of dogmatics. At that time mankind looked back to the past, deriving greatness from having come forth from God. The temple-building, which with the Israelites began with the making of the tabernacle, is the central place of the cult in pre-Christian, and also in the greatest period of Christian life; it stood as a great power in the focus of all life. And the giving of the Law, with all the many prescripts and commandments, lays hold of and permeates the whole of human life; all *ethics* in the widest sense and politics are included.

Creation

From this point of view, the gospel appears new to us in its human greatness and above all in John's Gospel. It is not only because it begins with an account of creation, with a pure myth of creation, to use the phrase in the sense of a pictorial truth. The most inner story of creation that has ever existed, the story that enters into the divine Being itself, is here placed facing all previous mythology. We are made a part of the pure and great evolutionary rhythm of the cosmos, and can read in it our own history from God and to God. Moreover, John's Gospel also speaks openly of the necessity of a new birth, of a *new creation*. We shall have to speak of this when we look at the story of Nicodemus (John 3). A new 'Let there be' is spoken. Those who would be Christians must look at the new beginning, must live out of the new beginning. The feeling that a new creation has been begun ought to be the feeling permeating the life of the Christian. This is more than was meant during the last centuries by 'the new birth', and it includes it. It is not merely the 'conversion' of the individual, but it is a beginning of the new creation of the world. We are no longer amid the evolving of the old creation. And so for us the story of the earlier creation has receded into the background. We are to breathe the air of the beginning of creation; we are to stand amid the glory of a new, awakened, higher creation.

Temple

In the same way, the word 'temple' may also acquire a new meaning for us. 'But he spoke of the temple of his body' (2:21). Here once again we must make a fundamental study of the individual details regarding the 'building of the temple' in John's Gospel. In the first *Letter*, we spoke of the meaning of the dedication of the temple (John 10), the saying concerning worship of God 'in spirit and truth' that requires neither Mount Gerizim nor Jerusalem as the place where it is fulfilled (4:24). And it is completed by the destruction of the old Temple and the setting up of the new Temple, fulfilled in the presence of the disciples and of doubting Thomas. Here again we are to take great events into our thinking and perceiving. We can reach the heights of John's Gospel only when there are Christians who feel their own bodies to be temples in which they live, worship and serve; these must be their bodies that have been built anew by Christ. This has to be taken quite literally.

In the future, temples and 'houses of God'—and there will be very glorious ones—will be the reverse of what they were in early times. In the past, the temple was built in such a way as to educate human beings. In a sense, the temple was placed over the human being, so that a person might evolve in accordance with it. In the coming age man will increasingly create the house from within—the house that will be like him. In the highest sense only that temple will count in which the risen human being feels s/he is at home, which the risen person feels to be their greater covering, through which they can pray as they are able to do through their body.

These thoughts throw a special light upon the difference between the Gothic cathedral and the Greek temple. The Greek temple trained the restless, easily-moved Greek to harmony, rest and equanimity. For it has been rightly said that one ought not to be deceived, but should understand that what the Greek praised most—*sophrosyne*, calm self-command—was *not* what he possessed naturally, for he lacked it. He was formed by the calmness, the weight, the even nature of the stone. The Gothic was quite different. It was grandly contemptuous, as no other art, of stone—of stone as earthly material. It built man into the stone. The Gothic cathedral is the man or woman who prays, who has impressed him/herself into the stone, and has left nothing of the stone except what resembles him/herself.

The temple-building of the future need not be so violent. It can take loving notice of the nature of its materials. It can make a deeper discovery of the relationship of nature to the human being. It can feel it is related from of old with nature. Yet it will still build from within outwards. The temple of the body into which Christ entered will find its likeness in the coming temple. The feeling of the temple, the worship of the temple, the glory of the temple, will be fulfilled above all by a man or woman in the house of his/her own body, in which Christ makes His abode. The old nature of religion will be changed into something new. And there is all too much of the old nature of religion in Christianity today.

The 'new commandment'

It is with such sacred connections that the 'new commandment' (13:34) Christ gave to His own should be received. Here one always feels one should emphasis the word 'a'—the 'one' great commandment of the King. And one is justified in thinking so, for the other gospels speak of 'a' commandment 'upon which depend all the law and the prophets' (cf. Matt. 20:40). The moment the 'one commandment' appeared amid the multitude of religious precepts, the human being for the first time really became a single being. His 'I' now gathered all the wealth of the soul to one point. It is not possible to see more readily all the tremendous novel greatness of Christianity than in contemplating how, in the place of the many religious commandments, from that time forth the one single commandment came, or, to put it more exactly, shall come, that is, love. It had, of course, been prepared by the whole course of the history of religion; it was the redeeming word towards which that history had been pressing forward. The human being no longer looks outside for that by which he shall be guided; he creates from within that which ought to be. For this nothing but free, creative love can be law and commandment. The world of the old ordinance, which, as it were, was breaking up into individuals, will give itself from within a new ordinance by love's free creative power. One can scarcely think that out boldly enough: every ordinance laid upon humanity from without and from above is in reality still Mosaic. And the time of Moses passed away when Christ came. In the Christian future there will be only free, realized ordinances, and yet there will be complete harmony. Those who do not yet dare to imagine this, to foresee it, do not yet see Christ's kingdom. It might be put in this way as well: in heaven there are neither tablets of stone neither collections of commandments, but the 'angels' act in all things out of their own nature and inclination—and yet the whole is a majestic organism.

One would not venture to speak with such boldness upon the Earth were not the very strongest force, the very clearest example of true love unchangeably present on the Earth. For this reason Christ adds to the new commandment, the new comparison, 'as I have loved you' (13:34). It is only when we look to Him, to His manner of loving and His deed of love, that our tremendous venture can succeed.

The Cross

The cross of Christ itself stands as the greatest comparison in the world: the greatest 'as'. If we examine John's Gospel we find two kinds of 'as'. One points upwards like one arm of the cross, for example, 'as the Father has sent me, so I send you' (20:21). Another points away into space, like the other beam of the cross, for example, the saying here, 'you love one another; even as I have loved you' (13:34). He answered (Luke 10:27), 'You shall love the Lord your God with all your heart, and with all your soul, and with all your strength, and with all your mind;' (cf. Deut. 6:5); 'and your neighbour as yourself' (cf. Lev. 19:18). But we must actually feel the two beams of the cross in an ever more living and spiritual manner, in the sense of the twofold comparison that we experience right through the whole of John's Gospel. The cross has been set up upon the Earth; its arms stretch out for ever into the heights and breadths, full of meaning, mighty in their significance. The cross is still used in Christianity too much as if it were a kind of charm, very often even when one feels one has been redeemed by the cross of Christ. But it is the divine rune in which the whole content of heaven and Earth stands before us. Feeling the cross vividly as the writing that has been written upon the Earth by God's own hand, when one adds the sense of the historical deed of revelation, and one even feels the historical occurrence upon Golgotha to be the life and spirit of this outward sign, then the sign of the cross will become *the Christian sign* in the fullest sense, so that nothing ought to happen in the kingdom of Christ without this sign.

Streams of life

One can wander through John's Gospel tracing everywhere the love of Christ. Indeed, story by story, deed by deed, word by word, one can hold one's ear to the pulse-beat of love. Thus one would dwell by the streams of life.

If we have to pick individual examples, we would recall the conversation with the Samaritan woman at Jacob's Well (John 4), in which may be found more wisdom, higher wisdom in conversation, higher teaching on how to converse, than in any book of 'good manners'. How Christ treats the simple person as a brother would treat her, takes her by the hand in order to lead her up to His high level by the nearest way, is for us an eternal example. Or, in contrast to this, the whole struggle of Christ with 'the Jews', especially in John 8, where the decisive battle for the earthly period of time was fought out—yet to be discussed in detail—but in which through the preaching of the spirit the revelations of love shine out, even embodying themselves in them. We have not yet fathomed the depths of the way in which Christ's love, with complete purity, ever and again makes the misunderstandings and ill-will of people the occasion for letting new truths flash into the world, of giving new gifts to people.

Every individual standing before Christ in John's Gospel might be studied in the light of the love that falls upon him from Christ.

- This is true even of Pilate, with whom Christ, when a prisoner, struggles for his soul when He speaks into the Roman's ear the word 'truth'—in such fateful circumstances, with so much that lies behind it.
- There is Judas. Even down to the Last Supper, when Christ hands him the sop, not to betray him to His beloved disciple, but to woo him for the last time by a deed of friendship, indeed, even in the High-Priestly Prayer itself in which his traitorous deed is accepted as a world-necessity—Judas is continually redeemed by Christ.
- There is Peter. What skill in the pastoral office did Jesus show in dealing with him! It is the high school of the pastor, not only of the priest, that we see in this.
- There is 'the disciple whom Jesus loved', who might rest upon the breast of Christ, as Christ above 'in the bosom of the Father'—'As the Father has loved me, so have I loved you; abide in my love' (15:9). Those places that speak of this disciple are even by themselves a little history of love.

Highest Song of Love

But Christ's Farewell Discourses, and not only His High-Priestly Prayer, are quite especially a great Song of Love. We simply do not notice with what complete lack of understanding the nearest disciples keep breaking into what Christ is saying, because it is all taken up by Christ and transformed in His soul into a new revelation of love. What an example this is! Here we have not only a sermon about love, but a continuous act of reconciliation and a deed of transfiguring love. If one has ever felt that which lives behind the words to which Christ's transfigured nature—that glory of heaven which came down to the Earth—has risen, then one knows that this is *the* medicine for human beings, medicine in a far higher sense than ever medicine was hitherto. 'Having loved his own who were in the world, he loved them to the end' (13:1).

From this last and highest song of love, whose end is love, we can receive a further impression of that which we have already perceived in the High-Priestly Prayer, namely of that which moves to and fro from the heavenly world to the earthly world; of that high impulse towards heaven that is constantly conquered by the free act of love with which Christ repeatedly turns back to His disciples, looking on them once more and sealing them as His own.

The act of love upon the cross takes place, as it were, behind a curtain—as the holiest part of the Mass, or Liturgy, in the Orthodox Church does. Man took no part in the greatest thing that was ever done for him. He knows it not; he scarcely even dreams of it. Great words are never spoken when great deeds are done. Christ had indeed clearly foretold His death and its meaning, also in John's Gospel. We have already seen how He spoke of the 'lifting up' of the Son of man. But we always notice the same delicacy and restraint which we have perceived in Him in the narration of the Washing of the Feet, in the parable of the Good Samaritan, and everywhere else when He speaks of love. 'I am the good shepherd. The good shepherd lays down his life for the sheep' (10:11). Here again He is speaking in a picture and not, as it were, of Himself. Certainly, a few sentences later comes the great announcement of love until death—almost the only one in John's Gospel—which is unsurpassed in its clarity and freedom.

> For this reason the Father loves me, because I lay down my life, that I may take it again. No one takes it from me, but I lay it down of my own accord. I have power to lay it down, and I have power to take it again; this charge I have received from my Father [10:17-18].

These words breathe such inner certainty and purity, such a divine knowledge and divine will, that we feel we are here walking upon the highest heights of an 'I'. The divine soul of Christ lies open before us. When we go through these words in meditation, uniting ourselves to them in our will, we actually make the soul of Christ our homeland. These words of Christ are as the inner side of the cross itself, and here again we see the two beams of the cross; He points upwards to the Father, and outwards to His own, for whom He gives Himself.

According to John's Gospel, Christ spoke three times upon the cross itself. These three sayings are *three deeds of love*. A 'Yes' to human beings, a 'Yes' to the Earth a 'Yes' to the Father; these are Christ's three last sayings before He died.

- A 'Yes' to human beings; He can speak it only to those of His own who yet remain, and between the disciple whom He loves and His mother, He founds a new Church.
- A 'Yes' to the Earth: yet once more He accepts and completes His becoming man, by saying 'I thirst'. In this last request there is something unspeakably humble, something which fulfils all earthly being.
- A 'Yes' to the Father, Whose work He now gives back into His hands: 'It is finished!'

Through this account given by John there shines again the open secret of the Holy Trinity.

- In the Church that Christ leaves behind Him upon the Earth, there lives the *Holy Spirit*.
- In the confession of His need, the *Son* speaks upon the Earth.
- In the work, now completed, the *Father* is speaking.

With his last words, Christ has once more written upon the Earth the secret of the Holy Trinity. He has baptized the Earth in the name of the Father, and of the Son and of the Holy Spirit.

One may look from the most different sides at the great revelation of love in John's Gospel. Rudolf Steiner, in his cycle of lectures on John's Gospel,[77] has shown from esoteric insight how the seven 'signs' in John's Gospel represent at the same time an inner progress in the power of self-devotion, revealed in Christ. To each successive miracle there belongs more power of self-devotion than belonged to the previous one. Then, in death and resurrection the revelation of love was completed. Such a method of study helps us surmise what secrets of the Bible will be discovered when people are mature enough to understand them. Much, very much, is still waiting for people.

For contemporary people as we are, it is important to know whether John's Gospel describes any clear way to the heights of love—a 'way of initiation', if we wish to use that phrase once more. The Last Discourses of Christ give an account of this: 14:15-24; 15:9-16. It is as simple and clear as possible. Christ has revealed love; we must look repeatedly at this love; by doing so, we shall learn to live in this love; living in this love is shown by our 'keeping the commandments of Christ'; in this way one becomes at home in it. Then He Himself comes and sets up His abode in us; and with Him comes the Father, whose dwelling-place we ought to become. This is the way into divine life; every person may progress on this path.

Many things yet strike one when looking at the history of Christianity. It should be quite clearly perceived that it is not simply Christ's deed, but much rather Christ's nature which awakens our love, or rather the deed of Christ, as a revelation of His nature, as the self-sacrifice of His nature. When it is said that Christ's deed has brought us divine grace, whether it be that one thinks, 'it has first made it possible', or, 'it has revealed it and proved it', one has not yet reached the heights of John's Gospel. Here we are not dealing initially with a proclamation, not initially with a deed, but with the substance of a being and with the gift of a being that has been brought into humanity *by* the proclamation and the deed. It is tremendously important to perceive this clearly. It is more than an extraordinary historical act. And it is more than a new revelation in our consciousness. It might be said, 'It is the material for a new world'. Only we must represent this 'material' in a wholly bright and spiritual way. It can exist only in an 'I', an ego. He who lives in this material, in this essence of love, lives in a new world. He who creates from this material, creates a new world. One can represent to oneself this substance of a new world neither tangibly enough, nor spiritually enough. One can, in meditation, actually draw it into oneself as breath, and, when it comes higher, even drink it, when it comes still higher, even eat it. This will seem strange to many people today, if not repellant, but it has to be put into words.

The German word *Liebe* can mean much in meditation. In all three words *Licht*, *Leben*, and *Liebe* ['light', 'life' and 'love'], the German spirit reveals its close relationship to John's Gospel, through having formed these words in such a spiritual way. In the sound represented by the letter 'L' there lies something creative, formative. Rudolf Steiner draws attention to the way in which the artist shapes his lips into a kind of point, as in the letter 'L', when he is in the act of creating, just as children do when writing. What is being created appears in the 'I'—pure light in which the 'I' is the living centre, as in the German *Licht*. The 'B' is that which cares for something, sheltering and protecting. What is sheltered in the *Liebe* is spoken by the 'E' that is earthly in its nature. One consequently passes through a drama, as it were, as one proceeds in meditation from sound to sound, letter to letter, of the word *Liebe*. What is creative, divinely creative, stirs in people. It brings forth the light of the 'I'. This 'I' turns consciously towards the Earth lying beneath it, its protective, indeed, one might even say, its brooding power.

The whole process recalls the Act of Consecration of Man: the creative word, the new 'I', the power of transubstantiation, the communion. We are speaking of an actual eating of the substance of love. If such talk seems to be too coarse, we are reminded of the end of Goethe's *Faust*:

> For this is the spirits' food,
> Which the freest ether holds,
> Eternal love's revealing,
> Which to blessedness unfolds.

In these lines, Goethe has said something higher about love than is said when the personal grace of God is thought of as being for human beings alone. Love is 'the food of spirits'. The more we become spirit, so much the more does love become our food. But anyone who has not yet access to such a thought may begin with what lies above eating, drinking and breathing, namely, with fire. It is truly a part of the experiencing of love, to experience it as a primal fire; as the fire of a new creation; as the Act of Consecration of Man speaks of the fire of love which is 'creative of being'. The fire of life, the *true* fire of life, is love.

Here one sees the complete contrast with Buddhism. *Nirvana* means 'extinction'; love is fire. It is the exact opposite. Buddhism and Christianity agree that the ordinary life of man is no life. Buddhism makes the great attempt that had to be made before Christianity, and which was the greatest thing there was before Christianity appeared. It sought, so to speak, to withdraw from life on the one side, on the side of complete extinction of the spark of life. The human 'I', which has realized the nothingness of the earthly life, extinguishes man, as he is, upon the Earth. Christianity sets up the exact contrary. The heavenly fire of Earth lays hold of earthly being, places itself in the place of the earthly spark of life, permeates man with light, making him for the first time truly a human being.

Buddhism was right, until a new Prometheus brought fire from heaven and planted it upon the Earth. Buddhism will always be right where there is not Christianity, and will always be in what is most spiritually clear and decisive. Buddha and Christ are fighting for the Earth, or rather, Buddha would have, or shall we say *has*, long perceived that he was the last and deepest preparation for Christ. Humanity as a whole has not yet become conscious of this spiritual struggle for humanity, which is being fought out in those heights where spiritual questions are decided without hatred or enmity, when spiritual realities come to grips.

Here we arrive as a point that is especially important. It is essential to perceive that *human beings only become truly human through love*. How is a human being who is entirely devoid of any feeling of love? Such must seem very strange to us, like a mask, because in this one, as in a mask, we have a form that is not made alive by the spirit. Think on the other hand of a wicked man upon whose face, as he looks at a child at play, a gleam of love lights up. The most horrible, devilish face will have on it a breath of beauty if a faint trace of spiritual love passes through the soul. The 'Son of man' is 'lifted up' by the cross; by that power to give of oneself and to lift oneself up into the heights, which is the essence of love. One may really say that lovelessness is the real heathendom. The lovelessness of a person is the measure of his/her heathenism, even if s/he names the Christ, or is even a Christian preacher. John's Gospel teaches us to feel that lovelessness is heathenism. A death-dealing breath of coldness, of destruction, proceeds from every loveless word and from every loveless act. Thereby a person dies. This mankind will increasingly come to experience.

Hence we also see that love, on one side, is God, but consequently on the other side, Golgotha. Where love is experienced, only as blessedness, there is certainly Lucifer, but not Christ.

At the end of the novel *The Man Who Was Thursday: A Nightmare*, which G.K. Chesterton [1874-1936] wrote against bad detective novels, the protagonist sees a mighty vision of a huge, superhuman face.

He revolts against it: why do you permit all the frightful wickedness that takes place on the Earth? Then the countenance grows yet greater, but over it lies an expression of immeasurable suffering. 'Can you drink the cup that I drink?' (Mark 10:38). When a person becomes more open to the world around him and is no longer shut up within himself, but has become receptive towards his fellow human beings and the world, then his sufferings through others increase immeasurably. This is a law which none can escape. This is connected, too, with an actual opening out of the 'astral body', so that indeed the fullness of life that streams into a person becomes significantly greater, but so also does the fullness of their sufferings. A ruffian can torment a helpless person without being moved to any expression of soul by their cries except laughter. A person whose soul has been 'opened' would feel the cries of the tormented person as if they came out of his own soul. One cannot experience love without being drawn into the tragedy of God. One suffers them along with the sorrows of others, and suffers, too, with the sorrow of God, because there is so little love. This alone is Christian love, and not the weak sentimentality to which people have distorted and debased Christian love. And there is only one means to protect oneself against the latter—namely to live ever more resolutely in the divine love itself. Only with access to the highest divine strength can anyone bear the full weight of Christian love. But for this Christ was given to humanity. For this He came down to us. Nietzsche knew this, and he often said that a person has to die if he loved human beings. And consequently he refused to love them. He did not know that there is a power by which one may yet remain in life, may remain in *joy*.

In writing such studies today one is enveloped and oppressed by the question: How does such a thing exist in the face of the hard and burning need of the age? Is not something quite different necessary? Who would have time for this or need of it, or a sense of it? And yet the whole organization of the Earth, the whole evolution of the Earth becomes comprehensible only when one speaks of love. A visible, material world, such as our earthly world, had to come into existence so that there might be beings who had passed through the experience of being entirely released from the immediate union with the divine. If this world had never been, then in the spiritual realm there would have only been beings who perceived only so much of the divine as was compatible with their being united to the divine in their innermost being. Consequently, there had to come into existence in this visible, material world, a human body such that the being who lived in it had the possibility of being shut away from others, of coming to them from outside, and even of living in its own house, as it were, facing the divine world. Consequently, in this human body, too, which was entirely shut off, an 'I' had to mature and evolve, so that what we call freedom might grow within it, and that finally, out of this freedom, love might freely arise. Looking at all this in the context of the history of the Earth, we have before us a sublime, sovereignly divine undertaking. Every citizen of the Earth ought to be joyfully aware of their dignity, because in their 'I' each can bring forth real love out of freedom, and so help a high cosmic thought to come into actual being. Who can say what worlds must have preceded this one, so that one day this cosmic plan might be realized!

A person can be led to the divine thought for which they were created only by the divine hand, by the divine Son Himself, Who entered the Earth's evolving for this end, and took His part on Earth, sharing its bitterest sufferings and death. And at every moment when love is enkindled out of the human 'I', in the sphere of freedom, all the heavens share in the joy of a sublime divine revelation. People ought to know this. And all their needs upon the Earth ought to be perceived and overcome in this consciousness, and with this knowledge in their hearts.

The divine thought of mankind lies before us when we speak of the 'I' that unfolds love in freedom. And this thought is so mighty and so unequivocally convincing that even Friedrich Nietzsche, the greatest opponent that Christianity has ever had, could not evade it. He wished to find a cosmic thought that was higher than love. But he could only put 'love for what is farthest away' in opposition to the Christian love of one's neighbour.[78] But if 'the person that is farthest away', the man of the future, is the man to whom I can do the most good, then s/he that is farthest away *is* my neighbour. This contradiction has not produced a surpassing of Christian thought, but only a highly spiritual explanation of it. Consequently, the evangelist, who has most spiritually seen the revelation of life in Christ, found afterwards in his letters the great words that sum up his own life, words in which humanity itself has found its greatest answer to Christ, has most joyfully acknowledged Christ:

> No man has ever seen God; if we love one another, God abides in us and his love is perfected in us. By this we know that we abide in him

and he in us, because he has given us of his own Spirit. And we have seen and testify that the Father has sent his Son as the Saviour of the world. Whoever confesses that Jesus is the Son of God, God abides in him, and he in God. So we know and believe the love God has for us. God is love, and he who abides in love abides in God, and God abides in him [I John 4:12-16].

See what love the Father has given us, that we should be called children of God; and such we really are [I John 3:1].

Letter No. 10

A World-Historical Conversation

Moving on from our general survey of John's Gospel, we now consider a single passage in its context. By doing so, we enter into the gospel in a new way. We choose the beginning of the Farewell Discourses. Words of farewell, similar in form, play a special part in world literature. The best of all farewell words are those of Socrates with his disciples, as Plato has preserved them, and Buddha's parting words to his disciples. If we study side by side the accounts of these farewells an elevated mood enters souls. What is humanly noble in Socrates's words and what is spiritually sublime in the words of Buddha are combined in a higher harmony and irradiated with golden light in the words of Christ that have been preserved by the evangelist.

No one need feel compelled to believe that these words were spoken exactly as they are given in the gospel. Who, though, in his spirit and soul can have better retained the way Christ spoke—the evangelist John or we? We come nearer to the truth if we imagine the evangelist has most faithfully preserved in his soul and spirit what was said, that all the important words were essentially spoken in this way, and that the connections and order of the parts give a true picture of what then occurred. But in those hours Christ said much more. Neither the fullness nor the glory of what was then spoken could find sufficient room in the soul of even such an evangelist. And yet the shining of the divine Sun through this soul is quite real, conveying what is essential and decisive. It was not only that human memories were then more pictorial and more faithful. Not only was their reverence for the revelation given to them more deeply and more undisturbed. Through the devotion of their souls, their capacity to reach to the inner word and to know directly out of the divine world what was in accordance with that world, and sprung from it, was much more living than we can imagine today. One cannot be grateful enough that at least *one* disciple has handed down this portrait of Christ as He is as taking his leave.

The sacred act of the Washing of the Feet is concluded. Christ had introduced it as an act of the Mysteries (13:1). It was indeed like a solemn Mystery-consecration of a quite new kind.[79] And the last struggle for Judas is also past, 'So, after receiving the morsel, he immediately went out; and it was night' (13:30).

No painter in the world can paint a more awe-inspiring picture than this. The door opens, and for a moment the black night is seen, into which Judas disappears—Judas whom Leonardo himself represented as being dark. And now, after the door is closed again, Christ says (13:31-35):

> 'Now is the Son of man glorified, and in him God is glorified; if God is glorified in him, God will also glorify him in himself, and glorify him at once. Little children, yet a little while I am with you. You will seek me; and as I said to the Jews so now I say to you, "Where I am going you cannot come". A new commandment I give to you, that you love one another; even as I have loved you, that you also love one another. By this all men will know that you are my disciples, if you have love for one another.'

In the previous *Letter* we said we have to take these words as actually a new giving of the law. They are as decisive, and still greater than the law-giving upon Mount Sinai. At this moment, all commandments and laws of the world went to their rest. Though it is very far from being understood, let alone fulfilled, yet in this hour a new order of the world began. The Jews preserved the tables of the law that were given upon Mount Sinai in the Ark of the Covenant within the holy of holies; the true disciple of Christ writes this command of Christ in his inmost soul, letting it shine forth there, and he stands often before it, beholding its light.

It is the foundation stone of a new world that is sunk into him. This foundation stone bears a golden inscription, written by Christ Himself. In truth, the disciple of Christ ought to feel as if he carried in his heart this golden gleaming inscription, written by Christ's own hand. And with the words 'as I', he is received into the ranks of a nobility. It can be felt in all its depths that now *humanity* really begins, now that people have no more law and no more compulsion imposed upon them from without. But each has a sacred law of his own, and this is no longer a law, but an '*I*' that feels and acts within him—a new 'I', the highest 'I', and the most beloved. Where people feel this, and make it a reality—that they no longer need any sort of law and order, because love rules everything within and rules rightly—then a first ray of the coming kingdom of Christ falls upon the Earth.

At this moment, one of the highest moments in the world's history, Peter intervenes. He is the first of *four disciples* who now in succession interrupt Christ's words. And again it seems as if, before our eyes, a deeply ashamed confession is made, when we are openly told what the disciples had to say at such moments. It is as if the Evangelist John wished to say, 'Yes, we actually behaved in this way! We cannot deny it! And we cannot but confess it, so that our confession may be of use to you.'

(1) Peter's question

'Lord, where are you going?' (13:36). What has taken place in Peter? Has he heard anything at all of what Christ has been saying? He is like a child, who has somehow understood from what his mother has been saying, that she intends to go away, and now in a fear he does not understand, can think no other thought than that.

One might expect Christ to rebuff Peter, who was so little able to enter into the highest thoughts that were so supremely important for Christ. But here, as in all the succeeding passages, we scarcely notice how stupidly and awkwardly the disciples intervene, because Christ receives their words with such sublime calmness; with such purity and goodness raises them to the heights, making them the occasion of new revelation. How *we* lack presence of mind and soul when we are asked clumsy questions!

'Where I am going you cannot follow me now; but you shall follow afterwards' (31:36). With complete freedom Christ passes from the sayings about love, to speak about the other world. But at first He gives Peter no answer to his question; instead He answers the distress in Peter's soul, which lies beneath his question. And He holds Peter back, as He may have held him back countless times: 'You cannot follow me now.' Yet at the same time He comforts him, 'Later'.

There is no word, however, that Peter can bear to hear less than the word 'later'. He had shown this at the Washing of the Feet, when Christ said, 'What I am doing you do not know now, but afterward you will understand' (13:7). Here again Peter shows his comparative impatience, 'Lord, why cannot I follow you now? I will lay down my life for you.' Then with a deeply earnest gesture, Christ raises His hand, 'Will you lay down your life for me? Truly, truly, I say to you, the cock will not crow, till you have denied me three times' (13:37, 38).

How did Christ know this? We do not speak in the old dogmatic way of an abstract 'omniscience'. But the pictures of what was to come stood clearly before His soul, in so far as He was obliged to know them in order to find His way through the difficult hours that lay before Him. Such things are not so rare. It was as if the divine angels were gathered lovingly around Him, ready to reveal to Him all that might lighten His heavy way. We know today that important events that are predestined, are already there, that they hover around people, and that when people have the capacity to read them, then they do so. An experience I once had made clear to me how such things happen. On the day when I had a serous fall in the mountains, I told my companions before the fall, indeed, even before the decision to set out upon the expedition, story after story of such falls, so that it seemed to them to be quite uncanny when they remembered it later. How did this come about? The picture of what was to come was about me, but was unclear; I was not fully conscious of it. And yet it was in such a way that it stirred my fancy continuously out of my unconscious. Many people have had similar experiences.

But why did Christ say this to Peter? Or why had He not told him this *before*? Christ was trying to do what the cock would later do, to awaken Peter! If there had been anything that could have awakened Peter, it would have been this appeal to his warm heart. Now or never Christ could once more come to the help of His first disciple. Destiny should not be thought of as a dark power that, indeed, takes its stern course, but even at the last moment it may take a different one.

It is also striking that the cock is so often in fairy tales the picture of the awakening of the 'I', and that it is Peter who will soon say, 'I am *not*!' Is this chance?

The mixture of goodwill and incomprehension, of a devoted heart and blinded eyes, in which Peter lived, could not be treated with more love or with greater wisdom.

Rome

But now, behind Peter, we see a whole great history of Christendom. What is here revealed to Peter has also been the character of Roman Christianity in all the centuries of its history. It was not by chance that Peter went to Rome. Three points strike us in particular. Roman Christianity has interested itself more in the place whither Christ *goes* than in Christ Himself. It has been a *Christianity of the other world*. People were told how to get to heaven. It has looked at the world after death. And consequently it has had no loving eyes for this Earth—although it has well known how to rule over it.

But a second characteristic has been this: Roman Christianity has always been great in 'following Christ'. We would call attention here to an especially arresting trait in John's Gospel. In the passage we are considering, Christ says to Peter, 'You shall follow afterwards' (36), and at the end of the gospel Christ's last words to Peter are 'Follow me!' (21:22). It is as if the great Pastor of souls had not forgotten this one vow of Peter, and now when the hour for it has come, He takes it up again and brings it to fulfilment. Nothing more welcome could happen to a man of Peter's character. And so it was in the Roman Church that the book, *The Imitation of Christ* [by Thomas à Kempis] was written, and not only with the pen.

The third point, in which Peter and the Roman Church are dangerously alike, is the unaware part of the 'I'. When the words were spoken: 'Here I stand, I can do no other' [Martin Luther], the time of the Roman Church was really past. The 'I', the fully-awakened 'I', hovers still *above* the Roman Church and is honoured in the Pope, who is a substitute 'I' for the faithful for the purposes of knowledge and conscience. At the very end of the gospel, as it takes its leave, Peter still says, '*You* know that I love you'—but *still* Christ gives him the commission, 'Feed my sheep'. Because the fully-awakened 'I' was not yet come, there was always the danger of betrayal, which is always present where great feeling and great words do not yet come out of an 'I' that is continuously aware and certain of itself. Peter denied Christ to the soldiers: the Roman Church has done this, too, on a great scale. Much readiness to give one's life, and yet the danger of betrayal—those have always existed side by side in the Roman Church.

During these words of farewell one seems always to see the scene when Christ's gaze rests upon His disciples. The saying that spoke of Peter's denial must have been reflected in the dismayed faces of the disciples. Christ says to them:

> 'Let not your hearts be troubled; believe in God, believe also in me. In my Father's house are many rooms; if it were not so, would I have told you that I go to prepare a place for you? And when I go and prepare a place for you, I will come again and will take you to myself, that where I am you may be also' [14:1-3].

The word used here for 'be troubled' is the same word that played a great part in the Greek world [*ataraxia*], 'freedom from passion' or 'calmness', which was the Stoic ideal. Many tales were told by the Greeks of celebrated men who remained calm and steadfast in severe danger, and even maintained this attitude while they perished.

> Should the whole frame of Nature round him break,
> In ruin and confusion hurled,

> He, unconcerned, would hear the mighty crack,
> And stand secure amidst a falling world.

In these words of Horace,[80] we have the characteristic courage of the Stoic. Even if Christ Himself did not use the word, but spoke Aramaic, yet a new picture of calmness was introduced into the Greek world of ideals. In those days the saying of Archimedes was well known: 'Give me the place to stand, and I shall move the Earth.'[81] The Stoics sought this point outside the world in the individual 'I'. Christ points to it in the *higher* 'I'. If you no longer have faith in anything but God, if you trust in my 'I' and in nothing else, then there can come no trouble that can overthrow you, but on the contrary you can even 'move the world'. Christ starts from the momentary trouble. But what He gives is a help, is *the* help against all and every trouble that may come to us. If in the moment of a great trouble, or of a smaller daily trouble, we throw, as it were, our whole weight upon God, then we cannot be moved. We are standing upon firm ground, and can say, 'Here I stand. I can do everything, even move the Earth itself'.

Christ now leads the disciples from their momentary emotion over what He said to Peter, and brings them to the great trouble towards which they are all going. And at the same time He does answer Peter's question about the other world. But He answers otherwise than Peter wished; He answers both more and less than that. The impression is gained that every time Christ is touched, a source of revelation is opened up. He must have been so filled with divine revelation that only a slight touch was needed for a stream of revelation to pour over human beings. Christ tells Peter three truths about the other world. These three truths contain complete fullness of comfort. I *am there*. I *am working* there for you. I shall *fetch you* and *take you thither*. One need only let these three truths pass sometimes in spirit through one's soul, and one will learn what fullness of consecration is contained within them. And one need only consider what ideas of the other world existed in the Christianity of later times and especially in Roman Christianity, and one will feel how little Christianity is in it, how little of the spirit of Christ, with its purity and light. Think of the pictures of the Last Judgement that were painted in the Middle Ages, down to the *Last Judgement* of Michelangelo. Think even of Dante's *Divine Comedy*. And then reflect how heaven would have been represented in painting and poetry if such a saying of Christ had been completely understood. Here a marvellous 'I am' is spread abroad over the whole heavens.

'Where I am, you may be also' (14:3). This is like a musical motif, which will sound from now on throughout these words of farewell until it reaches its heights at last, where Christ stands before His Father upon the mount of prayer. 'Father, I desire that they also, whom Thou hast given me, may be with me where I am, to behold my glory which Thou hast given me in Thy love for me before the foundation of the world' (17:24). This is the will of Christ, the promise of Christ, which burns itself into the souls of all those who really listen to Christ's words. And no single thing that we may hear about the other world, either now or in the future, ought to sound louder in our hearts than this heaven of the music of the spheres filling our souls at such a promise. It is as if Christ were not troubled by Peter's question, but even rejoiced that he might enter this heaven for a moment. There can be no answer more divine that that which changes a most human question into the most divine revelation. Always, when we let the manner work upon us in which Christ lived among men and entered their questions, we have a picture before us. We see that, when someone touches Him, a star, as it were, rises from Him, and all these stars are formed into a starry vault of heaven. And this starry heaven *is the gospel; it really is He Himself.*

How are the words intended to be fulfilled, 'I will come again and will take you to myself' (14:3)? Does it mean only the disciples there present? Or all disciples? Ourselves included? These words, we believe, cannot be taken too literally or too sublimely. Many people in dying have told us that in the hour of their death their room has been filled with departed spirits who have come to share in the festival of their departure. They are not to be imagined as phantoms, or that they appear in external space. But it is an actual fact. And the higher someone evolves towards Christ, the greater will be the glory of Christ Himself that He comes to him in the hour of death. It need not always or exclusively be Christ Himself Who comes to fetch him. Christ has His servants. But in them is Christ Himself, as near as He alone can be. And at the close of Earth's history we really have to picture a great coming of Christ, to fetch all those to Himself, 'who by their bearing He can wrest from the death of matter' [the Creed of The Christian Community].

Just as sublime as this prospect is the other truth, that His activity in the other world has always to do with His disciples. Everything is directed to one end—to prepare a place for them. Every time a person who has died passes over to the other world, the other world is changed. It is not a fixed place that awaits people, but itself consists of the spirits who inhabit it. But through Christ the greatest transubstantiation is accomplished.

Out of what Christ says here, a light falls upon all those who have died. With guiding, gentle kindness, Christ points the way by adding, 'And you know the way where I am going' (14:4).

In Christ's words lay an additional, clear answer to Peter's question, 'Lord, where are you going?' (13:36). It is as if Christ replied, But you know that, Peter! But He gives this correction in the most gentle manner possible, and not at once, but after He has given him every chance of finding his own answer. But this, too, is not understood.

(2) Thomas and India

Peter, indeed, says no more. But another disciple, Thomas, breaks in, 'Lord, we do not know where you are going; how can we know the way?' (14:5). In *Letter* 8 we tried to feel how nobly Christ's words broke forth: 'I myself am the way, and the truth, and the life' (14:6). Here we would add that this saying is directed to another point of the compass than that directed to Peter, namely towards India. Again we hear the voice of a simple disciple, and through it speaks again the history of the world. It is, of course, not meant that a conscious conversation of this kind is taking place. But in Thomas we see standing before Christ a man who, according to the legends, later became the Apostle of India. Thomas is indeed deeply related in his soul to India. If one of the disciples had had to be chosen to be the Apostle of India, then according to the description of the characters of John's Gospel, the choice must have fallen upon Thomas.

Thomas is by nature brooding and melancholy, and deeply connected by destiny with death. We remember how before the raising of Lazarus he says, 'Let us also go, that we may die with him' (11:16). *Death* was the great experience in India. Its iron inevitability was always present there to a brooding, melancholy mind. On the other hand, the Indian strove with all his might to *see*. It was not the intimation of the heart, but spiritual perception to which his mind was directed. It was vision that he strove after in his Yoga-exercises. How intimately this type of spirit is related to Thomas, the disciple, who wished to see the Risen One alive before him (20:25). And the words he uses in the passage we are studying are again intimately Indian in their nature. *Where is the way?* For thousands of years the Indian sages and saints had been asking this question as they sought the path of release.

'Then the most venerable Brahmin went out of his home into homelessness, to find the path of release'—we find these words countless times in the Indian texts. And Buddha also taught the 'noble Eightfold Path'. Just as we have had before the threefold spiritual nature of the Roman, so now we have the spiritual nature of the Indian presented to us in three essential traits. And to these three traits the threefold saying of Christ now replies:

- 'I am the Way', He says to those who through thousands of years have sought the Path.
- 'I am the Truth', He says to those who wish to *see*, and whom He will lead in Thomas to a new kind of seeing.
- 'I am the Life', He says to those who feel they are fast bound in the Mystery of death.

Might one not have found in this threefold saying of Christ a sublime indication of the 'mission' of India? Just as out of Christ's preceding words, the Catholic Church might have taken a hint for its further development. It is not important to bring to the Indians the Protestant theology of the sixteenth century when it has become unsuited to the present age. But it is important to connect one's teaching with the Indian character and bring the Indian directly to Christ. And one would have had the most illuminating, guiding words in this saying of Christ. Again we cannot marvel enough at the depths that lie in the gospels—or at the things of the future that within them are waiting upon people's understanding and readiness of will. For since this saying of Christ was spoken, no future mission to the Indians ought to be possible that passes over these words of Christ, or which does not *proceed out of* these words of Christ. Such missions would have done more, and would yet do more than the missions that Gandhi expressly rejects for the new, independent India. But Gandhi also is seeking the Way, like Sadhu Sundhar Singh [1889-1929, a remarkable Christian missionary],[82] and Rabindranath Tagore [1861-1941]. The ancient Indian longing still exists in these men, and is still unreleased.

To what does and did the Indian seek the way? The answer to the question is unequivocal. He is seeking the way back to the lost Paradise. He is seeking either the Tree of Knowledge in his striving after knowledge, or the Tree of Life in his exercises. These two kinds of striving can be distinguished quite clearly in the history of India. Recall that in *Letter 8* we said expressly that it is the way to Paradise that Christ leads, that Christ *is*, and that in the two sayings that follow, the two Trees stand before us—the Tree of *Knowledge*, 'I am the truth', and the Tree of *Life*, 'I am the life'. What Christ has to tell us is that in His '*I*' all this *is*. Receive my 'I' into yourself, and in a quite inner and spiritual way you have therein the way back to the Tree of Knowledge and the Tree of Life! Up to now, Indian wisdom wished to extinguish the 'I'. But with all His might Christ confronts the Indian nature and the Indian longing with His own 'I AM'. 'I am the way, and the truth, and the life.'

Christ adds yet another weighty sentence, 'No one comes to the Father but by me'. There is no more world-embracing proof of the truth of this sentence than precisely—India. Where has God been sought with more resolution, more readiness for sacrifice, more spirituality, than in India? India has been the great land of the seekers. And what did they find? Unity, sublimity, immeasurability, the All—but the 'Father'? The truth of this saying of Christ has often been doubted. But can anyone name in the whole of the world's history a single person who has come to the 'Father' without Christ? For this reason the Indian seeking, and in it the most mighty seeking of the soul of humanity in general, ended in Nirvana. 'If you had known me, you would have known my Father also; henceforth you know him and have seen him' (14:7). When we understand them rightly, these words are much more alive than as they have been translated by Luther. Once again we stand marvelling before the miracle that such words have come from a human mouth. What a marvellous mood must exist in such a spirit that can speak thus of itself, not in foolish, sentimental overestimation, but with such pure clarity! But perhaps the best of all protections against overestimating oneself is to think one's way with reverence into such a saying. What Christ is in the earthly world is just the example for all human existence. Man ought to be just such a picture of God for others to see! How far this is from being so, meditation on such a saying shows us. But as we meditate we receive formative forces, 'are being changed into his likeness from one degree of glory to another' (2 Cor. 3:18).

(3) Philip and the Geeks

The word 'see' calls upon the scene the *Greeks*. Philip raises his voice. Wherever he is named in John's Gospel there is always something about seeing. First of all, at the beginning where he speaks to Nathanael: 'Come and see!' (1:46). Then again when the Greeks directly approach him on the Feast-day [the second Passover]: 'Sir, we wish to see Jesus.'

And then here, even 6:5, where Christ turns Himself towards Philip it happens that a multitude comes to Him after He had 'seen'. With the word 'going' there appears the Indian; with the word 'seeing' the Greek. It was the greatest thing for the Greeks, who had developed divine service through the eye to its height, that here before Christ they could step forwards. But the greatest of all for such seeing at that point was that they could not find themselves. Consequently, it is really the moment of the fulfilment of world-history for the Greeks that we are allowed to witness here. 'He who has seen me has seen the Father!' (14:9), Christ says in the third cardinal point of the way. But once again, it is indeed not only the historical Greek people but all who become spiritually related to Him. The fulfilment of everything that such people seek according to their natural disposition is there in Christ.

Equally, however, such people must enhance their need for seeing to a higher beholding. The sentence which precedes Christ's confession shows again how deeply and securely He rests in His self-consciousness. No evangelist could invent or imitate how, to the ignorant request of Phillip, 'Lord, show us the Father, and we shall be satisfied' (14:8) there breaks forth in mighty radiance, 'Have I been with you so long, and yet you do nor know me, Philip?' Further, this 'knowing' was veritably the Greek longing and the Greek talent, yet it is *here* that the Greek beholding and the Greek knowing finds its highest end. In Philip's 'we shall be satisfied' there gently resounds 'then are we fed' (cf. 6:6). And whenever a Greek spirit comes to Christ he has in these words the fullness of soul-nourishment for all time.

It is especially striking that the whole of Christ's speech that now follows, for which Philip had given the initial impulse, was to be heard at one time by Greek ears (14:9-21). We are all the more called upon with regard to the 'motif' of seeing, if one may so call it, in that it repeatedly resonates in the words towards the end of the speech. 'Yet a little while, and the world will see me no more, but you will see me; because I live, you will live also' (19). 'He who loves me will be loved by my Father, and I will love him and manifest myself to him' (21). The speech closes with these words, which we can feel as addressed to the Greeks. And, thinking upon the words, 'I will *manifest* myself to him'—Gk. *emphanizein*—who will not think of 'theophany', the appearances of the gods, which plays such a role in Greek literature? Here we also see what new eyes are to be bestowed upon the Greeks. Through the whole of the conversation the word 'love' is used ever more clearly. To the Greek *eros*, 'love' another and higher love, *agape*, is contrasted; for it is historically true to say of the Greeks that a second characteristic of theirs is the search for the true love. Here the Greek love also receives its highest goal—Christ. But it is worth noticing, Christ immediately guards this love against that which is merely aesthetic, giving it its fundamentally moral character. He does so expressly twice: 'If you love me, you will keep my commandments' (14:15). 'He who has my commandments and keeps them, he it is that loves me' (21). In this connection, the greatest fulfilment of all love is revealed: 'he that loves me shall be loved of my Father, and I will love him' (21). Here, with deep reverence, we perceive the Greek world being led upwards to its loftiest heights. This is pastoral cure of souls on the highest possible level. Those that seek for love have never heard anything greater, said in all simplicity.

From here one looks back to Plato and to all that he has said about love. One first sees how the peak, upon which one is now standing, towers high above what formerly seemed to be so high. A holy trinity of love is here revealed to our eyes. We stand upon the highest mount of worship that human beings can climb. Who cannot now hear the first gentle intimations of that which sounds forth in super-earthly sounds at the end of the High-Priestly Prayer, the Great Intercession, 'I in the Father and the Father in me, and I in you'? Indeed, these words appear here too, quite expressly, and in the divine threefold chord, which is so much loved by the Evangelist John, or rather, in which he lives, 'Believe me that I am in the Father and the Father in me' (11). 'In that day you will know that I am in my Father, and you in me, and I in you' (20). From the standpoint of *love*, the Greek looks forth in vision into the secret of the Holy Trinity. Would that the Greek spirit, which later formulated the dogma of the Trinity, had remained on this height! Here it is not a dialectical definition, but a love that sees, a seeing love, which Christ pointed out to the Greek spirit. Let a person immerse himself as deeply as possible into a true Greek soul, like that of Plato, and from there it let him look up to the Temple that here is built in shimmering light upon the height, and he will feel no contradiction to the Greek spirit, but rather its purest and highest achievement.

The Greek was indeed an 'I'-person. Greece fell through the individualism of its peoples and its personalities. 'I in the Father and the Father in me.' 'You in me and I in you'—in these words lie their redemption; and the redemption and transfiguration of individualism, all 'I'-manhood. All this is so free, so pure and bright that we have quite forgotten that we have come to it out of Judaism. Individualism and the quality of *eros* never reached such heights in Greek history that they could have failed to work destructively—each in its own way. Here, in these words of Christ, we see them reconciled. And yet not in any compromise, but in such a way that each finds at the same time a greater height than it had ever found in Greece. In this love there is no longer anything sickly, or anything of purely material enjoyment, or of mere aestheticism. Nor is there any longer self-will in this. Starting from the completely uncomprehending question of Philip, Christ, Who understood the inmost feelings of Philip's soul, had led us on to this fulfilment of the world's history. It is only a question of what spirit is speaking, and the simplest question, the most uncomprehending request, can become transparent, and through it we can see the highest history of the world.

In addition to these two characteristics of the Greek spirit, for a third we might think of the Greek gift of oratory, of the joy which the Greeks always had in *speech*. And strangely enough Christ now begins at once to speak about speaking. 'The words that I say to you, I do not speak on my own authority; but the Father who dwells in me does his works' (10). Are we wrong in saying that in this one saying of Christ there is healing for all the errors to which the Greek was led by his gift of speech? 'I do not speak on my own authority'—that is the one magic saying by which speaking can be healed. Wait until something higher speaks in us. Allow this really to speak through us. Let nothing speak, but what is higher than us. In this way the word becomes the organ of revelation. By this it is gifted with incredible strength. By this it is able to do magical deeds. Wherever the work has become small, or false, it was because the lower, or the ruined 'I' has laid hold of it, or still has it in its power. In their later history, from the time of the Sophists onwards, the Greeks brought the word into disrepute. Here the word is restored to them in its sacredness.

We have now already entered into the second consecration of the word. 'My Father ... does his works.' In *Letter 2* we have already studied this saying of Christ in another connection. Here we see the word as weapon and tool, hallowed because it is the *first* new instrument of creation that is given by the World-Father into the hand of man. No greater tool can at present be given to man. But this tool can be evolved, till it reveals a higher power to create. Man has not to play with the word but to *create* with it, being conscious of the majesty of the word's World-power. Here again, it was the Greek's love of playing with the word that was so disastrous for Greece.

In John's Gospel we shall often experience that world-history appears before us on a grand scale—spiritual world-history that did *not* occur in reality, but which might have taken place, which ought to be taking place *today*, and which shall certainly take place *one day*. How can it be that all this is simply there in John's Gospel? Certainly neither in the sense that Christ wished expressly to say all that we have described above, nor that He consequently intentionally spoke over the heads of the disciples to the peoples of the world about world-history. Much rather, that through those men who spoke to Christ, and through their peculiar characteristics, great connections of events in the history of the world passed intimately into Christ's soul. The souls of those who spoke to Him lay open to Him; thus could He read the whole course of the history of the world that must come from souls like these. In the soul of every true Indian, Greek or Roman there lies the whole history of his people—at least as far as these peoples shape their destiny out of their own spirit and nature. This is the secret.

A true pastor of souls, answering the simple questions of anyone, would still today answer quite unconsciously, in such a way that the other might ask, How do you know me? For where do you know my thoughts? From where do you know the dangers with which my soul is secretly struggling?

Thus here we have the Saviour of Greece, as we had previously the Saviour of India and the Saviour of Rome. But we ought not to press any such viewpoint one-sidedly. It is evident from all that has been considered as spoken towards the four points of the compass, we ourselves who do not belong directly to any can have much to think about. At certain points, though, what is said breaks quite clearly through what concerns the various nations, into a region embracing the whole of human life, in which we may no longer think of any individual people, but of *humanity in general*. It is just this which is so beautiful, giving us so great an example, that the inherited characteristic is so completely accepted as it is, and yet through it Christ presses on to human nature as such. Much could be said about the fact that it is always, today, too, and in all future times, a great day for humanity when differences are so delicately felt and completely accepted. Then, through and along with this, what is higher is found in community. This is not only an example of how the nations ought to live together, but also a model of how one character ought to hold dialogue with another.

In this conversation starting from Philip's request, three truths help us feel we are now emerging from the planetary world of the nations, into the world of the fixed stars, the world of universally human truths.

[i] Christ speaks of the *Spirit* He will send to the disciples. The Spirit 'whom the world neither sees nor knows' (17)—again a gentle echo of the Greek world—is here promised for the first time, at the moment when human beings, the Greeks first of all, wish to have God as near as possible before them. Later we shall discuss in their own context the passages in which Christ speaks of the Holy Spirit. Then

[ii] after Christ has led on from *'word'* to *'work'*, He proclaims the truth of the *greater works* which His disciples will do in His name. We shall have to discuss this saying as well in its context where we discuss Christ's works and the works He lays upon His disciples.

[iii] The third truth, shining as a star in the heaven of fixed stars, is the promise of *prayer in the name of Christ*. Those sayings, too, in which Christ speaks of this inmost connection with His disciples, we shall bring together, allowing them to work upon us in all their fullness. At first we only briefly glance on the *man of the Holy Spirit, who prays inwardly, and outwardly performs miracles. This is the human being as he lives in the soul of Christ*. And yet it is not accidental that the first picture of this superman flashes up here, where the Greek speaks, who loves and fosters a *humanity*. A person, filled full of the life of the Holy Spirit, constantly inwardly united with humanity to the living Christ, from Whom by prayer he derives his life, and outwardly working mighty deeds; a person in whom God Himself is lying hold of the world—this is the shadow here of the *superman*.

(4) Judas

Our glance now falls upon the fourth man, taking his turn to speak. It is Judas. His name betrays him as here the representative of the Jewish world. He is expressly distinguished from the other Judas, 'not Iscariot' (14:22). When Christ appeared, Judaism was split into two portions, the part that went with the disciples and with Paul, and the part that went with Caiaphas and the Pharisees. As we proceed, we have to bear in mind the contrast between these two kinds of Jews, and of Judases. In the word of Christ Himself there is a division. 'If a man loves me'—'if a man love me not'. These are the two Judases.

But the saying of Christ, after which the representative of Judaism enters the conversation, is very distinctive, 'I will manifest myself to him' (21). It sounded not only in the ear of the Greek. Much more did all that made up the Jew await with passionate earnestness the 'manifestation' of the Messiah. That Christ would not reveal Himself to *all* the world in His Messiahship, was the reason why Judas Iscariot became so impatient, and why he wished to compel Christ to reveal Himself. The other Judas at least *asks*, 'Lord, how is it that you will manifest yourself to us and not unto the world?' (22). That the appearance of the Messiah was inward and not outward, that it had to do only with those who were receptive and was not to astonish the whole world, was the twofold stumbling-block over which the Jewish spirit, both then and now must find its way. Wherever the outward appearing of Christ is looked for today, there we still find the Jewish spirit in the midst of Christianity. It is particularly in America—among the 'earnest Bible students' and similar sects, that one finds this spirit.

Looking more closely at the words Christ speaks to Judas, we notice in them how fully, even apart from this one saying, the redemption of Judaism is to be found. What was especially sacred to the Jews, was the word of the Old Testament. 'Moses has said' was used to beat down all resistance. 'The word of the Lord came to me' was the proclamation of the prophets to the people. 'The word which you hear is not mine but the Father's who sent me' (14:24). This saying of Christ's is for all, but in particular for the Jews who, unlike the Greeks, would not hear of the image of God, but who held entirely to the word of God, and not to human speech, like the Greeks, but to the *word of God*.

'If a man love me, he will keep my word, and my Father will love him, and we will come to him and make our home with him' (23). Here we reach one of the leading sayings of John's Gospel. It is also worthy of thorough study—the word 'word'. 'My word', that is the Word, the 'I am'. This Word, which Christ Himself *is*, as living, divine Spirit-Word—this Word should be borne within us human beings. Then in this Word the Father Himself comes to us. When this comes home more clearly to our consciousness than is possible in the usual translations, if we read, 'the Word that I am', then we have a new and sublime approach to John's Gospel. Christ indeed never said directly in John's Gospel, 'I am the Word', but that lies in the expression 'my word' that comes so often. And in the Revelation of John, too, it is said quite expressly, 'I am the Alpha and the Omega' (Rev. 1:8; 21:6; 22:13), for that includes the whole alphabet; it is *the Word* in which all the letters are contained. Is it not remarkable how Christ here speaks of the Word, bringing into the Word the great decision that separates the two Judases from one another in the Word; how He Himself, as the 'Word' of decision that He is, addresses in Judas the Jewish people? Also the phrase 'make our home with him', which is here emphasized more than it is anywhere else, speaks to hidden feelings that were especially active in the Jewish people. For among them stood the *Temple*. This Temple will be destroyed. But here a new Temple is being built. The creative word enters into man. Love prepares for it the inner warmth, in which it can grow and create. Thus it creates the new Temple, which is God's true abode. Along with Christ the Word, there enters Christ the 'I', and in him the Father Who dwells in Him. In this small space we have, consequently, side by side, a new prophecy—the 'word'—and a new priesthood—the 'home, abode', the Temple. *The Jew is redeemed.*

Again, we are surprised at the fine distinction between the way in which the Holy Spirit is spoken of to the Jews, and the quite different way in which it was previously spoken of to the Greeks. Christ spoke to the Greeks of knowing this Spirit, of receiving this Spirit, of seeing the Spirit. He says to the Jews that this Spirit 'shall teach you all things, and bring to your remembrance all that I have said to you' (26). It is as if He said, 'It is also the fulfilment of the synagogue'. There sat the teacher of the Jewish people. There the members of the Jewish race were reminded of all that Moses and the prophets had spoken. This synagogue, Christ is saying here, you will bear within yourselves in future, and the teacher will be the Holy Spirit. Is this all chance? Is it all an imagination of the evangelist? We hold it by far most probable that Christ knew right into their inmost feelings, what sort of men He had before Him, and that the evangelist has retained a true impression of this trait of Christ's character.

And now Christ raises Himself again above the particular people standing before Him, into the general case of humanity. It is true that the saying about peace is still applicable to the soul of the Jew. There in the East, people have wished each other peace, as often as they have greeted one another. When Christ takes His leave He gives a great greeting of peace, but one that *leaves behind* to the other that which another had only *wished* for him. 'Peace I leave with you, my peace—the peace which I am—I give to you: not as the world gives do I give to you' (27). The millions of wishes of peace that people have exchanged for thousands of years have been unreal words. But He, Christ Himself, is the living, actual, effective greeting of peace. That is what these sublime words are really saying. Again they are divided into three parts. And through them there shines the primal, living fact of the threefold Godhead.

- 'Peace I leave with you': we are in the world of being, of the Father.
- 'The peace which is in me, I give to you': we are in the world of Christ, in the world of the Son.
- 'Not as the world gives give I to you': peace seeks to be realized in its special nature: we are in the world of knowledge, of the Spirit. In a holy rhythm the angelic worlds pass before us. Never has the thousand-year-old greeting been spoken with such full significance, with such character, with such intense spiritual reality.

Concluding words

The words that Christ speaks to His disciples in the following verses are like angels that spread their wings over us. He really is leaving His peace behind Him on the Earth. 'Let not your hearts be troubled, neither let them be afraid. You heard me say to you, "I go away, and I will come to you". If you loved me you would have rejoiced, because I go to the Father; for the Father is greater than I' (14:27, 28). It is quite marvellous how the joy of Christ, which lives within Him, breaks forth here, as He thinks of the nearness of the Father. And it is just as marvellous, how it is only expressed, because He thereby hopes to help the disciples. And again it is marvellous to see in what a restrained and gentle way all this takes place. Such words, simple as they may sound, are real miracles of the soul. For the sake of one such saying, our deepest love might be bound to Christ. 'And now I have told you before it takes place, so that when it does take place, you may believe' (29). 'The Father is greater than I'—this saying alone calls for a new theology in which it is possible to think of the Father as greater than Christ, and Christ yet of the same nature as the Father. The mathematical dogmatics of logical dialectic cannot attain this fact. This we must bear in our consciousness—that Christ is entirely of like nature with the Father, and yet the Father is 'greater'. How gently does Christ now call the attention of His disciples once more to the importance of every word which He is now speaking to them when He says, 'I will no longer talk much with you'. And with what majestic calm and greatness does He let them share with Him as friends. 'The ruler of this world is coming. He has no power over me; but I do as the Father has commanded me, so that the world may know that I love the Father. Rise, let us go hence' (30, 31).

Again we have to thank Rudolf Steiner for the knowledge that this last saying, which has caused much difficulty to commentators because no one knows how to conceive a 'going hence' at this point.[83] It refers to that which is inner and spiritual. A new inner sphere, or level, has been reached. The former sphere of the conversation, in which Christ answers the requests and questionings of the disciples, and deals with the different types of human being in world history, is now left. From now onwards, Christ speaks *entirely out of Himself*. He tells the parable of the vine, which is the true vine.

We too shall follow Him into this sphere. But let us review once more. The four peoples to whom Christ has spoken as to the four quarters of heaven, are also what are called the four human temperaments. One may learn an immense amount about how to deal with human beings by looking back once more over the conversation from this viewpoint.

- Peter was *choleric*. Christ calms him. But he also awakens him. For he is in danger of being overcome by his temperament, in the realm of the feelings. Christ gives its due to Peter's power of will, 'You will follow me.' But He raises him into an awareness of the 'I', into clarity of spirit.
- Then the *melancholic* man appears in Thomas. Christ meets him with an announcement that is full of meaning. He bestows on him an illuminated soul-life, which is full of joy and significance, 'I am the way, and the truth, and the life'.
- In Philip, who is so easily 'satisfied', we see the typical *sanguine* person. He is set to work inwardly, strongly and richly, but in such a way that he sees all possible things shine out far above him, which he does not yet possess, and for which he is called to exert all his strength.
- Last comes the *phlegmatic* person, Judas. But in him we feel that power that the phlegmatic man often contains deep within himself. He receives a mighty arousing; he is brought face to face with most serious decisions.

From this viewpoint, too, such a chapter is rich, endlessly rich. We feel ever and again what wisdom and kindness, both human and divine, lies hidden in such a World-conversation.

Letter No. 11

The Springtime of the Disciples

A special radiance lies over the narrative of John, Chapter 1. We experience, as it were, a kind of higher springtime. The special position in history of the first Christians enabled them to receive Christ as out of humanity's winter hopes. They rejoiced in the coming of a new spring of mankind. They repeatedly looked back to those first days; all the glory of its sunshine is gathered together and shines through the narration. Simple as they are, that is what makes these descriptions so arresting.

We feel the same again in the final two chapters of John's Gospel. The spring glory that lies over them has a stronger radiance, and is filled, as it were, with joy of soul. Having once perceived this glory that like a gold background behind landscapes fills the background of these stories one can conceive of nothing higher than to gaze for ever into this light, which is part nature, part spirit; which is nature that has become spirit. This is the 'glory' of which John's Gospel is always speaking. 'Father, I desire that they also, whom Thou hast given me, may be with me where I am, to behold my glory which Thou hast given me in Thy love for me before the foundation of the world' (17:24).

In these *Letters*, when we came to speak of love, as it lives in individual nations, we were obliged to say of the Teutonic people that the innermost notes of joy sound forth when they speak of Balder. Balder is the god of the spring. But not only of the spring as we experience it today. The Teutons sought a nature that blossomed in the spring, a nature illumined and permeated by the spirit. This appears, too, at the height of German history, in Goethe. With what elemental forces did the German spirit in him seek for the spirituality that rules in nature! This is the case from Walther von der Vogelweide down to the Classical and Romantic poets, and even to poets today. Its much-boasted inwardness is mirrored in the revelation of nature, or rather the inwardness in man finds the inwardness in nature and chimes with it in religious accord. In this way German people experience their God. Consequently, his religious fulfilment is not a Christianity that is far from nature, but a Christianity in which the divine countenance shines forth out of nature. Such a Christianity is only dawning. But for this reason the Germans ought to have a special sense of the Balder light of fulfilment that lies over the first and the last chapters of John's

Gospel, even if in them nothing at all is said about nature and everything blossoms in a spiritual spring.

Yet all such introductory thoughts are not great enough to act as a frame for the mighty events that we are about to witness. They can at most tune the harp so that the spiritual song may sound forth from it.

Chapter 1

What happens falls again clearly into three parts:

- First we see the witness of John the Baptist concerning himself, then
- the witness of the Baptist concerning Christ, and then
- the experience of the first disciples when they meet Christ.

John the Baptist

What is called the Prologue that comes first has been discussed in the little book, *Das johanneische Zeitalter*, 1925 ['The Johannine Age', Chapter 3: *'Von der werdenden Welt'*. Eng. tr. see p. 16ff. above], and we may discuss it here later. In the Prologue, John the Baptist was the only person who towered up into the spheres that lie above our world. 'There was a man sent from God, whose name was John' (1:6). The word 'man' awakens in us the question whether it doesn't have some special meaning in such an important position. Is something meant to be said about the *human being* himself? And in fact, what follows is a description of the human being himself, as he ought to regard himself: 'sent from God', 'His name is "grace of God".' (Cf. Luke 1:63.) It might almost be said that in these two sentences the Old and the New Testament, the pre-Christian and the post-Christian period are characterized in their innermost nature. Sent here upon the Earth by God and accompanied by divine blessings, thus man was led through the first part of earthly development. The glory of the divine gift slowly faded. But when he who had been sent by God had become increasingly the Prodigal Son, then he received the blessing of Christ—grace. And now there came to life within him what he had earlier received from above. Man's true name was proclaimed—'the grace of God'. So that God's grace may shine forth brightly, man was created and sent to the Earth. So John is really *the* human being as such. For this reason he has the right to appear in the cosmic heights.

It is not only the peculiar distinction of John that he is a 'witness to the light', but it is also the World-task of humanity itself. Man can wish for himself nothing higher or more beautiful than to be a witness of the light upon the Earth.

From 1 John and elsewhere out of John's Gospel, one can hear that the writer had before him in the spirit such people who valued John the Baptist so highly that they played him off against Christ Himself. The experience of many people, in meeting John the Baptist, must have been so powerful that it filled their minds and hearts entirely and left no room for them to receive Christ. On his journeys, Paul, too, met disciples of John who knew nothing of Christ or of Pentecost (Acts 19:1-7). One may easily suppose that the writer of John's Gospel had himself originally belonged to those groups and that he always wished to make clear to his former friends that John himself expressly pointed to Christ, and that consequently they were being unfaithful to their master John when they glorified him at Christ's expense.

John's witness to Christ

In this Chapter 1, John appears significantly three times as a 'witness' for Christ.

- This is first emphasized in verses 7 and 8. 'He came for testimony, to bear witness to the light, that all might believe through him. He was not the light, but came to bear witness to the light.'
- Then once more within the sublime, super-human Prologue: 'John bore witness to him, and cried, "This was he of whom I said, 'He who comes after me ranks before me, for He was before me'".' (1:15.)
- And then comes the third statement of the witnessing work that now reaches its fulfilment in the concrete reality of history.
- The first saying (1:6 & 7) shows John, as it were, in his metaphysical nature.
- The second (1:15) shows him in his place in the history of the world.
- The third shows him in living, historical fulfilment.

And, that John might be shown most strongly in his character of a witness, this third account is itself divided into three parts.

- The Baptist speaks about Christ to the Pharisees (1:19-28).
- Then he speaks about Christ, without naming individuals, to the whole congregation of his hearers (1:29-34).
- And then he speaks once more about Christ to his own nearest disciples (1:36-37).

With special emphasis, John the Baptist, of whom certainly there must have been much that is interesting and valuable to be told, is given only this significance, that he was a witness to Christ. In this posture, as pointing to Christ, Christianity has portrayed him in many hundreds of pictures.

But is not all this of purely historical importance? If so, we should entirely misunderstand John's Gospel. We recall how John is first before us—'a man'. In this concrete, historical account it is made clear in what way a person must be qualified if he is to know Christ—to what sort of man Christ can reveal Himself. Here is no dogmatic talk about repentance that must precede faith, but we are shown a man who has such a knowledge of himself as is necessary for a true understanding of Christ. John does not speak of his sins, but he grasps what is more essentially human and more profound: 'I am the voice of one crying in the wilderness, "Make straight the way of the Lord", as the prophet Isaiah said.' (1:23.)

In the language of the Israelites, which lived in their prophets, we have here the exact characteristics of the man who is the suitable vessel for Christ. And this man is portrayed from his inmost depths, from his '*I*'. This 'I' feels it is 'unspeakably lonely', deserted and lost in the world. Do we know this feeling—to be without Christ? The feeling of fear in the world; the feeling that we belong somewhere quite other than to the world as we experience it; the feeling of the king's son who has gone astray? Buddha's preaching is but another expression of this experience. Buddha said, 'Thou, O man, dost not belong to this world with thine inmost being'. But he could not say, 'Make straight in the desert a highway for our God!' (Is. 40:3). He could only say, 'Seek for the way out of the desert—walk the noble Eightfold Path'. From John the human 'I' like an empty Grail cup is raised to the heights. All human longing becomes a 'cry in the wilderness'. And when we place besides this that other picture that immediately succeeds it, 'I saw the Spirit descend as a dove from heaven, and it remained on him' (1:32), then in this second picture we see the *full* cup of the Grail. The empty cup of the Grail raised up—the cup of the Grail filled from above, that is the right beginning of the 'gospel of the I-AM'.

The 'I' becomes conscious of its loneliness, which really means its godlessness. It allows this lack of God to grow into a mighty longing, a knocking at the gates of heaven, and it becomes a 'cry in the wilderness'. Thus, in itself, it is only a voice. It is no longer concerned for what it is out of itself. But this 'voice' is predestined, as it were, for the 'word', whose bearer it ought to become. From such a viewpoint, this introduction, this confession, is exactly right for the gospel in which the *Logos*, the cosmic Word proclaims itself.

Throughout his gospel, this is also felt by the other John [the Evangelist], who here speaks to us of John the Baptist. He is a 'voice' for his word, and consequently never names himself. Only he is not a voice out of the 'loneliness', but a voice out of the 'fullness'. 'From his *fullness* have we all received, grace upon grace' (1:16). Thus he clearly says, before he speaks of John the Baptist. And his message would not be, 'Prepare the way of the Lord', but expressed in the spirit of his gospel, 'Make a dwelling-place, a home within, for the Lord'.

With John the Baptist, the confession of what he is is preceded by the confession of what he is *not*. 'I am not!' Thus, very significantly, begins the gospel of the 'I am'. If we read this story of the 'I am not', then comparisons spontaneously arise with the people of our own time. Why are so many people unable to realize a great man? Because they *themselves* wish to be somebody. A joke is told of someone who was asked whether he was a Kant*ian* or an Hegel*ian*. He replied, 'I myself am an *ian*!'

In the days of John the Baptist, a Leader of men appeared as a Prototype of what two thousand years later first became a reality for a large number of human beings. When people are asked today to realize they are sinners so that they may receive Christ as their [personal] Redeemer, we can really say that we are pushing them back into the spirit of a past age. We are grateful to anthroposophy for the knowledge that our age of the consciousness-soul was preceded by the age of the mind-soul. The latter lived more in great objective cultural contexts. It was right then to take the individual more in the way he behaves in these connections, even with respect to the divine law. From this time comes the awareness of sin, suggested by preachers, with the remoteness, as regards their actions, of individuals from the divine law. But the age of the 'consciousness-soul' succeeded, with an emphasis on the individual 'I' in its freedom and personal characteristics. To this there corresponds another need of redemption, because a changed feeling of selfhood has appeared. It is less remoteness that is felt, than emptiness. Undeniably, remoteness is naturally still present, but the experience of selfhood becomes still more inward.

This feeling of a nameless loneliness in the contemporary world leads to many suicides. Religion has not understood how rightly to approach this nameless feeling of loneliness and lead it to redemption. It always seeks to win people in the old way, and that does not succeed. Moreover, if the word 'nameless' is the right word for this feeling of loneliness, this closely agrees with the fact that John the

Baptist speaks of himself as a voice of longing, without a name. This realization that human needs are now quite different from those of an earlier age seems to us to be of great significance, in relation to the lack of success with the usual religious preaching and the demand for a new understanding and preaching of Christ. It ought to take as its starting point our inner human emptiness, the hidden fear of life, the increasingly bitter loneliness in the world, not only among our fellow creatures and the longing for fulfilment. This is taught by John's Gospel, when rightly understood. And the prerequisite for success is that we should not imagine we are more than we really are; we should scorn all pretence.

We could imagine a deputation, of such importance as the one sent by the Priests and Levites from Jerusalem, coming today to one of our leaders and questioningly attributing to them titles, like those suggested to John. Are you Christ? Are you Elijah? Are you the prophet? Can we believe that many would have sufficient character to say 'No' as directly as John does? Would they not avoid replying in such a way as to disturb the halo that had formed round their personality? Imagining such a deputation—as we would rightly express it in today's drastic language—paying homage to the new Bismarck, to the new Goethe—would anyone reject it so clearly and roundly as here John rejects the title of Elijah in order to point simply to Christ? In this one trait, the whole greatness of John's character stands before us; we understand why Providence could put just this man, and only this man, in this place as Christ's forerunner. Then John's character becomes still clearer when we perceive how each time he is not merely satisfied with giving the answer expected of him. Immediately, he adds to it a powerful call to repent. To the questions, 'Who are you? What do you say of yourself?' he answers, 'I am the voice of one crying in the wilderness, "Make straight the way of the Lord", as the prophet Isaiah said' (1:23). And to that other aggressive question, evidently prepared beforehand to shake his authority with the people, 'Then why are you baptizing, if you are not the Christ, nor Elijah, nor the prophet?' John answers, 'I baptize with water; but among you stands one whom you do not know, even he who comes after me, the thong of whose sandal I am not worthy to untie' (1:25-27).

Entirely great people may characterize themselves with a single phrase. We might place side by side the pure humility of John, and the assured authority with which he nevertheless speaks to these powerful envoys. The clear insight and decisive courage of his elevated character, the impressive, pictorial eloquence of his words, and at the same time his resolution in approaching the essential—here we have a living picture of this last and mightiest of the prophets.

A few details of the story could be mentioned, all indeed significant. 'The thong of whose sandals I am not worthy to untie.' On entering a house the guest's sandals were removed by the humblest of the servants so that he might cleanse his feet, leaving his dusty sandals outside. A living picture! A Guest really is seeking to enter the 'house of earth'. Of course, it is quite different with Him. He comes with spotless feet and enters an unclean house. Such a thought seems to thrust aside the decisive point of the picture, and yet it only strengthens it. For it is his overpowering sense of the holiness of this Visitor that lies at the heart of John's words.

Can it not be said here, too, as with the Communion, 'It is he who feels he is unworthy who is worthy; and he who feels he is worthy is unworthy'? These important people, the Priest and Levites from Jerusalem, would certainly not have felt they were unworthy to loose the thongs of Christ's sandals. On the contrary, they would have arrogated to themselves the right to decide whether Christ was worthy to enter the house. And because of this, they are placed into the background. That a great and celebrated national character, who had the courage to speak the unadorned truth to these important people more deeply than the lowest slave—that is particularly impressive in this picture at the threshold of the gospel.

And we have to look at this picture in connection with that at the end of John's Gospel, where Christ Himself bows down to wash His disciples' feet (13:3-20). The greatest man before Christ feels he is unworthy to untie the thong of His sandals before the washing of feet. And Christ proclaims His own new dignity as King of human beings by washing their feet. The gospel is rich in such contrasting pictures.

'This took place in Bethany beyond the Jordan', as the correct text reads (1:28); this is not without significance. So the two Bethanys, this one and the Bethany where Lazarus was raised, approach each other from opposite sides, and this tells us much. Bethany means 'house of need'. That is the Earth itself. The Baptism by John and the raising of Lazarus meet one another like the baptism with water and the baptism with the Holy Spirit. The first takes place 'beyond Jordan', at the entrance to the Promised Land. The other is 'near to Jerusalem' in the centre of the Holy Land. Already here John's 'preparing the way of the Lord', and the initiation of Lazarus-John appear in significant contrast—and yet united by the name of Bethany.

In a religious document like John's Gospel, every expression is important. 'The next day' (35)—is it not as if we were told that the divine reward for the selflessness of John is not long in coming? John had still to undergo a thorough searching of 'the heart and soul' before he had the real vision of Christ. He stood the test. When we ourselves have overcome one of life's severe trials, we shall often find, if we give heed, that some divine answer follows in our life—some recognition, some blessing, some moral advance.

But we have to notice too that a night separated these two events. We are often reminded in anthroposophy that experiences over which a night has passed, reappear changed and further developed. We are still little inclined today to notice such 'metamorphoses' of our spiritual experiences. But profound revelations can often be traced to them. 'He saw Jesus coming towards him' (1:29). Is this not an external picture of what John afterwards proclaims, 'He must increase, but I must decrease' (3:30)? When to this is added that Jesus afterwards sees Nathanael coming to him (1:48), the whole of the world's history again appears before us.

- Man sees Christ coming towards him—that is the first half of the world's history, history down to Christ's appearance on the Earth.
- Christ sees man coming to Him—that is the second half of the world's history, history after the coming of Christ to the Earth.

This man is called Nathanael, which means 'God-given'. 'The men whom Thou gavest me' (17:6 and 24). But the man who sees Christ coming to him is called 'the grace of God'. Is all this not perfectly transparent?

Looking attentively at someone who is coming to us, we can perceive very much concerning them, their character and destiny. This, too, is confirmed by anthroposophy. Speaking personally, I remember very well that moment when Rudolf Steiner, standing at the top of the stairs, received me on my first visit. One could feel as though one were illumined through and through by this calmly observant gaze. A caricature of this is Mussolini's custom when he receiving visitors, of making them approach him through a large hall, and gazing at them with piercing eyes, making them quite uncertain of themselves.[84] But having once grasped that this 'seeing a man come' in John's Gospel is not without meaning, then we may ask ourselves whether this were not an effective form of meditating upon those who are near to us. We see them coming to us in the spirit, as if out of cosmic spaces, as if sent by God as a gift, and we take their whole nature lovingly into ourselves. In trying to do this, we shall soon realize that even within such details John's Gospel gives what can be of the greatest value for our lives.

When he sees Jesus coming towards him, John says, 'Behold the Lamb of God who takes away the sin of the world!' We take this saying much too dogmatically. We ought to feel it in a living way, as the impression that entered John's soul as he saw Jesus. To attain this, let us cast aside old traditions, and recall our experience that sometimes occurs when we are confronted by a young girl in the first flush of youth, who had led a very sheltered life. You young, unsuspecting maiden, how will you fare in the world! 'I feel as it I ought to lay my hand upon your head!'[85] Such an impression, but transposed into the sphere of the active and heroic, must have gone forth from Jesus. There is One who is quite pure! And equally, utterly resolute. When it comes to a struggle with the world, there can be no going back. The great tragedy will come; and from an external viewpoint complete destruction in this world. But through such a defeat mighty powers of victory will arise, just as at the Passover, the sacrifice was blessed by all the people. All the feelings working through centuries of the history of the Children of Israel, at the sight of the sacrifice of 'the lamb without blemish' were now awakened all at once. 'Behold!' We can hardly form any idea of such an overwhelming impression as the tragedy proceeding from an incontestably pure being endowed at the same time with the relentlessness of perfect strength.

John speaks of the sign that had been given him, 'He who sent me to baptize with water said to me, "He on whom you see the Spirit descend and remain, this is He who baptizes with the Holy Spirit"' (1:32-33). Here John allows us to look into his prayers. People who have received a divine task, sometimes, in their hours of solitude, receive signs through which they can realize important events in their coming life. Such signs may possibly dip right down into their consciousness, having been received in another state of consciousness, but they rise to the surface when the hour has come. John himself could hardly have had this vision or received this sign had he not himself had hours of spiritual receptiveness, only neither 'hovering over him' nor 'descending upon him' but rather lightly touching him, as it were, with a breath. A breath of what we are to receive must be already in us, otherwise we cannot have it at all. Consequently, the hours of our profoundest intimations, prayers and longings are not unimportant, but in fact the most important in our life as preparations for that which is to come.

It is remarkable that here in the Greek text all the words for 'seeing' are used in turn: to see, to perceive, and to behold by intuition [v. 29 *blepei, ide*, v. 32 *tetheamai*], as if in this way full emphasis were to be laid upon its reality.

Yet I believe that in the present state of consciousness the dove does not rightly represent the form in which the Holy Spirit appears. Fundamentally, it is less a question of the outer shape than of something gentle and swift, of something quivering and hovering, wondrously white and shimmering. This above all was what the seer saw, if not externally but 'Imaginatively'. And consequently those theologians were on the right track who called attention to the fact that it was a *descending* like a dove, and not the *form* of the dove that was the actual point of the comparison in the original text. We picture this to ourselves as an Imagination of the Baptist's, of something transcendentally bright and luminous out of all the worlds and far spaces, suddenly, as it were, drawing itself together and vanishing into Him. But he who beheld this knew that this was no abstract light, but a being, a spiritual being.

We cannot directly understand how the gospel here too indeed speaks emphatically of Him Who comes after and yet was before. We can perhaps get some faint intimation of this when we hear of the immeasurable numbers given us in astronomy, and thereby feel the greatness of the universe. The Jews were a people who felt things in time, whereas the Greek felt them more in space. Thus the Greeks were more prepared for the body of Christ, and the Jews more for the blood. In the sacred Psalms of the Jews, it is said, 'Before the mountains were brought forth, or ever Thou hadst formed the Earth and the world, even from everlasting to everlasting, Thou art God' (Ps. 90:2). In another way, more with imagination than with thought, the Indians experienced the aeons. But as in the old spiritual schools the greatness of a being was known by its age—'Reveal the light of thine age!'[86]—so John experiences in that which surrounds him in time something spiritually towering above him, and at the same time sheltering him within. He experiences something of the 'from everlasting to everlasting'. If I go back into the past, Thou art there! If I go into the future, behold, Thou art there also.

What we are further told is externally as simple as possible, but on small occurrences hangs the weight of eternity. On the previous day John had seen Jesus coming to him; now he perceives Him as He *walks* on the Earth. Truly, the life of the Baptist here falls into two parts. Firstly he sees Jesus come but then he watches Him as He walks. This is also stated by the other evangelists, when they describe how in prison John hears of the works of Christ. Humble and resolute, John immediately brings to fulfilment his saying that Jesus is greater than he, at the very point which touches him most closely—he gives Him his disciples. In a delicately tactful way that does not infringe the freedom of the others, by putting them *themselves* to the test—a procedure in which we see the results of a training in the Mysteries—he does this, by pointing again to Christ: 'Behold the Lamb of God!' (36).

The first disciples

A delicate attitude of soul is here expressed in that the disciples do not immediately follow Christ when first directed to Him. By this they show once more their confidence in their former teacher. But when he points to Christ a second time, it is no longer possible for them, through their very confidence in him, to do anything but understand him and obey his instructions. It is, if a trivial comparison were permitted to make things clear, as if a person more important than myself were to invite me to go before him into his room. I hesitate the first time; but if he repeats his invitation, it would be uncivil to refuse him. 'The two disciples heard him' (37)—they heard him indeed and followed Jesus.

All that follows unfolds like the solemn symbolism of a ritual. Calmly, the disciples follow Jesus and thus indicate to Him what they are seeking, but wait until He addresses them. For the first time their action symbolizes what afterwards filled their whole life. They follow Christ. Jesus turns round and 'saw' them, as they follow. This 'seeing' means with spiritual vision, but the unwritten spiritual ritual, as it might be called, now demands an express declaration from the disciples. Jesus, Himself, must introduce this with a question, 'What do you seek?', not '*Whom* do you seek?' 'They said to him, "Rabbi (which means Teacher), where are you staying?"' (38).

We have first to learn the significant spiritual language spoken here. It is far above our customary forms of speech; but there is no doubt, intercourse among human beings will in future times become again more illumined by the spirit. For this we are preparing ourselves when we give heed to the more delicate traits of such a story. The confession of the two disciples to Christ appears first of all in their form of address: 'Master'. John would not have laid such emphasis on the word had he not wished to stress it. Not everyone is called 'Rabbi'. It was in itself a request to become His pupils. A present-day experience may again be allowed. As a student, we had amongst us a budding scholar, now a well-known Professor of Protestant Theology. At that time he was studying the writings of the famous philosopher Eduard von Hartmann. He paid the latter a personal visit, introducing himself with these words: I have been occupying myself very considerably with your works, and should like to complete my studies with a personal impression. Thereupon he was promptly invited to coffee.

How much more refined and spiritual are the customs of these men of old. We breathe once more the training of centuries in the early spiritual schools—the Mystery centres. 'Master, where are you staying?' In this lay more than the asking for His address. Expressed in our language it means, 'We have realized in you a master from whom we wish to learn, but what we want from you cannot be obtained in an interview. We must ask your permission to be near you personally.' This was demanded by the early form of teaching given by a Master, in which the disciples were always with him. But in the question, Where are you staying? also lies the significant question: Where is your spiritual home? They did not only wish to hear his 'doctrine', but know 'from where he comes', where his home is in the *spiritual* sense. The same word for 'to dwell' [*menō*] is used here immediately above where it is said of the Spirit that it 'was abiding over Him', and is repeatedly used in Christ's parting words when He speaks of their 'abiding in Him', 'abiding in love', and says that His word will 'abide in them'. This is often the question that arises in our soul when listening to a man of religious significance. From what plane does he really speak? From what heights do his words come down to us? What is his inner state, that he can speak in this way? These questions lead one much farther than the mere question of his doctrine or opinions.

The two disciples put their question so that Jesus can answer in a number of ways without making them feel ashamed, and without being obliged to feel that He has shamed them. This also partakes of the delicacy of the spiritual intercourse of former times. Jesus receives them. He signifies His acceptance by a gesture and makes use of a formula customary in such circumstances: 'Come and you will see.' He opens His house to them—and also His inmost house, as they well understand. But He opens it to them in freedom. They have *themselves* to feel convinced. Already over this whole tender scene hovers that saying which they will hear later, 'He who sees me, sees the Father', and the Word which the evangelist has already said at the beginning, 'No one has ever seen God; the only Son, who is in the bosom of the Father, he has made him known' (1:18).

How chaste, spiritually, is the following sentence, 'They came and saw where he was staying; and they stayed with him that day, for it was about the tenth hour' (39). What does this reference to the tenth hour mean? Is it only a recollection, to indicate the importance of this day to them, so that every detail may be recalled to mind when speaking of only this one external matter? Is it only, as has also been suggested, a literary trick, intended to awaken this recollection? We shall only regain an understanding of such indications in religious documents, when we can clearly distinguish the various characteristics of the different hours of the day. Human experiences will then become far richer. We will know for what activities the various hours of the day are specially suited. To a certain extent, we shall be working in harmony with the favourable hour. Naturally, it was an advance in human history when, out of their own volition, people began to make themselves independent of the hours, for example, not simply to fall asleep at sunset, but continue to be awake, to struggle on and work. But it is a further advance when they can now return of their own free-will to the hours and so receive their blessing. Nietzsche, who anticipated so much, says in one place that he who at the first moment of the day seizes his newspaper is a barbarian.[87] For he does not know that at this time he is nearest to his good angel, and in a flash can receive revelations that later in the day would mean hours of toil. Just this first morning-hour is the genial hour; during the rest of the day we can scarcely catch up with its blessing.

What is the meaning of 'the tenth hour', four o'clock in the afternoon? It can be experienced as the hour of fulfilment. Previously the Sun was shining in the zenith until about three o'clock. Then it begins to decline. At the ninth hour (three o'clock) Christ died. But now the reflection comes down upon the Earth. The Sun's joy and blessing has been bestowed upon the fields; they, as it were, now ruminate on what has been. It is the time of fulfilment. It is different again when twilight approaches and 'the day is far spent'. This was the hour when Christ took leave of His disciples. They 'saw where he was staying, where he dwelt'. 'We beheld His glory.' 'Father, I desire that they also, whom Thou hast given me, may be with me where I am, to behold my glory which Thou hast given me in Thy love for me before the foundation of the world.' The bells all chime together over this hour. All surmises about the future, as so often at a first meeting, are now floating like soft melodies in the air.

Andrew and Simon-Peter

Now the first name is given, Andrew. But this name is not mentioned in order to emphasize his importance, but because Andrew is the brother of Peter. Peter was *not* one of the very first disciples. This is not said in order to place him into the background. But, here again, a law we frequently meet is fulfilled. 'The first adherents prove nothing against a doctrine,' Nietzsche claimed.[88] The great disciples come to light only gradually. We recall to mind Paul, a contemporary, but who at that time was still far from Christ.

Over the conclusion of this chapter lies the radiance of the word 'find'. Andrew first 'finds' his brother Simon. Did he seek him out? 'He says to him, "We have found Messiah", which, being interpreted, is the Christ.' Was he searching? Were they searching? The word *heurekamen* is the same as *eureka*, 'I have found'—the word used by the great mathematician [Archimedes] when he had solved his problem. But how differently does this 'we have *found*' stand, not only in this story, but in all the history of Israel. *'Found'*—all the prophets had waited for this.

Simon stands for the first time before his Master. And Christ here, with full authority, exercises a right belonging to a 'Master'—the giving of a name. Today, we have no idea of what the giving of a name should be, and at one time was: a result of a deep listening to a person's being—as a name was once bestowed in Paradise. The right thing would be to give a name at birth or in baptism, as one, as it were, hears their being in higher worlds. And consequently, too, Rudolf Steiner, despite his ceaseless activities, did not allow himself to be prevented from giving names to those children whose parents came asking him for the name. But to our knowledge he gave the name only on the following day. The intervening night is of significance. So, too, in the Bible, names of important leaders of humanity were announced to the parents in nocturnal visions by the angels. This is like the last remnant of that giving of names, which in past times was customary and felt to be right. In complete contrast to this is the contemporary mother who said she would have no objection if her children would choose new names to replace the ones she had chosen and which they did not like. Consequently, she wrote names on pieces of paper and what they then picked out became their name.

Like a premonition of a future age, the sentence in the baptismal rite of The Christian Community, with the giving of the name, speaks of awareness of the powers of light in the spiritual worlds penetrated by the power of the Christ-Community. Out of such a spiritual attitude the right name-giving may return some day. An echo of earlier times survived when the early Christians at their baptism received new names. But that name which Saul-Paul gave himself already shows that the old way of name-giving is over. He calls himself, more as a thought, the 'little one', the least amongst the Apostles. But Christ gave Simon son of Jonas his true name, as afterwards he gave Nathanael his, even if in that case no longer with the consequence that it would be outwardly used. In Simon's case, is the additional name 'son of Jonas' really only the name of his father? Or is it a Mystery-name indicating that Simon has previously passed through a form of Jonah-initiation—'within the whale', meaning in the interior of the Earth? We are reduced to surmises, as long as we have no better understanding of these early times. But it is certain that the name Christ gave Peter in no way characterized him as he initially appears in the gospel narrative—here he is easily swayed, is indecisive—but still the Peter as he can and ought to become, and after the story of Pentecost did become. This giving of the name, consequently, touched his deeper nature and thereby helped it to come to birth. How often is a person in our immediate circle helped when, ignoring his present stage of development, we invariably appeal to his maturer 'I' that we may have glimpsed in some special hour! Jesus did this, not by outwardly moralizing, but *every* time He addressed him as 'Peter' [= 'rock'].

From the gospels we know what tender consideration Christ always showed towards His forerunner. This first result of two disciples of John coming to Him will have been the cause of Christ journeying to Galilee (1:44). He was not of the opinion that John was there merely to bring disciples to Him. But He knew a greater circle of human beings would be achieved if the two worked separately. Such a considerate co-operation is rarely seen between great workers. It seems like an answer to the selflessness of John, who delegated his disciples to Christ. And again, it is like an answer from God, that only upon this path of consideration Christ immediately met two new disciples.

Philip

The first is Philip. In *Letter* 10 we met him as a Greek, a man of sanguine temperament. His sanguine nature is shown here in the vivacity and directness with which he immediately goes to summon Nathanael. But particularly for people of this kind, it is good for them to be given in a direct and simple way a great task to which they have to apply their whole will. Christ does this simply by saying: 'Follow me!' The hasty enthusiasm of the other man, of sanguine temperament, had for the time being been dampened by Christ when, to the youth who had said 'I will follow wherever you go', He had replied, 'Foxes have holes, and birds of the air have nests; but the Son of man has nowhere to lay his head' (Luke 9:57f.). The right way of treating sanguine people in particular varies very greatly, not only from person to person but even with the same person on different occasions. Furthermore, when in Luke 9, the different temperaments approach Christ, first the sanguine man, then the melancholic man who would first bury his father, then the phlegmatic man who would first say farewell—the choleric man appeared directly before in the disciples who wished to call down fire from heaven (Luke 9:54)—one may ask, whether in John 1 the complete circle of men who gathered around Christ is not indicated by these different types. And indeed, if Philip is the sanguine one, then Peter is again the choleric; in Nathanael we can see the melancholic, and the more phlegmatic type in Andrew, scarcely mentioned, but who in the fewest possible words informs Peter. Such a study is not without value. Completeness—fulfilment—is not only expressed in the fact that twelve disciples are gathered, as a picture of the twelve tribes of Israel and of the twelve cosmic forces that encircle the heavens, but also in the other fact that all the different types of human beings are included.

Once more the word 'find' appears. Jesus 'finds' Philip. Here, where it comes from Christ's own mouth, we feel for the first time its full significance. We might perhaps instead have said, Jesus met Philip. But when any great work is to be done in the world, the hidden leaders of destiny provide those that are ready to accomplish it. It is only a case of 'finding' them. With joy we experienced this at the beginning of the movement, The Christian Community. The people who were to accomplish this work had actually been sent into the world. And today, too, the question is not, How shall we obtain successors? but far rather, How shall we *find* the people who are waiting for us, who are ready for us? The whole progress of The Christian Community is a matter of seeking and finding. This is true not only of the priests but also of the members of the Community. It is not a case of enlisting people but of finding them.

That with this, what are called 'karmic complexes' play a part is shown by the very example of Philip (1:44). He came from Bethsaida, the town of Andrew and Peter. This may have led him the same way as the others. This one town, compared to the many towns of Israel, brings Christ a number of disciples. So, too, in The Christian Community, we find that often out of some unknown little provincial spot whole groups of people find their way to The Christian Community.

These stories in John 1 are a beautiful example of the way Christianity generally spread during the first centuries—from person to person—and how it will again spread today. Great advertisements are not of much use, but the meeting of person with person is. In this, guidance plays a part. We need only keep our eyes open and we shall 'find'. Philip 'finds' Nathanael and says to him, 'We have found!' After only one day in the new Christian community, he already brings another person to it.

Nathanael

In *Letter 4* we discussed the story of Nathanael. We pointed out that a new understanding is possible today for all these details: 'fig-tree', 'an Israelite indeed', 'to see under the fig-tree'. We also pointed out that Nathanael acknowledges the 'Son of God', and Christ does not refuse this homage, but responds with the phrase 'Son of man'. We also pointed out the inner construction of the story, how Christ at the beginning of His ministry is greeted as the Son of God out of John's prophecy, and from the spirit of the Mysteries in Nathanael. True Judaism confesses Christ before false Judaism fights against Him.

From the more ethical side, Nathanael's attitude could also be symbolically described. For example, the way in which he clothes his quite comprehensible prejudice, 'Can anything good come out of Nazareth?' (1:46) as a question and not as a denial. Would that all prejudices today were worded like his! On the other side, Christ does not go into this prejudice with him and refute it, but sets against it a higher fact. Notice, too, the way in which Philip treats Nathanael: 'Come and see!' He certainly does not spare him from making the resolution to come. He who will not come to see, or open his own eyes, cannot be helped—not even today, when coming and seeing may consist, for example, in the earnest study of certain books. Or notice how we are shown by this account what inner conditions are necessary for a knowledge of Christ—how John shows his fitness to become a disciple of Christ by his humility, and Nathanael by his honesty. The whole account is full of intimate teaching, as has also be repeatedly shown in edifying, expository literature.

It remains for us to point once more to the new 'initiation', appearing here quite clearly in contrast to the old initiation 'under the fig-tree'. 'You will see heaven opened, and the angels of God ascending and descending upon the Son of man.' The 'fig-tree', 'the Son of man', these are placed facing one another. The old initiation worked with the fine etheric forces of earthly nature. The new initiation is based upon new forces of revelation. The old initiation is connected with nature, the new initiation with the human being. The old initiation is an isolated occurrence, which, of course, worked in throughout the whole of life. The new initiation is to keep heaven for ever open above human beings, and draw them into conscious co-operation with the angelic world.

This first chapter of John's Gospel is like the mighty prelude to a symphony. At the beginning it speaks of the Son *with* the Father. Then upon the Earth He is acknowledged to be the Son of God:

- by the exoteric religions,
- by the prophets, and then
- by esoteric religion, by those initiated. And that the third element may not be lacking, Christ gives His assent thereto, although not expressly in words.
- Prophecy, sent in John to meet Him, sees the divine Spirit above Him. It had always been dedicated to the Spirit.
- And the teaching of the Mysteries, which was sent to meet Him in Nathanael, sees the human being in Him, the Son of man. It had indeed always sought for the human being.
- But the heavens opened above both of these, and beneath this the further history of the gospel is completed.

Letter No. 12

The Great Intercession: The High-Priestly Prayer (I)

The final prayer of Christ, as preserved in John 17— the more one sinks oneself into it the more one wonders that such a glorious witness to life can be here amongst human beings. A new radiance is thrown over the whole of humanity simply because this prayer exists among them. And no less great must be our amazement that humanity has been so little aware of this great treasure in its midst for all these centuries. As regards this gospel according to John, people seem like children who rejoice in the sparkling of their glass beads, without dreaming of the value of the diamonds in their hands.

Upon hearing the young Mendelssohn play Bach fugues, Goethe declared that it seemed to him as if he had witnessed God at the creation of the world.[89] In John's Gospel one feels immersed in the realms of music. Floods upon floods of hidden melody well up repeatedly. Unfathomable depths break forth into music. We feel as if we were on the edge of an invisible ocean; symphonies rise and fall around us. Fain would one catch and hold these melodies in the human spirit, and one knows that then *music* would be born for the first time upon the Earth, indeed, *speech* would then be born. But we do not feel as if we were present at the creation of the world but at the perfecting of the world, at the fulfilment of the world's consecration, or as if at the creation of a world that is to come.

In John's Gospel one can actually speak of musical 'motifs', interweaving into one another. All these motifs—the sublime joy, the gravity of judgment, the bright peace, the consecrated love, the sublime glory—combine once more in the last Prayer, the Great Intercession, in higher and more solemn tones and interwoven harmonies which no speech of man can describe.

When we attempt to penetrate what we experience in this, we have to seek still higher comparisons. When Buddha was released from this Earth, the spirit of this being who had attained perfection moved up and down through all the kingdoms of the spirit. In such a soaring upwards and downwards, we are told, he took leave of earthly life, as it were, with mighty strokes of his wings. Still more solemn and radiant is the upward and downward soaring of Christ's spirit in this farewell prayer. Whole worlds pass before us. It seems as if the spirit of Christ had been released from earthly being and were disappearing into far heights, and at the next moment He is with His disciples and enfolds them in blessing in His holy pinions. His mighty love for the Father draws Him upwards into the glory that is His home. Then His love for His disciples draws Him down again to the work that He willed to do upon the Earth. Our spiritual eyes see Him in the gateway between two worlds. It seems as if He were calling into the world of glory, that is, seeking to draw Him into itself, 'Yes! I come'—as if He had heard a call from hence that He may now come. It seems as if the question were arising in His soul, 'Have I done everything, everything, for those who are remaining behind?' Then He calls forth another blessing from the depths of the divine Being and presses His seal once more upon their life.

And we draw open yet another curtain before this prayer when we perceive Christ as He turns to His Father. Even someone who does not know what has been communicated from spiritual research, will find it illuminating to learn that in a spiritual world the mutual intercourse of beings is quite different from what it is in the visible world. There spirits are not separated from each other by a boundary wall, as the body can be in the visible world. Neither has one access to a voice there that can be heard as we know it. There only exists a different, far higher way of intercourse; beings stream out one to another. A being makes itself known by the power of what lives within, and so summons the other being also to reveal itself. In our life after death, we shall all learn this manner of intercourse. But already upon this earth, our intercourse with spirits of the higher world, indeed even our intercourse with those who have died, can only be carried on in this way. It may initially be an unfamiliar exercise and difficult to achieve, yet it opens much deeper regions of understanding and communal life.

If anywhere on the Earth we are led lovingly to such spirit intercourse, it is in this last prayer of Christ. Indeed, in such an insight lies the key to a true understanding of this prayer. One will no longer remark, as may happen in the academic theology of today, that the prayer 'repeats itself', or is of a 'doctrinal' character. The Father sends His nature in radiance to the Son; the Son returns it in radiance to the Father. That which is spoken in words is only the reflection of these spiritual lightnings. One can think of no higher grace than can be received than to be allowed to overhear this spiritual conversation between Son and Father. It is a training for life in higher worlds. Here one is taught right praying. Here Christ's wish is fulfilled, at the passage, 'Father, I desire that they also, whom Thou hast given me, may be with me where I am, to behold my glory which Thou hast given me in Thy love for me before the foundation of the world' (17:24).

17: 1, divine glorify

'When Jesus had spoken these words, he lifted up his eyes to heaven and said ...' Never, as we hear confirmed in anthroposophy, has it only an external meaning when the Bible tells of the 'lifting up of eyes'. And so Rudolf Steiner[90] translates it: *'Er versetzte sich in die Geistesschau'*, 'He transposed Himself into spiritual vision.' One need not consequently also avoid representing the raising of the eyes in an external way. On the contrary. This very picture of Christ gazing up to heaven seems to have remained unforgettably impressed upon the soul of the evangelist. By placing it thus at the beginning, he wishes that it may remain before our eyes during the words of the prayer that follows. In this way, supported by the picture in our mind, it will make this prayer an immortal possession for us.

The whole folly of recent biblical exegesis is expressed in the fact that an academic 'exegetist', moreover, particularly a believer, expresses the opinion that the 'looking up to heaven' shows that the prayer was spoken in the open air.

But neither do we want to overlook the teaching that every right praying is a 'transposing oneself into spiritual vision'. If this is not known today, it is because most people when they raise their spiritual eyes to heaven only perceive a faint dulled radiance. It is usually only a dark feeling of the existence of a higher power, or a dull remembrance of religious experiences reaching them from above, when they begin to pray. Prayer would become very different if we knew how to direct our eyes towards a heaven that is not like a bright wall, but is a clear spiritual kingdom in which we can see the Father holding sway. Whether we direct our eyes towards what is without, or turn them inwards and raise them, it is always a *world* into which we gaze.

And the first chord to be heard to cross Christ's lips, when this world becomes perceptible to Him, is the word 'Father'. The fullness of the way in which this word 'Father' sounds in the mouth of Christ is still unfathomed. This is no self-deception, but a perception made of feeling in which the higher perceptions are awakening. All the subsidiary musical sounds will thereby come forth if one perceives the main sound. If we could speak the word 'Father' as Christ speaks it, as He does, for example, in the Lord's Prayer, we should have in this alone the whole of Christianity, the true life, indeed, the transfiguration of the world.

During our whole life and far beyond it, we could learn and ever further learn how the word 'Father' sounds from the mouth of Christ.

In the Great Intercession, too, Christ's address to His Father, without any epithet or word of praise, 'Father' sounds strongly over the world. An indescribable modesty of the inner, spiritual attitude is spread thereby over the whole prayer. The word is seldom repeated. This also reveals the modesty, but also the inner certainty. Christ does not need to keep on addressing the Father, for He is before Him as one faces another human being in conversation. Besides the original address, the word 'Father' is repeated only three times, and then only for a special reason.

- 'And now, Father, glorify Thou me' (5);
- 'as Thou, Father, art in me, and I in Thee' (21);
- 'Father, I desire that they also, whom Thou hast given me, may be with me' (24).

Christ always speaks with emphasis to the Father when He seeks to fill Himself anew with the Father's being. It can be noticed, too, that the address becomes more frequent towards the end of the prayer, where it becomes more urgent in its entreaty. Here the address even changes its form twice. When He speaks of keeping them from evil, God the Father is addressed as 'Holy Father', then 'Righteous Father' when the shadows of the Last Judgement fall upon the prayer. How extraordinarily natural and true it is to turn to a special divine characteristic at these moments. Can one really believe that there is anything arbitrary, or invented by the evangelist? It is just such passages that disprove such an opinion. Nowhere has a better example of true intercourse with the Father been given than here. How would Christian worship appear if the spirit of this prayer had really entered into it! In what a pure world of prayer would we breathe, if we ourselves were to follow Christ upon this path of the spirit!

Those with a living sense of what was mentioned above concerning the intercourse between spirits will feel the living truth of Christ's first saying, as He looks into the countenance of His Father. 'Father, the hour has come …' Let us try to follow in our soul what took place then. Here, upon the Earth, stands the Son. Above Him, as though spiritually overarching, is the Father. When the Son looks up to the Father, what is the first thing that comes into His consciousness? It is the difference between the worlds in which they are now living—the Son is now in time, the Father above all time. For the world in which the Father lives, time in the earthly sense is no more. That is why the old Church saying declares that the Father lives in 'eternity'.

When *we* feel the living Godhead near us in all its overwhelming force, our first thought is for our sins. A feeling of our unworthiness and defilement rises first in our souls. Christ stands in purity before the Father. Purity breathes through His very first words. But still, in consideration of His destiny, He might have begun otherwise. Somebody else might have begun by saying, 'My life draws near its end', or, 'My destiny is approaching its darkest hour'. Christ feels He is *in time*, separated from His Father, when He stands there in time, where the divine will itself flows through time—where the pulse of the divine will can be felt in time. 'The hour is come.'

This is the first reaction in Christ's soul, when He feels He is face to face with the Father. But the profoundest knowledge of life lies behind this. Our life is indeed much less than we assume it to be—a ceaseless streaming away of the hours that contain a like number of minutes. It is much more a woven fabric in which at important points the threads become intertwined and then take on new directions. The hours that lie between serve to prepare or to work out what is determined in these decisive hours. That a person's engagement to be married, or their choice of profession are such hours, life itself clearly shows. But there are decisive hours, scarcely less important, that are more concealed; they often pass by unrealized but are not without significance. If we do realize them, it is as if a bell sounded somewhere, as if angels were holding their breath, watching to see how we shall decide. Whether, for example, we shall pay a visit, or go to a lecture, or take a saying to heart, ask a question, venture on a certain action—upon such a decision that may seem perhaps quite immaterial, the whole of our subsequent life may depend, indeed, more than one life. Far beyond this one life, decisions may be met again to which we scarcely gave heed at the time. And after death we shall see how important such hours were. It would be a modest but very fruitful advance in life, if we could observe every hour and notice in it whether such decisions might be slumbering. For we might also make those hours, in which nothing essential seemed to happen, decisive hours for our life.

Thus it is with the hours of our destiny. Everyone possesses, so to speak, their own time-piece, according to which their life is regulated, and which they must find for themselves. But time conceals for us many more secrets. The men of past ages have sometimes felt the lapse of the hours of the day to be, as it were, the passing over of presiding genii. Every fairy-spirit had her special blessing to give and asks of human beings whether they will allow it to be given. The Greeks showed a delicate perception of time when they spoke of the 'Hours' [*Horae*]. This perception was still alive in the monasteries of the Middle Ages where the hours of prayer were observed. Human life will become much richer and greater when people learn to work with these beings, to allow their strength to be bestowed upon them. The coarsest approach to this is to be able to distinguish the character of the morning hour from that of the evening hour.

Certainly, as anthroposophy also teaches, it is a significant advance when people are not tied as slaves to the 'commandment of the hour', when man began to be able to remain awake at night to work and struggle on at night. 'Sun, stand still over Gibeon!' (Joshua 10:12). When someone comes again today to the 'Hours', he comes as a free person with awakened insight. And so he can now summon to strive together with him those who were once his stern mistresses. But they help willingly, shaping life into the cosmic context more grandly, richly and deeply.

The seasons of the year also wish to come forward and bestow their blessings. Indeed, it is one of the tasks of The Christian Community to revive out of the traditional 'Church Year', in which there still lives recollections of those earlier sensibilities, a new Christ-Earth Year. In this the events of the year unite with the events of Christ's life into a great Life of the Year. It is not just by chance that in these days the early God of the Year of the Atlanteans has been rediscovered through scientific research; the God who, through the seasons, was in turn called Al (in the spring), El, Il, Ol, Ul (at Christmas), and thus distinctly points to the 'Logos'.[91] Through the Seasonal Prayers (the 'Epistles') of the Act of Consecration of Man [the Eucharist of The Christian Community], we are educated into a new harmony with the seasons of the year. Nature and Christ, so often and so painfully dissociated, are again united. Of more importance than our narrow individual life, with its daily needs and its longing for spiritual comfort, is that communal life with our Earth, speaking always of the Christ. The more enlivened time becomes for us, the nearer we come to Christ, for He lives in the realms of becoming.

It is from such perceptions we now contemplate 'the hour' (17:1) of which mention was made above; we see that world-history really divides into two parts at this very moment. Luther [and similarly the AV/KJV] translates 'Father, the hour has come; glorify Thy Son, that

Thy Son also may glorify Thee!' The word *verklären*, 'glorify', is one in which the genius of the German language expresses a profound spirituality. Can one express in a simpler and yet more striking way what happens when the earthly becomes translucent through a 'glory' pouring from within outwards? For this reason it is so deplorable when such a word, through constant usage, becomes so worn out that it no longer arouses definite ideas. How are we to choose words that they may awaken in us feelings as words did formerly? We could say, for example, 'Father, let Thy Son be manifest in His divine glory, so that Thy Son can then also bring to light Thy hidden glory'. For clarity, one could for once translate these words. But even they would become outworn, if we worded the whole of John's Gospel in this way. It is not the fault of John's Gospel but the fault of human beings.

The whole first half of world-history serves the end that the Son of God be revealed within a human being. There will be a continual enriching and deepening of the knowledge that all religions, Mysteries and cults, and even all outer world-events were directed to the great historic fact of the appearance of Christ among mankind. Yet the great significance of this revelation is not what Christ did and suffered, but that Christ died and rose from the dead.

For the glorification of which Christ speaks, is not only that which happens after His death, so that in a way He passes over His death, but *is* just this very death and the ensuing resurrection. This work Christ cannot accomplish by Himself, but has to place it into the hands of the Father. Here we see into the very depths of that co-operation of the Father with the Son, which is the real background of world-history. Even the rough hands of the executioners serve as the tools of what had been fore-ordained between Father and Son. Of this co-operation between the Son and the Father, we have already heard at the grave of Lazarus (11:41).

In the present instance, the curtain over the heavenly conversation behind world-history is drawn back still more. We see Christ standing before us as He converses with the Father, speaking in ultimate and sublime purity about the frightful event that is to take place on the Earth. But what is to be carried out hereafter, be it so tragically painful, is here spoken of as radiant, divine realities. A work of revelation is to be contemplated, of whose real divine content people—who on Earth are so loud and busy with their own importance—have no conception at all, but which appears here in its strictly spiritual aspect. And the Son, of Himself, asks the Father to accomplish this deed that is so gruesome in its outer aspect; in full consciousness and unity of will He resigns Himself into the Father's hands. If any person seeks to breathe divine greatness, here he may find it within his grasp.

That the Father should reveal the Son is the necessary condition for the Son's subsequent revelation of the Father. Only by dying and rising again will Christ be able to accomplish His real work. But henceforth His only desire will be to let the glory of the Father shine through Himself into human beings. What Christ has done up till now was only in preparation for this. He was waiting to commence His own work. But then begins the second half of human history.

Thus the Son stands in regal equality beside the Father. Before our eyes, Father and Son are sharing between themselves the history of the world. The realm of the Father is completed in the deed which He accomplishes with His Son. Then He passes on the kingdom to the Son. And now the kingdom of the Son commences. Here the Son says to the Father how He is prepared to take on the work of the Father, leading it further in the same spirit. We view the transition of the world-event from the Father to the Son.

17:2, power to give

A view upwards and a view downwards: thus Christ presents Himself in these first words regarding His whole position in the world. 'Thou hast given Him creative power over everything that lives in the earthly body, in order that He gives life that does not pass away to all those which Thou has given to Him' (17:2). As with a mighty sweep of twofold wings, we see Christ hovering above the world. It is the consciousness of the Son into which we are looking—in which we are permitted to share.

It is still difficult for many people today to understand that in Christ self-consciousness was present, as it were, in three circles. All three have the same centre, but the one always embraces and towers above the others.

> [i] The inmost consciousness is the consciousness of the *earthly personality of Jesus Christ*. What is meant by this we see perhaps most clearly in the story of the struggle in Gethsemane. In order to learn how to distinguish the other two consciousnesses, anthroposophical knowledge comes to our help [supplying details of the traditional esoteric teaching] that above humanity nine kingdoms of higher, spiritual beings rise up ever higher above humanity.

> [ii] Far above the angels and archangels is *Christ, the spiritual Prince* of those kingdoms that govern our solar system. It is He who descended to our Earth, and with Him all the greatness that was possible in our worlds.
>
> [iii] But again, over Him governs the *Logos, God the Son,* forming with God the Father and God the Holy Spirit the primordial Godhead, just as in the human being thinking, the feelings and the will are united. This Logos, God the Son, shone into Christ, lived in Him and found its full revelation for our world in Christ. Christ, as it were, is the focus through which God the Son can shine in the full glory of revelation into the world of human beings.

Whoever hears such a truth for the first time, especially someone coming from earlier religious ideas, will easily find this as something mythological or Gnostic. They will feel that for them the living unity of the personality of Christ is thereby destroyed. In reality there lie in this knowledge, or recognition, the answers to many questions that the contemporary thinking person has to pose. How can the highest God of all the thousand worlds make precisely this poor Earth the place of revelation of His Son? Is it not naive earthly pride in the face of all the starry worlds just to think such a thing? How can indeed a God live on the Earth at all? How do humanity and divinity relate? One will see that these questions, which the contemporary person has to ask, destroy the old Christian view if new insights do not appear. Or rather, they have long since destroyed them, and only a small bunch of old stalwarts still defend themselves defying death behind a barricade.

In particular, a testimony to life as the High-Priestly Prayer is cannot be understood at all unless one has an inkling of these truths. But then, it belongs precisely to the most splendid things how Christ rises to the consciousness of the Son in these opening words and again in the ending words, how He then is living in the Christ-consciousness, and at some passage even inclines to approach the earthly consciousness of Jesus over which certainly all the heavens are open, for example, in the words, 'for their sake I consecrate myself' (19). It is a free hither and thither, or rather, it is like an expansion of consciousness and a drawing together again. Living observation frees us completely from the fear that the unity of the personality might be destroyed and something schematic, abstract and mystical be put in its place. What we experience is so clear and alive; it brings out so fully the riches of the real personality that, in reading the sayings of Christ, we very quickly accustom ourselves to these intuitions.

If we take a trivial example from life, it is as if a king's son were speaking, in the first place as man to man with a friend. Then, through the coming of a messenger, we are reminded of his status as Prince, then finally through the appearance of his father he is filled with the feeling that he is the son, in particular of this father, yet he is still always the same person who does not contradict himself in anything. When Christ looks upon humanity, then the Christ-consciousness—it is always a case of less or more—stands more in the foreground of His soul. When He looks upwards, the Christ-consciousness is enlarged to the Son-consciousness. The ascent and descent through these spheres is at the same time a part of the soaring upwards and downwards through the higher spheres, of which we spoke at the beginning.

Of course, one can simply look at the undivided personality present in full inner harmony. Whoever wishes may pass over these remarks. But an approach to them can be made easier by the following picture. In a dark cave, a person may have a mirror into which the Sun shines. What he has in this mirror, made of earthly matter—if the mirror is clear—is the actual Sun in its totality, with its powers of light and heat. Yet outside in the sky stands the great and mighty Sun, illuminating our entire planetary world. This Sun may be the friendly image of hidden primal light, which for other worlds shines quite differently and only for this world presents the visible form in the sky—presents it, however, quite legitimately and revealingly. All these three Suns are in fact one. The picture, nevertheless, is inadequate. For in an 'I' the unity, or rather the undivided situation, is still more complete. It is but like an expansion or contraction of the 'I'-consciousness. The Christ-consciousness is now more strongly and now less strongly irradiated by the Logos-consciousness. But it is just this, in the figure of the Christ Who, walking throughout the gospels, is the deepest attraction. If we had more understanding of the intimate things we are allowed to experience in their very heart and core, we would feel drawn into this revelation of Christ. Of almost every parable and deed of Christ, one can say which consciousness was most prominent in it. But the highest revelation of the consciousness of the *Son* is revealed to us in these words of John's Gospel.

'Thou hast given him power over all flesh.' The word '*flesh*', especially when it is heard in John's Gospel, has become *even more soul-less* for us, more weakened through the Fall of man, than it was for people of that time. The Evangelist John, as also the Apostle Paul, understood by it the bodily nature, as it became through the Fall of man. The bodily nature, consequently, is not only permeated by all kinds of sinful appetites, but it has also become more coarse and materially solid. If this is doubted, one may observe the difference between the blossoming tree in one's garden as it appears after having eaten a heavy meal, especially if accompanied by drinks that dull the mind, and its appearance after an hour spent in studying John's Gospel. In the latter case, the blossoming tree is, as it were, transparent, a messenger of the spirit, indeed, as if it were living and speaking of divine things. In the former case, it seems as if it had been extinguished, standing there stunted and dead. It may perhaps be said that it is the fault of the observer and not of the tree. But it is just the point that one realizes that *a tree is something quite different for a human being and for an angel.* If there were no coarse, materially organized being like human beings, there would be no coarse material tree. We can set aside the question whether the tree is material *only* to the sight now, or as Paul indicates in Romans 8, whether all nature did not sink into a coarser materiality with man and for man's sake. This touches upon deep universal Mysteries. But human individuals can experience how the tree in front of their house can be redeemed along with themselves, or at least begins to be redeemed, when they themselves become more spiritual. The old tree, so moribund, so coarse, begins to disappear; a new tree, as from Paradise, begins to blossom. And we can experience similar things with every flower.

Human beings, however, have become 'flesh' on the side of sensory life. Even the word 'body', according the Bible, is too good for the human being as he is today. And over all creation that has fallen into this sphere of sin-ravaged materiality Christ has received full 'power'. This word, too, was much more alive and spiritual for people of that period than it is for us today when every administrator of the law has 'power'. The creative, divine spirits, the 'powers', '*Gewalten*' as they are translated by Luther, are called *Exusiae*, the 'Spirits of the fullness of Power [of Will]'. Through them the work of creation was carried out. In the very words of Christ there sounds something of the forces and majesty of a new creation. Out of this world that has fallen into the depths of sin, Christ brings forth a new creation. That is His World-mission, His 'power'. He is able to bestow 'eternal life', the life of a higher sphere where the transitory nature of the sensory world is unknown. Things transitory and death itself are overcome in this 'eternal life'. Christ is there as a new creation of the world.

At the very beginning of this prayer, it is as if Christ is simply answering questions that come to life within Him at the sight of the Father.

- 'Where art Thou?' That is the first question that seems to come from the Father's being, Who is entirely one with the Son, and yet now lives in a different world. The answer is returned: 'I am here in time where Thy will is to be fulfilled.'
- 'What is this will?' comes the question. The answer: 'The work of divine revelation.'
- 'By what right dost Thou accomplish this?' 'By the right of the plenary power that is committed to me.'
- 'Why has this power been committed to Thee?' 'Because men have fallen into the sphere of sin, and must be raised again into the world that is above sin and death.'

We are to think of this conversation as being of a supremely intimate and delicate nature; as a raying out from being to being. In the nature of the being lie the questions, and out of that nature come the answers. There is nothing doctrinal in them. The divine Son places Himself before the Father, and the Father before the Son; it is a divine revelation of the nature of the Godhead into which we are brought. It is a conversation carried on in higher worlds, a converse of spiritual beings.

Nevertheless, we can sense these worlds out of our own earthly experiences that still contain a shadow of higher things within themselves. Let us suppose someone has a friend, of whose penetrating gaze he is convinced. When this questioning eye rested on him, would he not begin of his own accord to tell of what had happened since they last met, and which perhaps required justification? There are cases known of children who, when a parent looked at them, began of themselves to tell of things of which the parent could have known nothing. This is also the beginning of converse between beings. From this we may look up to the illumined heights in which the Son meets the Father.

'Whom Thou hast given Him.' Why does Christ remind us of this limitation of His power? Does He seek thereby to excuse the lack of result in His works? Or to justify the smallness of the fruits of His life, which are these few poor disciples whom He can offer the Father? An interpretation of such a saying is too narrow, if such questions pass through our soul. By these words He is grounding His work still more deeply in His Father, or, as one might also say, He is drawing it more deeply out of the Father.

Here we notice that in this prayer Christ stands in such purity before the countenance of the Father, that He never says 'mine', except in the one saying, 'all mine are thine, and thine are mine' (10). And once He speaks of 'my joy' (13). He does not speak of *His* work, but of 'the work which Thou gavest me to do' (4). He does not speak of His own words, but of 'the words which Thou gavest me' (8). He does not speak of His disciples, but of 'those whom Thou hast given me' (9). He does not speak of His glory, but of 'the glory which Thou gavest me'.

The emotions of soul that we share here, as Christ stands in the full light of the divine clarity and cannot utter the word 'mine', help us to look deeply within Him. They lead us by the safest and most natural way into the relationship of the Son to the Father.

How easily the word 'mine' crosses our lips as we pray, my need, my work, my loved ones. But this is just a sign that we are very far from understanding the clear light in which Christ stands. We learn from His example. If He had used the word 'mine' in this prayer, there would have been something intervening between Him and His Father. And this He cannot bear. It is *only* of 'my joy' that He speaks. The *joy* over what the Father gives Him, that is His portion. Now there is nothing left to separate Him from the Father.

We may first learn, perhaps, to follow Christ upon this inner way in respect of those people whom we love. What, then, are human beings? Are they something that should be studied by themselves, as if they had suddenly grown out of the ground before us? We usually, indeed, do study them in this way. And this is precisely unreal. No person would exist had not the Father bestowed upon them a portion of His own life. Man lives by the gift of the Father's life. And as all people, whether they know it or not, bear within themselves the gift of life from the Father, the Ground of the World, as such the individual human being is given us for that moment in which we meet, when I speak with them, when I befriend them. As secret gifts from God people pass through life together and pass on. Hence the respect that sometimes lays hold of us—though we may not be clear about its origin—when someone crosses our path.

If this is so, then the meeting of two people is a conversation of the Father with the Son. We mean now the Son in us. Every person who crosses our path is a question put by the Father to the Son in us, a request of the Father to the Son in us, a task given by the Father to the Son in us. 'Those whom Thou hast given me', not only the people who are especially united to us are to be regarded in this way, but all those into whose lives we come, even if only with a passing greeting.

Today, we can but dimly imagine what loftiness of intercourse between people can come from pure perceptions, and we can but faintly imagine out of what a deep union with God such a saying arises, such a perception, such an intercourse. *To hold fast* in our lives an inner attitude of such solemn greatness will as yet not be possible to us. We can also trace in other passages in the gospel when a disciple came to Christ that He felt: He is *given to me by my Father.* And furthermore, he is given to me in order that I should give him super-earthly life, as it exists in the Father alone, when I give the Father to him and him to the Father.

In quiet meditation we can enter in imagination into such heights of humanity. When two people meet, a supersensible occurrence takes place. An interchange of gifts takes place between two sovereigns. Indeed, the Father is giving a gift to the Son and the Son to the Father. It is not a question of what another 'offers me', or 'means to me', but the radiance of a meeting of Father with Son lies in *every human conversation.*

Only with reverence can we approach these pure inner realms. But are they not given us in order that they may penetrate us? How different is this even from wishing to 'win people for God'! From the Father people come to Christ as a gift, and the Son replies to the Father by putting divine life into the soul of those who have already received their natural life from the Father.

17:3 Eternal life

Christ has spoken of super-temporal life, of life that outlasts the time of this world, because it belongs to a higher sphere. But even *this* saying He has to connect much more deeply with the Father. People have frequently spoken in general and very abstract terms of 'eternal life'. In doing so they have not walked in the path of Christ. And still less have they noticed what Christ now gives as the content of this super-temporal life. 'And this is eternal life, that they know Thee the only true God, and Jesus Christ whom Thou hast sent' (17:3). Do we not feel that with each ray of knowledge coming to us out of the divine world, we are raised into a sphere where time and death have no more meaning? Perhaps no age was ever further from this saying than our own, and surely no age has ever more sorely needed it. The talk here is of knowledge. Our age takes pride in its knowledge. But of *this* knowledge it knows nothing. And it is just this knowledge that would be its redemption.

We recall the ancient legend of Seth. Seth, the late-born [third] son of Adam and Eve, returns once more to Paradise. When, for an instant, the door is opened for him, he sees the tops of the Tree of Knowledge and the Tree of Life *have grown together and become intertwined*.[92] Who was the first to have this dream-vision into the future of mankind? Once the two Trees were separate. That was in the far past of humanity. That was the prerequisite for the Fall of man from Paradise. But while men on Earth were going astray, in the heavens a new age is being ushered in, a Paradise of the future. The redemption of humanity is already there, where the two Trees have grown together; whoever eats of the Tree of Knowledge, at the same time eats of the Tree of Life. And whoever eats of the Tree of Life also eats of the Tree of Knowledge. Now let us look again at the saying of Christ: 'This is eternal *life*, that they may *know* Thee.' Paradise has come. The tops of the Trees are intertwined, indeed, they have become wholly one.

From the saying of Christ, let us look again to that of Goethe: 'To acknowledge God, where and how He reveals Himself, that alone is blessedness upon the Earth.'[93] Do we not find in this saying a Johannine imagination concerning Christ? Does not another kind of knowledge stir there, aside from church Christianity, feeling its way gently but instinctively along a new path? Because the word 'know' has become darkened for him, Goethe says, quite in the Johannine sense, 'acknowledge'. Is not this the ushering in of a new Christian age? Did Goethe know how near he came to the sacred precincts of John's Gospel?

As we have often said in connection with anthroposophical ideas, our present knowledge is very closely connected with death. Its only certain knowledge is that connected with death; in man it perceives only what it dead—anatomy; in nature—death in physics; in the cosmos—death in astronomy. As soon as it goes into the realms of the living, uncertainty begins. There are no certain methods of investigation; pure empiricism and hypothesis begin to hold sway. Only because we regard this as the only possibility, we do not notice that our knowledge is only adequate to deal with that which is dead. Furthermore, our knowledge itself leads to death. Even those who do not know anthroposophical research and the death-producing processes that takes place in the brain in every act of pure perception by the intellect, can grasp out of their own personal experience how this intellectual knowledge and thinking can produce a laming, weakening, calcifying effect. Those who are able to live strongly and consciously in this *kind* of knowledge, experience out of its very essence death grinning at them. And this kind of knowledge has today even penetrated into theology; though strongly repudiated, it is still enthusiastically practised.[94]

If there were no other kind of knowledge, this would be the death of humanity, quite literally and in every respect. But can we, amid the whole modern world-outlook of science, of natural science and even philosophy, put our trust in any other kind of thinking? Here we should name the philosophical writings of Rudolf Steiner, especially *Truth and Knowledge* and *The Philosophy of Freedom*. In them, out of the pure theory of knowledge, the way is traced towards another kind of knowledge; indeed, in the highest sphere, in the sphere of philosophy, we find a breakthrough into the Johannine kingdom: '*Becoming aware of the idea within reality is the true communion of man.*'[95] Consider this sentence in connection with the saying of Goethe, quoted above. Compare the ages where the two were spoken and the kinds of spirit from which they proceeded. Then place beside them from John's Gospel this saying of Christ under consideration. Such a comparison is a real spiritual joy.

But why is 'becoming aware of the idea within reality' a communion? Because when rightly grasped, the idea immediately brings a piece of God's life into our spirit. No one need first become a philosopher in order to share in this communion. Such a perception in the sense of a communion can be reached, for example, when meditating on a tree in blossom, as described above. Only, it is necessary to penetrate beyond blind sentiment and intellectual surmising to a real meeting with the spirit. The human spirit meets the divine spirit, and the divine spirit, when we meet it, can do no other than give us communion, receive us into its life.

It is very clear in John's Gospel how mankind is taken everywhere to be *spirit*, not merely *soul*. By thinking of oneself, of one's blessedness or salvation, of the grace that is bestowed, one remains mostly in the *soul*-sphere. In thinking wholly of God and of sharing in the divine life, one is transformed from a soul-being *into a Spirit-Man*;

- then one walks among spirits, living with them in the spiritual worlds;
- then one rises to the higher Christianity, to Johannnine Christianity;
- then one 'sees' God.

Formerly, to see God meant inevitable death. But Christ has taken this curse from man, as he has taken so many others, and changed it into its opposite—'to see God', He now says, in complete contrast to the olden days, 'is *life*'.

From this other kind of 'recognition' in John's Gospel there also arises another 'truth'. 'The only true God.' We have no idea how dry and barren we feel the word 'truth' to be, as compared with what we felt in ancient times, even when we speak of the search for truth. The word 'truth' was then not taken in the sense of logical correctness—that scarcely existed in those times—but of living reality. The 'only true God' is the God Who is the ultimate reality behind all things. The Greek word *monos* has thereby an additional nuance of 'remaining'. From this you receive a more living impression than in our word 'one'; the one Who remains when all else has passed away. Our phrase 'all in one', or 'all in all', that we would use here also has the nuance of alone, but at the same time in language it has the beautiful meaning that He Himself is all One, and that in Him everything finds its ultimate unity. This is not to be taken as simply a playing with words. When we begin to understand and to use language in a living manner we come much closer to many things and among them an understanding of the Bible.

In the High-Priestly Prayer itself there is such a 'recognition', a seeing right through everything to the One Who is behind everything. We have just seen this when, in Christ's avoiding the word 'mine', we saw behind the work, behind the word, behind the disciples, behind the glory, always the same living reality. This is the 'true', the 'eternal life'. Here it is lived out right before us.

But the question now is whether we ourselves, having thus perceived the meaning of the ultimate living reality, have experienced this higher stream of life flowing through us, have been received into a super-temporal sphere, have received this quiet, spiritual communion? We can experience all this *everywhere*, and then the whole of life will be one continuous communion. Again, when we here follow after Christ through the ways of His soul, we enter into this kingdom of life.

This is also expressed in the fact that Christ immediately places besides the Father 'Him Whom Thou hast sent' (3). He knows that we do not have this recognition of ourselves, but that we must awaken it by contact with Him. He knows that He is there so that, by His example, this Living may be realized, this perceptive life may be kindled, and that, above all, it is kindled by *sight* of Him. Those who look on

Christ experience communion. To see Him and to feel that He is sent, that He would not exist unless some Person higher Who has sent Him was standing by Him—this is the best beginning of higher knowledge. From this starting-point it can be developed.

By the word 'sent', Christ names Himself also as the archetypal Apostle (it is the same word) and thus shelters Himself with His whole work in the Father. Previously He saw human beings coming forth from God; now He sees *Himself* as He places Himself facing Himself—also coming forth from God. He receives Himself as a gift.

Let us now be courageous enough to apply this word to ourselves. From the beginning John the Baptist was placed before us as he who was 'sent'. 'There was a man sent from God whose name was "the *grace* of God"' (1:6). This is the picture of man himself. We can experience no higher feeling about life than when we feel ourselves wholly as sent to this Earth. Then we come from the Father and go to the Father—like Christ.

17:4

'I glorified thee on earth, having accomplished the work which Thou gavest me to do' (17:4). No more sublime or exemplary farewell to a life-work can be conceived than that which we experience here. This will appear especially clearly before our soul if we imagine that *we* must today take leave of our life-work. In this hour the gulf between what we have willed to do, and what we have accomplished, will lie oppressively upon our consciousness. Our whole soul will be filled with the wish that we might go back once more and do everything better. We shall be aware of so little good in our work, in comparison with the many stains that will appear through our neglect. And this cloud lying there above us and our work is our unfulfilled destiny. We feel that we must first accomplish that, before we can be in full harmony with the divine world.

How clear, on the contrary, is the heaven lying over the work of Christ. 'I have accomplished the work which Thou gavest me to do' (17:4). With such calm purity that cannot be more perfect, He looks back upon His work. And as if for a sign that this calm purity really fills His whole consciousness and His conscience, He remains not a moment longer by His work, but turns calmly to His Father, 'glorify Thou me in Thy own presence with the glory which I had with Thee before the world was made' (17:5).

17:5

Here we witness incomparably sublime life-processes. We see, as it were, a great in-breathing and out-breathing. A human being is breathed out by God to his life upon the Earth, and breathed in again to life in God. Shall we be courageous to imitate the greatness of such a life-process in ourselves, perhaps in the evening when we go to rest? To enter into the glory we had with God, before our life began? Such a 'glory' was ours, even if not consciously as Christ's. We lived as a divine thought in God. To find again the glory we then had, is the highest task given for our inner life. We are near to it every evening when we go to rest, and every morning when we come out of the divine world in which we have rested.

All the life in all the worlds is like a great out-breathing and in-breathing of the Father-God. This exhalation and inhalation takes place most sublimely when worlds proceed forth from God and return again into Him. This is a life-process that occupies *millions of years*. The Indians called their two world-conditions *pralaya* and *manvantara. Pralaya*—the resting of the world in God, *manyantara*, the proceeding out of God to a new process of evolving. Through a deep necessity, human beings have a likeness and after-image of this cosmic process daily in their sleeping and waking. People will increasingly come to perceive in everyday experiences the reflection of great cosmic occurrences. And between the great cosmic occurrence and the little daily happening lies the alternation of earthly life with a life in the divine world, such as we experience at birth and death. Here, too, we are looking upwards to heights that human life will reach only in the future.

The way thereto would be an evening prayer, such as we could gain from a remembrance of these words of Christ. If in our sleep at night we could more consciously enter into 'the glory that we had with God' before our life began, and if this glory could then shine through our daily life, then our whole life would approach nearer to Christ's life, and our farewell to life would partake more of this glory. As long as our sleep does not conform to this rhythm we can only prepare for this greatness through meditation. For the most profound content and the highest striving, even in meditation, is to find that glory we had in God, as divine thoughts. We can really take as a daily meditation this saying of Christ: 'And now, Father, glorify Thou me in Thy own presence with the glory which I had with Thee before the world was made' (17:5). Christ may say 'before the world began', and out of such a meditation our life would acquire its radiance. We would then increasingly understand and live out in our lives those words Christ speaks immediately before, 'I have caused Thy glory to shine forth upon the Earth' or 'I glorified Thee on Earth' (RSV). If we feel that the words 'I' and 'upon the Earth' are especially emphasized here—as is very likely considering the verbal construction—we have the meaning of the 'I' and the meaning of the Earth expressed as simply and comprehensibly as possible. Through millennia the 'I' was developed upon the Earth in order that through it the world of Glory of the Father might come to shine through the Earth. The Earth is the place of revelation. It will have fulfilled its meaning and reached its goal when the divine glory has succeeded in shining through the sensory world. The Eucharist is very closely connected with this highest task of the Earth. The task can only be fulfilled through the 'I', that is to develop on the Earth. And only when the 'I' has completely evolved, also in the Eucharist, can it attain its full height, inspiring man's earthly life with highest soul.

When we notice how Christ describes His earthly work, we make a remarkable discovery. He chooses three different expressions for it.

- 'The glory of light which Thou hast given me I have given to them' (22, cf. 4);
- 'I have manifested Thy Name' to them (6);
- 'the love with which Thou hast loved me, I give to them' (26).

Are we wrong in finding parallels in these three descriptions of His work to the three higher kingdoms, which according to spiritual science Christ opened to human beings?

- The kingdom of Imagination is that next above human beings, leading them to supersensory vision—the glory of Light.
- The kingdom of Inspiration leads him beyond this, into a supersensory hearing—the Name.
- The kingdom of Intuition leads human beings into the fellowship of that higher life—Love.

By this example we may perceive the difference between what the Bible tells us and the results of anthroposophical research, but more especially their points of contact. Again, we follow the *path of Christ* into these higher kingdoms of Imagination, Inspiration and Intuition when we seek to train *through Christ Himself* our vision for the higher glory of light, our hearing for that higher music, our feelings for a higher life in love. John's Gospel and anthroposophy are exceedingly close, and the difference of time and manner of approach explains the difference between them. Thus spiritual training and education concerning Christ are quite near to one another when one understands how to perceive.

17:6-8

'I have manifested Thy Name to the men whom Thou gavest me out of the world.' As in ancient times to see the Godhead was thought to be dangerous to life, it was also forbidden to pronounce His name. In those days there was still an acute awareness that in the name is really expressed the nature of the being. People consequently did not feel pure enough to take the divine Name upon their lips. And now Christ openly says that He has revealed the divine Name! In what purity and safety He stands amidst this world of dangers! This He can only do if He feels He is to be the divine Name. He was Himself 'the Word'. The divine Name was not spoken, and people felt they were impure before it, because they felt that it could only be expressed through one Being and Life. This even has now taken place. The whole cosmos awaited this hour. This was Christ's work. And henceforth it is no more forbidden; it is the highest work that people can do on the Earth—to speak the divine Name. But in the manner that Christ spoke it—one Being and Life. This is no longer dangerous, since the coming of the great Prototype.

Now we see Christ's gaze, which has been resting upon the divine glory, slowly turn to the disciples. Out of His Father's hand He solemnly receives them once again. 'Thine they were, and Thou gavest them to me' (6). If we try again in meditation thus to receive out of the divine hand those who are nearest to us, we shall find what ennobling forces for the whole world He enclosed in a single sentence of this kind. A consecration is breathed out over mankind, and a consecration over ourselves as well.

And yet there is no suspicion of exaggeration here. What Christ has to commend in His disciples is unspeakably little—so little that we are not conscious of it in the higher sphere into which Christ's words take us.

- 'They have kept Thy word' (6).
- 'Now they know that everything that Thou hast given me is from Thee' (7).
- 'They have themselves received the words Thou hast given me;
- and know in truth that I came from Thee;
- and they have believed that Thou didst send me' (8).

Is that not somewhat little? There are no great words about their knowledge, no great hopes for their actions. It is only—they have received the revelation. Therein lies great comfort for us.

Christ could have wished the highest amongst human beings as His disciples. But He only needs those who 'receive His word'. And we only have still to notice a subsidiary sound, 'they have *themselves* received them' (8). In the 'I' and in freedom is the word of World-creation laid.

And yet there sounds behind Christ's words a secret triumph. Those who have themselves most frequently to speak of divine things will be the first to feel this. After doing so, one often comes away deeply oppressed by the feeling that one has not succeeded in expressing what lies most deeply in one's heart, in making people love the greatest. But at another time we have the conviction their hearts *have* received it! Just as little as the soil can reject the seed of corn sown in it, so little can their souls free themselves from what has entered into them. It will work, if not now, then later; if not in this life, then in another life. One has to experience this exalted feeling: it is within them! if one would understand the gentle note of triumph and joy sounding in these words of Christ. 'They have themselves received Thy Word.' The effect of this will continue to work throughout the whole of world-history.

Once more Christ re-affirms that He has spoken no word to mankind, but 'that which His Father gave Him'. 'The words that I say to you I do not speak on my own authority' (14:10). We cannot take such words literally enough. When Christ had to speak to people, He quietly waited for the words which His Father 'gave' Him. And what was then given, He gave to others. We can experience this in the High-Priestly Prayer. A conversation was always a twofold occurrence for Christ. Whilst He was speaking to people, His soul was in converse with the Father. In no other way did He speak to people. *For this reason* the Father was speaking to people when Christ was speaking. Are we excluded from such heights? When we endeavour to speak a *good* word to people, we can experience that this word arises out of profound depths within us. Then indeed it requires courage to give back that which has been given to us. But to pass on the gifts of God is the highest work that can be given to us in life.

Let us glance once again at the teaching concerning faith and knowledge, which quite in passing Christ gives us in the last words of this part of the prayer. Had this teaching been observed, then the whole of the present-day confusion in Protestant theology would be impossible. 'They know in truth that I came from Thee; and they have believed that Thou didst send me' (8). Is it not quite clear that here knowledge precedes faith? It can never be otherwise, unless faith includes within itself some resemblance of what is untrue. The truth must always first be realized as true before it can be confessed in 'faith'. Only, this act of recognition preceding faith has today sunk into such darkness that it is no longer acknowledged—not even in theology. But this is only another sign of the weakness of present-day 'faith'. With what extraordinary delicacy and correctness is the distinction made here, and articulated. That we should know from where Christ comes, requires knowledge. But that one should confess Him as the One who is sent, is a matter of the heart's devotion, of faith. Christ never required faith from anyone who had not this knowledge beforehand. Knowledge and faith are related to one another as the Sun to the sea. The Sun must rise. Then it is mirrored in the sea, and the sea rejoices to greet it.

These words say this clearly enough. We are entering the Johannine age, in which this will again be realized. Then will the way be clear for an understanding of that knowledge which can release us and lead us out of the intellectual age.

First 'landing place'[96]

In examining the inner course of the prayer down to this moment in which it passes over entirely into a prayer for the disciples, we discover that we have been witnessing a kind of incarnation of Christ, a gradual descent of Christ from the heights to the kingdoms of the Earth. The prayer begins in those heights where 'the Word is with God'. Every prayer is also a gradual revelation of the divine world. Our prayers usually begin in the lower kingdoms, with our needs, and it is much if they gradually mount ever higher. The profound glory of Christ can also be seen in the way He is here revealed in His most inner and ultimate reality before His Father, and then descends step by step.

Is it presumption to wish to follow this descent in our thoughts? Christ said, 'You shall see heaven open, and the angels of God ascending and descending upon the Son of man' (1:50). He will surely also allow us, divining and worshipping, to look at His own descent.

We are allowed to look into this last and highest relationship of the Father to the Son, of the Son to the Father.

- At the beginning of the prayer we hear that the Father glorifies the Son and the Son the Father. A delicate tint from this eternal activity in the supreme heights lies upon Christ's work on the Earth.
- When then mention is made next of 'power over all flesh', and of 'eternal life', for 'as many as the Father hath given', a breath wafts down to us from the kingdom of the Seraphim. It is told of them that the ultimate ordering of all human life rests in their hands.
- Next, the Cherubim look down upon us through Christ. To them are entrusted the shining rays of the spirit. Their light shines into all human knowledge. 'This is eternal life, that they know Thee' (3).
- The Thrones, which now follow in this descent through the angelic Hierarchies, are mighty beings of will, whose mighty power is felt in the solidity of the Earth, but also in all action of the human will. The 'Earth' appears, the 'I', the bearer of the will upon Earth, and the 'work'. 'I glorified Thee on Earth, having accomplished the work which Thou gavest me to do' (4).

At this boundary of the uppermost trinity of Hierarchies,[97] Christ stops and looks back at the glory He had with the Father. 'And now, Father, glorify Thou me in Thy own presence with the glory which I had with Thee before the world was made' (5).

The descent continues into the 'Hierarchies of the Sun', into the kingdoms of the spirit that rule throughout our solar system.

- Here work the *Kyriotetes*, the Lords and World-Guides, the Spirits of essential Wisdom, through whom pulses Christ, the Lord (*Kyrios*).
- Then the *Dynameis* (the World-Mights), to whom is entrusted all life that is manifested in movement.
- Lastly the *Exusiae* (the Revealers), Spirits of Power or Authority, who have implanted into us the 'I', with which we are called into earthly being.

In the saying, 'I have manifested Thy Name to the men whom Thou gavest me out of the world', we see how Christ, the *Kyrios*, takes over His earthly work out of the higher worlds, indeed, from the Logos itself. To the people who were given Him, He restores, as it were, the Logos itself. 'They have received Thy Word.' Out of the Word, then, come the words which He has given to human beings. This is further approximation to the Earth; it is already the moving life of the Dynameis. Such 'cosmic force', such 'fullness of life', also dwells in the words of Christ. But a further step down into the history of the Earth is made when people 'know in truth that I came from Thee; and they have believed that Thou didst send me' (8). This knowledge and faith are the great forces that human beings use in their 'I's through the gift of the Exusiae, the Spirits of Power; knowledge through the spirit, confession and faith with the will.

Only those who know nothing of these kingdoms mentioned above, or only know of them theoretically without a sympathetic approach, can think such considerations remove Christ further from us. We are, as it were, witnesses of the way in which He brings all the highest and best of these kingdoms with Him down to the Earth. A real repetition of His Incarnation, of His descent, is taking place before our eyes. The Christ, in Whom the 'fullness of the Godhead dwells' (Col. 2:9), reveals Himself before our eyes. Dionysius the Areopagite[98] describes the nine angelic hierarchies; here they are before us. The whole living, integrated personality of Christ allows Him to look through Himself into the kingdom of the angels. And the angelic kingdoms look with and through Him down to the Earth. The song of the angels during the holy [Christmas] night is here again, but now in the living deeds of a Man.

We cannot be grateful enough that this [Great Intercession] has been given to us. And those who have walked this path with us can never again think that in front of them lies the product of an evangelist. Great does the evangelist become, in whose spirit all this can be mirrored. Greater is Christ, Who thus revealed Himself in the human spirit. And we, too, may attain to greatness if this is reflected in our spirit.

Letter No. 13

The Great Intercession, the High-Priestly Prayer (II)

We have often pointed out the fact that when John's Gospel reaches its highest levels it always falls into a threefold rhythm, even in its very first sentence.

- 'In the beginning the Word already was,
- and the Word was with God,
- and the Word was a God.'

If we had fine organs, adapted to observe inner realities, this first sentence would show us that John's Gospel is inspired. This is not to assert, as has often been said over the centuries, that here the Mystery of the Holy Trinity is indicated. The process is much deeper, much rather in the spiritual than the intellectual sphere. Certainly, in these three phrases there lives the Three-in-One:

- the Father can be realized in the first phrase speaking of Being;
- the Son in the second phrase speaking of relationship, of love;
- the Spirit in the third, where there is recognition and naming.

The evangelist would perhaps be astonished if he heard this—and yet he would agree.[99] Perhaps he himself knew—we suggest no more than 'perhaps'—only that he was in the world of truth when he wrote these words. He knew he had not begun to write until he had felt he was entirely within that world. Readers can perceive this in the threefold sentence, aware of their own understanding for that world. The evangelist raised himself to these heights in which it is felt that truth is spoken, truth that stretches far beyond the individual's consciousness. Naturally, this again does not mean that spiritual wisdom, as distinct from intellectual wisdom, is something unconscious. If it were so, we would long ago have conjured up long past ages of humanity. What the evangelist tells he certainly knew. But he need not necessarily have known everything that appears in his words. For one sacred instant he shared in the life of the Holy Trinity itself. His spirit joined in the highest rhythm of the life of the primordial Godhead, even if—and this is what is so precious—he did so in a truly human manner.

The first three petitions of the Lord's Prayer, without our having initially to take this fully into our consciousness, lead us into this pulse-beat of the primordial Godhead, likewise the story of the

Resurrection in John's Gospel with its three double pictures. So also does the Great Intercession, the High-Priestly Prayer, which has always been felt to be differentiated into three parts (there are different opinions where the division lies between the first and second parts). And we can also clearly see the countenance of the Holy Trinity shining through the three parts. Only it is possible—and one has to accustom oneself to such fluctuationgs of aspect when dealing with higher truths—to see the Father more in the first part, and the Spirit more in the third part, or vice versa. Here we are in a position to perceive the reason for the difference. If one thinks more of the subjective side, of that which is going on within Christ's spirit, then this first part is more a seeing and perceiving, and consequently belongs to the Spirit, whereas the third part is more a uniting of Himself to the divine will, and consequently belongs to the Father. If one thinks rather of the objective side, of that which is revealed in Christ's spirit, of that which is perceived through Him, then in the first part, which looks more to the will from which everything proceeds, we have more the Father. In the last part, in which the goal of the world to which human beings are to be led shines out, we have more the Spirit. It is from this more objective side that we would now look. The second part, in which struggle and sorrow upon Earth appear before us, belongs above all to the Son.

To many people such considerations may appear questionable, or at least less important. For us they strengthen our certainty of the perfect inner organization of such prayers. The Great Intercession, the High-Priestly Prayer, comes to light in remarkable inner parallels to the three first petitions of the Lord's Prayer—to which this twofold method of study is also applicable.

- The first part of the Great Intercession is like a life-school for the first petition: 'Hallowed be Thy Name.'
- The third part will give to us the very thoughts that we need if we would fulfil the will of God: 'on Earth as it is in Heaven.'
- The second part shows us what we expect of it, both from below and from above. It is of great importance to see the High-Priestly Prayer thus in the light of the Lord's Prayer, and the Lord's Prayer in the light of the High-Priestly Prayer. The latter then seems to fill the requests of the Lord's Prayer with living content, and to be a guide for those who, like an inner circle of disciples, would wish to pray, as it were, close to Christ.

17:9

'I am praying for them; I am not praying for the world but for those whom Thou hast given me' (17:9). This is the only passage in the Great Intercession where, initially, a shadow might pass over our soul. Why does He not pray for the world? Why does He leave it so completely outside? Was it not in most pressing need of His prayer? But one can only ask these questions as long as the way is not noticed in which the world appears in the third part of the prayer—how it is to be led to knowledge of recognition and to love. In seeing this, a great cosmic law appears. This is the swiftest and surest way to the salvation of many. Why?

The destiny of those who are set apart and sent before is never easy, and it is the less easy the more inward the tasks for mankind are for which they are set apart. They awaken the resistance, the dislike and even the hatred of others. But this is in the deepest sense *good*. By the rejection they incur, they are brought to the most severe trial. By the opposition they arouse their own strength increases. By this severity of criticism with which they are confronted, both objective and personal, they are led into great depths, are protected from becoming light-minded, and above all from being self-satisfied, as they might become for the part they have to play in history. Out of the opposition, they meet the opportunity needed to give their utmost spiritual and physical power to their work. In this way the good cause is itself best strengthened. The opponents who attack a good cause, themselves hammer, as it were, the steel until it become so strong that they can be overcome by it. Such laws of destiny, true of all historical evolution, proceed out of the deepest wisdom.

A struggle such as this naturally can also end tragically. It would not in fact be good if one knew in advance for sure that it would end victoriously. But one can know for certain that if a good cause is utterly lost it can be for one of two reasons. Either the time was not yet ripe for that cause, although it may have been good that it appeared, or those who represented it were too small and weak for their task and so drew it with them into their own downfall.

For such reasons Christ says, 'I do not pray that Thou shouldst take them out of the world, but that Thou shouldst keep them from the evil one' (17:15).

In political life we know that anyone coming forward publicly will have their private life investigated so that, at a suitable time, they may be overthrown. What happens in religious life is still worse. It is as if all the devils conspired together to thrust such people into evil. Then with their claims that they are 'renewing' humanity, they become a derision, even to themselves. The temptation is often very subtle, for example, to make what is religious impure by using political methods. Often the temptation is surprisingly coarse, tricky and dangerous. Those who represent any new and great cause do indeed need to be 'tested, proved'. It points to the way Christ continues this first petition. 'Sanctify them in the truth.' To be on probation expresses faithfulness to what is realized as true (*wahr*). The word in German, *bewähren*, 'to prove', *sich bewähren* 'to prove oneself', carries the stamp of the same spirit.

To a person who cannot enter into Christ's method of prayer, the logical sense of these words may appear very strange. 'I pray for them ... for they are thine' (17:9). We recall how many people say to us that they feel no desire to pray for anything, for God knows everything much better than they do. Why should they interfere? From this point of view, try to find a way into this movement of soul: 'I pray for them ... for they are thine.' That means, if they were not thine, then I would not pray for them—but *just because* they are thine, I pray for them. In following this spiritual path, one can learn more of value from true prayer than one can from long study. What is true prayer, when seen from this viewpoint? It is the strong echoing by the will in the individual soul of what is felt to be the divine wish. It is the awakening of the divine will in one's own will. It is a co-rulership with God—for which He waits. In this region is the highest prayer.

17:10

Christ, however, cannot now stop short at the word 'thine'—as before He could not stop at the word 'mine'. 'All mine are thine, and thine are mine.' The spirit of Christ here rests in this consciousness as the eagle rests in the sunlight. And out of this consciousness 'my joy' breaks forth. The first actual request that Christ utters in this prayer passes immediately into thanks. Everywhere the 'glory' that He has with the Father is, as it were, immediately before the door, and it is always drawing Him thither, and ever it is drawing Him back again from thence to the Earth.

Is it still believed that all these movements of soul we are privileged to witness are the personal possession of the evangelist? What, for example, is the whole of [Nietzsche's] *Zarathustra*, in comparison with the sublime poetry of humanity that we have before us in the few verses of this prayer? If we take the nearest comparison that offers itself, the Socratic dialogues of Plato, an answer can be approached. For no one can doubt that Plato himself might have been just such a figure as he represents Socrates to be. Plato describes his own ideal figure in Socrates. But no one can think that the evangelist himself could have so closely inwardly resembled the picture he places before us. A Figure that shone into him must have given him the gospel. But it is very probable that not all that was contained in this Figure could have been reflected even in this faithful and youthfully pictorial memory.

We cannot be glad enough that at least so much has been given. 'They have kept Thy word' (17:6). 'I am glorified, revealed, in them' (17:10). What Christ expressed at that time is especially true of this disciple.

Looking back again to the sayings of Christ that we have just heard, it may be a similar experience to that of gaining the best view of a high summit, not from the valley, but from a neighbouring hill, even if it is lower. Here we recall two sayings of other writers. Meister Eckhart once said: 'I bethought me, one day: if God does not will as I will, then I shall will as He does.'[100] And then he was glad. One can still feel his joy today. And yet this is only on the way to the saying that we now hear from Christ: 'All mine are Thine ... and Thine are mine.' The other quotation is from a poet of our own time, Gustav Schüler,[101] perhaps in the highest hour of his life:

> *To God till now I always said / 'My God, my God, Thou must!'*
> To do aught else I did not dare, / For then I knew nought else to trust.
> But now I say—'We both shall do, / of this or that, as it may be.'
> And truly no one can conceive / How God now looks on me.

The poet was scarcely aware that he had caught a glimpse of that hour that can be found here in John's Gospel. But the fugitive flash in the poet's heart of this moment of joy lies in eternal brightness upon the Christ's soul. *'All that is mine is Thine,* and what is Thine is mine.'

Although we cannot observe every individual detail in the exposition of this prayer, yet we can observe how Christ does not repeat the word 'all' in the second half of the sentence. 'All mine are Thine, and Thine are mine.' It is only a difference of emphasis, not of meaning, but in the first half of the sentence the joy is based on the fact that *all* that is mine is Thine, and in the second the joy is based on the fact that what is Thine is also mine, and the 'all' is not emphasized. Could we have ever believed that we could come inwardly so near to Christ as, for example, we are in such a study?

'I am glorified—revealed—in them.' Here Christ says something more than He said earlier in the first part of His prayer concerning His disciples. He sees *His* picture shining in their souls. Thus they carry His seal. And what *we,* too, bear in our souls of the picture of Christ is the most important thing in us. By this Christ knows us as His own. The highest thing for which the human soul was created is that it can become the mirror of Christ's glory. In meditation, in prayer, we can do nothing higher than simply to let the picture of Christ, Christ's being, shine into us, stamp itself upon our souls. With this the true 'I' enters into our soul. '*I* am revealed in them.' And also of this higher 'I' in ourselves, it is true that 'All mine are Thine and Thine are mine'. This 'I' is so built and formed that it can bear within itself the whole wealth of the divine glory, that when it bestows its 'mine' upon the 'Thine', it conversely also sees the whole divine plenitude of the 'Thine' made into its 'mine'. And this is '*the* joy', '*my* joy', the joy of the 'I'.

17:11

'I am no more in the world, but they are in the world, and I am coming to Thee.' Ever and again through this sublime hymn, 'I am no more in the world'. Christ was, indeed, passing into the decisive act of His life, but at the same time He has already withdrawn from the world and is accomplishing the act from without, and from above—when this is perceived, one has also the picture of the manner in which the people of the future will increasingly learn to live. It is known in anthroposophical spiritual science that in the far future people will steer their way through earthly life from without and from above. Their true 'I' will be above them and will go through life as one would use a limb. But from one's own surmises something of this can already be known. It is really the same as is said in the New Testament, by Paul, 'Our citizenship / commonwealth is in heaven' (Phil. 3:20). In the clearest and most perfect way this fact is lived out before us by Christ Himself.

*

It was mentioned above [*Letter 1*] how John's Gospel is divided into two parts. As a background, the whole of part one presents the message, often repeated, '*I come* from the Father'. This is replaced in part two, '*I go* to the Father'. This second part is quite clearly introduced, and the change is accomplished before our eyes, so to speak, at the beginning of the washing of the disciples' feet (13:1). The mood reaches its highest point in the Great Intercession, 'I come to Thee'. When noticed, it can become through meditation an extraordinary help in our life. Our life is enclosed between the portals of birth and death. Human life reaches its highest when, upon these two portals there shines the light of these two sayings of Christ, 'I come from the Father', and 'I go to the Father'. The external earthly events of being born and of dying scarcely remain for us. In their place the deeper truth has come. And everything shines in spirit and in a likeness to God. Connecting these two sentences with what was said in the previous *Letter* about the in-breathing and out-breathing of God, we see in our little, everyday life an image of the highest Life of the World, then we see once more how the life of Christ 'reveals' the highest Mysteries of the world. But it is also true for us that 'what is Thine is mine'. If at least sometimes, as we go to sleep and as we wake up, a breath of this greatness came to us, we should learn to look quite differently at the human being and at human life.

As an extension of the first address to God the Father, there hovers above Christ's prayer for His disciples the words *'Holy Father'* (17:11). One cannot read these words without regretting that this name of God has been transferred to the Pope at Rome, has not retained the exclusive meaning that befits it. By this transference much of its essential force is taken from it. For this name was not given by Christ to any man, not even for the best of all Popes. Yet if the saying can be re-won by the individual, it is like a temple from which consecration streams forth upon us from all sides.

'Holy Father, keep them in Thy Name, those whom Thou hast given me, that they may be one, even as we are one.'

The experience awaiting us here has to be re-won for ourselves, out of our abstract present. It can be achieved initially by remembering what a protection the name of a beloved or revered human being can be when we think of it at the right moment. Its effect can be like a charm. At the moment in *Tannhäuser* when the protagonist in the Venusberg says, 'My salvation is in Mary' (Act 1, Sc. 2), the whole world of temptation sinks into nothing. Richard Wagner's works are especially rich in such pictures of intimate soul-events. We know but little of the higher art of life, if we have not to hand within us the names of the most beloved and most revered people so that we may avail ourselves of their magic. In this case the magic is accomplished within ourselves. Forces of consecration stream over us. Help comes, transformations take place, which we ourselves had never expected.

But in the name *'Christ'* such helping forces are prepared for us, that one can perceive it to be the highest and holiest magical power upon the Earth. It is not only that we change ourselves when we speak the name of Christ with our whole soul, feeling lifted above the need of the hour and protected against dangers. But when we are able to speak the name of Christ inwardly in the right way, a sacred power of helping spirits is by our side, and in that moment we know that 'no harm can befall us'. Even the sequence of sounds may be of help, as Luther also felt when he composed his hymn:[102]

Fragst du, wer der ist?	Ask ye, Who is this same?
Er heisst Jesus Christ!	Christ Jesus is his name.

Above all we may find that the help comes so quickly that we ourselves may be unnerved, and comes so strongly that we immediately feel the victory within ourselves. 'Holy Father, keep them in Thy Name, *those whom Thou hast given me.*'

We may also take the name of God, which Christ here speaks, and, as it were, gives to us for these moments, to clothe ourselves with it as with a garment in which we may pass through temptations. If his uniform can protect an officer from much whereto he might allow himself to be led astray as a private man, how much more must the name of God surround us like bright spiritual armour, against which nothing can prevail if we will only allow it to enclose us strongly enough.

The *'keeping from evil'* (15) has here become *'keep through Thy Name'* (11). This is carried still further in the prayer: *'Sanctify them in the truth;* Thy word is truth' (17).

This glorious saying of Christ has also to be made accessible to us through our own experiences. Perhaps we have heard a talk given by someone whose sincere and conscientious efforts in pursuit of the truth were everywhere evident. It was as if a pure breeze were wafting around us. It was as if we were walking in clear, high rooms. If we took notice of ourselves after such a talk, we could feel that we *had been changed* by it. It was as if we had been *thoroughly cleansed,* as if we had bathed in pure water. The goddess of truth had passed through our ranks and has consecrated human beings. Certainly, in the future the benefit received from such hours will be more strongly felt in such a collective experience, than in the individual recognitions we may have reaped. Meeting one person in this way is like a baptism, especially when they are pure through and through. Whereas from another person whose passionate, untrue nature is let loose upon us, we may receive the impression that we have been defiled.

With 'truth' in particular, we can experience that, at certain depths, truth and holiness are one. A certain purity is necessary in order that the truth can be mirrored in us. And again, out of the deep tranquillity of truth, purity streams into us. 'Blessed are the pure in heart, for they shall see God' (Matt. 5:8). The completion of this saying is, 'Sanctify them in the truth, Thy word is truth'.

Anthroposophy realizes that the Spirits of Wisdom are also the Spirits of Holiness.[103] In the exalted kingdoms of the angels, wisdom and holiness flow out of *one* [rank of] being.

We have certainly to think about 'truth' in a more living way than is required in the research institutes of the present day. Christ also said, '*I am the* truth'. In the passage we are considering, 'truth' and 'Thy word' are placed together. Every truth, even biological and physical truth, is a word spoken by the Father, the cosmic Father. And every word spoken by the Father is living truth. Christ is *the* Word. And every word spoken by the cosmic Father is the living truth. Christ is *the* truth. If Christ is realized as *the* word and *the* truth, then one divines all.

Moreover, one single saying of Christ, if it is experienced strongly enough in meditation, can become a baptism, can 'sanctify in the truth'. And so this prayer is also a most excellent saying with which to begin meditation. 'Sanctify us in the truth, Thy word is truth.' Then the fact that the three words, hale, healing, hallowing (*Heil, Heilung, Heiligung*), resembling one another, can be felt to be especially full of blessing. For the word 'hallow' in the ancient tongues [NT Gk. *hagiazo* and OT Heb. *q-d-sh*] has not simply a moral sense; it has the sense of 'consecrate'.

From these considerations it is also easier to understand that the prayer continues, 'that they may be one, as we are one' (17:11).

With this saying, we have entered the holiest temple of John's Gospel. Why should it be such great happiness to be 'one'? Now, let us look at the different kinds of happiness. There is a happiness in love of the body, and many people scarcely know any higher happiness than that. There is happiness of the senses and may stop short at this, for example, in music. There is happiness of the intellect. The Greek researcher felt it when he cried out, 'Eureka! I have found it!' But there is also happiness of the 'I'. And since Man is here on Earth in order to develop the 'I', the happiness of the 'I' is, as it were, the highest among the kinds of happiness named here.

But wherein consists the happiness of the 'I'? Let us first ask, what is the sorrow of the 'I'? And the sorrow of the 'I', the real deep sorrow of the 'I', is loneliness. Many people will not admit this. They will say, 'I like best to be alone.' But this only means they do not value the company in which they have to live, that they prefer to seek their company for themselves, for example, in their books, amid the great spirits of the past, or in their memories, amid the revered men into contact with whom their own destiny has brought them. Few people have known the really great sorrow of loneliness. And it is a terrible sorrow. This is shown by the fact that the people who have known this sorrow—and they could only know it if they were living without faith in God—divide themselves into two people, simply in order that they may be able to bear being alone. The most striking example of this is Nietzsche. We have evidence in his works that he knew the frightfullness of real loneliness. And for that very reason the figure of his Zarathustra was such a 'happiness' for him.

If loneliness, real loneliness, is the sorrow of the 'I', the happiness of the 'I'—and our example, Nietzsche, proves this, too—is unity, a being one. As little as people know of the sorrow of loneliness, they also know little of the happiness of fellowship. In fellowship, in unity, we grow above our own narrow 'I' into a greater 'I'. And for this our 'I' on Earth is destined. And consequently the gospel of the 'I', John's Gospel, ends with the sublime outlook—'all one as we are one'. Marriage, too, in which two become one, is a prophecy of this fulfilment. And it is a fundamental fact of human life on the Earth, just because it is meant to be a prophecy of this fulfilment. For this reason, the gospel of the 'I', begins with the 'I' in loneliness (John the Baptist) and ends with the 'I' in unity (John the Evangelist). The highest happiness of the human 'I' is to expand his little 'I' to a big 'I', and to live out of the bigger 'I', out of the biggest 'I', out of the divine 'I'. And as we near the end of this prayer we shall hear all the bells peal out this fulfilment, 'One as we are one'.

17:12

Perhaps nowhere does Christ let us look more deeply into His inner relationship to His disciples than He does in the words that follow:

> While I was with them, I kept them in Thy Name, which Thou hast given me; I have guarded them, and none of them is lost but the son of perdition, that the scripture might be fulfilled.

In noticing how Judas is spoken of here, we learn something new about the opposition every great cause arouses. From the beginning

Christ sees *right through* Judas. The way in which Judas, who has just gone out to betray Christ, is mentioned only in passing and to quote the Scriptures, shows Christ's harmoniously free and balanced feeling in which no breath of personal bitterness can be detected. In the background of this blackest deed in the history of the world, world-necessities appear, as it were, casting a veil over it. The very name, 'son of perdition', as the traitor is called here (12) before the Father, instead of 'Judas', thereby indicates that he had fallen into a power that made him its servant. One cannot say this excuses the deed; that is not possible. But Christ looks beyond the human weakness to higher events. Beyond the dark deed, He seeks the power from which the deed proceeds, and again, behind this power, the divine will that permitted it. It becomes possible that the thought of punishment or retaliation is very far from entering the soul of Christ. Even in the face of this deed, Christ is only concerned with retaining and revealing His love and trust to His Father.

'That the scripture might be fulfilled'—even such a saying has to be understood in a much more living way if we are to think in accordance with the Bible. We can think of every prophecy as of a vessel that stands always ready, waiting, and into which by the fulfilment its content is poured. In asking where the deed of Judas is prophesied in the Old Testament, John's Gospel itself gives the answer, 'He who ate my bread has lifted his heel against me' (Ps. 41:9, John 13:18). Could we say that in these words of Christ a gentle prayer for Judas is given? We think not. Yet everything has been done that could be done for the man Judas, if his betrayal is fitted into the cosmic framework, leaving no trace of a personal feeling of injury in Christ's soul. We might express it as follows: if Judas, before or after death, learns to see his deed with the eyes of Christ, then he is purified from it. He sees it in its superhuman contexts and feels deeply for the first time to whom he has united himself. But he is also lifted above himself through the super-personal vision of his Master. He can free himself and need no longer feel that he had left behind in the soul of his Master a wound that will never close. The purity, truth and greatness of the vision that we see here, and for which we have not only to thank the evangelist, should be taken to heart and inspire anyone who has to deal with opponents of any great cause. It should only be borne in mind that he himself can never face his opponents so free from guilt as Christ stands here. 'Sanctifying the opponent' might perhaps be written above this passage of the prayer.

But how are we to understand the statement that, when with His disciples on the Earth, Christ protected and kept watch over them Himself in the name of the Father?

Let us again approach from our ordinary experience what we are told here. A person can most easily notice that he is surrounded by a spiritual atmosphere when, not intensely concentrating, he allows his spirit to move more freely. Then involuntarily perhaps, he thinks of a distant friend—and next day a letter arrives from the friend. This friend had been holding him in his thoughts and consequently the thought had 'occurred' to him. Those who know such experiences, and particularly those who have made themselves attentive to them through special discipline, know of this 'atmosphere' that can surround a person.

Here intercessory prayer enters a new phase. Is it meaningless if a mother surrounds her child with a protective mantle of good thoughts? Of course, the child may consciously or unconsciously out of his own 'I' resist the 'influences' that are seeking an entrance into his soul. But someone who has such influences around him is differently placed in the world from someone who is unguarded. It will one day be realized that the angels are given quite different possibilities of leading and inspiring such people when they meet such vibrations—to use a hackneyed word—from the human side. They then find it easier to work for human beings. And human beings themselves can notice that a loving power, a power of healing and awakening, is around them coming to meet and help them. As soon as we think of such a one again, we see them in this protective mantle of prayers and wishes, a mantle that is of great delicacy and easily torn, but of great value. Can one measure what such knowledge means for the future of human fellowship?

Shall we now venture to learn about what Christ, according to His own words, has done for His disciples? He has built around His disciples the divine Name, 'whom Thou gavest me', the Name 'Father', perhaps 'Holy Father', and in this divine protection He has kept and 'watched over' them. In this divine Name lived a whole world of angels. This Name itself is like a guard of angels.

If we attempt in such ways to stand by our neighbours, if we are courageous to take spiritual things ever more seriously, we shall soon notice that we are standing at the entrance gate to rich spiritual experiences. One of the first will be the stern reality of evil and the mighty reality of good.

17:13
'But now I am coming to Thee; and these things I speak in the world, that they may have my joy fulfilled in themselves.'

Faced with this sublime saying of Christ, we will not pause over the difficulties of pious critics: how Christ could suddenly 'speak in the world', since He had previously said He was 'no more in the world'. It is necessary to understand how Christ is passing here from one world to another, indeed, how He is actually living in two worlds at the same time. His voice is sounding in the earthly world; His spirit is already radiant in the heavenly world. This is the secret of His 'joy'. We have already seen people dying whose bodies were being torn in the death struggle, over whom their departing spirit was living in freedom and gladness. Yet this was violent when compared with the free and natural calm in which Christ stands here before us.

How abundantly this lives in Him, Christ has not only said but proved, since even the darkest cloud, like Judas's deed, was instantly dispelled in the light of this joy. What a power that joy must have had! And it is not only the deed of Judas, but the whole frightfulness of the coming martyrdom that passed away before this joy. It is a sunrise in which the darkest valleys begin to shine and there is no more darkness at all. Here Christ has really revealed *the* joy. And could people but understand their Bible, then Christ as He stands thus amid betrayal and slander, as He passes into the darkness of torture and death, and yet shines in the pure joy He has from His Father, would be able to help all people carry out their own destiny. In an age when humanity is drawing near to almost hopeless darkness, people would have in this figure of light a source of joy that would make them able to carry not only themselves but all the others through that darkness.

One can, as it were, try to feel ways in which people express their joy and hear the sound that rings out from that joy. Thus one can hear the songs of joy of the liberated Indians, 'In highest joy we live: blessedness is our food, like the gods that are rich in light'.[104] One can tap the spiritual joy of Plato when he makes Diotima, the divine woman, sing the praises of the heavenly Eros.

Such efforts are the right preparation to receive within us the joy that radiates in John's Gospel, and above all in this passage. This joy is so pure and so certain, so strong and so true, so 'I'-clear and so illuminating that it is surely possible to say, now for the first time I learn what true joy is. Until now, people have rejoiced too little. They 'have not known', and they do not yet know, what joy is. They mistake

Diotima of Mantinea, by Jósef Simmler, 1855

distorted pleasures for joy, and in their intoxication they cannot be sufficiently pitied. They do not guess, or guess only feebly, that they are really created and born for joy. But to us it is given to have an inkling of it as we look back upon this joy of Christ, in the 'glory of the Father' that He bore within Himself.

'But now I am coming to Thee.' This simple saying contains all joy. And can we not speak it anew before every meditation and before every prayer, and so follow upon its inner way the soul of Christ, which has revealed itself to us for this very purpose?

Joy 'in fullness', in 'the fullness of perfection'—this is in the Greek the same word we hear at the beginning of John's Gospel. 'From his fullness have we all received, grace for grace' (1:16).

'The fullness', 'the *pleroma*' was once the name for the whole heaven of the gods, for the heavenly hosts in their totality. This echoes in the words of Christ. And it is true that if we can not yet consciously possess the angelic kingdoms, nevertheless we can have them in their reflection—in the joy that we see in Christ. It need not depress us that this is 'only a feeling'. For Christ Himself says that He has said all this that we may have His joy in ourselves (15:11). One day such joy will be like a bright rainbow composed of the whole choir of angels. Indeed, we can see in the individual words of Christ the glory of the different angels passing before us. Every word Christ spoke can be regarded as the last earthly mantle of an angel of Christ belonging to His heavenly hosts. Through the individual sayings of Christ, when we let them act upon us long enough and deeply enough, we may enter into the fellowship of the angels.

Joy is the inner side of *love*. This again is shown by this prayer in a most living way. The knowledge that He is loved by the Father changes within Him to joy. Joy and love are two names for the same thing. Because the human being is created for love, he must be filled with joy. For only out of joy can a person love. And because man is created for joy, he must stream out in love. For only in love can joy live. We never have any time to fill our hearts with joy. And yet in joy we would fully unfold our flower, as the plant can unfold its flower only in the sunlight.

We ought to 'have', to 'possess', the joy of Christ in 'perfect fullness' in ourselves, not only to feel it now and again when we behold Christ, but have it within ourselves as a possession, not only as a mirror as long as the Sun shines, but to allow ourselves to be illumined as a wandering star is by the Sun, to have its own light and its own warmth.

'In ourselves', we have to see the 'I'-nature of this joy. The *power* of this 'I' in joy manifests itself in the way in which Christ makes the hardest of destinies into a free act. And it shows itself in the way in which, in this darkness, Christ shines forth from within. When this has become the core of our life, then our 'I' is 'full' in every sense the word can have. Beethoven's *Ninth Symphony* [in which Beethoven, setting Schiller's 'Ode to Freedom' to music, thereby changes the word '*Freiheit*, freedom' to '*Freude*, joy'] is such a human document because it draws so near to this secret of the filling of the 'I', but the greater 'I' in joy. Then *above* there is the fullness and *below* the fulfilment. Then the 'I' has been filled because the divine fullness from above has entered into it. And now we see for the first time for what the 'I' was created and what a miracle it is that was so created.

17:14

'I have bestowed on them Thy word; and the world has hated them because they are not of the world, even as I am not of the world.'

The verb usually translated 'give', in the Greek has a more living meaning of 'bestowing' than it has with us who give so thoughtlessly at times. Our translation, consequently, uses the latter word in order to bring home to ourselves for once what a gift the word is which Christ has given us.[105] Words that we speak to others are gifts given to them. And all kinds of gifts are to be found among them: secret poison, and pure gold. Indeed, the gifts that we bestow in our words have the advantage of having many properties that other gifts never, or only seldom, possess. In one word we can bestow our whole being and life, without ourselves losing them. By a word, we can make a present to another person that will always accompany and refresh them. In a word a person can also sow a seed from which a whole garden may spring up. We people do not yet know how to make a gift. If we did, life could become infinitely richer. And precisely in words, we as yet scarcely know how to bestow a gift. And yet with them we could give most, in such a way that the other is least embarrassed and we ourselves least impoverished. Nor do we understand how to carry words with us as treasures. Yet this would be the condition of our real understanding of Christ's saying, 'I have bestowed upon them Thy divine, spiritual Word'. The Word that Christ *spoke*, the Word that He has *accomplished*, the Word that He *was*, that is the great gift to humanity, gold and seed at the same time, the Being and the Life of God Himself—and yet contemplating us ceaselessly, from our own innermost soul. The more living the way is in which we understand the miracle of the Word, the more living is the way in which we look into Christ.

However, the shadow that accompanies the divine gift of light is 'the world's hatred'. Christ clearly considered it very important that His disciples should be free from illusions. He wished once and for all to guard them from the disappointments with which they were threatened, and from that crippling of the soul-life which is otherwise unavoidable. Goethe achieved the wisdom of realizing that in order to guard oneself against its many small disappointments, it would be best to expect nothing from life, once and for all. Christ in the same way seeks to fortify His disciples with the same inner greatness for the struggle in the world.

'If the world hates you, know that it has hated me before it hated you. If you were of the world, the world would love its own; but because you are not of the world, but I chose you out of the world, therefore the world hates you. Remember the word that I said to you, 'A servant is not greater than his master'. If they persecuted me, they will persecute you; if they kept my word, they will keep yours also. But all this they will do to you on my account, because they do not know Him Who sent me' (15:18-21).

Nowhere else did Christ use these words. He who believes he can achieve more in the world than Christ places himself above Christ. In this is a warning, and yet much more—comfort. Whoever is moved by the divine glory of the revelation of Christ, is overwhelmed by the feeling that if this revelation were only put before the souls of people in the right way, they would all be richly blessed thereby. But Christ wished to take away from His disciples all hope of doing the divine work in the world with greater success than Christ and all the hope of destroying opposition, or of escaping hatred. Christ laid great stress on this. Thereby, in the face of all optimism He implanted into His struggle for the world its tragic character, even beyond death, and He assigned a tragic fate to all His followers in that struggle. The danger is only that His disciples will too hastily attribute to Christ, instead of to themselves, the blame for the opposition that comes to them from the world, and that Christ will suffer more because of His bad disciples than His good disciples suffer for Christ.

But the 'hatred' of the world immediately leads Christ back to the ultimate and deepest cause of that hatred. Two worlds are here colliding. And Christ clearly wished to arouse His disciples to its very living reality. This knowledge has a redeeming quality, in the sense that we do not then feel so much that individual opponents are wicked individual people, but that we—who have already begun to do so in wars between nations—may see through the war into the character of the worlds that are here in conflict. This lifts us above many personal irritations that otherwise weaken our power or debase the struggle. Christ wishes the struggle to be maintained on the plane of purity and strength, illuminated by the earnestness of His last decisions.

17:14-16

Perhaps no age is better prepared than our own for this saying of Christ. In the earthly world—this can clearly be seen—the tendency is towards the abyss. Intellectualism and materialism had to develop in the sensory world. That was a profound necessity in world evolution. But now they are revealed as mighty forces that are leading the world towards destruction. All outer advance is mere illusion. This world can only be 'saved', to use the biblical expression, or much rather, only human beings can be saved. A 'new world' comes down and takes up the life-and-death struggle with the old world. We cannot sufficiently realize the magnitude of this struggle. The earthly sensory world was a gigantic hazard for the Godhead. For this sensory world by its very nature is sliding down into the abyss. That is its character. And only because it gives the opportunity for a new world-creation in its very midst, can it be justified at all.

Here we cannot raise, much less solve, all the questions that quite justifiably occupy the serious thinker. Christ Himself here is not teaching but praying. We shall place what is happening as two pictures before our soul. When an illness is treated by injections patients summon up all their forces to throw out this injection. A fever is set up; outwardly the intruder disappears—only to reappear within the body as a healing power, where it continues to work. A similar febrile process has often appeared in the body of humanity when healing was introduced into it from the Spirit. This took place most strongly when everything conspired to cast out Christ—cleverness, hatred and force—just at that very time when healing was taken into the sick body of humanity. The great process is reflected wherever human sickness and human salvation face each other.

We see the same law from another side by recalling the deed of Arnold von Winkelried during battle. A wall of lances stood facing the Swiss army. But Arnold Winkelried drew a handful of the lances towards himself, and in transpiercing himself broke a way through.[106]

Those who have to bring in that which is divine have to draw the 'hatred' of the world upon themselves in order to draw it out of the world. They are subject to the same sacred law that was revealed in Christ's death. When this law has been realized by its opponents, they avoid making outer martyrs, and rather seek for deceptive means of opposing this sacred law, without doing themselves any good.

'The world'—we are amazed to see the calm and certainty with which Christ includes in that phalanx even the acknowledged leaders

Winkelried's Death at Sempach by Konrad Grob, 1878

of that religion which in His time was by divine ordinance the highest religion. Perhaps the Jews never had better Rabbis than at that very time—Hillel, Gamaliel, and in Alexandria the great philosopher Philo. And yet, 'they have not known Him who sent me' (cf. 17:25).

17:17

As we study side by side the petitions that Christ makes to His Father for the disciples, the great prayer He gave them, the Lord's Prayer, rises before our souls. 'Keep them in Thy Name' has a twofold meaning: 'Keep them from the evil' and 'Sanctify them in the truth'. The Lord's Prayer takes a definite course from the first petition 'Hallowed be Thy Name' to the last, 'Deliver us from the evil'. The High-Priestly Prayer, the Great Intercession, takes the same course, as it were, in the reverse direction, until it has sheltered the disciples within the holy name. Certainly, the Lord's Prayer, as it is expressed in words, could have scarcely fitted into the style of John's Gospel, but the same spirit pervades it. And just this comparison of the two shows their differences and their profound similarities. But what is always manifested in Christ's life of prayer, and is powerfully shown in the Lord's Prayer, as here in this prayer, is the deep and holy dread of the uncanny power of evil.

How different in this respect is our age that thinks itself prejudiced not to regard evil with the same equanimity as the good, that whenever possible would always assure us that only a weakling can fear evil instead of going boldly through it. It is only lack of the deeper experiences of life which betrays people to such arrogant viewpoints. In his Farewell Discourses Christ's greatest anxiety with regard to His disciples was: How can I secure protection for them against the mighty spiritual forces threatening them? He knew just in this matter that human beings cannot help themselves; they need help from above, and that this help must be sought in prayer. Consequently, He Himself prayed before them, as if to tell them for what above all they should afterwards pray. The higher a person rises, especially in sanctity, the more seriously do they take the power of evil.

17:18

'As Thou didst send me into the world, so I have sent them into the world.' Word by word this part of the prayer is meant to work upon the *new self-consciousness and the new feeling for life* of the true disciples. They were to feel they were sent. From above only, were they to learn to live and to work. We should need a whole life, and more than a life, in order to acquire the inner attitude that Christ wished to arouse in them. Can we not, as we wake up in the early morning, sometimes hear as though spoken by Christ Himself, 'I send you into the world—as my Father has sent me'? The world is our place of work but not our abode. Some Christians today feel the world as their place of abode, and their religion possibly a private chapel in it, into which they can sometimes go, but which does not mind if they desert it for a while.

However, we have not yet asked how it can be said that they—the disciples—are not of the world. Let us again consider the relationship of the age to the Earth. It is, of course, true on the one side that the whole of earthly history serves the evolving of the human 'I', but only 'the "I" in loneliness', or to 'the "I" as God', can this evolution proceed from out of itself. The prophet in the wilderness and the Caesar on the throne are the two ultimate forms of evolution that can be given to the 'I' by the Earth. The whole content of this 'I' must be bestowed from *above*, as the cup of the Grail is filled from above. Consequently, Christ says with such emphasis, 'I am not of the world' (17:14, 16). The 'I' as it is really predestined *comes from above*. The Son of God infills the Son of man. And all those who join Christ are consequently 'born from above' (3:3). We ought to feel this in a very living way. And it is good if we sometimes feel it in the midst of daily life, perhaps during some idle moment, waiting for something or other. Then we can experience the 'I' entering into the earthly body from above. And then we ought to feel this not only for one blessed moment, but out of this 'I' take up the whole life-and-death struggle with the old world that is our destiny here. Every age that has been filled by Christ with its true content is the seed of a new world. But the seed has to burst through the Earth in which it is laid, if the Earth is not to become its grave. Even the least disciple of Christ ought to be conscious of being the firstborn of a new world. It is not at all a question of having any special 'mission', although that may also be the case—it is the most central of all things, namely, being sent with the 'I' itself that is born in a higher world—in Christ—and now returning thither. This mission ought to become a daily exercise that we practise not only in the morning, but whenever possible as we enter upon a new piece of work.

17:19 Atonement

The sublime composure evident in such disciples is based on exalted words of protection. Firstly, 'Sanctify them in the truth; Thy Word is truth' (17:17). But just in this, it is remarkable that Christ cannot stop short here, that He knows a deed has to follow the prayer: 'for their sake I consecrate myself, that they also may be consecrated in truth' (17:19).

Now we come to the most high-priestly words of the Great Intercession. In earlier times the high-priest entered the holy of holies [on one day of the year, the Day of Atonement] with the blood of the sacrificed in order to secure consecration for the sins of the people. Here we see Christ Himself entering the holy of holies and offering His own blood for the healing of mankind.

This saying can be looked at from a variety of viewpoints. We can try to reproduce within ourselves the inner movements of soul expressed in these words. Many human prayers consciously or unconsciously follow the course that after praying the persons feel relieved of the necessity *themselves* of doing anything for the cause for which they have prayed, because they have 'given it over to God'. But the right inner attitude towards the divine world results from the feeling that we cannot pray for anything whatsoever without at the same time offering ourselves to do the utmost towards its realization. No prayer in which there remains even a vestige of the feeling that we will 'see what God will do' is a real prayer in the spirit of Christ. In this respect the transition from 'sanctify them' to the words 'I sanctify myself for them' is forever an example for all His disciples. A request is made only in the spirit of Christ, if it inwardly moves and inspires the person who made it to fulfil that request to their utmost.

Another approach to this saying is when we consider what results from it for all moral endeavour. A person who has reached a certain level of inner development may notice that all motives for further moral striving suddenly fail them. Perhaps this is seldom admitted to oneself, but still in the bottom of the soul an attitude of mind may exist that can be expressed as follows: 'Why should I keep on striving so energetically? I have already attained a quite respectable result. Life becomes too uncomfortable if I am so hard upon myself. And other people do not value it.' When even in passing such feelings spring up, there is every reason to ask whether this whole 'striving after perfection' has not up till now been built on crumbling foundations. This person has been looking for praise from others. They have been asking—even if quite unconsciously—for their own self-satisfaction.

Christ's saying that we are here allowed to hear comes from quite a different region of the soul. It builds morality upon new foundations. 'For their sake I consecrate myself, that they also may be consecrated in truth.' We have already remarked that here the truth, and only the truth, is cited as the source of all moral purification. But we have also to keep in mind that not only morality in the narrow sense, but the complete consecration of man is referred to. The 'sanctifying of Himself' for the disciples means not only the devotion unto death, but also that inner rising to those heights where death for others becomes possible—'sanctification' unto sacrifice. And since self-sacrifice for others is the highest of moralities in the Christian sense, in those words there consequently lies the true and ultimate foundation for all 'seeking after holiness'. Thus, when the perfecting of the self is the actual goal of moral purification, one is not yet approaching Christian ideals, but still those of Greece.

In the same way, the moral life of the Middle Ages, in as far as it had self-perfecting in mind, to say nothing of self-satisfaction, or recognition by men, and of heavenly 'blessedness', was not yet Christ-like even when it made use of Christian words and thoughts.

'Christian morality' is purely and simply that we should ourselves strive to rise ever higher, in order thereby to draw others ever more after us, in order to become progressively better in that work of the Father, the Ground of the World, for whose completion we have ourselves asked in prayer. We are here looking towards those heights of striving for Christian sanctity, and here alone is the true foundation and direction of all morality, even of everyday life. It becomes a work of love. However, neither of love to God or of love to people, nor yet of love to God as well as love to people—but of love for people, which at the same time is love for God and the love of God Himself. The person who is inwardly united with this high-priestly saying consecrates themselves to humanity as a priest of Christ, 'I consecrate myself, that they also may be consecrated in truth.'

But how can that come to pass, that others are consecrated when Christ consecrates Himself? The most ordinary experiences of life can again help us. Many people are occasionally moved by the question, 'What can I do to make the world better?' To this there is one certain answer. We can do nothing more perfect to better the world than becoming better ourselves. In the last resort, when we see the 'badness' in the world, the answer can only be, 'then *I* must become *better*'.

When a human being becomes better, then at the same time they always make their whole surroundings better. That is a cosmic law. It certainly often does not seem so. The apparent effect will frequently be that people become worse, that all the evil in them first comes out. 'Hate boils over.' When Saul was a witness of Stephen's martyrdom, he was 'still breathing threats and murder against the disciples' (Acts 9:1). This was the way—to Damascus. This Damascus may delay its coming for years, even for a lifetime, or for several lives, perhaps for whole periods of the world. Yet we can feel the triumph: If I myself become better I am at the same time doing what is best for the healing of the people whom I meet, indeed, even for the healing of the whole world.

This was also the wisdom to which Goethe arrived at the end when, at the conclusion of the last scene of *Faust*, Gretchen asks the Queen of Heaven what she can do for Faust, and the answer comes:

> *Mater Gloriosa:*
> Rise up! To higher spheres induct him,
> Feeling thee, he will follow on thy way.

This, in his old age, is Goethe's advice to all world-reformers. '*Wenn er dich ahnet*—when I divine thee'—from the supersensory viewpoint there is always something that divines because it is itself from above. If it does not succeed in this way, it will certainly not succeed in any other, least of all in the way of helpless moralizing, preaching at others.

To make the world better we start at the point within our grasp, that is, ourselves.

Our improvement is a concern of the whole world, not simply our private affair. If we are only considering ourselves the thought may arise, 'A little sin is also quite nice!' But the very greatest moral force to which we can attain can be derived from knowing, that 'if I become better, I make the whole world better'.

Second 'landing place'

Let us look once more at the whole of the second part of the Great Intercession, which is addressed to the Earth, to people and their sufferings and struggles.

If we enter into this temple, in which Christ is praying for us, we derive from His soul all the feelings that bring us nearest to Him, and which He wished to awaken in His disciples.

Christ leaves His disciples in a clear and wholesome, but serious, frame of mind. Everywhere it is the very simplest words that He speaks both about them and to them, but everywhere behind these words the ultimate depths open up. Out of these depths a heroism breaks forth that can never be surpassed and which yet touches even the most ordinary things.

Can anything greater be said to the disciples than that they are 'not of the world'; that they are 'sent' out of another world into this world; that they can always acquire this consciousness again by looking up to Christ, Who is also 'not of this world', but has sent them into this world 'even as' He Himself was sent by the Father? We are given a new feeling about the very grounding of our life when we know we are not only fighting for a 'good cause', nor only for a great Master, but for a *new world*. Such a fundamental realization of life may communicate itself to all individual actions and bring them into true greatness.

Can anything more serious be said to the disciples than that they will draw upon themselves the 'hatred' of the whole world, but that this is their task, in order to draw it out of the world; that in this respect they will not be better placed than Christ Himself? And at the same time will they not be raised above this hatred, since they are permitted to see its backgrounds, and so be raised into peace?

Can anything more inspiring be said to the disciples than that Christ has prayed for them, and consequently is still praying for them? That above all He has two requests to make for them—that they may be kept from evil, and may be sanctified in the truth?

Can anything more helpful be said to them than that Christ has sanctified Himself *for them*, and will further sanctify Himself for them?

Or can anything more joyful be said to them than that they will carry the joy of Christ within themselves in fullness; that for this He has given them His word and His example, and gives these again in His last injunctions, that as the Transfigured One He will dwell in them and that they shall share with Him the 'mine' and 'thine' with the Father?

The other gospels tell of a 'sending forth' of the disciples. Here, too, is a sending forth. In a sense it is the counterpart of the external sending forth. The moment of leave-taking becomes the moment of the sending forth, and thus it is raised above all that is merely sentimental, becoming an act of heroism. A mission and a fitting out for it—all that we need!—Christ is giving to His disciples, before He ascends into the 'glory' of the Father.

We cannot but think that in the future the true disciples of Christ will come repeatedly and let themselves be consecrated by the words of the prayer their Lord and Master has spoken for them. This prayer is the true consecration of the disciple. And meditation upon it is the ritual of the consecration of the disciple, is the inner consecration of the priest by Christ, the High Priest Himself.

Letter No. 14

The Great Intercession, The High-Priestly Prayer (III)

Now Christ lifts up his gaze above and beyond the struggle of the present time and gazes into distant ages. The eagle of John's Gospel soars majestically upwards and circles high above us. If we are able to receive into ourselves the spirit of the last prayer, then henceforth the goal of the Earth will shine over us, remaining like a radiant star in the heavens. And the star beckons us still higher. It helps us foresee also the super-earthly goal of humanity. It is like the golden door to the heavenly glory itself. Humanity has nowhere else beheld its true goal, the goal of the Earth, and the super-earthly goal, so clearly revealed as in these words of Christ. When once this has been seen, then life begins to acquire clarity and greatness.

17:21

'I do not pray for these only, but also for those who believe in me through their word, that they may all be one; even as Thou, Father, art in me, and I in Thee, that they also may be in us, so that the world may believe that Thou hast sent me.'

In German there is a word that expresses extraordinarily graphically what it wants to say: the word *Zwietracht*, 'discord'. In this can be heard the hissing hate and the crashing of struggle. When Christ, with the feelings of a higher world powerfully present in His heart looked to the Earth, He saw how discord was tearing people apart; He saw how precisely the true divine goal of the Earth is endangered.

There is another German word that is equally graphic. Placing this word next to the first, the redemption of discord is, as it were, painted before us. This is the word *Eintracht*, 'concord'. In the syllable *ein*, a calm harmony can be heard. It can be found right into the single speech-sounds. But the strange thing is how the second syllable becomes quite different. We no longer hear the clash of the struggles, but the profound, powerful force emanating from the common ground in the striving.

It is truly not frivolous to listen to what the genius of language teaches. Within the Germanic world in particular discord has devastatingly governed throughout history. Consequently, precisely the spirit of the Germanic world is appointed to take up these last proclamations of Christ and convey them to the world. If the Germanic people are to develop the individual spirit, then they are called to listen to where in the gospel of the 'I' ultimate salvation shines forth. Here are received consecration and a task in the world. Already the word *Eintracht*, 'concord', is a prophecy and a consecrating music. For it says as clearly as any word can, that unity is not to be gained in any sentimental reconciliation, but only in united endeavour for a common goal.

One would wish that this prophecy live more clearly in the spirit of all those seeking anywhere to bring about unity in everyday life. One cannot 'fabricate' unity. One can only create concord. In cases of need people know instinctively that only 'concord' can save them. When an adversary from without attacks, then the parties within the state unite themselves surprisingly quickly; each person knows at once that the other has also power to contribute, and that this power is indispensable for the whole. In difficulties between married couples, too, it would always be right to ask whether both parties were not pulling different ways, and whether unity could not be reached by some 'pulling together'. If this cannot be done, for example, in a common effort for the good of the children, or for some external or spiritual reason, then community in marriage can scarcely be maintained. But in pulling together for some goal, *the higher 'I'* is already present, and in this the two people may find their way to fellowship.

Never has concord been founded in a greater spirit than here in the Great Intercession. And never has the power that leads to concord been more surely revealed. For here the concord between Father and Son is placed before humanity as the image and power of concord. And the diverse human beings are all raised up into the Son. So will be fulfilled in the highest sense what a German word unconsciously prophesies—the word *Ver-sohnung* [= 're-son-ing']—reconciliation.

Earlier in these *Letters*, we took the opportunity of considering in a great historical context the unity of which Christ is speaking here. Three times unity was proclaimed in a religious way, sounding like a mighty bell above humanity.

- The first time was in early India. There people were taught by holy teachers to seek the One from whom all things have proceeded, and in the All-One to let the soul stream out in calmness and greatness. This was a unity that people experience in their *feelings*, in the *past*.
- Again the bell sounded, but quite differently, when the spirit of the Israelites apprehended God as the One Who is *above* all others, and turned away from the many in order to serve only the One, the Greatest. This was the unity to whom the human *spirit* rose in prayer in the *present*.

- And now, for the third time, in John's Gospel we hear the bell tolling forth the great unity, but now in the human will, indeed, for the 'I' of people who have fallen to pieces in their will. This is the unity that seeks to come not *before* being, nor *above* being, but *after* being, as the perfecting of being, as the *future* in which the many is not denied, as it was by the Indians, and not disowned as it was by the Israelites, but in which it will be permeated by the divine 'I' that ensouls and transfigures all things.

In endeavouring again to perceive with our eyes the whole of religious history in John's Gospel, we see the proclamation of Christ that in this prayer there is to be the ultimate fulfilment of religious history. For spirit and feeling also are brought to fulfilment where the 'I' active in the will unites with the goal of the Godhead, there shining forth.

It has already been suggested that we have to learn to feel the word 'one' quite differently if we would enter into Christ's feeling about life. Such words can make us aware how much the abstract intellectual character of our time has altered the spirit of words. To 'become one' is not a very attractive ideal in an epoch mainly logical and mathematical. But in this passage of John's Gospel, we can still feel how alive numbers must have been in an age that brought forth Pythagoras, and which within the Mysteries perceived cosmic secrets in the interplay of numbers.

We may also approach John's Gospel more in the sphere of thought. We recall, for example, the very end of Hegel's *Phenomenology of Spirit/of Mind* [1807], where he is inspired to use poetical language. Schiller's line, 'From the cup of the whole realm of being, infinity wells up to him',[107] is transformed by Hegel in his philosophy into, 'From the cup of this realm of spirit infinity wells up to him'. That Hegel writes here 'this realm of spirit' where Schiller evokes 'the whole realm of being', shows their difference more livingly than volumes of cultural history could show it. In the same way, Hegel cannot become reconciled to a sentimental idea of immortality, but feels the necessity of returning through infinity to unity, '*his* infinity'. Here we find the greatest modern philosopher on the way to John's Gospel. John's Gospel also journeys from the 'fullness', in which it rejoices at the beginning to 'unity', only even more decisively than Hegel. 'That they may know Thee, the All-One God, the real truth.'

But even 'unity' loses in John's Gospel its last contact with Indian thought, which it still retains with Hegel. It is not 'unity', but 'union'. 'I in the Father, and the Father in me', Christ's words as He spoke to human beings. 'Thou, Father, in me, and I in Thee'—thus He speaks from an even higher level when He stands before the Father in prayer. And here the locked gates of the holy of holies are solemnly opened and before our eyes Christ enters in.

The 'I' itself was still 'locked up' in the human being, like the holy of holies in the Temple at Jerusalem. Now the veil is torn asunder. The one, eternal High Priest enters in. And while He says, 'even as', He hands over, as it were, the key to this sanctuary of humanity.

We endeavour to understand for ourselves from ever new angles what then took place. It was always the goal of those longing for the highest to become entirely one with God. Much that was sublime and holy was given to them. But there was a difference: the union took place in 'ecstasy', and consequently not yet in a mind fully awake. It occurred in secluded places of the Mysteries, or in the 'desert', and usually more in the feelings than in the consciousness. Consequently, also, the union was only of a passing nature and not enduring, although such hours might control the whole life. And, lastly, human beings were united to an individual god, perhaps tribal god—and even if the highest God may have shone through this tribal god, He was not yet united to the highest Father, Who was first revealed to mankind in this all-embracing union and purity through Christ.

Past forms of religious union live on in the human community in forms that are becoming increasingly degenerate. For example, in 'possession', whether it appears as 'insanity'—which is by no means always the case—or whether it is artificially brought about by narcotics or by ecstatic dances. But since these are no longer suited to this age, or to the human consciousness of today, it is always a lower being that empowers people at such times. The spiritual condition of the Hebrew prophets was far above such conditions. But it also was passing, was still 'ecstatic' and connected with their tribal nature. That which Christ would give us is far above this, and words fail when we seek to describe this glory destined for human beings—this true glory of mankind.

Let us suppose the human being owns a jewel in which he can focus all the hidden divine rays, as in a burning-glass, that he carries this jewel, hidden invisibly in the middle of his royal forehead, between his eyes, and that in this house of light he could let the divine beings of the cosmos pass out and in, and also could illuminate with this light all the events and realities of the Earth. In which case, it would shine in every direction like a secret lighthouse. And let us suppose that he himself lived in this focus of light, and governed himself from out of himself, guided his body and directed his life. If he felt this invisible diamond of light as the dwelling of all wisdom and purity, as the living seal of his own divinity—then we should have the first impression of the way in which the 'I' will live in human beings of the future. As such a jewel, in which the Sun shines, which itself becomes a piece of the Sun's life, yet remaining entirely itself, indeed, is now for the first time fully itself, so does the higher human 'I' live with Christ, and through Christ with the Father.

Today, we can only faintly surmise such a life but it is really true. 'I and the Father are one.' This also applies to the 'I' rising up in truth and light. It applies to us in the measure in which it can live in us. When we then speak and act, we are truly speaking and acting ourselves—now for the first time really and truly ourselves. And yet it is the Father Who is speaking. In this community is contained the greatness of man and his happiness. 'Thou, Father, in me and I in Thee', 'That they also may be in us' (21)—not only as Luther [and the AV/KJV] translates it, 'that they may be one in us', but 'may be in us'.[108] The picture we thus take into ourselves would also suffice for a lifetime meditation. For in it we have in respect of time, the evolutions of whole worlds and, in respect of space, the whole fullness of the cosmos. We can have such an 'I' forever in us, and not merely transitorily, we can have it fully consciously within us, and not only in conditions of ecstasy; indeed we can have it in a super-consciousness that we are now only learning to comprehend. In this we can draw near to the highest God, and speak with Him as with a 'Thou' quite within ourselves; we can speak to the greater 'I', which we are also ourselves. We can go to and fro between the lesser 'I' and the greater 'I', which no longer lives merely over us, but also in us, after it has built its dwelling-house within us. And we can be certain that we go to meet infinite 'glory'. Here we have it in print, and there it is *the* glory, full of grace and truth.

And as this vision extends upwards to the 'glory'—into the fellowship of the Father with the Son, which shines through everything with transcendent light, so now towards worldly depths mighty forces ensuring victory over the world are entrusted to Him. 'That the world may believe that Thou hast sent me' (21).

We have already met the word 'believe' in this connection, 'all that believe in me through their word'. Let us not overlook that here again in the simple words a great cosmic progress is described.

'Thy word—my word—their word.' In this metamorphosis lies the whole path of the 'word' through the world. If this were only sometimes meditated, especially by those who speak in the name of Christianity, the word would regain its sacredness—and would be able to sanctify. 'Sanctify them in the truth; Thy word is truth' (17). The introductory prayer to the reading of the gospel in the Act of Consecration of Man leads us the same exalted way.

We ought to notice how much more alive the word 'through' is in the Greek language [*dia*]. In this there is much more the meaning 'right through'. And that the two words 'through' and 'on account of' are *one* word in Greek, and differentiated only by the case of the following word, also points in the same direction. With us such words have degenerated through abstract logic.

Our word has full weight only when the word of Christ is present in it, which is the word of the Father. But then those who receive it can pass right through our word, and on this path meet the divine 'I'. If then they affirm the divine 'I' in their own 'I', then they 'believe'. And in such belief they receive the divine 'I' in their own 'I'. It would be good to take this whole inner process as described in John's Gospel, clearly and livingly into our soul. We would then know what to do and what not to do if we wish to 'preach the gospel', be it to a few or to many people.

Let us now look at the other saying, 'that the world may believe that Thou hast sent me' (21). We need not say that this implies a promise that one day the whole world will turn to Christ. Although Christ is not in doubt about this, yet He speaks quite fully, because it is up to the world to make the decision, and because it depends upon the power of the disciples' words how much they will achieve in the world. The result of the struggle for the world is well known. But it must be fought. And it must be fought in the hope of the greatest possible victory. In this struggle nothing is gained by deceptions or self-deceptions. A higher spiritual bearing is expected from the warriors, so that without any illusions they can apply their full strength in the consciousness that only thus the highest can be gained for the world.

We can see the same thing still more clearly in what follows, 'That the world may know that Thou hast sent me and hast loved them even as Thou hast loved me' (23). Why is 'know' used here, when formerly (21) 'believe' was used? Is it done arbitrarily? Is it the choice of the evangelist? In John's Gospel all these words are used in a very living manner, and consequently with changing meaning. We have heard one saying in which 'to know' goes before 'to believe', and we have linked our studies to this (v. 7). But sometimes in John's Gospel, faith—in which, however, some knowledge is already implied—progresses to complete and clear *knowledge*. Such a passage is found, for example, 8:24 and 8:29. And even the saying in 17:3, 'this is eternal life, that they know Thee', points to this higher knowledge, in which knowledge in faith is purified in man's consciousness to an ultimate transcendent apprehension of truth. It is the same in the sayings about the world. The world indeed will know, and now let us notice what precedes this saying, 'that they may become perfectly one' (17:23). The more perfection in unity is reached by the disciples, the more there is knowledge in the world. And yet the world then stops short at the perception that the Father loves the disciples, and there is no talk of the love that the Father has to the world; that is, as far as the world is and remains the world—and does not come over to join the disciples. Indeed, it seems as if here a world-future were shining through, into which the world already gets an insight but cannot yet find the inner connection with it. This will perhaps be attained in a future epoch of the world, but the ground for this has already been implanted in the present world-epoch. We venture too far, perhaps, when we utter such thoughts here in connection with the words of Christ. But at any rate they point in this direction. Christ wished to save His disciples completely from illusion, and yet asked them to stake their lives on the task of converting the whole world.

17:23

Now let us turn once more to the saying, 'that the world may know that Thou hast sent me'. Does there not lie in this thought that the world would certainly *not* believe that Christ was sent by the Father *if* there were *no* Christian community? The decisive meaning, too, of The Christian Community here presents itself to us—its ultimate meaning and its highest responsibility. Christ's last gift and promise rest upon it. This can never mean that any organized body could exclusively appropriate this saying of Christ. It can only mean that it must stand by this saying of Christ, to test itself thereby, to strengthen itself thereby and to make the whole purpose of its life an exemplary fulfilment of Christ's saying.

One thing is certain—and all history proves it—that all other ways of convincing the world of Christ's mission do *not* lead to the goal. An individual who appears before the world, preaching 'the word', even if that person embodies the word, makes an impression upon individuals, but not on 'the world'. It was the same with Christ Himself. In order to make an impression upon the world, only one thing is strong enough—that the world should really *see* Christian community.

But has not this way also failed? It sounds sentimental to the people of today to hear said of the early Christians by the 'heathen', 'See how they love one another!'[109] And yet in that lay the real power which increased their numbers. It was not the spiritual warring of their apologists, not the witness of the martyrs, but just a new *power of life* had entered into humanity, which made Christianity into a world religion.

What was going on probably seldom entered men's full consciousness. But they felt, 'Here the divine aim in the creation of the world shines out! It is not the individual man struggling for self-perfection; it is *humanity* which is the divine will'. They felt how the 'I' in the human being breaks through into a higher sphere when, along with others, it finds itself within a greater divine 'I'. They felt an awakening to a higher life in love. The sorrow of the 'I' in its loneliness was suddenly revealed when redemption became visible.

This was an experience of the 'I', and was more than a sublime experience in the feelings or even than an individual experience of the spirit. It was to a certain extent the earthly experience for which the human being had unconsciously waited—which is why it was so overwhelming. The meaning of human existence flashed forth the purpose of earthly history, and the divine thought in the creation of the world. But thereby the divine mission of Christ dawns upon people. 'That the world may know that Thou hast sent me.' Without Him the world would have no meaning.

It is perhaps not so very easy to make clear to oneself what the world would be today without Christ. People speak about how *little* Christianity has so far achieved. But when we read Caesar's *Gallic Wars*, or Livy's *Histories*, or even Thucydides, we can feel the darkness before the dawn that still pervades these accounts. Deep down in man's being the question must have arisen: If all this continues, what is life worth? And precisely this something, deep down within the human being, which was secretly looking for the meaning of life, beyond war, ambition and passing glory, felt it was awakened and gathered hope when, out of a community of human beings, the Spirit of Love spoke to it. Now a new future hailed the human being worthy of life, awakening in people's hearts a new longing and a new strength.

Did a similar thing happen later in Christian history? When we think of Francis of Assisi—certainly, he himself made an enormous impression upon people, but the community of the new life, among his followers, first attracted them. So it was repeatedly when new monastic Orders were founded. And the Protestant Churches? We recall how often communal singing was the convincing thing. There, fellowship was experienced in a common spirit. If today the Protestant Church is in a state of disintegration, its weakness is a lack of the power to form community. Wherever it succeeds in awakening community the Protestant Church still flourishes. The [Roman] Catholic Church is assured of its unity in the person of the Pope; it is just this imposing 'unity' that exercises the strongest attraction on so many souls who feel they are 'deserted' without a greater ego.

From the words of Christ's revelation we have to learn ever more what The Christian Community alone can make flourish for its life. Perhaps it has never been harder than in our own time to create genuine community among human beings. Human beings have become much more unbending, capricious and obstinate than in earlier times when traditional ties still warmed their hearts. From sheer discontent and individual isolation people now unite themselves into great unions that follow the same aims. But those communities are either Unions bound together by material interests that extinguish the human individuality altogether for the sake of an idea that is but an interest; or they are blood-ties of an egoistical nature that falsify the greater 'I' seeking to enter into human beings.

The greatest and most dangerous union of interest that has ever been seen is the Bolshevik International. One can perceive ever more clearly how within it the individual 'I' is sacrificed to the Moloch [= idol] of an abstract ideology that has laid hold of people's minds, but which dries up the main-springs of life. On the other hand, Nationalism thrives on egoistical blood-ties. Merely to speak of a blood-tie is today half a lie, and even more than a half-lie. They are communities of destiny, communities of culture, but they threaten to narrow and to destroy in autarchy, in egoistical self-sufficiency, the divine plan for humanity.

Just in such an age The Christian Community was founded [1922]. But the small number of its members at present ought not to divert attention from its divine mission. Here is a Community really founded around the 'I in the Father, and the Father in me'. In the Protestant churches the individual preacher comes too much to the fore, and in the [Roman] Catholic Church the hierarchical figure of the Pope. In The Christian Community people gather as closely as possible around the 'I' of Christ present at the altar, preaching and acting.

> Preaching: I in the Father.
> Acting: the Father in me.

The Catholic will say, that also happens in the Mass. It is unnecessary to convince him or her that this does not *happen*, but rather that it does not happen in a way fully in accordance with things as they are today.[110] The human 'I' has developed beyond the ancient form of the Mass. It demands that it should be approached in a different way from what was necessary in the first 1500 years of Christianity. In The Christian Community, community is really founded around the 'I in the Father, and the Father in me'. Consequently, in this particular age when community and the 'I' are so important, in Christ's expectation towards The Christian Community we have to realize the full earnestness of our undertaking and its importance in world-history.

People who see above them the greatness of the truth of Christ, Who fulfils all humanity's need, cannot entertain an arrogant thought. For them it will be their mission to fulfil to their utmost, in the station of life to which they are called, what Christ has willed for all humanity, or rather for the whole body of disciples, and of serving Christ's will as ideally as possible. The message Christ gave, according to His sayings, has been accepted. But what will lead us forward in world-history is not the truth of our preaching, not even so much the power of consecration in our worship, but the real growth of a community *in* its divine worship, *in* its congregational meetings, and *in* its acts as a congregation. If in all these there is a reflection of the saying 'I in the Father, and the Father in me', then 'the world will believe that Thou hast sent me'.

Out of this clear insight into the ultimate goal of the world, we must acquire the full content of what love means. Our conception of love is far too low. Many people are disgusted today by the stuffy atmosphere, the impure sentimentality, the hidden selfishness that so often passes for love, even in the name of charity. Love is in no sense just sweet happiness of soul or blessedness impregnated with sentimentality; when taken seriously it means taking over into our own soul the trials and troubles of others; it demands the most resolute courage and the most steadfast strength. Only the feeling, 'I can do no other' [Luther] can make us penetrate with real love into our neighbour's troubles. But behind this feeling, 'I can do no other', there is the secret urge of our 'I' towards its goal, towards an uprising into a greater 'I', or much rather, to its resurrection in a higher 'I'. In this way, we experience *God* in love. There is no salvation for any of us except in our becoming a *humanity* completely penetrated by that Spirit of Love that through all cycles of time has been weaving between the Father and the Son. The *Spirit* of Love must fill us to overflowing—the feeling comes spontaneously—and so as a real 'fulfilment'. Only when we have grasped that without love, no spirit has understanding, no will has fire, no 'I' has existence, and no God can dwell in us, then strikes the hour of Love. 'That they may be *in us.*'

17:22

'Whom Thou hast sent'—scarcely has Christ spoken these words, before He looks again upon His work with the eyes of His Father, to judge of its permanency, 'The glory which Thou hast given me I have given to them, that they may be one even as we are one' (17:22). Christ draws from His mission not lordship over what is beneath, but only responsibility towards what is above. From these words we shall learn what is to be our greatest responsibility in life. Those who have succeeded in bestowing upon others all they themselves have received of divine revelation have accomplished the highest they can do with their lives. And just because we long to bestow more upon people, we ourselves continually seek to draw more from the divine world. Should it ever be that our whole life is suffused with the highest and most divine attainable, then our life has reached its goal.

Christ regarded as His greatest gift to humanity, 'The glory which the Father has given me'. But He Himself never spoke of grace. He never used the word—this we especially note—but the 'glory' the Apostles perceived in Him was 'full of grace and truth'. We ought repeatedly to meditate upon the words, 'the glory Thou hast given me I have given to them'. Then of themselves the questions would follow: How much of divine glory, of divine revelation has life brought to *me*? How can I bestow it even more fully upon them? How can my life in its smallest details be suffused by the highest that is given me? For, as we can vividly feel from these passages, that which shines out from our being is of decisive importance. Important as all individual spiritual knowledge may be, that higher quality behind everything is the radiance of our being. Can we say, 'The glory which Thou hast given me'—even if it were but little—'I have given them'?

17:22, 23

'That they may be one even as we are one, I in them and Thou in me, that they may become perfectly one, so that the world may know that Thou hast sent me and hast loved them even as Thou hast loved me' (17:22, 23).

Here again we come across the word 'perfection', or 'fulfilment', sounding through John's Gospel. Christ has fulfilled the work which the Father gave Him to do. He bears within Himself perfect joy; here He speaks of the perfecting of the disciples. And, as His last word on the cross, 'It is finished' (19:30). Can we fail to notice this? Or how in the world of that time the word 'perfecting' or 'fulfilment' must have sounded, when the word 'initiation'—the coveted initiation in the Mysteries—had the same sound? *'Telos'* means the 'goal' or 'fulfilment', *'telete'* 'initiation' or the 'consecration',[111] *'teleiōsis'* the 'perfecting' or the 'consummation'. Since everyone in the Greek-speaking world of those days must have known the word *'telete'*, it follows that John's Gospel—without suggesting a direct relationship with the Mysteries, or even mentioning them—was to appear as the book of the fulfilment of the Mysteries for humanity.

This consummation, quite different from that in the Mysteries, yet transcends them. There an individual human being was led to initiation that consisted in a union with the Godhead, in 'becoming one'. Truly, in this one sentence we can find the Mysteries clearly proclaimed to all the world. Human beings do not *lose* their 'I' in the Godhead, but they receive a greater 'I'. So Christ says, 'I in them, and Thou in me'. Human beings are not perfected as *individuals*, for the human being as an individual[112] can never become 'man'[*Mensch*]. But as Goethe has said, 'Mankind is the only real man' [*Mensch*],[113] so Christ says, 'That they may be one even as we are one'. Consecration, or initiation, is not a goal reached once and for all, but a condition in which true life first begins. To use a modern expression, it is not static, but dynamic. Perfecting is not reached from below, it is bestowed from above. Perfecting does not consist in abstract moral perfection, nor moods of sentimental feeling, but in love, in the love with which the Father loves the Son, and all creation in the Son. Human beings become not only one with the Father of the world in their thinking, they are this, too, for they have 'known' him—nor do they become one with him only in their feeling—yet they are also this, for love is the highest feeling—but above all, they become one with the Father in their *will*, in their 'I'. And this is the highest of all. We can well imagine how the preachers of Christianity entered the circles of the Mysteries. They were steeped in these truths, having received into themselves the light of John's Gospel, as it shines forth from the Great Intercession, the High-Priestly Prayer.

This consecration was not accomplished in the strictly guarded seclusion of the temples where it was forbidden on pain of death to mention it, but the solemn spectacle became an historical fact and was addressed to the whole world. 'That the world may know ...'. With amazement the world beholds its sacred drama fulfilled.

Truly, we can say the ultimate goal of human knowledge is indicated in the love wherewith the Father loves the Son. From the most diverse aspects this is the ultimate wisdom to which all thought and research will lead us:

- physics and chemistry, when they become more spiritual and have perceived the spiritual interplay of the various forms of 'matter';
- astronomy, when once the harmony of the world of the stars has been perceived;
- history, when the hidden will behind the guidance of mankind has become clear;
- but also the invisible world of the spirit, when human beings rise ever higher to see the love of the Father to the Son shining through all the angelic realms.

However, it is the life of the disciples among themselves that is meant to be the source of the inspiration from which the world receives this illumination. What a lofty task for a Christian community! And yet, again, not as the 'heathen' once said about the first Christians, 'See how they love one another!' but more truly and more comprehensively, 'the Father loves them'.

Buddha still believed that someone would find perfection only when they released themselves from the world. Christ's power is far greater. In Him the human being does not find perfection *through* the world but *in* the world and *for* the world. With the silver light of the Moon, Buddha leads his followers into the far spaces of Nirvana;[114] with the golden rays of the Sun the human being returns victoriously back to the world in Christ.

United with Christ, the human being shines as the same light, and fulfils upon the Earth a new working of the Sun. In the beginning of the Bible we are told of the creation of humankind; here the fulfilment is announced.

17:24

'Father, I desire that they also, whom Thou hast given me, may be with me where I am, to behold my glory which Thou hast given me in Thy love for me before the foundation of the world.'

Christ's vision is now concerned with things far beyond the world. High above the earthly goal He lets the goal of future worlds, which has to be represented in His disciples, shine out before us. 'That they may behold the glory that is mine.' In this passage three phrases reveal special truths.

> [1] First, Christ here says for the first time '*I will*'. Before he said, 'I pray'. In freedom and sovereignty He appears as the Son before the Father. Now he enters again into His divine kingdom. As long as He was on the Earth, He adapted Himself to earthly conditions. This was struggle and trial, and consequently praying. Now we see Christ reign, indeed the true Son of the Father, for His will is none other than that of the Father. What the Father has given Him He returns to Him. This is really the meaning of the whole of earthly history. That also which is given to *us*, we ought to return, and for this end need an 'I' of free will. And consequently an earthly life in which it can grow and find itself.

Yet in the shade of meaning between 'I pray' and 'I will', the difference between our present-day world and our future world is as clearly and briefly expressed as is possible. Upon the Earth we can pray, the Earth is the place of prayer. Angels cannot pray as we can but they can worship. This is the distinction that is also always made in the Bible. When we ourselves ascend to a higher plane, we work out the will that is in us, moreover, that will which comes into being in us through the contemplation and worship of higher powers. But we are not placed so externally in respect of those higher powers, nor are we so shut off from them as our earthly prayer presupposes.

> [2] The second point to notice is the way in which Christ here speaks of His disciples. They are to be 'with Him'. Upon the Earth He wills to be *in* them. In the higher world they are to be 'with Him'. A weighty and essential distinction! Upon the Earth, where there is such great variety of being, the joy of the disciples consists in their being wholly filled with Christ, in being one with Him. In the higher world everything interweaves and is not so separate. There, joy consists in feeling one is an individual 'I'—the product of earthly history, in remaining conscious of this history and yet being closely united with Christ.

> [3] But the third point of importance is that here the *'I am'* that sounds throughout the whole of John's Gospel, appears once more, but now in its highest revelation. 'I will that where *I am*, there they may be with me.' Here, at the end, the 'I am' makes itself known. It reveals and bestows upon us its world. The more the 'I am' lives in us, the more it will cause the realm belonging to it, so to speak, to shine around us. And after death it will lift us with itself into this realm. This is the reason why the 'I am' wills to live in us—because only thus can it bring us to the place where it has its home.

As a beholding of His glory, Christ describes the highest life to which He will lead His disciples. Here, at the most majestic part of the gospel, we have the same words that we met at the beginning. 'We beheld His glory.' There, at the beginning, it took place on the Earth, here, at the end, it is promised for the higher world. But when on the Earth, it is perceived in prayer—in meditation—it is the right preparation for the higher life.

How have we to think of this beholding? Certainly, as the perceiving of individual revelations, through which everywhere, Christ's being, the Christ-'I' shines, but also as the beholding of the Christ-'I' itself, in the glory of its being of light and love, until we are entirely united with it.

At the moment when this is apprehended, all beholding acquires another meaning. What is seen every day upon the Earth is also a preparation for the highest life. The whole content of our sense impressions now acquires a new and deeper significance. Will not the person who on the Earth has succeeded in reaching a clear, objective 'recognition' thereby also acquire a training for the higher world?

If the external beholding is of such importance, then by the inner *training* to behold we are led directly to the highest life. Consequently, too, spiritual vision, to which anthroposophy shows the way, is not so meaningless as those constantly assert who do not know it, in particular certain theologians. This one saying of Christ, that He wills that His disciples should learn to behold, ought to protect us against such errors. It is simply not known how in such beholding there is communion—the higher it reaches, the greater it is—nor, that worship presupposes vision and consists in a viewing with our whole nature, even with our will and its whole capacity for devotion and sacrifice. When we see without eyes, the eye changes into an image of what we see. This is only a hint. Into that, O man, which you *behold*, thou shalt be changed! Can we speak so disparagingly of vision in relation to faith when we have read John's Gospel? Ought we not much rather to seek in faith for the dim beginnings of vision?

Again a great human document may serve as a pinnacle from which to look across to the high summits of the Johannine heights of worship.

> Take note, Socrates, all thou canst! He who has so far been trained for love, will at last as love's final consecration, behold a wondrous sight, and witness the great story of creation. He will behold the Beautiful that mirrors itself in beauty, mirrors eternally in itself. And what is beautiful otherwise will be only its reflection, and part of it. 'And here, beloved,' cried the prophetess, 'here if anywhere is life worth living, where thou dost perceive eternal Beauty. Believest thou, that thy life or the life of another would then still be fettered and base, if thou couldest look thereon and dwell near that miracle?[115]

One cannot read these words of Plato in *The Symposium* alongside the words of Christ without being deeply moved. Indeed *here* belong, where Christ says: That they may 'behold my glory which Thou hast given me in Thy love for me before the foundation of the world' (17:24). For these words of Christ are their fulfilment. And nowhere have they been approached so nearly as in this hymn of Plato. What is there still lacking? That we should rise from love of beauty to love of that very love by which we are contemplated through the gaze of an ego-being, indeed of the Father, the Ground of the World. The two words 'beauty' and 'glory' placed side by side say everything. Beauty (*Schön*) comes from 'shine / appearance' (*Schein*). But appearance points back to *revelation*. Revelation (*Offenbarung*) is the same word as glory (*Herrlichkeit*).[116] 'That they may behold not only eternal Beauty itself, but the shining revelation of my "I", my Ego, in which lives the Father.' A light bandage still lies over Plato's eyes. But where else, outside Christianity, has there been a more prophetic vision of Christ, as He is revealed in John's Gospel?

'Here, if anywhere, is life worth living, where thou dost perceive the eternal Beauty,' says Plato. 'This is life eternal that they should know Thee, the only true God,' says Christ. In Plato we might still sense a last suggestion of egoistical joy and also a suggestion of uncertainty, but these disappear in the solemn call of the risen Sun, appearing in the words of Christ. Across the centuries Plato and John greet one another as representatives of humanity.

'Thou didst love me before the foundation of the world.' The word 'foundation' is such a fitting expression for the physical world. But now Christ looks back to those aeons of joy *before* the world began. They will return, but quite changed. The difference is again expressed in very simple words; in the words 'with me'. This is the gain of evolution.

We have realized that the greatest content of our external life is that we should ray forth that glory which has been bestowed upon us; now we realize that the content of our inner life is to behold the glory bestowed in Christ. Our life passes between these polarities, and always when we gaze upon Christ, we are where He is, even when still on the Earth. This the evangelist tells us at the beginning by testifying, 'We have beheld his glory' (1:14). Who does not yearn for more of this glory within oneself?

But there is a law that everyone receives as much glory as, for the time being, one can bear. Yet, however little we can at first obtain of this glory, in this reciprocal process our life henceforth proceeds; the more glory we learn to ray out, the more we can receive from within. And the more we acquire within, the more we can bestow outwardly.

17:25

'O righteous Father, the world has not known Thee, but I have known Thee; and these know that Thou hast sent me.'

Here again the world and the 'I' stand opposite one another. But how firmly does the 'I' stand! Never did an 'I' face the world more freely and victoriously. Whoever would stand for Christ must, as an individual 'I', also be able to face the whole world. And they can feel and learn from these words how to do this without undue force or arrogance.

Our amazement at these words increases as we consider all that is included in this 'world'. For example, the whole religious world of the Jews. It did 'not know' the Father, however much it preached God, and however earnest and intense was their striving after righteousness. The saying of Christ becomes fully comprehensible when we see that here He does not only touch upon the fact that the Jews could not realize God as Father,[117] but the more fundamental distinction between Yahveh and God the Father. Yahveh, the God of the Jews, rayed down to them high divine qualities, but God the Father is still higher and greater. And through this distinction—one cannot say antithesis—*between Yahveh and the Father-God, the struggle of the Jews with Christ can be partly explained.* Whoever understands the historical sources of the first centuries of our era, knows that similar statements have often been made in Gnostic writings, even if these accounts have been handed down through people who no longer understand the meaning of the Gnostic doctrine. These doctrines had frequently become misrepresented and degenerate.

The whole world has 'not known the Father', even the non-Jewish world; in spite of all the surmises of God held by the nations and their various forms of divine worship, Christ felt that His knowledge surpassed all theirs. Of the disciples themselves, He does not yet say in this passage that they have known the Father, but only that they have known *Him* Whom 'the Father has sent'. It appears as if in these words Christ made His final reckoning with the world. This isolation does not disquiet Him for a moment. His reliance on God is much stronger than the whole world. With sublime calm He looks upon His work, from which He has already begun to retire, and He can only place this rejection by the whole world into the sphere of divine justice. It is not a case of love which deceives itself about these realities, but purified, considered observations and judgment of the worlds that there stand in opposition.

From our ordinary experiences, we can consider the events concealed behind these words. How often does it seem to us, when we are profoundly moved in our souls by experiences of God, that people are ignorant of the Father, to an astounding and disconcerting degree. It is as if all that which was so clearly revealed to our souls had not really existed. 'They know not what they do' (Luke 23:34). Then one seems helpless. What can we do when we have done all we know? Are they blind or guilty? We can only place it before the farseeing vision of divine justice. If undercurrents of life and profound inner necessities are evolving, then we can only leave it to divine guidance to find the right way. But let us consider that where there is no knowledge of the Father, there is no 'life'. The world just lacks life and will continue to lack it in spite of all external speed and pomp.

Deeply moved, the spirit of Christ turns back again to the beginning of the prayer. Indeed, He has done His part.

17:26

'I made known to them Thy Name, and I will make it known.' Even unto death and after death He will declare it, for He is and remains 'the Word'. Therein also lies all that He will still be able to do in future cycles for the salvation of that world, which has not known Him. In this is also comprised our eternal task for the world. We also are to become 'the word'. And what happens to the world is the concern of divine justice and not of our judgment.

'The love with which Thou hast loved me may be in them, and I in them.' This is the last phrase of the High-Priestly Prayer. Can we conceive any conclusion of the gospel of the 'I am' that could be more essential or comprehensive? And although we may be quite convinced that the evangelist could not have remembered every detail, yet surely he retained this final sentence in his memory? With what feeling and with what intonation may this 'I in them' have been spoken? May it not have been spoken with such authority that it should resound throughout all human history?

And it does sound on. Out of these concluding words of the Great Intercession, the High-Priestly Prayer, we hold the authority with which in every celebration of the Act of Consecration of Man we pronounce the words 'Christ in you!' [plural]. In them throughout all Christian worship, this parting gift of Christ lives on. And whoever even once perceives this connection will ever and again through this saying look back to the hour in which Christ stood before His disciples, summing up His whole work in this one single phrase: 'I in you.' Evermore do we hear this last greeting of Christ to His own.

If anywhere, then from these simple, powerful words of Christ, we can perceive what Christianity really is.

- Not a dogmatic doctrine for the head, but 'I in them'.
- Not a sentimental feeling for the heart, but 'I in them'.
- Not a fanaticism in the will, but 'I in them'.
- This is great, this is free—and it is boundless.
- It is entirely calm—and full of power.
- It is many-sided—and yet central.

This Christianity we have still to learn. We open wide the doors of our inner being, that this 'I' may dwell therein. And it is as if a temple were illumined with light from within. If we feel we are a temple, looking inward to the radiant light that burns there, and by this light it is made living, is ensouled, then we have come near to this saying.

'The love with which Thou hast loved me may be in them.' When we perceive this parallelism, we are in the realm of the loftiest mysticism, or much rather, in the realm that all the mystics through all the centuries have looked for, and about which they had only dim forebodings and no clear insight. We will not embark on obvious speculations, pointing to the similarities of these two sayings. Perhaps we might say that the love wherewith the Father loves the Son, when condensed into our 'I', and radiated back to the Father, may be the Son. But our thoughts, which live in the world of dialectical logic, do not yet grasp these ultimate truths, and only awaken new questions, to which we can supply no answer. So we shall initially content ourselves with knowing that the content of this 'I' that would live in us, is love—not merely grace, which turns towards our unworthiness and impurity, nor yet merely the love that comes to the divine kernel of our being, but the love wherewith the Father loves the Son. What an exalted goal is thereby given to our inner life! Millions of years alone will be required for us even gradually to approach this goal, after it has become a light within us. If we consider this as far as we are able, as the *real content of our 'I'*: the love wherewith the Father loves the Son; if we think of this content as shining out in all our actions, our words, our thinking, feelings and will—the love wherewith the Father loves the Son; then the real archetypal picture of the human being will begin to shine out in our spirit. This Johannine proclamation rises far beyond all Protestant preaching, even far beyond everything up to now achieved by Christendom.

Practical life

Let us recall our thoughts from these distant heights to the quite tangible and practical things of our life. We wake up early in the morning. Our 'I', which during the night dwelt in the realms of unconsciousness, is here again. We let Christ shine into this 'I' of ours. He lives in the inmost part of our being, as the divine 'I' for which our lower 'I' was only the forerunner and custodian. Our higher 'I' that is a part of Christ—Christ, Who for us guards and keeps within Himself our higher 'I'. And now let us bring the content of this 'I' into our consciousness. It is love. But love in its very highest form, as the love of the Father Himself, and as the love for the Son Himself. Shall we not experience something from this:

- that really in everything to which we turn our love the Son would be awakened?;
- that continuously loves in us *that which is coming into being?;*
- that we ourselves continuously share both in the life of the Father and of the Son?

- in the life of the Father in as far as we love, and in the life of the Son, in so far as we receive into ourselves what we love, and let it radiate back to the Father?;
- that in this way without ceasing, the Father greets the Son, and the Son the Father?;
- that this twofold fact is possible through the love in which the two become one?;
- that so the very highest life—and this is the love of the Father to the Son and of the Son to the Father—remains in us forever, and yet is always changing?;
- that the reflection of this sublime life can radiate throughout even in the smallest trifles of life?

'Here, if anywhere, is life worth living.' Indeed, this only is 'life'.

Now we see man's being shone through by the very purest light with which it can be illuminated. All further evolvings of the world, however many there be, can contribute nothing higher; they can only raise this one thing to an ever higher perfection. We spoke of our earthly goal, and of a super-earthly goal. We see them simultaneously as an external goal and an internal goal. And they are the same. The outward goal is to shine forth in the revelation, in the 'glory' that has become ours. This holds good for this Earth, and perhaps in another more exalted way also for future worlds. The inner goal is to share in the love wherewith the Father loves the Son, and certainly holds good for all cycles of time to come. Here we share the highest thoughts that were ever conceived about mankind.

The Paradise Legend

In order once more to bring these lofty thoughts for the *Earth* into our consciousness as clearly as possible, let us place two pictures before our soul. The first is *from the Paradise legend*. We have already been led to the two Trees, the Tree of Knowledge and the Tree of Life. We saw how their tops have grown into one another. 'This is *life* eternal that they may *know* Thee.' Now, at the end of the Book of Revelation, they receive new names, their ultimate, sublime names. 'Knowledge' is now named 'glory'. The glory, the radiant revelation from above, must come to meet knowledge. And all knowledge receives its final goal in the revelation, in the glory of the Father Himself. And *'life'* is now named *'love'*. It is not possible to call life anything higher than love. Do we understand the likeness and the difference? If we have understood why the 'Tree of Knowledge' is now called 'glory', and the 'Tree of Life' 'love', we have grasped the meaning of the whole evolution of the Earth. For the two Trees of Paradise could only acquire these names after long periods of history in which humanity through darkness and sin could progress to the 'I', to revelation, and to love. In these final words of the High-Priestly Prayer, the Great Intercession, we have reached Paradise again, but bringing with us the whole result of earthly history.

- What we might have had as knowledge in Paradise is shone through by what has been able to be revealed in the earthly world as the glory of existence.
- What might have been to us life in Paradise is shone through by what has been revealed in human history as love.
- Human beings as they have now become, may look up to another Paradise, where they live with their spirit in the divine glory, and with their being in the divine love.

The Lord's Supper

The two sayings have now been understood from the viewpoint of Paradise. With the other picture that we would place before the soul we can understand them now more deeply *from the aspect of the Lord's Supper.* The body of Christ—that is the glory which is destined for human beings. For in the body, as it originally was and has become again in Christ, all worlds and all revelations are represented. And if we succeed in bearing the living body of Christ within ourselves, then we know that we ourselves have had bestowed upon us in earthly form and in a human way the fullness of all divine revelation, the whole edifice of divine glory. Through all the members of our body we look into the worlds of divine revelation. But the blood of Christ is no other than love itself. The noblest products of all the Earth are gathered into the blood, until they become the bearer of the life of love, indeed, they have even been transformed into overflowing love. 'Glory' and 'love' are bestowed upon us in every Lord's Supper. And every Lord's Supper is a training in 'glory' and 'love'. This is the light and the fire of the primordial Sun, of God the Father.

Third 'resting place'

From these last heights let us look back once again at the way we have come. Is not what we have experienced together like a great 'Lord's Prayer upon the Mount'? First of all we stood in the full glory of the divine Name. 'Transfiguration' shone upon life, upon mankind and its work, upon knowledge and all forms of human activity. The divine

Name was divine ordinance made visible. What it means to hallow the divine name upon the Earth is revealed as we looked back upon Christ's life. But then we descended to the battlefield of the Earth. Amid struggle and sorrow we saw the disciples press forward for their Master; protected and consecrated by Him for their earthy battle. Thus, and not otherwise, in simplicity and hardship and not in the glory of the vision of light, but in dark striving with continuous hidden effort, 'comes' 'the Kingdom of God'.

But then the Castle of the Holy Grail rose up.[118] The earthly goal and the super-earthly goal became visible. We saw what the divine will should be on the Earth, 'as it is in the heavens'. 'As Thou hast loved me so ought they to love one another; so that the world may behold love. As we are one, so shall the disciples become one in glory.' The Mystery of all being is announced to the whole world. Out of heaven, out of the being of the Father with the Son, love breaks through upon the Earth, and it will fill all things.

When we see that the Great Intercession, the High-Priestly Prayer, is a development of the Lord's Prayer, then both of them become greater for us. In seeing in the Lord's Prayer a radiant constellation of three stars, we have now entered into the starry worlds.

> [1] But we have also received a baptism, than which we can receive no greater—but here we should receive it ever anew. Nowhere does the countenance of the Father look into human life as it does in the first part of this prayer. We hear Him speaking to His Son and messenger concerning their history, concerning the word and the work, concerning life and being, faith and knowledge. The Name of the Father is written upon the Earth, and we enter into its glory.
>
> [2] The Son in the second part of the prayer writes His Name on the Earth and in our souls. If anywhere we are brought to the knowledge of the Son's being, then it is here. We see Him before us, sharing 'mine' and 'thine' with the Father. We see how fullness of joy shines forth from Him, how He turns to His own upon the Earth, how He guards them and watches over them, and how He sanctifies Himself for them.
>
> [3] In the third part, the Holy Spirit is not indeed mentioned by name. And yet we can nowhere receive Him so intimately from out of Christ Himself as here. Light illuminates the distant cycles of time. The sacred wisdom concerning all ultimate Mysteries descends upon human beings, consecrating them into those who have wisdom and love—the world, meanwhile, knows them not. Father, Son and mankind in

> which lives the Holy Spirit, become one. The primordial history of the Holy Trinity resounds over the Earth. For someone who would wish in divine solemnity to be baptized directly from heaven, here the sanctuary is laid open.

These are in fact *the* highest thoughts that can be held upon Earth, *the* highest feelings that can be kindled in our souls, *the* highest impulses of the will that can awaken in our life. With ever-renewed light, the jewel of this prayer shines out. Do we not also see Christ standing as Prophet, High-Priest and King?

- In the first part of the prayer He is above all the Revealer, the Preacher of the divine will, the Prophet.
- Then he assumes the garment of the High-Priest, sanctifying Himself for His disciples.
- But then, in the third part, when He says 'I will', as a King He mounts the throne of a new kingdom, that of humanity united in God.

Has the past, present and future of humanity ever been more steeped in holiness than in this prayer?

- The past: we return to our first origin when we lived as a thought in God Himself, and like Christ shared His glory with Him, though all unconsciously.
- The present: it brings the sacred task of a cosmic struggle that we have to wage for Christ, to which we are sent, in which we are watched over, but not protected from sorrow and enmity, but are drawn from within into a deep hallowing, because Christ draws us with Him.
- The future: we see the final goal before us, we receive sure guidance for all our human work, we perceive how our own 'I' is absorbed in the heights of divine glory.

Because these are *the* highest thoughts, *the* highest feelings, *the* highest impulses of the will that have ever lived or could ever live within a human being, we could wish for no more ideal passing from life than that we might be received into the glory that Christ in this prayer has bequeathed to us upon the Earth. We do not know whether it will be granted to us to approach our death consciously, but should this be so, then a time might come in which we might leave behind all external earthly thoughts, when we should have a right to fill our soul with that which filled Christ Himself, when He 'went to the Father', and of which He spoke in His wish that we should follow the shining path by which He went.

For this reason it is the custom of The Christian Community in the simple last sacrament, for those who desire it and who wish to have their dying sanctified, to surround them with the words of the High-Priestly Prayer. At this time human beings have the right, like St Francis, to let all joy break forth in their soul like the buds of spring. Now all pettiness and trouble pertaining to the Earth may withdraw, and what has been laid of greatest worth as a germ in the soul, be allowed to sprout. If the exalted words of this prayer are then surrounding us, it will be as though there were angels sheltering us with their wings. And when death comes, these angels, folding their wings around us will carry us up, as upon the chariot of Elijah, where Christ would have us be. 'Father, I desire that they also, whom Thou hast given me, may be with me where I am, to behold my glory which Thou hast given me in Thy love for me before the foundation of the world' (24). The whole of earthly history dies away. The heavenly heights receive us. Christ, at the same moment, as it were, has given us the password with which we may knock at the gates that separate life and life. We are most surely near Him when we pass into the glory into which He Himself rose; the glory that He left behind like a bridge of light leading from the Earth to Him. So we speak that 'I in Thee' with which we answer His last wish: 'I in you.' And this greeting He knows, and to this greeting He opens the gate.

However, in order that we may be able to do this in the last hours, when perhaps our soul will lack the power to soar, and when it can only lie in the remembrance of its better moments, we will practise it in the quiet hours during life. Then all these angels will become our friends so that we can call them by name. In this prayer, 'death is swallowed up in victory' (Is. 25:8, I Cor. 15:54). We no longer notice that this is what is called death! Consequently, we can take death into our life in no more glorious way than through this prayer. In this prayer there is nothing but death, death of the old nature and the old life, death of the old thinking and will, the death of the old 'I'. And in this prayer is nothing but life: new being, new vision, new will, a new 'I'. Death is no more. Whoever follows the path of this prayer, moves in freedom out of the world of death into the world of life. And they do it in every moment of treading this path. They 'see death no more in all eternity' (8:51). Over their soul sounds the rejoicing that echoing from Christ moves us so profoundly throughout the whole of this prayer: '*I come to Thee.*'

FINIS

Consecration of the Disciples (John 21)

(Die Christengemeinschaft, 6. Jg. 3, Juni 1929, pp. 73-7)

Peter denies

Peter denied his Lord at the fire of coals. At the coal fire he confessed Christ. Already the early Church Fathers pointed this out. But is the wonderful symbolism seen here? The black coal speaks of darkness and evil. It is dug out of the depths of the Earth. It derives from a process of death. But meeting the fire it gives light and warmth.

Such a process took place with Peter. When he denied his Lord he went out, and it was night. The darkness around him was the outer symbol of the darkness within him. Then Christ kindled the fire of love in this darkness. And now Peter burned brightly, giving light and warmth to the first community.

We do not know a picture simpler and more eloquent than this for the Mystery of evil in the world. However dark and black evil is on Earth, when it meets the fire it gives more light and warmth—all the more wisdom and love. The world is not so simple that one could divide it like a bad drama into the bad characters and the good ones.

Does this mean we should commit evil so that good can arise? Already Paul answered this—decidedly not! In devoted prayer we behold the divine that holds sway and take part in it! Turn evil into good through love!—this is demanded by Christianity at large. This may not always succeed on Earth. But the people are more than their life on Earth. Approach the coal as fire. Perhaps it takes a long time until it catches fire. But then it transforms all the more into light and warmth.

Soul-care that redeems

I do not know how those who deny a true resurrection of Christ can deal with this story at the end of John's Gospel. Do people believe that the first community would have realized Peter as a leader from the beginning after he had denied Christ, unless some event had happened? Do people believe that Peter himself would have found the strength of certainty at Pentecost without any self-accusation, if he had not experienced a meeting with Christ and been forgiven? Is it believed that anyone in the group of the first community could have been found who could have made up the tremendous soul-care of the story of Peter with all its human splendour?

Peter denied his Lord three times. Three times he is allowed to make it good before the disciples—without even a single word mentioning the painful denial. He is also reminded of his earlier presumption, again only indicated, yet clearly so. 'Do you love me more than these' (John 21:15). And when he understands and in his answer does not maintain his earlier presumptuousness above the others, then this wonderful rebuke, as serious as it is tender, is dropped, and everything is steered towards the main matter of the heart. The best in Peter is addressed—his love for Christ. This best, against all the rest that lives in Peter—his pride, his ambition, his passionate nature, his unthinking impulsiveness—is increasingly strengthened and geared towards a divine aim. For all time a question is burned into Peter's soul, with which he can now transform himself. He enters into the fire and in his words one notices that he writhes and struggles. But he holds out and emerges with a heart that completely trusts in Christ. 'Lord, you know' (v. 16)—in place of his earlier self-trust. The denial is answered by a new and greater trust. The trust again is answered by a new, now complete self-giving. The self-assured Peter surely feels himself as if built into a divine great trust, after he was freshly created through the question. Everything dark and flickering in him is smelted away through the pure fire of Christ's question.

One can search the whole world for such an example of pastoral soul-care. Anyone who has seen it once knows this signature. A whole world-history lives in this simple narration.

Advance in love?

But the story has more interesting depths when one looks more precisely at the Greek text.[119] The Greek language has three words for love: *ερος* [eros], *φιλεῶ* [*phileō*], *αγαπᾷο* [*agapāo*].

- The first word does not occur in the Bible. It lives in the eroticism of the present day and has left the path which Plato in his *Symposium/ The Banquet* has so wonderfully portrayed as *eros*—approaching quite close to Christianity.
- The second word we meet in *philo-sophia*, the 'love of wisdom', but also in each Philip, the 'lover of horses'. It shows a love based on inclination, on feeling [= friendship, affection].
- The third word [*agape*, unconditional love] is the one which Christ raises in the High-Priestly Prayer (John 17) towards the highest life, when He prays that the love with which He loves His Father may be in the disciples and become their new soul.

In John's Gospel when the disciple is mentioned 'whom the Lord loved', the word *agape* is used. Of Lazarus it is said before he was raised, using the word *agape*, also in the expression, 'Lord, he whom you love is sick' (John 11:3). But in order that we see that both are not simply different, but can merge into each other, even for the disciple whom the Lord loved, the word *philia* is sometimes used. Interestingly, it is Mary Magdalene who brings the message of the Resurrection to the disciple whom the Lord loved, in the spirit of *philia*.

And now a profound dialogue unfolds at the Lake of Gennesaret between the disciple who had denied and the Lord, Who wants to call him afresh. Since our language [hardly] allows anything else, we translate the word *agapão* with 'to love' or 'dearly love', and the word *phileo* [usually also translated 'to love'] with 'cherish', 'hold you dear', or 'have affection for'.

> [i] Christ asked Peter, 'Simon, son of Jonah, do you love me more than these?' Peter answers, 'Yes, Lord, you know that I hold you dear'.
>
> [ii] Christ asks once more but no longer repeating the reprimand, after He has attained His aim, 'Do you love me?' Again Peter answers, 'Yes, Lord, you know that I hold you dear'; he does not dare use the word *agapão*.
>
> [iii] Then in the third question Christ also takes over Peter's word, 'Do you hold me dear?' He [too] no longer asks using *agapão*. And now comes Peter's last answer, 'Lord, you know everything, you know that I hold you dear'.

What has happened? Christ has accommodated Himself to Peter's level. He was not able to raise him to the heights of *agape*-love. But He nevertheless realizes his *philia*-love. He confirms to him that with this love in his heart he can assume the pastoral care of the first community.

The Church of Rome

What we see here with Peter reflects the future history of Roman Christianity throughout the centuries. The Roman Church showed the 'first love'. Humanity that was in need of care was entrusted to it. But this love was not yet the *agape*-love of which John speaks, although it does shine out of some lights in the Roman Church. It is more the love of the heart than the love of the spirit. Powerful feeling, which is raised to a strong discipleship—the Catholic Church was great in the imitation of Christ, as also its choicest devotional text by Thomas à Kempis concerns this imitation. Precisely this phrase Christ spake to Peter, 'Follow me!' It is like an answer for the one who had first asked, 'Where shall we go?' (John 6:68) and who later wanted to follow again, where he still could (John 13:36, 37). But also in this narration the spirit of the not yet fully awake 'I' can be felt, such as in the denial scene. Peter said to the servants, 'I am not the one ....'. In the Greek way of expression, it says, 'I am not'. It really was not his 'I'. It was not present in that hour. Only his fear and his secret plan were present. But now, too, when he answers Christ, he places his 'I' outside himself, 'You know that I cherish you'. He puts his 'I' into Christ; such a deed is fine, noble. But John would not have spoken like that. Through the mouth of John the 'I am ...' has been proclaimed to the world, and here something else is prepared than what lives in the 'You know' of Peter. The 'I in them' of which the High-Priestly Prayer prophecies will come one day, and only to the extent to which this 'I' is present can the *agape*-love come about.

But initially the 'You know' lives on in the Roman Church. The trust in authority is the basic character of Roman Christianity. The not fully awakened 'I' does not live in it. The [Roman] Catholic Christian feels the Pope, the representative of Christ, like his higher 'I', not yet in himself, but above himself, willingly leaving to him the higher insight and his final conscience. The name of 'You know' the Catholic Church has always justified through the biblical word; even when the words seem to go against human insights and human 'I'-consciousness. In the name of 'You know' heretics were burnt contrary to one's own human feeling, when a biblical phrase or a Papal injunction stood against them.

The character of Roman Christianity is threefold:

- trust in authority in the spiritual life,
- transmutation of emotion in the life of the feelings,
- faith in discipleship in the life of the will.

It is astonishing how exact this Christianity in its most noble characteristic has its picture in Peter whom we see before us. And Christ has realized this Christendom.

Christ's commission

The commission, too, that Christ gives to Peter we have to investigate more precisely in the Greek text. Luther [also KJV and amost all the others] translates Christ's words almost the same. But then it appears only like a strong seal on the mandate. This does not correspond to the magnificent progress of the story. Christ's three mandates translated into our language would run:

- take my lambs to pasture,
- lead my sheep,
- take my little sheep to pasture.

The taking to pasture is more than the leading. A feeding is included here, not only a leading. And when Christ speaks for the third time of the little sheep, then one does not only think of the sick and weak, as happens sometimes, but can hear the diminutives with the sense of a special love, which go to the heart and are carried by the heart.

We consequently see a threefold elevation of rank carried out. Its prerequisite is ever greater love. For as the question burns itself more deeply into the soul, it awakens each time a self-realization and a more tested confession. Only according to the degree of love is one carried aloft in the divine realm. The story shows this in a living way. The elevation of rank does not consist of ever greater bliss but in ever higher commission.

- In the same way as Christ with special emphasis has given the little ones and those unprotected—also elsewhere [in the Gospel]—to the special care of the disciples, initially their care is first given to Peter. 'Take my lambs to pasture'. It is always the mark of a genuine Christ-attitude that it condescends. Thus the Christ-attitude had first to prove itself. This does not concern mastering the teachings of a schooling, but care of the children in the spirit of Christ.
- Then the second thing is leading the adults. To this there already belongs greater love, not merely wisdom, but love. Here too the expression is taken from the shepherd's profession and not that of the ruler.
- The third element is caring for the life of adults in the sense of feeding with divine nourishment. And for this there belongs the greatest love of all. Leading of souls can have no other task in the spirit of Christ than guiding into the divine aim—all one in Me, and replenished with divine nourishment, that they may behold My glory (cf. John 17). If one takes this will into oneself, then one becomes a true leader to one's fellow human beings. Especially today people are wrestling with the 'problem of leadership'.

It is unimaginable how Christ leads Peter to the height of his task. Repeatedly He merely directs His gaze towards him, asking 'Do you love me?' One has to relate this story of Peter to oneself and experience it oneself. Then one realizes that in this question, which certainly has accompanied Peter his whole life, the entire human heart and especially all passions are smelted, purified in the purest fire.

In psychology, it was noticed long ago that one cannot call on the will; one has first to awaken the feelings if one wants to inflame the will. If one succeeds in awakening the right feelings in the human being, one does not then need to address the will, it breaks forth of itself. In the famous speech of Mark Antony in Shakespeare's *Julius Caesar*, Mark Antony seemingly subdues the moment when feeling wants to pass over into the will; through this he demagogically effects, as it were, an elemental outbreak of the will. In the pure heights of the Act of Consecration of Man, too, the passage 'to Thee be turned my willing' is immediately followed by the words expressing the power of the will springing out of the feelings that unites with Christ Who lives in the Father's life. If we wish for a feeling united with Christ, then there is nothing better than to place ourselves under Christ's question, 'Do you love me?' Then everything in our soul disappears into the fiery power of this question. We feel how, out of the answer to this question, a new life arises. These are not religious phrases but ultimate realities. Ultimately nothing remains but the pure divine all-knowing—'You know'—and the beginning of love in us. One can well imagine that this experience is a pre-taste of the judgment after death.

In his *Sartor Resartus* [1836], Thomas Carlyle [1795-1881] has placed two chapters adjacent to each other, 'The eternal No' and 'The eternal Yes'. It sounds like such a world-important 'No' when, directly before the story of Peter, the disciples answer Christ's question, 'Have you nothing to eat?' with the answer, 'No'. The world without Christ offers no nourishment that can satisfy the soul. This 'No' is powerfully confronted with a 'Yes' that Peter speaks after the question, 'Do you love me?' The true world-history rests in this 'No' and 'Yes'. To place one's own life consciously ever again into this 'No' and 'Yes' is in the greatest style—repentance and faith.

A truly 'new' life is only that in us which is born out of pure love for Christ.

Three comprehensive 'motifs' basically exist for the human will. It is always love. But it is either the lower self-love, as with Émile Coué [1857-1926], 'Every day in every respect I feel better and better'. Or, it is the highest love of self, which makes people feel distinct from the world as in the pure Yoga practice. Or it is the divine love of self, love to the I-AM, which is in Christ and is born out of Christ.

But this love has to know that it chooses death.

> When you were young, you girded yourself and walked where you would; but when you are old, you will stretch out your hands, and another will gird you and carry you where you do not wish to go [John 21:18].

In the first Christian community, Christ's words were related to Peter's death on the cross—and rightly so. For it could not yet be realized livingly enough that indeed the cross itself is a picture of the new person who receives his will completely out of the divine world. The hands are spread out like receptive organs to the will of the universe. The strict girdle of inner control of a greater life is borne, like the Christ of the Book of Revelation. One does not go one's own path, but the divine path. Indeed, one can always feel one is in the world as is described here of Peter. In this there also lies a death, a death of the old human being who on the cross of the world dies into the resurrected human being. And the 'world', too, always pays with 'death', although this death today has taken on other forms.

In this consecration of the disciples, Christ places before the disciples:

- the strength of this new activity; love to Him,
- the aim of the new activity; leadership of humanity,
- the destiny of the new activities; death which leads to resurrection.

'Follow me'.

The other disciple

And yet John's Gospel ends by regarding another disciple. It is of greatest world-historic importance how here the disciple who loves the Lord and the disciple whom the Lord loved face each other. There are two kinds of Christianity, the one following the other. The second could not be without the first. Christianity from below or Christianity from above. Seen from another point of view, Good Friday Christianity in which death is shown, and Easter Christianity living from the words, 'I come'. With this word, 'I come', John's Gospel ends—as John's Apocalypse begins with it. 'I am'—this is John's Gospel. 'I come'—this is the Apocalypse of John. The one who has written the book 'I am' was also allowed to write the book 'I come'. Both belong together.

But here we approach a final Mystery of the disciples, a Pentecost Mystery. What is the difference between the disciple who loves the Lord and the disciple whom the Lord loves? With the second disciple, all his own ability to love is taken up, transformed into the love living in Christ Himself. This disciple no longer loves with the love that is in himself, but he loves with the love that is in Christ. With the love with which we love Christ, we pass over into Christ Himself, and then we love with the love that is in Him. This is a natural development, but it is good to experience it fully consciously and to do it.

The Medieval mystics were accustomed to say: The eye with which we behold God is the same with which God beholds us. This one can say about the spirit-eye. In Christ's sense it is still more comprehensive; it also includes love of being (*Wesensliebe*). Thus we are raised to the last and highest saying, which John reports of the Christ Who prays the High-Priestly Prayer—'that the love with which Thou hast loved me may be in them, and I in them' (John 17:26). If our own love does not live in us, if in us the love of Christ is alive, then according to the same law, the love of the Father is fulfilled with us, which beforehand was fulfilled with Christ. Christ, too, did not love with His own love, but with the love of the Father.

This is the true discipleship, to love God and the world with which God loves Himself. As simple as our narration sounds, it leads up to this world-height.

John's Gospel, Chapter 17
(Revised Standard Version)

1 When Jesus had spoken these words, He lifted up his eyes to heaven
and said, 'Father, the hour has come; glorify Thy Son that the Son may
glorify Thee, 2 since Thou hast given him power over all flesh, to give
eternal life to all whom Thou hast given Him. 3 And this is eternal life,
that they know Thee the only true God, and Jesus Christ Whom Thou
hast sent. 4 I glorified Thee on earth, having accomplished the work
which Thou gavest me to do; 5 and now, Father, glorify Thou me in Thy
own presence with the glory which I had with Thee before the world
was made. 6 I have manifested Thy name to the men whom Thou gav-
est me out of the world; thine they were, and Thou gavest them to me,
and they have kept Thy word. 7 Now they know that everything that
Thou hast given me is from Thee; 8 for I have given them the words
which Thou gavest me, and they have received them and know in truth
that I came from Thee; and they have believed that Thou didst send me.

9 I am praying for them; I am not praying for the world but for
those whom Thou hast given me, for they are Thine; 10 all mine
are Thine, and Thine are mine, and I am glorified in them. 11 And
now I am no more in the world, but they are in the world, and I am
coming to Thee. Holy Father, keep them in Thy name, which Thou
hast given me, that they may be one, even as we are one. 12 While
I was with them, I kept them in Thy name, which Thou hast given
me; I have guarded them, and none of them is lost but the son of
perdition, that the scripture might be fulfilled.

13 But now I am coming to Thee; and these things I speak in
the world, that they may have my joy fulfilled in themselves. 14 I
have given them Thy word; and the world has hated them because
they are not of the world, even as I am not of the world. 15 I do not
pray that Thou shouldst take them out of the world, but that Thou
shouldst keep them from the evil one. 16 They are not of the world,
even as I am not of the world. 17 Sanctify them in the truth; Thy
word is truth. 18 As Thou didst send me into the world, so I have
sent them into the world. 19 And for their sake I consecrate myself,
that they also may be consecrated in truth.

20 I do not pray for these only, but also for those who believe in
me through their word, 21 that they may all be one; even as Thou,
Father, art in me, and I in Thee, that they also may be in us, so that

the world may believe that Thou hast sent me. 22 The glory which Thou hast given me I have given to them, that they may be one even as we are one, 23 I in them and Thou in me, that they may become perfectly one, so that the world may know that Thou hast sent me and hast loved them even as Thou hast loved me. 24 Father, I desire that they also, whom Thou hast given me, may be with me where I am, to behold my glory which Thou hast given me in Thy love for me before the foundation of the world. 25 O righteous Father, the world has not known Thee, but I have known Thee; and these know that Thou hast sent me. 26 I made known to them Thy name, and I will make it known, that the love with which Thou hast loved me may be in them, and I in them.'

Appendix: The Word from Inner Listening[120] Twenty Years after the Death of Friedrich Rittelmeyer

'Music of the Soul, Music of Life'—this motif touches on a most intimate element in Friedrich Rittelmeyer's character, but one that dominates from deep beneath the surface. A primordial ringing pulsed with the blood in his veins, similar to how he himself heard it rustling, speaking, singing in the biblical books, especially in John's Gospel.

In this respect, in the times when Dr Rittelmeyer was still preaching in Protestant pulpits, one was always left with an indelible impression, and not so much in the sermon itself, however poetically rich the language in which he clothed his preaching, but above all in the very sparingly balanced, short liturgy he spoke just preceding the sermon.

I was introduced to the inaugural sermon he gave in Berlin in August 1916—by one of those fateful coincidences that a good destiny had prepared for me—without knowing who he was. Almost more than the sermon, what impressed me, what amazed me, was that there was such a thing—the way he spoke two sentences from John's Gospel before mounting the pulpit. Many people from his time in Nuremberg have confirmed this impression. And this experience was repeated over and over again. You were witness to an aural event of an otherworldly kind, as, for example, when he spoke the verse at the end of 1 Timothy (6:16) in the liturgy he had put together himself, 'who alone has immortality and dwells in unapproachable light, whom no man has ever seen or can see. To him be honour and eternal dominion'. It was very puzzling. One had a direct experience of worship and the sacraments in a Protestant service with its sermon. A celebrant's resonance of words greeted you, which at first you could not decipher. It was a mysterious music of the soul that echoed from the depths. It couldn't just be the warm South German way of speaking sounding in the sober North German realm. After all, the people in Nuremberg, who were not unfamiliar with the special Franconian dialect, also stood before this miracle. A supra-personal Mystery of the soul was revealed.

One had to say to oneself: This is a speaking that is based on a mysterious hearing, a concentrated listening. Every word, every syllable is meditated through in many ways. Indeed, even more—it is almost as if a person who has been silent all his life, indeed who has piously practiced silence in inner activity, were born again and is now taking the floor. To speak of a musical element that resonated with it would be a far too scantily searching for words. It was not music in the usual sense; it was metaphysical music. A meta-music rang from unfathomable depths in spiritual undertones into and through his being. When he spoke on his own accord, in the pulpit or at the lectern, this music was also there, but it was carried and produced by a very unique element of will. This note of will must have been all the more enigmatic, the better you knew it in the great delicacy and sensitivity that never left him. From whence did this note of will come? Albert Steffen described it like this:

> You had to have seen him as a speaker, like a tree in a storm, with the power of the word blown through right into the feet. He did not make life easier for people, but he made it bearable, so that with their burdens they could walk even more nimbly.

One can almost say of Friedrich Rittelmeyer that he spoke with his feet, that is, through the way he stood. As a result, a deep bass flowed into the music, which he allowed into his speech, a primordial resonance as if from the roots of the world.

*

This was shown from another side when you were recognized by him as a friend and were allowed to observe from close up how he prepared his lectures. He prepared them word for word until the very last years. Michael Bauer, the dear friend of Rittelmeyer, who had little opportunity to hear him because of his illness, but always tried to be spiritually present when he knew that he had to speak here or there, sometimes asked him with his amiable impatience, 'When are you going to stop preparing your lectures verbatim?' But you have to understand that Rittelmeyer did not think of what he wanted to say. It was actually a kind of thought-hearing that he practiced. What he was about to say, he heard, not in the usual but in a more intimate sense. And what he heard he wrote down. And then the riddle was that what he wrote down was indelibly written in his memory and came back in the same imprint. This would not have happened at all if it had been a thought-element in the usual sense. The type of notation was more verbal than conceptual, that is, it was a poetic-musical type of concept. It is a living with the word, yet not with what was superficial in it, but with what every word has as a hidden continuation reaching back into the root depths of the world. This was what he lived with, how he worked. And the intimate hearing of the soul available to Rittelmeyer was an infallible tuning fork for truth and authenticity.

It was extraordinarily impressive to hear the two of them speaking side by side, Rittelmeyer and his friend Christian Geyer, who was ten years his senior. They sounded wonderful together and yet it was so different. When Geyer spoke, he had a bright element of thought at his disposal that simply flowed. In the *Sebalduskirche* in Nuremberg, I have experienced several times how the many people in the full church laughed heartily together during the sermon. Here such a happy element did not contradict the deepest piety. Once I sat in a lecture by Dr Geyer at the University of Berlin next to Rudolf Steiner, and I have never seen him laugh so heartily and cheerfully as in these five quarters of an hour. Something radiated there, one can hardly describe it—it was more of a glow than a ringing, it lifted one up, whereas, through the undertones in Rittelmeyer's speech, one was connected to the depths, to the centre of the Earth. With Geyer the thought-element was uniquely ensouled, whereas with Rittelmeyer it was more the words, the speech. Nevertheless, with Geyer, who lived very much in music, one could have spoken of a musical element in the word, but it was more a music of light sent from the air. It was interesting to see and hear the two of them play music together. When they played piano duets, Geyer had to follow his younger friend, as in other things. Geyer liked to take us younger ones with him when he played the organ in the Church of St Sebaldus at dusk. This roared along mightily; he could find no end—it just took him away. In my opinion, Rittelmeyer's deeper musicality came out best when he played Beethoven. But in the last decades he no longer played so much; he limited himself to a few pieces—as in many choices in his life he took the musical element selectively. A few pieces, but ever and again in such a way that he listened hard until he once again experienced the background, the deeper layers, of which even the composer himself might not have been aware. He followed the sound to the heart of the world. He was very occupied with the fact that Rudolf Steiner once said to him that, perhaps in his next life on Earth, he would be able to do something important for the further development of music.

*

Inner hearing, the musical sense, understood metaphysically, was actually Rittelmeyer's organ of truth. That is why he was a liberal theologian for a while, which was so strange. A really pious 'Bible criticism' has actually only been experienced from him in this one case—a completely unbiased critical thinking together with the most inner piety. What did Rittelmeyer bring to this area? To hear the wrong tones in the other [writers]. His hearing was very fine. Nobody heard false notes more quickly and more precisely than he did. The ear of truth also allowed him to recognize the voice of truth when he first heard Michael Bauer and then Rudolf Steiner speak—although Rudolf Steiner's language was so demanding in its strict thought-content that one can hardly imagine a greater difference in tonality than that between the language of Rittelmeyer and that of Rudolf Steiner.

And that brings me to what I actually want to say. Rittelmeyer was the representative of conscience in a really archetypal manner, just as it can still exist in our age. One speaks of the 'voice of conscience', but actually the conscience is more an ear than a voice, because it is important to hear this inner voice. Speaking and listening, so to speak, merge into one another. Here lies the innermost nerve in Rittelmeyer's character in general. And this conscience was his organ for the world situation. With this ear of the heart he heard the voice of his contemporaries; he heard, so to speak, the sounds and noises of what else was going on in the world.

I believe that, because of his nature, he comes closest to understanding the prophets of the Old Testament. These have had the ability to listen to what God speaks, what He speaks in destiny, and what He speaks as a call for the needs that lie ahead. And so the prophets of the Old Covenant, out of their concern for mankind, spoke the words that they had heard from God before the people. The role of Friedrich Rittelmeyer was actually similar. As for the ability of his conscience to hear him speak, he said what he felt needed to be said in the present moment. Thus he stood there. The Old Testament itself uses the image of spies standing on the watchtower and looking out, but actually it's more of an eavesdropping than a peeping. Just as in the old days one put one's ear to the ground and then heard the enemy coming, even if he was still very far away, so Friedrich Rittelmeyer found out by inwardly listening what is happening. A musical element of the most holy kind. He listened to it, for example, in Luther's language, especially in Luther's hymn 'A safe stronghold is our God'. Ever and again he meditated listening to such formulations. The music in it was, for example, the reason why he loved the Christmas song '*Es ist ein Ros entsprungen*' ['A Spotless Rose: Lo, how a rose e'er blooming'], which he loved so much, preferring it sung very softly and slowly so that one could hear in it the music of the soul. So he listened to John's Gospel. The voice of Jesus was familiar to him. He knew the sound as if he had heard it with his ears back at that time. But the voice of Christ was also familiar to him; he thought he could tell the difference. He was even familiar with the voice of the Logos. To be able to distinguish the voices was the ripest fruit of his dealings with the Bible.

And so he was the voice of destiny, through which he felt called and found the courage to be obedient to this voice. He has come, an inspiration for our great benefit, and we are blessed to have had him in our midst for many years. He will always remain in our midst.

Emil Bock

Further Reading

Friedrich Rittelmeyer:

—*Meditation: Zwölf Briefe über Selbsterziehung,* Verlag der Christengemeinschaft, Stuttgart,1929. English translation by M.L. Mitchell, *Meditation: Guidance on the Inner Life,* The Christian Community Press, London, 1932/69; Floris Books, Edinburgh 2012. Emphasis on the 'I-am' sayings.

—*Vom johanneischen Zeitalter,* Band 5/6 of the series *Christus aller Erde,* Verlag der Christengemeinschaft, Stuttgart, 1927 (Eng. trans. 'The Johannine Age', tr. A.S. in MS).

—*Das Vaterunser als Menschwerdung,* Urachhaus, Stuttgart 2015 (Eng. trans. 'The Lord's Prayer: Becoming Human', tr. A.S. in MS).

—*Das Vaterunser, zehn Kanzelreden,* Chr. Kaiser, München 1920/23, Eng. tr. *The Lord's Prayer,* tr. S.M.K. Gandell, Macmillan Co., New York 1931/ The Christian Community Bookshop 1931/ Floris Books, Edinburgh 2017; online: https://archive.org/details/in.ernet.dli.2015.264494/

—*Ich bin: Reden und Aufsätze über die sieben 'Ich bin'-Worte des Johannesevangeliums,* Urachhaus, Stuttgart 1951/92 (Eng. trans. 'I AM: Addresses and Articles on the Seven 'I-am' sayings of John's Gospel' tr. A.S. in MS).

—*Christus,* 1936 (Eng. trans. *Christ,* tr. A.S. in MS). Essentially a Johannine text.

—*Jesus: Ein Bild in vier Vorträgen.* Heinrich Kerler, Ulm 1912, 1914/ Chr. Kaiser, München 1920. Online: https://archive.org/details/jesuseinbildinvi0000ritt/page/n1/mode/2up/ Eng. tr. *Behold the Man* available online: https://archive.org/details/texts?and%5B%5D=Friedrich+rittelmeyer&sin= (rev. A.S. in MS). Emphasis on the Synoptic Gospels.

—*Das Heilige Jahr: Hilfe zur inneren Belebung der Jahreszeiten.* Stuttgart 1930/ Eng. trans. *The Holy Year: Meditative Contemplations of Seasons and Festivals,* tr. Alan Stott, Floris Books 2019.

—*Deutschtum,* Stuttgart 1934 (Eng. tr. 'The Teutonic Spirit' by A.S. in MS).

Rudolf Frieling:

—*Das heilige Zahl im Johannes Evangelium* (1933), in *Gesammelte Schriften zum Alten und Neuen Testament*, 4 Bde., Bd. 4, *Studien zum Neuen Testament*, Urachhaus, Stuttgart 1986 (Eng. tr. 'Sacred Number in John's Gospel', in 'Frieling Rarities', tr. A.S., Temple Lodge, forthcoming.)

Hermann Beckh:

—*Das kosmische Rhythmus im Markusevangelium* (1928/61), Stuttgart 1928/61. Eng. tr. *Mark's Gospel: The Cosmic Rhythm*, tr. Alan Stott, TL 2021.

—*Das kosmische Rhythmus in Johannesevangelium.* Eng. tr. *John's Gospel: The Cosmic Rhythm*, tr. Alan Stott, TL 2021.

Rudolf Meyer:

—*Das Wiedergewinnung des Johannesevangelium*, Urachhaus, Stuttgart 1962 (Eng. 'The Recovery of John's Gospel', not yet translated).

Christoph Rau:

—*Struktur und Rhythmus im Johannes-Evangelium*, Urachhaus, Stuttgart 1972. (Eng. trans. 'John's Gospel: Structure and Rhythm', tr. A.S. in MS.)

—*Der Vier um den Einen; Wesensart un spiritueller Hintergrund der Evangelien*, Dr Dieter Winkler Verlag, Bochum 2008. (Eng. 'The Four around the One: The Gospel—Essence and Spiritual Background', tr. A.S. in MS.) The literary form of all four gospels.

Kurt von Wistinghausen:

—*Der verborgene Evangelist: Studie zur Johannes-Frage*, Urachhaus 1963. (Eng. trans. 'The Hidden Evangelist: the Question of John', with 7 articles from *Die CG* 1984-85, on '*Dreizehn Jünger: Mahler-Wissen im Mitelalter*', 'Thirteen disciples in paintings of the Middle Ages', etc., tr. A.S. in MS. Chapter 6 of the book appears in *Father In*, No. 5, pp. 88-103.)

Emil Bock:

—*Tübinger Apokalypsebeiträge. Einigen über das Geheimnis der beiden Johannes, mit einem Beitrag von Johannes Hemleben. Studien Material für die Priester*, Heft 1, Archiv der Christengemeinschaft, Stuttgart Juni 1995, 27-47 (Eng. tr. A.S. in MS). [The 'Zentralarkiv der Christengemeinschaft' is today housed in Berlin.]

Adolf Arenson:

—*On the Christ-Mystery (2) (Elijah—John—Lazarus)*, lecture given at the Memorial Celebration of Rudolf Steiner's death, Stuttgart, 30 March 1931, and again Dornach 15 April 1931. Tr. from the German by Harry Collison (typescript German and Eng. trans. as pamphlet available in some anthroposophical libraries, ed. with updated refs. A.S. in MS).

Henry Scott Holland:

—*The Philosophy of Faith and the Fourth Gospel*, John Murray, London 1920, reprint editions: Kessinger 2006, Palala Press, Generic, etc.

John A.T. Robinson:

—*The Priority of John*, SCM Press, London 1985; Wipf and Stock 2021. John 'got it right—historically and theologically'.

Margaret Barker:

—*King of the Jews: Temple Theology in John's Gospel*, SPCK 2014. The background to the Fourth Gospel is temple tradition.

Notes

1 *Die Christengemeinschaft (Die CG)*, 15. Jg. Nr. 2, May 1938. 36-39: Memorial issue, F. R. 1872-1938.

2 Two central foci for Rudolf Frieling (1901-86) were the renewed liturgy and John's Gospel. Earlier in his career he joined Rittelmeyer in holding conferences on John's Gospel. In *Die heilige Zahl im Johannes Evangelium* (1933), Eng. tr. 'Sacred Number in John's Gospel' (in 'Frieling Rarities', Temple Lodge, forthcoming) Frieling takes up and develops further some of Rittelmeyer's discoveries. Frieling also refers to Hermann Beckh's work on John's Gospel (1930), Eng. tr. *John's Gospel: The Cosmic Rhythm* (2021); he also wrote a Foreword to the second edition of Beckh's *Der kosmische Rhythmus im Markus Evangelium* (1960, in which Beckh's Appendix is curiously omitted); the complete text is translated as *Mark's Gospel: The Cosmic Rhythm*, Temple Lodge 2021, with additional material—*Tr. note.*

3 F. R., *Das Goetheanum*, 11. Jg. 1932. 128f.

4 F. R., *Das Goetheanum*, 11. Jg. 321f.

5 The most probable word intended here is the Aramaic verb *qm*, also present in the call of Christ 'Talitha Kumi'—*Ed.*

6 Chapter 3 from F. R., *Vom Johanneischen Zeitalter*, Stuttgart 1927. Pp. 35-53.

7 Ernest Renan (1823-82), French expert of Semitic languages and civilizations, philosopher, historian and writer, published his enormously popular and influential *Vie de Jésus* in 1863, Eng. tr. 1864. It is a scholarly book, largely based on John's Gospel, and highly controversial. Jesus is depicted as a man but not God; the gospel miracles are rejected. With its ingredient of racial polemic the book upset both Jews and Christians. Albert Schweitzer gave a lavish yet deeply ironical assessment of Renan's work in his important *Quest of the Historical Jesus* (orig. Germ. ed. 1906, expanded 1913, Eng. tr. 1910/2001)—*Tr. note.*

8 The rendering of the verb 'already was', used, for example, in the Knox version, the *New English Bible* and *Revised English Bible*, the *Translator's New Testament* (London 1973: 'already existed') and William Barclay ('was already there') is more true to the force of the Greek than the more usual rendering 'was'. It also distinguishes the German *'war'* used here, from *'ward'* used subsequently, e.g. v. 14 *'Und das Wort ward Fleisch'*, and in Rittelmeyer's own translation also appearing in v. 6, *'Da ward ein Mensch'*—*Tr. note.*

9 The indefinite article is favoured by Rudolf Steiner and is found, for example, in *The Gospel of St John*, Hamburg, Lect. 4 (GA 103). Today the same expression is found as a major article of belief among Jehovah's Witnesses in the *New World Translation of the Bible*, John 1:1—*Ed.*

10 The term appears in many of Böhme's works as one aspect of the inherent polarity of the will of God, that aspect which turns towards objectifying the Absolute as Divine Nature. *Theoscopia* (1622) points out: *Gott will sich selber, und ist ein Gegenwurf seiner Selber …—Ed.*

11 The Prelude to Wagner's music drama *The Rhinegold* (premiere 1869), one of the wonders of orchestral composition, begins with a deep bass E♭. The music, lasting several minutes, rhythmically unfolds using only the three notes of the chord of E♭-major. The choice of key is important, as Beckh points out. (The only possible precedent would seem to be the martial-sounding toccata opening of Monteverdi's *Orpheo* (1607), from opera's nascent period. This piece is based on the continuously sounding three notes of the chord of D-minor, with only the briefest addition of other notes in the melodic runs)—*Tr. note.*

12 The Hebrew Yohanan, usually rendered 'Jah is gracious'.

13 Again following Rudolf Steiner's translation as found in Lect. 4 of *The Gospel of St John*, Hamburg (GA 103).

14 Cf. Rudolf Steiner, speaking on the 'second mission of the Archangel Michael', Dornach 20 Nov. 1919. *The Mission of the Archangel Michael.* GA 194.

15 Colossians 1:16 (*archai*).

16 *'Das Ich'* is normal German. The first person pronoun, not normally a noun in English, consequently requires inverted commas. For the most part this translation simply renders the word as 'the "I"'. This cardinal concept in a work on John's Gospel does not really require any apology. Some explanation, nevertheless, should not go amiss: 'ego', the Latin equivalent—another foreign word—occasionally appears, though not in order to suggest its technical meaning in some schools of psychology. To translate everywhere with 'self' might also suggest other connotations, not part of the author's meaning. 'Individuality', 'person' and 'personality', technically developments of the simple word, should ideally be reserved for those occasions, though 'person' is used in the translation where the author's meaning would allow it. Moreover, this word helps the admittedly real issue of translating *'der Mensch'*. This gender problem posed by the English language has been respected, although an invariable use of 'the human being' tends to border on pedantry; a balanced approach has been attempted. S/he is a little odd, so a varied treatment involving the non-grammatical partial use of the plural, the impersonal 'one' form, the use of 'people', and 'person' as noted above, and, indeed, of the generic term itself—bearing in mind English usage of several centuries—seemed more natural and in keeping with the author's meaning, who wrote almost 90 years ago. The generic meaning of 'man', after all, was ever distinct from the other, the gender meaning—*Tr. note.*

17 René Guenon suggests 'He Who causes to be'; Martin Buber also has interesting things to say on אֶהְיֶה אֲשֶׁר אֶהְיֶה, *ehyeh ašer ehyeh*. The original translates literally as: 'I am who I am.' Since the Hebrew lacks a future tense, some translators prefer the phrase: 'I will be what I will be'—*Tr. note.*

18 A summary of the indications found in Rudolf Steiner, *Building Stones for an Understanding of the Mystery of Golgotha*, Lect. 3, RSP, 1985, pp. 62-65—*Ed.*

19 The Athanasian Creed, the *Quicumque Vult* (from the opening words, 'Whosoever wishes'), technically speaking, is not a liturgical creed, but rather a late fifth or early sixth century Christian statement of belief emphasizing Trinitarian belief, attributed to the Church Father Athanasius—*Tr. note.*

20 Quotation untraced—*Ed.*

21 *Italian Journey*, second visit to Rome,1787, letter of 6 September—*Ed.*

22 Julius Hart (1859-1930), German literary critic, author of numerous works including the collection of poems, Sansara, Bremen, J. Kühtmann, 1879.

23 The Jewish Shema, Deut. 6:4.

24 Hermann Cohen, 1842-1918.

25 A collection of *Märchen* published under various imprints. Richard von Volkmann (1830–1889), a prominent German surgeon and author of poetry and fiction, published under the pseudonym Richard Leander, *Träumerei an französischen Kaminen*, Breitkopf und Härtel, Leipzig, 1871; reissued Alfred Scherx 1947; Hamburger Lesehaft, 1986; Forgotten Books, 2016.

26 *Thus Spoke Zarathustra*, Part 2, 20, 'On Redemption'.

27 The key thought is that inspiration is 'unconscious', spontaneous and unpremeditated, whereas 'conscious' expression is deliberate and premeditated. It is a pre-eminently important example of a widespread dualistic thinking that fails to survive scrutiny.

The author here may be speaking for many, yet on the other hand his particular contribution should also be noted. Rittelmeyer was a pioneer in pointing out the musical nature of Inspiration. His claim that the gospel derives from direct vision is endorsed by his colleague Hermann Beckh, who also published on John's Gospel; both also draw on Rudolf Steiner. Yet, that Rittelmeyer is emphatic about a split in consciousness rather reflects his own situation and training as a Westerner than that of the evangelist himself. Today we are given a wealth of evidence from first-temple theology as reconstructed by Margaret Barker that the Fourth Evangelist and Apocalyptist records his own 'heavenly ascent' in the terms of that tradition. This suggests the evangelist was *aware* of using 'the melos of mathematics' (a phrase of an arch-Johannine writer Novalis). This all shows self-knowledge if anything does. The corollary coming into question here is the assumption—not only of theologians—that modern techniques enable scholars somehow to be placed in a more elevated position to pronounce on those who wrote the New Testament.

From a twenty-first century perspective, there seems no sound reason to suggest the evangelist—acknowledged as 'musically' inspired—was *consequently* somehow intellectually inactive. Since Rittelmeyer, further critical investigation of the structural rhythms of the John's Gospel (see 'Further Reading' below) supports this observation. A fuller survey of the evangelist's initiation—of the *total* human being—is revealed in Hermann Beckh's magisterial two-volume work on the gospel—*Tr. note.*

28 Father Richard Meux Benson (1824-1915), founder of the Cowley Fathers, the 'Society of John the Evangelist', puts the thought as follows: 'Every Christian knows Whose blood flows in his veins'—*Tr. note.*

29 The phrase is Luther's—*Ed.*

30 In Judaic tradition the Elect One, or Messiah, has been held back since before creation; in both the *Bahir* and *Zohar* a portion of the uncreated Divine Light has been 'withheld' since before creation and will appear with the advent of Messiah—*Ed.*

31 See: R. Steiner, 'The Son of God and the Son of Man', lecture at Munich, 11 Feb. 1911 (GA 127).

32 The subtitle and numbering of paragraphs here is editorial. Rittelmeyer here claims the phrase 'Son of man' is mentioned twelve times in John's Gospel; his study does not strictly follow the sequence. RSV mentions the phrase technically thirteen times, a couple are, as it were, duplicated on the occasion they were spoken, and not all are from the mouth of Christ: 1:51; 3:13,14; 5:27; 6:27; 6:53; 6:62; 8:28; 9:35; 12:23; 12:34, 35; 13:31—*Tr. note.*

33 J.W. von Goethe, *Theory of Colours*, 'Introduction'.

34 Fr. Schiller, 'Resignation', 1784 /85.

35 Ex. 21 and 22. More generally, the majority of Jewish commentators (Onkeles, Ibn Ezra, Rasag, Rashbam and Rashi's second reading) interpret the word 'Elohim' to mean 'Judge'—*Ed.*

36 Rittelmeyer refers especially to Luther's *'Otterngezücht'* 'brood of vipers' Matt. 3:7 and Luke 3:7, indicating a rather contemptuous expression. Rudolf Steiner's understanding is represented in *The Fifth Gospel,* Lecture 5, Berlin 13 Jan. 1914 (GA 148)—*Ed.*

37 Clement of Alexandria, in Eusebius, *Ecclesiastical History*, 14.2.

38 Thus Papyrus p. 75 (Vatican), Codex Sinaiticus, Codex Ephraemi, Codex Bezae, all followed in the Westcott and Hort text—*Ed.*

39 Rudolf Steiner, *The Gospel of St John*, Hamburg, Lecture 5 (GA 103).

40 Meister Eckhart, Sermon: *Qui audit me, non confundetur.* Sermon 24, 30.

41 On this whole subject, see F. R. *Meditation*, Letter 4. Edinburgh: Floris Books, p. 42.

42 Der Alltags-Christ, 116, in *Menschliches, Allzumenschliehes* I, 1878, Eng. tr. *Human, all too Human: A Book for Free Spirits.*

43 See, R Steiner, *The Fifth Gospel,* lect. Christiania, 6 Oct. 1913 (GA 148).

44 *Thus Spoke Zarathustra*, Part 3, 9, 'The Return Home' / 'The Home-Coming'.

45 *Frohliche Wissenschaft*. Aphorism 254.

46 *Thus Spoke Zarathustra*. Part 3, 4: 'Before the Sunrise'.

47 Cf. my book *Theologie und Anthroposophie*, Stuttgart, 1933, p. 83.

48 Rudolf Steiner, speaking on the 'second mission of the Archangel Michael', Dornach 20 Nov. 1919. *The Mission of the Archangel Michael*. GA 194.

49 From *Thus Spoke Zarathustra*, Part 2:3.

50 See e.g. GA 320: *Spiritual-Scientific Impulses for the Development of Physics.*

51 Lecture, Berlin, 28 Jan. 1907. GA 96.

52 Shekinah, Shechinah, or Schechinah (Biblical Hebrew: שכינה), is the English transliteration of a Hebrew word meaning 'dwelling' or 'settling' and denotes the dwelling or settling of the divine presence of God, His manifestation.

53 The tradition that John the divine wrote his gospel in old age is challenged today. See, for example, John A.T. Robinson, *The Priority of John*. London: SCM Press 1985 and *Redating the New Testament*, London: SCM Press 1976—*Tr.*

54 Following Rudolf Steiner's translation, e.g. Hamburg *John's Gospel*, Lect. 1 (GA 103), Rittelmeyer also puts the indefinite article here. To some biblical theologians this is questionable—*Tr.*

55 Band 5/6 of the series *Christus aller Erde*, Verlag der Christengemeinschaft, Stuttgart, 1927.

56 See note 27 above—*Tr. note.*

57 Sin is 'lawlessness' (I John 3:4), chaos, rebellion, apostasy—*Tr. note.*

58 See note 27 above—*Tr. note.*

59 Verlag der Christengemeinschaft, Stuttgart,1929. English translation by M. L. Mitchell, The Christian Community Press, London, 1932/69; Floris Books, Edinburgh 2012.

60 Goethe, *Theory of Colours*, 'Introduction'.

61 Rudolf Steiner, *The Spiritual Beings in the Heavenly Bodies and in the Kingdoms of Nature*. Lect. 1, Helsinki, 3 April 1912. GA 136.

62 Rudolf Steiner, *The Gospel of St John*, Hamburg, Lect. 4 (GA 103), Anthroposophic Press, 1973, p. 67.

63 From his Preface to the New Testament.

64 'Goethes Kritik an der Reformation', in the Journal *Die Christengemeinschaft*, Vol, 6. August 1929. 129-32.

65 Goethe, *Faust*, Part 1, II, 2, 'Faust's study'.

66 Both poems are found under 'Kleinere Gedichte' in Vol. 8 of the 1846 *Complete Works.*

67 Quotations from *Thus Spoke Zarathustra*. 2, 10; 3, 15; 3, 2.

68 *'Gott anerkennen, wo und wie er sich offenbare, das ist eigentlich die Seligkeit auf Erden.'* Goethe, Maxims & Reflections, No. 353. Goethe, *Maximen und*

Reflexionen. Aphorismen und Aufzeichnungen. Nach den Handschriften des Goethe- und Schiller-Archivs hg. von Max Hecker, 1907. Aus dem Nachlass. Über Literatur und Leben.

69 Friedrich Gottlieb Klopstock (1724–1803), German poet, best known for his epic poem 'Der Messias'.

70 It has been said that Klopstock's hymn 'Die Auferstehung' at the funeral of Hans von Bülow in 1894 gave Gustav Mahler the inspiration for the final movement of his second Symphony. Mahler incorporated the hymn with extra verses he wrote himself to bring a personal resolution to this work.

71 The 'danger', or tendency, named here with the personal names of cosmic, spiritual beings, is the universal polarity of *expansion* and *constriction* found in spiritual, psychological and physical phenomena in human life and in the environment. 'Enthusiasm' needs 'system' for both *alone* are extreme and, when too hot or too cold respectively, are unproductive. Divide the human being, says Steiner, and you find 'a kind of melody', a triad: 'Christ—Lucifer—Ahriman' (lecture, Dornach 31 July 1915. GA 162); Christ as the middle principle fosters the creative human balance: here 'form' and 'content' harmonize—*Tr. note*.

72 *Thus Spoke Zarathustra*, I, 20.

73 In Norse mythology, 'Baldr, Balder, or Baldur, the beautiful', son of the chief god Odin and Frigg, was one of the most beloved of the gods, representing the animating force behind the beauty of life at the peak of its strength and energy. The death of Balder, in Steiner's explanations, stands for the extinction of early clairvoyant faculties. Cf. Hermann Beckh, 'Meeting Rudolf Steiner', in *Hermann Beckh and the Spirit-Word,* Anastasi 2015. 26:

> What there in the consciousness of humanity has sunk down, had to sink down through an 'iron world-necessity', formed the content of a lecture on Balder given in Dornach, on Good Friday, 2 April 1915 (in GA 161). It remains unforgettable for everyone who had the good fortune to hear it. Especially this lecture was an experience of the word in a unique manner, a rhythmic, musical revelation of the word and of the etheric forces of the life of nature weaving in it. Right into the sound and rhythm of the speech, one could feel this life of nature, the 'weaving beings in meadows and in forests'. The entire sacred feeling of wellbeing in which the soul of our Teutonic predecessors still lived within that etheric-enlivening of nature, the Balder-element, sounded like a wonderful rhythmic music through the words and mood of that lecture. With the highest seriousness of knowledge and the highest profundity of knowledge, indeed tragedy of knowledge, everything in that lecture was lifted into a purely artistic atmosphere, was purest poetry. It could be felt that the one speaking was himself living in the 'sacred ether of the plant world'—*Tr. note*.

74 F.R., *The Holy Year*, Floris Books, Edinburgh 2019, pp. 16-19.

75 F.R., 'Jüngerweihe', in *Die Christengemeinschaft*, Juni 1929. VI. 3, pp. 73-77.

76 Cf. F.R. *Meditation*, Letter 6, pp. 91-103; *The Holy Year*, 'The washing of the feet', pp. 53-6.

77 R. Steiner, *The Gospel of St John* (GA 103) Hamburg, 18-31 May, 1908.

78 *Thus Spoke Zarathustra*, 1, 16.

79 The reader is referred to our books, *Meditation*, pp. 19-103, and *The Holy Year*, 'The washing of the feet', pp. 53-6.

80 *'Si fractus illabatur orbis, / impavidum ferient ruinae'*— *Odes* 3.3.7-8, tr. Joseph Addison.

81 The tr. in the text, and 'Give me a place to stand, and I shall move the world' are the most commonly quoted translations. Said to be his assertion in demonstrating the principle of the lever; as quoted by Pappus of Alexandria, *Synagogue*, Book VIII, c. CE 340. 'Give me a place to stand and with a lever I will move the whole world' is a variant deriving from an earlier source than Pappus: *The Library History of Diodorus Siculus*, Fragments of Book XXVI, as tr. F.R. Walton, in *Loeb Classical Library* (1957) Vol. XI.

82 C.F. Andrews (1871-1940) an English-born missionary to India, educator and social reformer, wrote *Christ in the Silence*, London: Hodder & Stoughton 1933, a meditative study of the Fourth Gospel, comparable in style to Rittelmeyer's meditative approach, also works on his friends Gandhi, and *Sadhu Sundar Singh: A Personal Memoir*. New York: Harper & Brothers, 1934—*Tr. note*.

83 Cf. the meditative deepening of R.H. Benson, *The Last Passover*, Vol. 2, Part 1, London 1895, 452-57. Without detracting from any spiritual insights, investigation of the text may also be noted. In his reconstruction of the original, C.C. Torrey presents the evidence that the famous riddle of 14:31 is easily solved as a Semitic textual problem, a 'slight corruption of the Aramaic'. The words and their order are 'all certain', but there is 'a very common omission of one of two consecutive *alephs*'. In English translation, the later part of 13:31 would run: '… that as the Father has given me commandment thus I do, I will arise and go hence'. 'Go hence' is a frequently used expression for dying. See C.C. Torrey, *Our Translated Gospels: Some of the Evidence*, London / New York 1936, 133, 135, 138-40; and *The Four Gospels: A New Translation*, London / New York 1933—*Tr. note.*

84 Benito Mussolini (1883-1945), Italian politician and journalist who was the leader of the National Fascist Party. Prime Minister of Italy from 1922-1943.

85 Two lines from Heinrich Heine's (1797-1856) lyric 'Lied' in the *Buch der Lieder*:
'Du ist wie eine Blume, / So hold und schön und rein; / Ich schau dich an, und Wehmut / Schleicht mir ins Herz hinein. / Mir ist, als ob ich die Hände / Aufs Haupt dir legen sollt, / Betend, dass Gott dich erhalte / So rein und schön und hold.'

86 From Rudolf Steiner, *Mantrische Spruche—Seelenübungen* II, GA 268.

87 Cf. 'To get up in the morning, in the fullness of youth, and open a book—now that's what I call vicious!' Nietzsche in *Ecce Homo.*

88 *Nachgelassene Fragmente*, 1880-82, Nr. 11, in Vol. 9 of the current *Kritische Studienausgabe* of Nietzsche's works.

89 Cf. *Goethe's Letters to Zelter*, edited A.D. Coleridge, G. Bell & Sons, London, 1892, p. 293.

90 GA 269 Nr. 5, Evangelien-Texte Übertragen von Rudolf Steiner.

91 During the early 1930s many in Germany were impressed and misled by the publications, touching on Atlantis, by Herman Wirth (1885-1981)—*Ed.*

92 R. Steiner, 'The Significance of Christmas from the Perspective of Spiritual Science', Lect. 8 of GA 97, Leipzig, 15 Dec. 1906; translated J. Hynes in *The Christian Mystery*, 'Prologue', Anthroposophical Press, 1998. The image of intertwining is not in the 'ancient legend' as represented by *The Golden Legend* of 1298—*Ed.*

93 J.W. von Goethe, *Maxims and Reflections*, No. 539.

94 In this context, two literary examples of the artist's protest against the prevailing materialism of the nineteenth century may be mentioned:
(1) a short but penetrating monograph on a most renowned novelist in the language: Donald Perkins, *Charles Dickens: a New Perspective*, Edinburgh: Floris Books, 1982;
(2) an in-depth study of the most quoted texts after the Bible and Shakespeare and which are translated into a record number of languages—which itself demonstrates that the story has achieved the status of myth: Lewis Carroll's Alice books. Under the guise of 'nonsense', *Alice in Wonderland* portrays the heroine's self-education as an inner journey through four stages of initiation, based on the four days from Maundy Thursday to Easter Sunday: John Docherty. *The Literary Products of the Lewis Carroll-George Macdonald Friendship*. Lampeter & Lewiston NY: Edwin Mellen Press 1995—*Tr. note.*

95 R. Steiner, Chapter 6, 'Goethe's Way of Knowledge' in *Goethean Science* (GA 1). Spring Valley, New York: Mercury Press. 91, emphases original—*Tr. note.*

96 This added subtitle is taken from S.T. Coleridge, *The Friend*—*Tr.*

97 The nine angelic hierarchies are arranged into three triads—*Tr.*

98 Dionysius converted to Christianity by the preaching of Paul (Acts 17:34). An early sixth-century writing employing Neoplatonic language, *The Celestial Hierarchies*, appeared under his name. Today, the author of this work is referred to as 'Pseudo-Dionysius the Areopagite'. This treatise could represent the oral Mystery tradition from earlier centuries, and is taken as such by Rudolf Steiner—*Tr. note.*

99 Cf. note 27 above.

100 Cf. Master Eckhart, On the Lord's Prayer—*Ed.*

101 Gustav Schüler (1872-1938); see *Wo bist du Gott? Gedichte des Trostes und der Zuversicht*, Norderstedt, 2002—*Ed.*

102 The lines are from the hymn *Ein feste Burg ist unser Gott* (tr. Thomas Carlyle).

103 Rudolf Steiner, *The Mission of the Individual Folk-Souls*, Lect. 8; GA 121, p. 136.

104 The quotation condenses verses in the Dhammapada as cited by Hermann Oldenberg, *Buddha: Sein Leben, seine Lehre, seine Gemeinde* (1882). Recent edition, Europäischer Literaturverlag, Bremen, 2014, p. 239—*Ed.*

105 For the Gk. *didomi* Rittelmeyer prefers *schenken* ('bestow') to *geben* ('give')—*Ed.*

106 The story is told in the anonymous Sempacherlied celebrating the battle of Sempach, 1386. It was illustrated in a large painting by Konrad Grob (1828-1914) in 1878—*Ed.*

107 Schiller's *Philosophical Letters*, 1786, Chap. 1—*Ed.*

108 Rittelmeyer here refers to Luther's translation *'in uns eins seien'*; the accepted Nestle Greek reading is *autoi en hymin ōsin* which is followed by the RSV 'that they also may be in us'—*Ed.*

109 Reportedly said by the Romans as recorded by Tertullian (c.160–c.220) in *Apologeticus*, 197—*Ed.*

110 For information: at the time of writing (early 1930s) the Mass was still celebrated in Latin; celebration in the vernacular and other revisions have taken place through the Second Vatican Council, 1962-65—*Tr. note.*

111 The classical Greek τελετή, meaning initiation in the Mysteries, does not appear in the N.T.—*Ed.*

112 An 'I' always implies a 'you'. Cf. Wilfrid Richmond, *An Essay on Personality*, London: Edwin Arnold, 1900. 18, reprinted Kessinger 2007: 'The individual person is an abstraction, not a reality. The individual emerged into personality out of the family …' William Blake concludes 'There is no Natural Religion' (1788) with what has become a well-known saying:

> He who sees the Infinite in all things, sees God. He who see the Ratio only, sees himself only. Therefore God becomes as we are, that we may become as he is.

'The Ratio', the mental abstract, is a condition of the practical life. He who sees that alone—and this we need not, and indeed must not if we would truly live—sees himself alone. Why should anyone be interested in a display of my aches and pains, being but the inside of a curled-up wood-shaving?—*Tr. note.*

113 In his autobiograhy *Dichtung und Wahrheit [Poetry and Truth]*, 1812, Book 9.

114 Various relationships between Buddha and the Moon had been extensively revealed some seven years earlier with The Christian Community

publication of Hermann Beckh, *Vom Buddha zur Christus*, 1925, complete Eng. tr. *From Buddha to Christ*, Temple Lodge 2019.

115 From *The Symposium* 211.

116 Rittelmeyer is considering the word *doxa* in the koiné Greek.

117 Close to New Testament times, the prophets did have flashes of insight regarding the Father of the nation: cf. Malaci 1:6, 2:10. However, before Jesus, nobody claimed that God was *his* Father—*Tr. note.*

118 '*Götterburg*' in the text ('mountain of the gods', 'divine mount') is perhaps open to several meanings at the same time—the Grail Castle, the castle of Wotan in Valhalla (Wagner and others), Luther's hymn '*Ein feste Burg*' ...—*Ed.*

119 Distinguished scholars are divided on the significance of the Greek words for love. The interplay of synonyms is a feature of the writer's Greek. This prompts almost all translators, including the *Translator's New Testament*, to use the one English word. In his commentary on John, F.F. Bruce (author of commentaries on all the books of the New Testament) summarizes the situation. He concludes that it is 'precarious ... to press distinction between the two synonyms here' (*The Gospel of John*, Pickering & Inglis, London 1983/ Eerdmans, Grand Rapids, Mich. 1994, p. 405). However, for all its temporary virtues, an 'agnostic' stance becomes increasingly outdated in the face of in-depth scrutiny of expositors, such as Fr. Rittelmeyer, Arthur W. Pink, and others, who explore the larger context, not to mention the extensive attempt to render the writer's meaning in *The Amplified New Testament* (1958), already suggested long ago in Chr. Wordsworth's sadly forgotten masterpiece of N.T. scholarship (1861) and Westcott's classic commentary on John (1880)—*Tr. note.*

120 Emil Bock, *Die Christengemeinschaft*, 1958, 78-80.